Encountering Kālī

Encountering Kālī

In the Margins, at the Center, in the West

EDITED BY
Rachel Fell McDermott
and Jeffrey J. Kripal

UNIVERSITY OF CALIFORNIA PRESS
Berkeley Los Angeles London

University of California Press
Berkeley and Los Angeles, California
University of California Press, Ltd.
London, England

Library of Congress Cataloging-in-Publication Data

Encountering Kālī : in the margins, at the center, in the West / edited by Rachel Fell McDermott and Jeffrey J. Kripal.
p. cm.
Includes bibliographical references and index.
ISBN 0-520-23239-9 (cloth : alk. paper)—ISBN 0-520-23240-2 (pbk. : alk. paper)
1. Kālī (Hindu deity) I. McDermott, Rachel Fell. II. Kripal, Jeffrey John, 1962–
BL1225.K3 E62 2003
294.5'2114—dc21 2002073269

Manufactured in the United States of America
12 11 10 09 08 07 06 05 04 03
10 9 8 7 6 5 4 3 2 1

The paper used in this publication is both acid-free and totally chlorine-free (TCF). It meets the minimum requirements of ANSI/NISO Z39.48–1992 (R 1997) (*Permanence of Paper*). ⊗

For David
April 25, 1939–April 25, 2000

Is my black Mother Śyāmā really black?
People say Kālī is black,
but my heart doesn't agree.
If She's black,
how can She light up the world?
Sometimes my Mother is white,
sometimes yellow, blue, and red.
I cannot fathom Her.
My whole life has passed
trying.
She is Matter,
then Spirit,
then complete Void.

It's easy to see
how Kamalākānta
thinking these things
went crazy.

KAMALĀKĀNTA BHAṬṬĀCĀRYA

Among the most surprising findings [of psychoanalysis] is the way in which the dream-work treats contraries that occur in the latent dream . . . an element in the manifest dream which is capable of having a contrary may equally well be expressing either itself or its contrary or both together. . . . In psychoanalysis opposites imply no contradiction.

SIGMUND FREUD, *Introductory Lectures on Psycho-Analysis*

CONTENTS

ILLUSTRATIONS

ACKNOWLEDGMENTS

This volume is the end result of a long process of collaboration between many people across many shores. It began twelve years ago, when Rachel and I were both living in Calcutta and became fascinated with the goddess's innumerable ritual, iconographic, and mythological forms: street art, poetry and song, iconic image, hagiographic text. A few years later, as we were each finishing our dissertations, John Stratton Hawley suggested to us that we hold a conference on Kālī at Barnard College, an idea that struck us both as timely and inspired. This we in fact did, in September 1996, under the rubric "Encountering Kālī: Cultural Understanding at the Extremes." For their help with this event, we would like to extend a special thanks here to Jack Hawley for suggesting, encouraging, and guiding this process; to Provost Elizabeth Boylan of Barnard College and Professor Irene Bloom, chair of the Department of Asian and Middle Eastern Cultures, who graciously granted us funds to organize and run the three-day event; to the conference's participants, student assistants, and various audiences; and to Stephen and Karen G. Livick for gracing the walls of our meeting room with dozens of immense color photographs of the goddess in some of her different Calcutta incarnations. It was both a memorable and a remarkably colorful event.

We would also like to thank Reed Malcolm, our editor at the University of California Press, who took a special interest in this project and guided it through its many review and production stages at the Press. Five anonymous readers appropriately prodded us to make a number of important changes; we are grateful for both their support and their criticisms, which we are certain helped produce a much better book. We would also like to thank Cindy Wathen for all the work she put into the details of the book's production, Peter Dreyer for his excellent copyediting, and Venantius Pinto for the beautiful art that graces the cover and the silhouettes that open each chapter. A special word of thanks is also due to the essayists themselves, who endured a very long incubation period and wrote what we believe is a collection of fascinating essays on one of the most remarkable divinities the world has seen—the Hindu goddess Kālī.

Finally, I would like to express publicly my own gratitude to Rachel, much to her chagrin, no doubt, for her dedication to this long process and, most of all, for taking upon herself the brunt of both the conference and the editorial work when I was living in another state, had other professional or personal responsibilities to tend to, or simply lacked the requisite energy for the project. Our names appear together on the cover, but let no one doubt that it was Rachel's *śakti* that finally brought this volume into being. May it now dance, like the goddess herself.

Jeffrey J. Kripal

ABOUT THE CHAPTER SILHOUETTES

My work incorporates my interaction with a broad range of media, suitable to bringing out energies manifest in ideas that relate to what I call "meshes of the continuum." These meshes are a weaving of my mind, experienced through being touched by truth—a flow of relationships and events stemming from the evolving archaeology of my existence that began in India. I draw and paint to realize fragments and wholes, through a layering process using traditional as well as digital media. "Layering" is a metaphor to express whatever I wish to contain in space: the memory of time, deity, culture, power, and compassion, and my existence as a Christian amid myriad religiosities. These elements are brought together spatially in what becomes for me a layered mandala. I use color as discrete units of energy in an attempt to portray an ineffable, archetypal numinosity. I assign meaning to evolve a new whole, energized by my breath and charged with a vision from a sanctuary of "knowing."

To arrive at a contemporary visualization of the Corpus Kali, I began looking for a model whose life and art spoke of an intense sexual energy. The Lolitaesque renditions of Kali as seen in Indian calendar art and popular posters were simply not reasonable models of inspiration. I see her as a dancer, always moving in relationship to a chronology of timelessness. In the dancer and choreographer Martha Graham, I have found an appropriate conceptual model for Kali. Her dances and technique come in part from a deeply sexual source. The image on the cover of the paperback edition of this volume is a homage to the Kali in Graham. Kali luxuriates in a very Graham-like expression of movement that thrusts the glory of her being out at us. It sings its eroticism right down to the particular velvet dark-blue that contains her energy in perfect equipoise. Kali's dark, luminous color and the expression on her face at once make her accessible emotionally and yet distance her from intimate communion. Visualizing the Goddess in this way stills the nervous system; one is becalmed under the fiery yet benevolent stare of the Devi, the luxuriant Goddess, the Mother and exemplar of intense feelings. Continuing to see her in the round, I have also created a series of fourteen drawings that appear as silhouettes throughout the book. These silhouettes help project the depth of Kali's force. She helps one belong, particularly in the nascent dawn of late capitalism. There is much to see and understand.

Venantius J Pinto

Venantius J Pinto was born on May 14, 1961, in Mumbai. In 1986, he received a BFA from the Sir JJ School of Applied Art, in Mumbai, where he majored in Design for Social Issues with an emphasis on illustration. He also received his MFA in computer graphics in 1991 from the Pratt Institute, in Brooklyn, N.Y., after completing a mixed-medium animated film, *Shunyata*, as a thesis project. He currently lives in New York City, where he works as a digital artist and uses art to pursue his ideas on social consciousness, religion, and sexuality.

NOTES ON TRANSLITERATION

Like the Goddess herself, the languages in which she is worshipped and described are various, with region-specific nuances. The contributors to this volume work in Sanskrit, Bengali, Hindi, Malayalam, Oriya, Tamil, English, and Trinidadian English Creole, each of which has its own transliteration, spelling, and pronunciation conventions. As far as possible, we have chosen to respect the integrity of each language—for instance, spelling the Goddess as Kālī in the north, Kāḷi in the south, and Kali in Trinidad and the United States. Several chapters open with explanations of relevant transliteration decisions; here we give a general overview for the volume, excluding, occasionally, the initial chapter by David Kinsley, who, in 1986, sometimes made decisions different from those that follow.

Certain Indian words—like ashram, babu, dharma, karma, maharaja, raja, sadhu, sannyasi, yoga, and yogi—have entered the English dictionary and hence are spelled here without diacritics or italics. Other terms, names of deities, and texts that are commonly recognizable to students of Indian religions are rendered as far as possible in their Sanskrit forms: for example, *avatāra, bhakta, darśana,* "Devī-Māhātmya," *pūjā,* Rāma, *śakti,* and Vaiṣṇava. Literary genres are capitalized and given diacritics but no italics (Maṅgalakāvyas, Maṇipravāḷam, Purāṇas, and Tantras), and anglicized adjectives are treated similarly (Purāṇic, Brāhmaṇical). All caste and tribe names, as well as proper names of people appearing only in their respective chapters or who are not widely known, are spelled according to local custom. The exception concerns famous people (and their organizations) who are known to or live in the West; these occur in their typical anglicized forms without diacritics: the Arya Samaj; Aurobindo Ghose; Bankim Chandra Chatterjee; Bhagwan Shri Rajneesh; the Brahmo Samaj; Guru Mayi and Siddha Yoga; Ma Jaya Sati Bhagavati; Maharishi Mahesh Yogi; Mata Amritanandamayi; Paramahamsa Yogananda; Ram Mohan Roy; Ramakrishna Paramahamsa; Sister Nivedita; Swami Bhaktivedanta, the Hare Krishnas, and the International Society for Krishna Consciousness; and Swami Vivekananda. Temple names (Kālīghāṭ, Liṅgarāj) are given regionally appropriate diacritics, but place-names are not; in some cases, the latter are spelled according to accepted anglicized forms (Banaras, Bhubaneswar, Calcutta, and Dacca). In addition, since all of the essays were written prior to the renaming of Calcutta as Kolkata, and since those that discuss Bengal are typically describing events in the colonial period, we retain "Calcutta" as the preferred spelling.

In the essays by Patricia Lawrence and Sarah Caldwell, deities' names are spelled according to Tamil and Malayalam conventions, respectively, except where noted; so, for example, A<u>n</u>umā<u>n</u>, Bhagavati, Gaṅgamma, and Kāḷi instead of Hanumān, Bhagavatī, Gaṅgāmmā, and Kālī. In Keith McNeal's study of Trinidad, where there is no local system of diacritics or transliteration, words appear as they are spelled or, more often, pronounced (*deota*, Parameshwarie, *shakti*).

Finally, aside from the essay of David Kinsley (chapter 1), where "goddess" is given throughout in lower case, and Roxanne Gupta's essay (chapter 6), where "the Goddess" and Her pronouns are consistently capitalized, the essays capitalize "Goddess" when indicating a particular deity or "the Goddess" as a philosophical absolute but use the lower-case forms "goddess" and "goddesses" for generic or plural referents.

Introducing Kālī Studies

Jeffrey J. Kripal and Rachel Fell McDermott

A PERSONAL PROLOGUE

Over the weekend of February 26–27, 2000, one of us (Rachel) flew to Hamilton, Ontario, to say good-bye to David Kinsley, who had been diagnosed with inoperable lung cancer a month before. Soon after receiving the diagnosis, David told me on the phone that he wanted to spend his last three months reviewing his life, being grateful for all its gifts, and saying good-bye to those who loved him. His house was a veritable pilgrimage site. Relatives, friends, colleagues, students, representatives of Hindu temples and organizations, local talk show producers, people whom he had touched in Hamilton—they all came. David talked with them, consoled them, cried with them. He was not afraid to speak of death, although he told me that he was afraid of dying; the pain, the decay, and the loneliness of the unknown frightened him. We also talked about the afterlife. What comforted him most, he said, was not some sense of personal immortality but a belief that he was part of the great cosmic cycle. His ashes, mixed with earth and water, would become new life. This view, he said, was primarily inspired by his work on the Hindu goddess Kālī, who represents the totality of life and death.

David's second book, *The Sword and the Flute: Kālī and Kṛṣṇa: Visions of the Terrible and the Sublime in Hindu Mythology,*[1] now continuously in print for over a quarter of a century, has justly earned him the affectionate appellation "The Father of Kālī Studies." The first accessible account of Kālī's textual and theological history to appear in English, *The Sword and the Flute* has influenced all of us who study the Goddess. David's appealing explanation for the religious attraction of Kālī—"Kālī's boon is freedom, the freedom of the child to revel in the moment, and it is won only after confrontation or acceptance of death"[2]—has drawn many into the study of this richly complex divine figure. And it also changed David; Kālī was a figure to which he returned again and again in his professional and personal life. The last class of his career at McMaster University, taught as scheduled in early April, three weeks before his death, was in his lecture course on "Health, Healing, and Religion." The topic for the day was the transformative effects of fatal illness, and although he did not mention himself as a test case, the three hundred plus students in the class knew of his condition and rose to give him a minutes-long standing ovation at the end. David was a man who was deepened, heartened, by what he studied, and this is what has made him such a powerful model.

Near the end of my February visit, David told me that he viewed me as a representative of younger scholars who found his work helpful and were now coming, in my person, as it were, to wish him well. Accordingly, and in this deeply personal spirit of friendship, collegiality, and hope, *Encountering Kālī* is presented as a tribute on behalf of all of us—scholars young and old—to this extraordinary scholar and human being.

ENCOUNTERING KĀLĪ: THE WESTERN CULTURAL CONTEXT

Since the 1970s, interest in goddesses and goddess-like figures has been on the rise in Western culture on both the popular and scholarly levels. For the past twenty years, for example, trade presses have generated numerous books on "the Goddess," New Age movements and feminist writers have appropriated different Asian and primal goddess figures as their own,[3] and Native Americans and ecological activists, often for very different reasons, have rallied around "Mother Earth." During this same period, scholars have continued to debate the role of culture, history, psychology, and gender in the construction and representation of these same goddess figures.[4] It is a mark of this social discourse that what scholars have had to say about goddesses and their natures has often been either largely ignored or actively challenged by the popular culture. Sam Gill's powerful historical study of Mother Earth in Native American cultures, *Mother Earth: An American Story,* in which he argues that the figure of "Mother Earth" was largely a Euro-American idealization of Amerindian culture, which Native American communities later appropriated and identified with for their own reasons, is a case in point.[5] At other times, this unfortunate "split" between popular and scholarly understandings of goddess figures has resulted in gross distortions and even demonizing representations. The portrayal of Kālī in the 1984 Hollywood movie *Indiana Jones and the Temple of Doom* comes immediately to mind. Here, Kālī is portrayed as a macabre demonness to whom crazed Indians and possessed priests (reminiscent in their actions of Incan legends rather than of Hindu texts) tear out the hearts of their innocent victims before lowering them into the steaming bowels of a molten pit. Needless to say, such grossly distorting depictions hardly advance the cause of cross-cultural understanding and could be easily avoided, or at least partially remedied, by a more active dialogue between the popular and scholarly levels of Western culture.

Happily, such cross-fertilizations are already taking place. Some scholars have "come out" as devotees of the Goddess or as members of various North American guru traditions, while others enter active and fruitful dialogues with these same American mystical traditions. On other levels, devotees read academic books and engage their authors via e-mail or through traditional correspondence, and nonspecialists and specialists alike "chat" together on Internet news groups. At other times, this cross-fertilization impacts more popular channels and appears in strikingly hybrid forms, not all of them uncontroversial. Hence "Goddess Kali Lunch Boxes," purchased over the Web, appear in college classrooms, beautifully adorned with traditional Indian popular art; the *Wall Street Journal* reports on the emerging market for Tantric sex weekends;[6] and the television serial *Xena, Warrior Princess* evokes angry protests from Hindu viewers, who sometimes gain support for their denunciations, and at other times do not, from scholars of the Hindu tradition.[7] Thus, as Kālī slowly becomes a recognized part of mainstream Western culture, her worlds become less and less bifurcated and her various proponents more conversant with one another's often very different perspectives. Many bridges, however, still remain to be built or at least imagined.

Encountering Kālī seeks to address some of these broad cultural issues by focusing on the complexities, promises, and problems involved in meeting and interpreting a specific Hindu deity, the goddess Kālī, both in her indigenous South Asian settings and in her more recent Western reincarnations. We conceive this volume as a vigorous example of what theoretically focused and historically responsible cultural studies can be, as well as a corrective to what we perceive as "wild borrowing" on the part of certain segments of Western culture. We are not in principle against such cultural borrowings—far from it—but we see it as one of our goals to provide a document that can, if nothing else, awaken people to both the difficulties and the potential benefits inherent in every act of cross-cultural understanding, including and especially a transforming encounter—cultural, intellectual, artistic, or mystical—with Kālī.

KĀLĪ: A HISTORICAL SKETCH

Kālī is a particularly powerful place to begin such a project, since many of the themes that arise in the modern appropriation of goddesses are unusually, almost fantastically, pronounced in her iconography, mythology, and ritual. As is true of most divine figures, Kālī is a deity with a long, multilayered history.[8] Although worshipped throughout South Asia, she has traditionally been most popular in geographically peripheral areas of the subcontinent, such as Bengal, Assam, and Nepal in the northeast, Kashmir, Panjab, and Himachal Pradesh in the northwest, and Kerala, Tamilnadu, and Sri Lanka in the south. While individual myths, rituals, and iconographic traditions may differ somewhat in each of these areas, Kālī is commonly perceived as a goddess who encompasses and transcends the opposites of life. She is, for example, simultaneously understood as a bloodthirsty demon-slayer, an inflictor and curer of diseases, a deity of ritual possession, and an all-loving, compassionate Mother. That Kālī often delights in shocking her viewers into new modes of awareness and emotional intensity is obvious to anyone who has witnessed her Bengali iconographic representations, which often present her wearing fetuses for earrings, decapitating men, sticking out her tongue for all to see, wearing a garland of chopped-off heads and a miniskirt of human arms, and living in cremation grounds. To make matters ever more complex, despite all of this, her devotees still insist upon affectionately addressing her as "Mā," or "Mother."

As far as can be reconstructed from literary and iconographic sources, Kālī's present complexity of character developed slowly during the course of at least two thousand years. Although she was probably originally a tribal goddess, by the epic and early Purāṇic periods (third century B.C.E. to seventh century C.E.), Kālī was absorbed into the Brāhmaṇical, Sanskrit tradition as a dangerous, blood-loving battle queen. Her first major appearance, for example, is in the "Devī-Māhātmya" (ca. sixth century C.E.), where she appears as the goddess Durgā's fury incarnate. Later, in Tantric ritual and philosophy (eighth to sixteenth centuries C.E.), she was elevated to an ontological absolute and identified with the dynamic ground of the universe. More recently, several devotional traditions (seventeenth century C.E. on) have claimed her as the loving Mother of all. Interpretations of Kālī, in other words, have evolved significantly over time. Although a male *mudiyettu* dancer acting the part of Kālī in a Kerala ritual may view her differently from a Banaras woman believed to be an incarnation of the Goddess, both are heir to an impressive composite layering of beliefs about Kālī, incorporating tribal, priestly, Tantric, and popular histories.

One of the most interesting developments in contemporary Western appropriations of this goddess is that she has been lifted out of the specificity of her several geographic, cultural, and literary South Asian contexts and fashioned into an ahistorical, archetypal, feminist figure. Some feminist writers, for example, have turned to her as an empowering model of female energy to do battle with the oppressive strictures of patriarchal social practices. And, indeed, Kālī seems to confirm their reading with stunning scenes of graphic violence: in one genre of popular poster, for instance, she effortlessly decapitates a male demon and stands on her corpselike husband while her female attendants cut off the limbs and heads of an opposing all-male army. Similarly, it is not difficult to see why New Age authors have seen in Kālī a radical sacralization of sexuality: the full-breasted Goddess is usually depicted naked and is often described as engaging her supine husband in sexual intercourse. Such Western interpretations of Kālī represent the most recent hermeneutical layer in her complex history. All of these layers, however, are tied together by a common social thread: she may be a bloodthirsty tribal deity, a goddess of esoteric Tantric rites, the Mother of devotional poets experiencing the political and social upheavals of eighteenth-century Bengal, or the Terrible Mother of universal female strength and rage, but in all cases, by her very multivalency, Kālī expresses transformative power (*śakti*). Whether marginalized or mainstreamed, apologized for or enthusiastically endorsed, such *śakti* both reflects and influences the aspirations of her votaries. Encountering Kālī, as we seek to do here, is definitely not for the meek.

THE SCHOLARSHIP: EARLY REACTIONS AND PRESENT PATTERNS

Western interest in Kālī has always been strong, if not overly favorable. Kālīghāṭ, for example, a famous Kālī temple situated in the area that is now Calcutta, has been a focus of curiosity from the time British merchants first settled there in the late seventeenth century. Eighteenth- and nineteenth-century diaries and travelogues of civil servants, missionaries, and tourists almost invariably include references to the Kālīghāṭ temple, which came to symbolize for such writers the idolatry, barbarism, and sheer otherness of non-Christian religiosity.[9] Kālī's alleged association with the Thugs, a group of Indian stranglers whose practices were stamped out by the British in the 1830s, also aroused Western censure and righteous indignation.[10] But perhaps most problematic of all was Kālī's association with the Tantric traditions, a family of Indian mystical traditions that variously employ erotic acts and symbols, many of them explicitly antinomian, in their rituals, philosophies, and myths.[11] Some Hindus countered such attacks on their Goddess and her traditions (attacks that, in many ways, mirrored those of earlier indigenous critical voices),[12] while others, influenced by Western values and reactions, either joined the foreign critique[13] or attempted to explain away her rough edges through various philosophical, allegorical, and apologetic strategies.[14] That Kālī needed such defense, justification, muting, and translation is eloquent and ironic testament to her "problematic" nature. Thus we can debate many of her aspects, but not the historical fact that she has been endlessly debated.

Such Western attitudes persisted well into the twentieth century, although the early decades of the century did witness the attempts of a few Western scholars to defend Kālī and the larger Tantric worlds in which she was ritually worshipped, philosophically understood, and mystically experienced in ecstatic and visionary moments.[15] This positive trend culminated in the many works of Sir John Woodroffe (1865–1936). The son of an advocate-general of Bengal, Woodroffe was an Oxford graduate, Tagore Professor of Law at Calcutta University, and a judge of the High Court of Calcutta. He was also a complex bicultural personality, a Roman Catholic who attempted in his life and writings to synthesize elements of British and Bengali culture. Writing voluminously on Tantric philosophy under the romantic pen name Arthur Avalon (as Kathleen Taylor has shown, almost certainly a code name for Woodroffe's intimate collaboration with Atal Bihari Ghose, who probably did most of the actual translation work), Woodroffe had himself photographed in indigenous dress before the Konarak temple (famous for its erotic sculptures), insisted on drawing out the similarities between Tantric and Catholic ritual sensibilities, and did not hesitate to quote a "European friend" who had experienced the power of an awakening *kuṇḍalinī* energy.[16] In all of this, he powerfully embodied the general doctrinal parameters (Tantra, eroticism, kuṇḍalinī, etc.), syncretic qualities, and discursive practices of much contemporary New Age thought; and indeed, his writings did much to inform and inspire this modern tradition of appropriation (astonishingly, many of his works are still in print after over ninety years). Although Woodroffe's publications are still important for the study of Kālī and Tantra—no Western scholar has even come close to the sheer volume, scope, and influence of his work—his books are difficult waters to chart because of their textual detail, inadequate referencing, and total lack of indices. Moreover, his work is marked by several cultural, moral, and philosophical biases that still color and in many ways restrict academic discourses on the Goddess to this day. For instance, his moralizing censorship of Tantric eroticism, his often forced cross-cultural comparisons, and his tendency to view the West as "scientific" and India as "spiritual" are all extremely problematic by contemporary scholarly standards. In the end, despite his early attempts to defend the Tantric tradition and its worship of goddesses, these difficulties—Tantra's infamous use of sexual metaphor and ritual and Woodroffe's own intellectual prejudices—led to a virtual scholarly neglect of the subject for the half century between Woodroffe's writings and the early 1960s.[17]

Beginning in the 1960s but flowering in the 1970s, Western interest in India, Hinduism, and Tantra grew in tandem with countercultural groups seeking meaning outside of Christian and Jewish norms. An early result of such interests has been works by Indian and Western authors that concentrate on Indian art. These may be less scholarly than the writings of Woodroffe, but they are no less influential in their attempt to present Tantra favorably to English-speaking audiences. Philip Rawson's *The Art of Tantra* and Ajit Mookerjee's *Kali, the Feminine Force* epitomize the genre;[18] here, Tantra and Kālī, respectively, are interpreted broadly, with almost anything sexual or goddess-related being brought under the scope of study. These works are themselves apologetic, seeking to rescue Indian religiosity both from overbearing moralism and from the perceived Western obsession with sex. Tantra and its goddess, Kālī, are more—are deeper, more complex in their spiritual and symbolic resonances—than a neophyte might think, such works implicitly argue.[19] Mookerjee's text, in particular, stands as a bridge between the scholarly and the popular in the interpretation of Kālī. His wide-ranging inclusion of ancient Indian "goddess" figurines and fertility symbols as part of Kālī's iconographic history is based more on symbolic and psychological association than on textual or art historical evidence, so scholars tend to view the book—valuable though it is for the labeled images of Kālī that Mookerjee collected—with caution.

Woodroffe and Mookerjee embody two different approaches to the rehabilitation of Hindu goddesses such as Kālī—one, elite, based on the translation and interpretation of Sanskrit texts, and the other, popular, deriving its source material from art. A third approach, through historical, textual, and psychological studies of devotees of the Goddess, has become increasingly important over the past decade. Inevitably, what we find in this third approach is a kind of historical revisionism designed to recover and restore the Tantric dimensions of the Goddess through her saints and mystics. Here we might call to mind Malcolm McLean's textual reconstructions of the eighteenth-century Bengali Kālī poet Rāmprasād with McLean's analyses of the singer's Bengali poems as essentially Tantric in doctrinal content,[20] and the several recent studies of perhaps the most famous Kālī devotee of all, the Bengali saint and mystic Ramakrishna Paramahaṁsa (1836–86). (During a recent visit to Boulder, Colorado, one of us [Jeff] walked into a sidewalk store selling South Asian art and religious items; the brass and clay statues of Kālī were arranged around a painted clay image of Ramakrishna seated in a yogic posture, as if to signal Ramakrishna's archetypal status among Kālī devotees, South Asian and Western alike.) As is well known, Ramakrishna has been the focus of numerous Western studies and encomia since his principal disciple, Swami Vivekananda (1863–1902), brought his message of the unity of all religions to the West at the first World Parliament of Religions in 1893. Most of the early English writers, lacking access to the rich fund of Bengali biographies, focused on Ramakrishna's perennialist message that all religious traditions lead to the same mystical goal; interest in his relationship with the goddess Kālī and her Śākta background was muted, if not actively suppressed.[21] Walter Neevel's 1976 essay "The Transformation of Śrī Rāmakrishna"[22] stands almost alone in its insistence on the Tantric nature of Ramakrishna's religious experiences and teachings until the 1990s, a decade that witnessed a rich spate of no fewer than seven major studies of Ramakrishna by Western and South Asian scholars, all focusing on the saint's remarkable sexuality, and many highlighting through a psychoanalytically informed method[23] the explicitly Tantric dimensions of that same sexuality.[24] It goes without saying that the picture of Kālī that has gradually emerged through such textual and psychological microstudies of historical figures has added an important new dimension to our shared "vision" (*darśana*) of the Goddess.

A fourth approach owes its origins to Cold War policies put in place by Western governments from the late 1960s. Newly funded area studies programs were established to train experts in the understanding of foreign cultures; situated at major universities, they provided vernacular language instruction and sent students to various parts of South Asia so that they could gain firsthand experience and familiarity with the peoples whose customs and beliefs they were studying. David Kinsley, at the time a graduate student at the University of Chicago, was one of the first who availed himself of this opportunity to turn his attention to Kālī. After a year in Calcutta—during which he spoke with Bengali devotees of Kālī and translated a number of Sanskrit and Bengali texts relating to the Goddess's history under the direction of a Bengali mentor—he published *The Sword and the Flute,* the first book in English to explore Kālī's meaning to her indigenous followers through a dispassionate reading of her vernacular and Sanskrit texts. In this reading, Kinsley advanced an interpretive framework in which some of the Goddess's more extreme characteristics, such as her famous violent nature, could be placed in their proper historical setting and understood as genuinely religious. Kinsley thus initiated a fourth method of studying of Kālī—an approach employing a mix of resources from history, texts, and field studies that asks questions concerning the theological and personal import of the Goddess to her South Asian worshippers. Since the publication of *The Sword and the Flute,* Kinsley's writing has become the starting point for all students' work on the Goddess, and many of the contributors to the present volume count him as an inspiration, if not an actual mentor.

As might be expected, however, the opening that Kinsley made into Kālī Studies has been enriched by the new interests, questions, and theoretical approaches of his followers. The overattention to Bengal as a region of study—natural because of the prominence of Calcutta in British history—has given way to the inclusion of all other regions of India, as well as Sri Lanka, Tibet, and Nepal. Thus, Indian vernaculars have been added to Sanskrit as a medium of study, and there are now as many field studies on Kālī worship as there are translations of her texts.[25] Scholars are also asking how

Indian women's relationships with Kālī differ from those of men,[26] or what Kālī devotion looks like when it is transported outside South Asia.[27] Finally, contemporary scholars are using a battery of sophisticated theoretical models, derived variously from feminist theory, psychoanalysis, structuralism, postcolonial theory, and postmodernism, to investigate further the subtleties of Kālī's meaning. Thus, in venturing into the study of Kālī, Tantra, and goddess-centered Hindu religiosity, the contributors to the present volume, by no means alone in their fascination with Kālī, are representative of a wider commitment among scholars of Hinduism to the elucidation and sympathetic investigation of her history and meaning in both South Asian and Western contexts. In this, they all write within a long discursive history richly troubled and amply inspired by a whole host of genres and personalities, from colonial and Christian denunciations to Woodroffe's existentially committed philosophizing to David Kinsley's eloquent phenomenological and historical analyses.

KĀLĪ AND THE HUMANITIES: THE MANY-ARMED DIVERSITY OF CULTURAL UNDERSTANDING

Precisely because we all write within this history—much of it ineluctably marked by the shadow of colonialism—and because we are explicitly approaching Kālī as a goddess of power and even of extremes, it is crucial that we not needlessly exoticize, demonize, or objectify her beyond what the texts and cultures we set out to study warrant. While some eighteenth- and nineteenth-century Orientalist writers, as described in the chapters to follow, may indeed have been guilty of this, projecting their fantasies of a morally corrupt East onto Kālī, such is neither our intent nor, we believe, the result of the work that follows. We are not making Kālī extreme. Rather, we are exploring and reflecting upon what her indigenous South Asian contexts have long acknowledged and even celebrated, the excesses of her power, sexuality, and violence, and the hidden potential of these energies to transform and liberate those who dare approach her. Indeed, every culture has its own category of the exotic; for those in the Hindu mainstream, this includes Kālī's various provenances—Tantra, tribal culture, historical links to social revolution, and a bloody temple cult—all of them both alluring and dangerous. The simple fact that Kālī's devotees frequently encounter her as "extreme" is more than established and supported, if perhaps unintentionally, by the presence of interpretive strategies that the indigenous cultures have adopted to explain away these more troubling aspects of her character and iconography. Several contributors to this volume were persuaded during the course of their fieldwork to admit more of the Goddess's off-putting characteristics than they had initially seen or intended. Sometimes this was because of straightforward claims made by their informants; at other times, the puissant underbelly of the Goddess emerged through an investigation of their informants' discomfort with the history of the deity for which they were seeking to provide an exegesis.

More recently, this goddess has taken on a life in the West, and here, when Westerners appropriate Kālī, they tend to turn to the very graphic and excessive features that indigenous cultures have rejected or tried to mollify: sexuality, social rage, and associations with battle. To complicate things further, these Western traditions often reinterpret these features in terms that are foreign and even incomprehensible to the Goddess's contemporary South Asian devotees. For example, Kālī is infrequently claimed as a feminist icon in South Asia. Nor is she often understood in her indigenous contexts as a symbol of the liberating powers of female sexuality. The extreme nature of both Kālī's original iconographic and textual history and her later South Asian reinterpretations are thus replaced by yet another extreme strategy, a bold act of cross-cultural borrowing and transformation. The ironic result is this: what traditional Hindu texts relate about Kālī and Tantra is often denied or explained away by different Hindu strategies of interpretation. To put it mildly, what Westerners tend to see in Kālī is not necessarily what Hindus see and appreciate. There are clear dissonances, then, between South Asian textual traditions and modern South Asian understandings, as well as between contemporary Western and South Asian readings. One of the primary goals of this book is to identify these dissonances and attempt to relate them critically to one another. Why, for example, do Westerners tend to emphasize the very characteristics in Kālī that Indians want to explain away or even deny? Should we privilege South Asian Hindu constructions of Kālī over Western constructions of Kālī, or are all of these different Kālīs equally creative imaginings performed within different historical and social contexts? Can scholarship and theoretical discourse shed some light on this moment of cross-cultural understanding? This certainly is our hope.

The essays in *Encountering Kālī* are divided into two geographically distinct parts: Kālī as she is represented and understood in South Asian settings; and Kālī as the Goddess of Western discourse, as perceived and practiced by scholars, psychoanalysts, feminists, and the votaries of goddess spirituality. It is our contention that wherever she resides, this complex goddess invites, and indeed usually demands, interpretive measures that are as radical and revolutionary as her iconographic forms.

Part I is devoted to Kālī's indigenous South Asian iconography, mythology, and symbolism. The six chapters in this section employ a variety of methods and situate themselves in different parts of the Indian subcontinent. We begin the volume by reprinting the chapter on Kālī in David Kinsley's book *Hindu Goddesses: Visions of the Divine Feminine in the Hindu Religious Tradition.*[28] This both gives scope to his voice and provides an introduction to Kālī's basic story for those who are unfamiliar with it, as well as acknowledging our indebtedness to his pioneering work. In this sense, we are like those legendary gods "with Indra at their head."[29] Kinsley surveys Kālī's Sanskrit and Bengali textual history, proposes likely reasons for her growing importance in Tantra during the medieval period and in devotionalism in late-eighteenth-century Bengal, and concludes by explicating her theological significance as a symbol of unconventionality, death, and the possibility of spiritual awakening.

Patricia Dold continues Kinsley's textual emphasis and phenomenological style in her "Kālī the Terrific and Her Tests: The Śākta Devotionalism of the *Mahābhāgavata Purāṇa*" by reporting on a late medieval Śākta text that glorifies the Goddess in her form as Kālī. As Dold demonstrates, the Kālī to emerge from this work is not simply a bloodthirsty, demon-slaying deity but also a magnificent mother, who tests and then lovingly rewards her devotees. Dold sees in this Purāṇa an early prototype of what later happens in the eighteenth-century Śākta *bhakti* poetry of Bengal: the Goddess is sweetened as her rough edges and extremities are increasingly downplayed and muted by devotion, public popularity, and modern sensibilities.

The next four chapters draw almost exclusively upon contemporary fieldwork—the first two providing further evidence of indigenous efforts to contain and mainstream the Goddess's theological and social implications. In "The Domestication of a Goddess: *Caraṇa-tīrtha* Kālīghāṭ, the *Mahāpīṭha* of Kālī," Sanjukta Gupta narrates in fascinating detail how the priests of Kālīghāṭ, Kālī's most famous temple in Bengal, have been systematically Vaiṣṇavizing her, removing as many reminders of her Tantric background as possible in their ritual regimens. Gupta's paper reminds us that public perceptions and elite priestly motivations, even if radically different, can exist alongside one another with little overt tension.

Likewise, Usha Menon and Richard A. Shweder, in "Dominating Kālī: Hindu Family Values and Tantric Power," demonstrate how the icon of Kālī trampling on her husband Śiva with her tongue extended has been almost completely reinterpreted in modern Oriya contexts; no longer a cue to Tantric rituals of sexual hierarchy reversal, this image is now understood by most contemporary devotees as reflecting culturally approved ideals of women's modesty and "shame" (Oriyan Indians stick out their tongues slightly in an act of embarrassed "biting" when they are ashamed). The "shame" the culture feels for its own Goddess is thus displaced and projected onto the Goddess herself in an interpretation that finds little, if any, support in the historical texts.

Patricia Lawrence's chapter, "Kāḷi in a Context of Terror: The Tasks of a Goddess in Sri Lanka's Civil War," is a chilling reminder that this goddess of extremes is not always hidden, masked by embarrassment, or made more "respectable." In war-torn Sri Lanka, Kālī worship is undergoing a dramatic resurgence, with Tamil devotees flocking to her oracles both for aid in embodying and interpreting the horrible injuries of war and to perform propitiatory acts of self-mutilation. Kālī here is an angry mother goddess who must be both appeased and quite literally inscribed onto the suffering bodies of her devotees in trance and political torture.

Roxanne Kamayani Gupta, in her "Kālī Māyī: Myth and Reality in a Banaras Ghetto," flips the coin and shows us a mysterious, spiritually masterful, and yet vulnerable Kālī in the form of a living incarnation. Kālī Māyī is an old woman, living in poverty, who acts as the priest in a small Kālī temple in Banaras. Although she is the catalyst for several transformative events in Gupta's life, Kālī Māyī is the victim of a local goonda, and it is Gupta herself, in an enraged and sympathetic response, who embodies the Goddess's compassionate revenge. Gupta concludes her chapter with a self-reflexive analysis of the shifting projections, identifications, and role reversals that took place between the Goddess, Kālī Māyī, and herself, and considers what they might teach us about the dissonances between Western and South Asian understandings of Kālī.

If Part I provides evidence for Kālī's associations in South Asia with blood and power, sexuality and Tantra—whether these be utilized or disguised—Part II turns decidedly to the West and investigates the various contours of her different Western representations. We begin with Cynthia Ann Humes and Hugh B. Urban, both of whose essays focus on the eighteenth- and nineteenth-century Orientalists and their fascination with, fear of, and religious and political censure of the black Goddess. Humes begins our discussion with "Wrestling with Kālī: South Asian and British Constructions of the Dark Goddess," an eloquent analysis of six different South Asian models of experiencing Kālī (devotional, apologetic, disbelieving, demonizing, dismissive, and sensationalizing or scandalizing), with a particular eye on indigenous South Asian literatures well outside the Śākta fold of the Goddess (e.g., Christian folklore, Jaina morality tales, and Buddhist hagiographies). While setting out the models and discussing in some detail the specifics of their different positions, Humes also relates these discourses to the later constructions of British colonialists, who employed many of these indigenous models for their own, very different ends. By so doing, Humes is able to document that British constructions of Kālī, far from being concoctions called up from nowhere, were in fact deeply reliant upon indigenous self-understandings and discourses, even if, at the same time, they took these prior models in some disturbing and often radically distorting directions (e.g., the infamous Thugee cult legend).

Hugh B. Urban's essay, "'India's Darkest Heart': Kālī in the Colonial Imagination," argues that Kālī was conceived by eighteenth- and nineteenth-century colonialists as the worst example of irrational Indian savagery. Such a reading of Kālī as the quintessential Other and the "extreme Orient" influenced Britons' dealings with the "Thugs" and led to the creation of a genre of Victorian novels centered on the lurid East. But such imagery always works both ways, and Urban also discusses the strategies of appropriation and subversion used by Indian nationalists, who turned this Orientalist Kālī against her colonial creators in their own literatures and actions. Urban's chapter thus complements that of Humes, for while not denying that British constructions of Kālī had a history, he demonstrates how their use of these histories forged a unique path.

With the next chapter, Jeffrey J. Kripal's "Why the Tāntrika Is a Hero: Kālī in the Psychoanalytic Tradition," we take up Western theory as both an arena for Kālī's descent into Western culture and a battleground for her proper representation and interpretation. Psychoanalysis is the Western hermeneutical tradition that has given the longest and most studied attention to Kālī. Interpreting the Goddess as a striking mythological embodiment of psychological patterns originating in Indian child-rearing practices and Brāhmaṇical social values, psychoanalysis, Kripal argues, can throw considerable light on such questions as why the male Tāntrika is called a "hero" (*vīra*), why Tantric ritual and language tend to "split" woman into a pure Mother and a sexually dangerous but attractive Lover, and why the Tantric traditions insist on their (in)famous synthesis of spiritual and sexual energies. To begin to answer such questions, Kripal outlines the twentieth-century psychoanalytic meditation on the Goddess through a series of mini-studies of prominent theorists and writers, offering, at the end, his own concluding reflections on what it all might mean for future studies of the Goddess.

Next we move to Keith E. McNeal's "Doing the Mother's Caribbean Work: On *Shakti* and Society in Contemporary Trinidad," which explores what he poignantly calls Kālī's "second exile," based on her double marginality in the West Indies. Exiled to Trinidad with her Indian devotees from her native South Asia in the nineteenth century, Kālī has been exiled again within Trinidadian society through a number of different colonial, economic, and Hindu processes of acculturation, sanitation, and religion-building. Even so, the Goddess has proven herself to be amazingly protean and syncretic on the island, capable of drawing on local practices and cultural dynamics in order to continue to meet the ever-changing needs of her devotees. To McNeal, this is a potent reminder of "the flexible and innovative power of *shakti* cosmology as a situated symbolic system," for this remarkable goddess unites in herself several seeming opposites—India and the West, power and oppression, Catholicism and Hinduism, and mysticism and psychiatry.

Sarah Caldwell then picks up this theoretical discourse and shifts it in a feminist direction with her chapter, "Margins at the Center: Tracing Kālī through Time, Space, and Culture." Here she calls for scholars of the Hindu religious tradition not to assume that what the Brāhmaṇical or geographic mainstream labels "marginal" really is so peripheral to people's lives. In regions and among peoples for whom Kālī is significant, she is central; indeed, it is the marginalized—women and tribals in particular—whose early involvement with Kālī may have given rise to the very conceptions of the Goddess that have informed mainstream, Brāhmaṇical, male thinking. Hers is, in effect, a call to see and recognize the women standing at the historical, ritual, and psychological margins of the Kālī traditions, while affirming that in their own spheres, Kālī is absolutely pivotal. Caldwell, in essence, exhorts a revisioning of the scholarly portrayal of Kālī as a deity of "outsiders."

Finally, we close the volume in the present with Rachel Fell McDermott's chapter, "Kālī's New Frontiers: A Hindu Goddess on the Internet." In two senses, McDermott's essay echoes the earlier contributions of Humes and Urban. First, the authors of her sources—websites, Internet news groups, and electronic magazines—are, like the Orientalist civil servants, missionaries, travelers, and novelists of the eighteenth and nineteenth centuries, not scholars in the traditional sense; mostly engaged in other professions, they imbue Kālī with personal, idiosyncratic meanings. Secondly, feminist and New Age proponents of Kālī have been criticized by Hindus living in the West as representative of a wave of neocolonialists; to some such critics, these Western interpreters and appropriators of the Goddess are every bit as insidious as those of the past two centuries. McDermott summarizes the various venues in which Kālī appears on the Internet and then discusses how the democratization of information media has affected the depiction of the Goddess.

ON THE MANY KĀLĪS

In sum, we might say that there are many Kālīs and many ways to conceive of these goddesses' presence in the religious histories of India and now the West. But is there some common thread, some pattern, a unity to be perceived beneath her many pluralities, be they historically, mythologically, or devotionally construed? It is most likely impossible to identify any such unity if we restrict ourselves to particular periods, cultures, or texts. The modern Bengali devotee of "Kālī Mā" will usually insist on the Goddess's gentle love and the emotional subtleties of *bhakti* and its *bhāva*s, or "moods," as the privileged means of access to her and as the predominant psychic places of her meanings. In a strikingly different way, the early-twentieth-century nationalist revolutionary will emphasize her violence, read her disheveled appearance as a symbol of India's unjust domination under the British, and even preach a sacrifice of "the white goat," that is, of the colonialist, as a means to rejuvenate her. The medieval Tāntrika, in still another hermeneutical move, will perform mortuary rituals in cremation grounds, induce altered states of consciousness with drugs, dance, and meditation, and engage in erotico-mystical practices to approach the same Goddess as an embodiment of divine consciousness, imploded back onto itself now, in an experience of bliss, being, and infinite freedom. The modern (or rather, postmodern) American devotee, on the other hand, may see in her unrestrained rage and her dominant position atop Śiva, that archetypal male, a potent symbolism for a religiously toned feminist project. In yet another perspective, the psychoanalyst or psychologically inclined anthropologist may see her as a projection of male fears about female sexuality, the devouring mother, and unresolved oedipal issues arising out of the particularities of Indian child-rearing practices. And so on and so on, through discourse after discourse.

It is difficult indeed to see what a devotee, a political revolutionary of the 1920s, a medieval Tāntrika, a postmodern feminist, and a contemporary psychoanalytic thinker might have in common. But not entirely impossible. For all of these figures and all of their Kālīs can be seen to represent together a kind of radical response to those many limit-situations of human experience in which the normal parameters of the world break down, frequently in the hope of something better or more adequate to the rich, often paradoxical textures of our lives (and deaths). Perhaps that is what we are after in the end—a new world to live and think and love in, a world big enough and honest enough to embrace the full scope and depth of human consciousness. Here Kālī beckons us, powerful, dangerous, fascinating, and paradoxical. Appropriately, those who seek to encounter such a Goddess respond to her multi-armed nature in equally diverse and even contradictory ways, through personal devotion, animal sacrifice, ecstasy, suffering, and, perhaps strangest of all, academic scholarship.

NOTES

1. David R. Kinsley, *The Sword and the Flute: Kālī and Kṛṣṇa: Visions of the Terrible and the Sublime in Hindu Mythology* (Berkeley and Los Angeles: University of California Press, 1975, reprinted 2000).

2. Ibid., p. 145.

3. For a representative sampling of Western writers finding solace and strength in Western and non-Western goddess figures, see Carol Christ, *Rebirth of the Goddess: Finding Meaning in Feminist Spirituality* (New York: Routledge, 1998); Elinor Gadon, *The Once and Future Goddess: A Symbol for Our Time* (New York: Harper & Row, 1989); China Galland, *The Bond between Women: A Journey to Fierce Compassion* (New York: Riverhead Books, 1998); Wendy Griffin, ed., *Daughters of the Goddess: Studies of Healing, Identity, and Empowerment* (Walnut Creek, Calif.: AltaMira Press, 2000); Rita Gross, *Soaring and Settling: Buddhist Perspectives on Contemporary Social and Religious Issues* (New York: Continuum, 1998); Lina Gupta, "Kali, the Savior," in *After Patriarchy: Feminist Transformations of the World Religions,* ed. Paula M. Cooey, William R. Eakin, and Jay B. McDaniel (Maryknoll, N.Y.: Orbis Books, 1991), pp. 15–38; Alf Hiltebei-

tel and Kathleen Erndl, eds., *Is the Goddess a Feminist? The Politics of South Asian Goddesses* (Sheffield: Sheffield Academic Press; New York: New York University Press, 2000); and Merlin Stone, *When God Was a Woman* (New York: Dial Press, 1976).

4. See Cynthia Eller, *Living in the Lap of the Goddess: The Feminist Spirituality Movement in America* (New York: Crossroad, 1993) and *The Myth of Matriarchal Prehistory: Why an Invented Past Won't Give Women a Future* (Boston: Beacon Press, 2000); Larry Hurtado, ed., *Goddesses in Religion and Modern Debate* (Atlanta: Scholars Press, 1990); David R. Kinsley, *The Goddesses' Mirror: Visions of the Divine Feminine from East and West* (Albany: State University of New York Press, 1989); Lote Motz, *The Faces of the Goddess* (New York: Oxford University Press, 1997); Elizabeth Puttick, "Goddess Spirituality: The Feminist Alternative?" in id., *Women in New Religions: In Search of Community, Sexuality, and Spiritual Power* (New York: St. Martin's Press, 1997), pp. 196–231; and Susan Starr Sered, *Priestess, Mother, Sacred Sister: Religions Dominated by Women* (New York: Oxford University Press, 1994).

5. Sam Gill, *Mother Earth: An American Story* (Chicago: University of Chicago Press, 1987).

6. "Naked Ambition: Tantra May Be Old, but It Has Generated a Hot Modern Market," *Wall Street Journal,* December 7, 1998, pp. A1, 6.

7. See discussion on p. 283–84 below.

8. The best general historical and textual surveys of the goddess Kālī include J. N. Banerjea, *Pauranic and Tantric Religion, Early Phase* (Calcutta: Calcutta University, 1966); Śaśibhūṣaṇ Dāśgupta, "Kālī-Debī o Kālī Pūjār Itihās," in his *Bhārater Śakti-Sādhanā o Śākta Sāhitya* (Calcutta: Sāhitya Saṃsad, 1960), pp. 63–89; Kinsley, *Sword and the Flute;* and Pushpendra Kumar, *Śakti Cult in Ancient India* (Varanasi: Bhartiya Publishing House, 1974).

9. See William S. Caine, *Picturesque India: A Handbook for European Travellers* (London: Routledge, 1898), pp. 336–38; Katherine Mayo, *Mother India* (1927; London: Jonathan Cape, 1930), pp. 13–19; J. Campbell Oman, "Kalighat and Hinduism in Bengal," in his *Brahmins, Theists, and Muslims of India* (London: T. Fisher Unwin, 1907), pp. 3–23; Fanny Parks, *Wanderings of a Pilgrim in Search of the Picturesque,* 2 vols. (1850; Karachi: Oxford University Press, 1975), 2: 104; and William Ward, *The History, Literature, and Mythology of the Hindoos,* 4 vols., 3d ed. (1817–20; Delhi: Low Price Publications, 1990), 4: 154–60.

10. The person principally responsible for identifying and checking Thuggee was Maj.-Gen. Sir William Henry Sleeman. See his *Thugs or Phansigars: Comprising a History of the Rise and Progress of that Extraordinary Fraternity of Assassins; and a description of the system which it pursues, and of the measures which have been adopted by the Supreme Government of India for its suppression* (Philadelphia: Carey & Hart, 1839). For other contemporary, scandalized descriptions, refer to James Hutton, *A Popular Account of the Thugs and Dacoits* (London: William H. Allen, 1857), and Edward Thornton, *Illustrations of the History and Practices of the Thugs and Notices of Some of the Proceedings of the Government of India, for the Suppression of the Crime of Thuggee* (London: William H. Allen, 1837). Cynthia Humes and Hugh Urban discuss the Thugs in more detail below.

11. An excellent introduction to the philosophical concepts, ritual practices, and textual foundations of Tantra may be found in Teun Goudriaan and Sanjukta

Gupta, *Hindu Tantric and Śākta Literature,* vol. 2, fasc. 2 of *A History of Indian Literature,* ed. Jan Gonda (Wiesbaden: Otto Harrassowitz, 1981).

12. A lot of the back-and-forth parleys between Hindus and Britons concerning Hindu goddess worship occurred in the local press, English mostly but also Bengali —see esp. the *Amrita Bazar Patrika, Bengal Hurkaru, Bengalee,* and *Hindoo Patriot*— from the 1830s on. Hindus challenged the British not to interfere, defended their goddesses, and criticized Christians for equal if not worse tendencies toward violence and uncouthness.

13. As early as October 1829, editorials in both the English *Calcutta Gazette* and the Bengali *Samācār Darpaṇ* expressed approval of the reduction in expenditure at the Durgā and Kālī Pūjās, crediting this (1) to Hindu recognition that such ostentation ran counter to the dictates of religion and sanctity—a point that the British had been trying to reinforce—and (2) to the spread of English education. See Mukul Gupta, "Early Editorials on the Puja," in *Statesman Sunday Magazine,* October 11, 1964, p. 10. In 1845, various Hindus joined together to establish the Hindoo Theophilanthropic Society, the object of which was to "exterminate" idolatry (*Bengal Hurkaru,* October 11, 1845, p. 410). By 1860, Hindus loyal to the British were substituting secular "polytechnic displays" in honor of peace in India for the annual goddess festivities (ibid., October 23, 1860, p. 3).

14. Many Hindus tried to translate the spirit of their religion into language that British observers could appreciate. Some said that the goddess festivals fostered communal harmony (*Bengal Hurkaru and India Gazette,* October 7, 1862, p. 2); others stated that icon worship was really only "an outward sign of inward faith" (*Bengalee,* September 23, 1876, p. 30); and still others tried to explain Kālī allegorically. For instance, the Christian convert Joguth Chunder Gangooly published a text on Hinduism intended to explain his former religion sympathetically to his Christian brethren; for his comments on Kālī, see his *Life and Religion of the Hindoos, with a Sketch of My Life and Experience* (Boston: Crosby, Nichols, Lee, 1860), p. 153.

15. Two notable examples are Edward Thompson and Arthur Spencer, trans., *Bengali Religious Lyrics, Śākta* (Calcutta: Oxford University Press, 1923) and Ernest A. Payne, *The Śāktas: An Introductory and Comparative Study* (Calcutta: Y.M.C.A. Publishing House, 1933).

16. Four of Woodroffe's works that are especially relevant to Kālī are *Hymns to the Goddess and Hymn to Kali* (London: Luzac, 1913); *Principles of Tantra,* 2 vols. (London: Luzac, 1914); *The Serpent Power, being the Ṣaṭ-Cakra-Nirūpaṇa and Pādukā-Pañcaka* (London: Luzac, 1918); and *Shakti and Shākta* (London: Luzac, 1918). For good introductions to his work, see Kathleen Taylor, "Arthur Avalon: The Creation of a Legendary Orientalist," in *Myth and Mythmaking: Continuous Evolution in Indian Tradition,* ed. Julia Leslie (Richmond, U.K.: Curzon Press, 1996), pp. 144–64, and *Sir John Woodroffe, Tantra and Bengal: "An Indian Soul in a European Body"?* (Richmond, U.K.: Curzon Press, 2001).

17. Two excellent exceptions, books prior to Kinsley's that treat Tantra in a balanced, scholarly fashion, are Mircea Eliade, *Yoga: Immortality and Freedom,* trans. Willard R. Trask, 2d rev. ed. (1958; Bollingen series, 56, Princeton: Princeton University Press, 1969), and Agehananda Bharati, *The Tantric Tradition* (London: Rider, 1965).

18. Philip S. Rawson, *The Art of Tantra,* rev. ed. (1973; London: Thames & Hud-

son, 1978); and Ajit Mookerjee, *Kali: The Feminine Force* (London: Thames & Hudson, 1988). Other similar texts by the same authors include Rawson, *Erotic Art of the East: The Sexual Theme in Oriental Painting and Sculpture* (New York: Putnam, 1968) and *Oriental Erotic Art* (New York: A and W Publishers, 1981); and Mookerjee, *Tantra Art: Its Philosophy and Physics* (New Delhi: Ravi Kumar, 1966) and, with Madhu Khanna, *The Tantric Way: Art, Science, Ritual* (Boston: New York Graphic Society, 1977).

19. Tantra was gaining a dubious notoriety in the West during the early 1970s, fueled partly by the India-looking counterculture and partly by Indian god-men such as Bhagwan Shri Rajneesh. Among his many published books, see esp. the five volumes of his *Book of the Secrets: Discourses on the Vigyana Bhairava Tantra* (Poona: Rajneesh Foundation, 1974), *From Sex to Super-Consciousness* (Bombay: Jeevan Jagruti Kendra, 1971), and *Tantra, the Supreme Understanding: Discourses on the Tantric Way of Tilopa's Song of Mahamudra* (Rajneeshpuram: Rajneesh Foundation International, 1975).

20. Malcolm McLean, *Devoted to the Goddess: The Life and Work of Ramprasad* (Albany: State University of New York Press, 1998).

21. For a discussion of this textual history of censorship, see Jeffrey J. Kripal, "Pale Plausibilities," preface to the 2d edition of *Kālī's Child: The Mystical and the Erotic in the Life and Teachings of Ramakrishna* (Chicago: University of Chicago Press, 1998).

22. See *Hinduism: New Essays in the History of Religions,* ed. Bardwell L. Smith (Leiden: E. J. Brill, 1976), pp. 53–97.

23. Psychoanalysis has been particularly central to the Western appropriation of Ramakrishna and goes back almost to the beginning of the Western tradition. Romain Rolland, one of Ramakrishna's earliest Western biographers, was, for example, deeply influenced by Freud and used his studies of Ramakrishna and Vivekananda to nurture an important correspondence with Freud that helped generate what would become the psychoanalytic theory of mysticism. For this fascinating story and an astute historical analysis of it, see William B. Parsons, *The Enigma of the Oceanic Feeling: Re-visioning the Psychoanalytic Theory of Mysticism* (New York: Oxford University Press, 1999). For a synopsis of this discussion, see Jeffrey J. Kripal, "Why the Tāntrika Is a Hero: Kālī in the Psychoanalytic Tradition," chapter 9 below.

24. In chronological order: Carl Olson, *The Mysterious Play of Kali: An Interpretive Study of Ramakrishna* (Atlanta: Scholars Press, 1990); Sudhir Kakar, *The Analyst and the Mystic: Psychoanalytic Reflections on Religion and Mysticism* (Chicago: University of Chicago Press, 1991); Narasingha P. Sil, *Ramakrsna Paramahamsa: A Psychological Profile* (Leiden: E. J. Brill, 1991); Catherine Clement and Sudhir Kakar, *La Folle et le saint* (Paris: Seuil, 1993); Kripal, *Kālī's Child;* Parama Roy, "As the Master Saw Her," in *Indian Traffic: Identities in Question in Colonial and Postcolonial India,* ed. id. (Berkeley and Los Angeles: University of California Press, 1998), pp. 92–127; and Narasingha P. Sil, *Ramakrishna Revisited: A New Biography* (Lanham, Md.: University Press of America, 1998).

25. For recent scholarship on Kālī and her relationship to other regional goddesses, see the following localities and studies: for Bengal, June McDaniel, *The Madness of the Saints: Ecstatic Religion in Bengal* (Chicago: University of Chicago Press, 1989), Rachel Fell McDermott, *Mother of My Heart, Daughter of My Dreams: Kālī and Umā in the Devotional Poetry of Bengal* (New York: Oxford University Press, 2001) and

Singing to the Goddess: Poems to Kālī and Umā from Bengal (New York: Oxford University Press, 2001), McLean, *Devoted to the Goddess,* and Suchitra Samanta, "The Self-Animal and Divine Digestion: Goat Sacrifice to the Goddess Kālī in Bengal," *Journal of Asian Studies* 53, no. 3 (1994): 779–803; for the central Himalayas, William Sax, *Mountain Goddess: Gender and Politics in a Himalayan Pilgrimage* (New York: Oxford University Press, 1991); for Kerala, Sarah Caldwell, *Oh Terrifying Mother: Sexuality, Violence, and Worship of the Goddess Kāḷi* (New York: Oxford University Press, 1999); for Nepal, Gérard Toffin, "A Wild Goddess Cult in Nepal: The Navadurgā of the Theco Village (Kathmandu Valley)," in *Wild Goddesses in India and Nepal,* ed. Axel Michaels, Cornelia Vogelsanger, and Annette Wilke (Bern: Peter Lang, 1996), pp. 217–51; for Orissa, Usha Menon and Richard Shweder, "Kali's Tongue: Cultural Psychology and the Power of 'Shame' in Orissa, India," in *Emotion and Culture: Empirical Studies of Mutual Influence,* ed. Shinobu Kitayama and Hazel Markus (Eugene: University of Oregon Press, 1994); for the Panjab Hills, Kathleen M. Erndl, *Victory to the Mother: The Hindu Goddess of Northwest India in Myth, Ritual, and Symbol* (New York: Oxford University Press, 1993); for Sri Lanka, Gananath Obeyesekere, *The Cult of the Goddess Pattini* (Chicago: University of Chicago Press, 1984) and Gananath Obeyesekere and Richard Gombrich, "Kālī, the Punitive Mother," in *Buddhism Transformed: Religious Change in Sri Lanka* (Princeton: Princeton University Press, 1988), pp. 133–162; for Tamilnadu, Eveline Meyer, *Aṅkāḷaparamecuvari: A Goddess of Tamil Nadu, Her Myths and Cult* (Wiesbaden: Franz Steiner Verlag, 1986); for Tibet, Andrea Loseries-Leick, "Kālī in Tibetan Buddhism," in *Wild Goddesses in India and Nepal,* pp. 417–35; and for Vindhyachal, Cynthia Anne Humes, "Vindhyavāsinī: Local Goddess Yet Great Goddess," in *Devī: Goddesses of India,* ed. John Stratton Hawley and Donna Marie Wulff (Berkeley and Los Angeles: University of California Press, 1996), pp. 49–76.

26. See Caldwell's *Oh Terrifying Mother* for a study of how ordinary Keralan women relate to the Goddess. For explorations of women gurus who worship Kālī, see Lisa Lassell Hallstrom, *Mother of Bliss: Ānandamayī Mā (1896–1982)* (New York: Oxford University Press, 1999), and June McDaniel, "Saints, Seekers, and Bhor Ladies: Bengali Holy Women," in *Madness of the Saints,* pp. 191–240. Several scholars are also investigating the attitude of women in nationalist political movements toward Hindu goddesses. See Paola Bacchetta, "All Our Goddesses Are Armed: Religion, Resistance, and Revenge in the Life of a Militant Hindu Nationalist Woman," in *Against All Odds: Essays on Women, Religion, and Development from India and Pakistan,* ed. Kamla Bhasin, Nighat Said Khan, and Ritu Menon (New York: Kali for Women, 1994), pp. 133–56, and Urvashi Butulia and Tanika Sarkar, eds., *Women and Right-Wing Movements: Indian Experiences* (London: Zed Books, 1995).

27. Rachel Fell McDermott, "The Western Kālī," in *Devī: Goddesses of India,* ed. John Stratton Hawley and Donna Marie Wulff (Berkeley and Los Angeles: University of California Press, 1996), pp. 281–313.

28. David Kinsley, *Hindu Goddesses: Visions of the Divine Feminine in the Hindu Religious Tradition* (Berkeley and Los Angeles: University of California Press, 1986), pp. 116–31.

29. Kinsley had been at the Kālī Conference held at Barnard College in September 1996, where most of the papers presented here were first submitted, but he died before he could revise his contribution for this volume. Using an old essay was a compromise to which he agreed six weeks before his death.

PART I

Kālī in the Texts and Contexts of South Asia

CHAPTER 1

Kālī

David R. Kinsley

The goddess Kālī is almost always described as having a terrible, frightening appearance. She is always black or dark, is usually naked, and has long, disheveled hair. She is adorned with severed arms as a girdle, freshly cut heads as a necklace, children's corpses as earrings, and serpents as bracelets. She has long, sharp fangs, is often depicted as having clawlike hands with long nails, and is often said to have blood smeared on her lips. Her favorite haunts heighten her fearsome nature. She is usually shown on the battlefield, where she is a furious combatant who gets drunk on the hot blood of her victims, or in a cremation ground, where she sits on a corpse surrounded by jackals and goblins.

Many texts and contexts treat Kālī as an independent deity, unassociated with any male deity. When she is associated with a god, however, it is almost always Śiva. As his consort, wife, or associate, Kālī often plays the role of inciting him to wild behavior. Kālī's association with Śiva, unlike Pārvatī's, seems aimed at exciting him to take part in dangerous, destructive behavior that threatens the stability of the cosmos. Kālī is particularly popular in Bengal, although she is known and worshiped throughout India. In Bengal, she is worshiped on Dīpāvalī. In this festival, and throughout the year at many of her permanent temples, she receives blood offerings. She is also the recipient of ardent devotion from countless devotees, who approach her as their mother.

EARLY HISTORY

The earliest references to Kālī in the Hindu tradition date to the early medieval period (around A.D. 600) and usually locate Kālī either on the battlefield or in situations on the periphery of Hindu society. In the *Agni-* and *Garuḍa-purāṇas* she is mentioned in invocations that aim at success in war and against one's enemies. She is described as having an awful appearance: she is gaunt, has fangs, laughs loudly, dances madly, wears a garland of corpses, sits on the back of a ghost, and lives in the cremation ground. She is asked to crush, trample, break, and burn the enemy.[1] In the *Bhāgavata-purāṇa,* Kālī is the patron deity of a band of thieves whose leader seeks to achieve Kālī's blessing in order to have a son. The thief kidnaps a saintly Brahman youth with the intention of offering him as a blood sacrifice to Kālī. The effulgence of the virtuous youth, however, burns Kālī herself when he is brought near her image. Emerging from her image, infuriated, she kills the leader and his entire band. She is described as having a dreadful face and large teeth and as laughing loudly. She and her host of demons then decapitate the corpses of the thieves, drink their blood until drunk, and throw their heads about in sport (5.9.12–20).

Bāṇabhaṭṭa's seventh-century drama *Kādambarī* features a goddess named Caṇḍī, an epithet used for both Durgā and Kālī, who is worshiped by the Śabaras, a tribe of primitive hunters. The worship takes place deep in the forest, and blood offerings are made to the goddess.[2] Vākpati's *Gauḍavaho* (late seventh or early eighth century) portrays Kālī as an aspect of Vindhyavāsinī (an epithet of Durgā). She is worshiped by Śabaras, is clothed in leaves, and receives human sacrifices (verses 285–347).[3] In Bhavabhūti's *Mālatīmādhava,* a drama of the early eighth century, a female devotee of Cāmuṇḍā, a goddess who is very often identified with Kālī, captures the heroine, Mālatī, with the intention of sacrificing her to the goddess. Cāmuṇḍā's temple is near a cremation ground. A hymn to the goddess describes her as dancing wildly and making the world shake. She has a gaping mouth, wears a garland of skulls, is covered with snakes, showers flames from her eyes that destroy the world, and is surrounded by goblins.[4]

Somadeva's *Yaśatilaka* (eleventh to twelfth century) contains a long description of a goddess called Caṇḍamārī. In all respects she is like Kālī, and we may understand the scenario Somadeva describes as suggestive of Kālī's appearance and worship at that time. The goddess adorns herself with pieces of human corpses, uses oozings from corpses for cosmetics, bathes in rivers of wine or blood, sports in cremation grounds, and uses human skulls as drinking vessels.[5] Bizarre and fanatical devotees gather at her temple and undertake forms of ascetic self-torture. They burn incense on their heads, drink their own blood, and offer their own flesh to the sacrificial fire.[6]

Kālī's association with the periphery of Hindu society (she is worshiped by tribal or low-caste people in uncivilized or wild places) is also seen in an architectural work of the sixth to eighth centuries, the *Māna-sāra-śilpa-śāstra.* There, it is said that Kālī's temples should be built far from villages and towns, near the cremation grounds and the dwellings of Caṇḍālas (very low-caste people) (9.289).

Kālī's most famous appearances in battle contexts are found in the *Devī-māhātmya.* In the third episode, which features Durgā's defeat of Śumbha and Niśumbha and their allies, Kālī appears twice. Early in the battle, the demons Caṇḍa and Muṇḍa approach Durgā with readied weapons. Seeing them prepared to attack her, Durgā becomes angry, her face becoming dark as ink. Suddenly the goddess Kālī springs from her forehead. She is black, wears a garland of human heads and a tiger skin, and wields a skull-topped staff. She is gaunt, with sunken eyes, gaping mouth, and lolling tongue. She roars loudly and leaps into the battle, where she tears demons apart with her hands and crushes them in her jaws. She grasps the two demon generals and in one furious blow decapitates them both with her sword (7.3–22). Later in the battle, Kālī is summoned by Durgā to help defeat the demon Raktabīja. This demon has the ability to reproduce himself instantly whenever a drop of his blood falls to the ground. Having wounded Raktabīja with a variety of weapons, Durgā and her assistants, a fierce band of goddesses called the Mātṛkās,[7] find they have worsened their situation. As Raktabīja bleeds more and more profusely from his wounds, the battlefield increasingly becomes filled with Raktabīja duplicates. Kālī defeats the demon by sucking the blood from his body and throwing the countless duplicate Raktabījas into her gaping mouth (8.49–61).

In these two episodes, Kālī appears to represent Durgā's personified wrath, her embodied fury. Kālī plays a similar role in her association with Pārvatī. In general, Pārvatī is a benign goddess, but from time to time, she exhibits fierce aspects. When this occurs, Kālī is sometimes described as being brought into being. In the *Liṅga-purāṇa,* Śiva asks Pārvatī to destroy the demon Dāruka, who has been given the boon that he can only be killed by a female. Pārvatī then enters Śiva's body and transforms herself from the poison that is stored in Śiva's throat. She reappears as Kālī, ferocious in appearance, and with the help of flesh-eating *piśācas* (spirits) attacks and defeats Dāruka and his hosts. Kālī, however, becomes so intoxicated by the blood lust of battle that she threatens to destroy the entire world in her fury. The world is saved when Śiva intervenes and calms her (1.106). Kālī appears in a similar context elsewhere in the same text. When Śiva sets out to defeat the demons of the three cities, Kālī is part of his entourage. She whirls a trident, is adorned with skulls, has her eyes half-closed by intoxication from drinking the blood of demons, and wears an elephant hide.

She is also praised, however, as the daughter of Himalaya, a clear identification with Pārvatī. It seems that in the process of Pārvatī's preparations for war, Kālī appears as Pārvatī's personified wrath, her alter ego, as it were (1.72.66–68).

The *Vāmana-purāṇa* calls Pārvatī Kālī (the black one) because of her dark complexion. Hearing Śiva use this name, Pārvatī takes offense and undertakes austerities in order to rid herself of her dark complexion. After succeeding, she is renamed Gaurī (the golden one). Her dark sheath, however, is transformed into the furious battle queen Kauśikī, who subsequently creates Kālī in her fury. So, again, although there is an intermediary goddess (Kauśikī), Kālī plays the role of Pārvatī's dark, negative, violent nature in embodied form (25–29).

Kālī makes similar appearances in myths concerning both Satī and Sītā. In the case of Satī, Kālī appears when Satī's father, Dakṣa, infuriates his daughter by not inviting her and Śiva to a great sacrificial rite. Satī rubs her nose in anger, and Kālī appears.[8] Kālī also appears in other texts when Satī, in her wrath over the same incident, gives birth to or transforms herself into ten goddesses, the Daśamahāvidyās. The first goddess mentioned in this group is usually Kālī.[9] In the case of Sītā, Kālī appears as her fierce, terrible, bloodthirsty aspect when Rāma, on his return to India after defeating Rāvaṇa, is confronted with such a terrible monster that he freezes in fear. Sītā, transformed into Kālī, handily defeats the demon.[10]

In her association with Śiva, Kālī's tendency to wildness and disorder persists. Although she is sometimes tamed or softened by him, at times, she incites Śiva himself to dangerous, destructive behavior. A South Indian tradition tells of a dance contest between the two. After defeating Śumbha and Niśumbha, Kālī takes up residence in a forest with her retinue of fierce companions and terrorizes the surrounding area. A devotee of Śiva in that area becomes distracted from doing austerities and petitions Śiva to rid the forest of the violent goddess. When Śiva appears, Kālī threatens him, claiming the area as her own. Śiva challenges her to a dance contest and defeats her when she is unable (or unwilling) to match his energetic *tāṇḍava* dance.[11]

Although this tradition says that Śiva defeated and forced Kālī to control her disruptive habits, we find few images and myths depicting her becalmed and docile.[12] Instead, we find references or images that show Śiva and Kālī in situations where either or both behave in disruptive ways, inciting each other, or in which Kālī in her wild activity dominates an inactive or sometimes dead Śiva.[13]

In the first type of relationship, the two appear dancing together in such a way that they threaten the world. Bhavabhūti's *Mālatīmādhava* describes the divine pair as they dance wildly near the goddess's temple. Their dance is so frenzied that it threatens to destroy the world. Pārvatī stands nearby, frightened.[14] Here the scenario is not a dance contest but a mutually de-

Figure 1.1 Kālī and Śiva. Gouache on paper, Kangra School, mid nineteenth century. Ann and Bury Peerless Picture Library. Reproduced by permission.

structive dance in which the two deities incite each other. This is a common image in Bengali devotional hymns to Kālī. Śiva and Kālī complement each other in their madness and destructive habits.

> Crazy is my Father, crazy my Mother,
> And I, their son, am crazy too!

Shyama [the dark one, an epithet of Kālī] is my
Mother's name.
My Father strikes His cheeks and makes a hollow sound:
Ba-ba-boom! Ba-ba-boom!
And my Mother, drunk and reeling,
Falls across my Father's body!
Shyama's streaming tresses hang in vast disorder;
Bees are swarming numberless
About her crimson Lotus Feet.
Listen, as She dances, how Her anklets ring![15]

Iconographic representations of Kālī and Śiva nearly always show Kālī as dominant. She is usually standing or dancing on Śiva's prone body, and when the two are depicted in sexual intercourse, she is shown above him. Although Śiva is said to have tamed Kālī in the myth of the dance contest, it seems clear that she was never finally subdued by him, and she is most popularly represented as a being who is uncontrollable and more apt to provoke Śiva to dangerous activity than to be controlled by him.

In general, then, we may say that Kālī is a goddess who threatens stability and order. Although she may be said to serve order in her role as slayer of demons, more often than not, she becomes so frenzied on the battlefield, usually becoming drunk on the blood of her victims, that she herself begins to destroy the world that she is supposed to protect. Thus even in the service of the gods, she is ultimately dangerous and tends to get out of control. In association with other goddesses, she appears to represent their embodied wrath and fury, a frightening, dangerous dimension of the divine feminine that is released when these goddesses become enraged or are summoned to take part in war and killing. In relation to Śiva, she appears to play the opposite role from that of Pārvatī. Pārvatī calms Śiva, counterbalancing his antisocial or destructive tendencies. It is she who brings Śiva within the sphere of domesticity and who, with her soft glances, urges him to moderate the destructive aspects of his *tāṇḍava* dance.[16] Kālī is Śiva's "other" wife, as it were, provoking him and encouraging him in his mad, antisocial, often disruptive habits. It is never Kālī who tames Śiva, but Śiva who must calm Kālī. Her association with criminals reinforces her dangerous role vis-à-vis society. She is at home outside the moral order and seems to be unbounded by that order.

THE LATER HISTORY AND THE SIGNIFICANCE OF KĀLĪ

Given Kālī's intimidating appearance and ghastly habits, it might seem that she would never occupy a central position in Hindu piety, yet she does. She is of central importance in Tantrism, particularly left-handed Tantrism, and in Bengali Śākta devotionalism. An underlying assumption in Tantric ideology is that reality is the result and expression of the symbiotic interaction of male and female, Śiva and *śakti,* the quiescent and the dynamic, and other polar opposites that in interaction produce a creative tension. Consequently, goddesses in Tantrism play an important role and are affirmed to be as central to discerning the nature of reality as the male deities are. Although Śiva is usually said to be the source of the *Tantras,* the source of wisdom and truth, and Pārvatī, his spouse, to be the student to whom the scriptures are given, many of the *Tantras* emphasize the fact that it is *śakti* that pervades reality with her power, might, and vitality and that it is she (understood in personified form to be Pārvatī, Kālī, and other goddesses) who is immediately present to the adept and whose presence and being underlie his own being. For the Tantric adept, it is her vitality that is sought through various techniques aimed at spiritual transformation; thus, it is she who is affirmed as the dominant and primary reality.

Although Pārvatī is usually said to be the recipient of Śiva's wisdom in the form of the *Tantras,* it is Kālī who seems to dominate Tantric iconography, texts, and rituals, especially in left-handed Tantra. In many places, Kālī is praised as the greatest of all deities or the highest reality. In the *Nirvāṇa-tantra,* the gods Brahmā, Viṣṇu, and Śiva are said to arise from her like bubbles from the sea, endlessly arising and passing away, leaving their source unchanged. Compared to Kālī, proclaims this text, Brahmā, Viṣṇu, and Śiva are like the amount of water in a cow's hoofprint compared to the waters of the sea.[17] The *Nigama-kalpataru* and the *Picchilā-tantra* declare that of all mantras, Kālī's is the greatest.[18] The *Yoginī-tantra,* the *Kāmākhyā-tantra,* and the *Niruttara-tantra* all proclaim Kālī the greatest of the *vidyās* (the manifestations of the Mahādevī, the "great goddess") or divinity itself; indeed, they declare her to be the essence or own form (*svarūpa*) of the Mahādevī.[19] The *Kāmadā-tantra* states unequivocally that she is attributeless, neither male nor female, sinless, the imperishable *saccidānanda* (being, consciousness, and bliss), *brahman* itself.[20] In the *Mahānirvāṇa-tantra,* too, Kālī is one of the most common epithets for the primordial *śakti,*[21] and in one passage, Śiva praises her as follows:

> At the dissolution of things, it is Kāla [Time] Who will devour all, and by reason of this He is called Mahākāla [an epithet of Śiva], and since Thou devourest Mahākāla Himself, it is Thou who art the Supreme Primordial Kālikā.
>
> Because Thou devourest Kāla, Thou art Kālī, the original form of all things, and because Thou art the Origin of and devourest all things Thou art called the Adyā [primordial] Kālī. Resuming after Dissolution Thine own form, dark and formless, Thou alone remainest as One ineffable and inconceivable. Though having a form, yet art Thou formless; though Thyself without beginning, multiform by the power of Māyā, Thou art the Beginning of all, Creatrix, Protectress, and Destructress that Thou art. (4.30–34)[22]

Why Kālī, in preference to other goddesses, attained this preeminent position in Tantrism is not entirely clear. Given certain Tantric ideological and ritual presuppositions, however, the following logic seems possible. Tantrism generally is ritually oriented. By means of various rituals (exterior and interior, bodily and mental) the *sādhaka* (practitioner) seeks to gain *mokṣa* (release, salvation). A consistent theme in this endeavor is the uniting of opposites (male-female, microcosm-macrocosm, sacred-profane, Śiva-*śakti*). In Tantrism, there is an elaborate, subtle geography of the body that must be learned, controlled, and ultimately resolved in unity. By means of the body, both the physical and subtle bodies, the *sādhaka* may manipulate levels of reality and harness the dynamics of those levels to the attainment of his goal. The *sādhaka,* with the help of a guru, undertakes to gain his goal by conquest—by using his own body and knowledge of that body to bring the fractured world of name and form, the polarized world of male and female, sacred and profane, to wholeness and unity.

Sādhana (spiritual endeavor) takes a particularly dramatic form in left-handed (*vāmācāra*) Tantrism. In his attempt to realize the nature of the world as completely and thoroughly pervaded by the one *śakti,* the *sādhaka* (here called the "hero," *vīra*) undertakes the ritual of the *pañcatattva,* the "five (forbidden) things" (or truths). In a ritual context, and under the supervision of his guru, the *sādhaka* partakes of wine, meat, fish, parched grain (perhaps a hallucinogenic drug of some kind), and illicit sexual intercourse. In this way, he overcomes the distinction (or duality) of clean and unclean, sacred and profane, and breaks his bondage to a world that is artificially fragmented. He affirms in a radical way the underlying unity of the phenomenal world, the identity of *śakti* with the whole creation. Heroically, he triumphs over it, controls and masters it. By affirming the essential worth of the forbidden, he causes the forbidden to lose its power to pollute, to degrade, to bind.[23]

The figure of Kālī conveys death, destruction, fear, terror, the all-consuming aspect of reality. As such she is also a "forbidden thing," or the forbidden par excellence, for she is death itself. The Tantric hero does not propitiate, fear, ignore, or avoid the forbidden. During the *pañcatattva* ritual, the *sādhaka* boldly confronts Kālī and thereby assimilates, overcomes, and transforms her into a vehicle of salvation. This is particularly clear in the *Karpūrādi-stotra,* a short work in praise of Kālī, which describes the *pañcatattva* ritual as performed in the cremation ground (*śmaśāna-sādhana*). Throughout this text, Kālī is described in familiar terms. She is black (verse 1), has disheveled hair and blood trickling from her mouth (3), holds a sword and a severed head (4), wears a girdle of severed arms, sits on a corpse in the cremation ground (7), and is surrounded by skulls, bones, and female jackals (8). It is she, when confronted boldly in meditation, who gives the *sādhaka* great power and ultimately salvation. In Kālī's favorite dwelling place, the cremation ground, the *sādhaka* meditates on every terrible aspect of the black goddess and thus achieves his goal.

> He, O Mahākālī, who in the cremation-ground, naked, and with dishevelled hair, intently meditates upon Thee and recites Thy *mantra,* and with each recitation makes offering to Thee of a thousand *Akaṇda* flowers with seed, becomes without any effort a Lord of the earth.
>
> O Kālī, whoever on Tuesday at midnight, having uttered Thy *mantra,* makes offering even but once with devotion to Thee of a hair of his *Śakti* [his female companion] in the cremation-ground, becomes a great poet, a Lord of the earth, and ever goes mounted upon an elephant. (15–16)[24]

The *Karpūrādi-stotra* clearly makes Kālī more than a terrible, ferocious slayer of demons who serves Durgā or Śiva on the battlefield. In fact, she is by and large dissociated from the battle context. She is the supreme mistress of the universe (12), she is identified with the five elements (14), and in union with Śiva (who is identified as her spouse),[25] she creates and destroys the worlds. Her appearance has also been modified, befitting her exalted position as ruler of the world and the object of meditation by which the *sādhaka* attains liberation. In addition to her terrible aspects (which are insisted upon), there are now hints of another, benign dimension. So, for example, she is no longer described as emaciated or ugly. In the *Karpūrādi-stotra,* she is young and beautiful (1), has a gently smiling face (18), and makes gestures with her two right hands that dispel fear and offer boons (4). These positive features are entirely apt, because Kālī no longer is a mere shrew, the distillation of Durgā's or Pārvatī's wrath, but is she through whom the hero achieves success, she who grants the boon of salvation, and she who, when boldly approached, frees the *sādhaka* from fear itself. She is here not only the symbol of death but the symbol of triumph over death.

Kālī also attains a central position in late medieval Bengali devotional literature.[26] In this devotion, Kālī's appearance and habits have not changed very much. She remains terrifying in appearance and fearsome in habit. She is eminently recognizable. Rāmprasād Sen (1718–75), one of her most ardent devotees, describes his beloved Kālī in almost shocked tones:

> O Kālī! why dost Thou roam about nude?
> Art Thou not ashamed, Mother!
> Garb and ornaments Thou hast none; yet Thou
> pridest in being King's daughter.
> O Mother! is it a virtue of Thy family that
> Thou placest thy feet on Thy Husband?
> Thou are nude; Thy Husband is nude; you both
> roam cremation grounds.
> O Mother! we are all ashamed of you; do put on
> Thy garb.
> Thou hast cast away Thy necklace of jewells,
> Mother, and worn a garland of human heads.
> Prasāda says, "Mother! Thy fierce beauty has
> frightened Thy nude Consort."[27]

The approach of the devotee to Kālī, however, is quite different in mood and temperament from the approach of the Tantric *sādhaka.* The Tantric adept, seeking to view Kālī in her most terrible aspect, is heroic in approach, cultivating an almost aggressive, fearless stance before her. The Tantric adept challenges Kālī to unveil her most forbidding secrets. The devotee, in contrast, adopts the position of the helpless child when approaching Kālī. Even though the child's mother may be fearsome, at times even hostile, the child has little choice but to return to her for protection, security, and warmth. This is just the attitude Rāmprasād expresses when he writes: "Though she beat it, the child clings to its mother, crying 'Mother.'"[28]

Why Kālī is approached as mother and in what sense she is perceived to be a mother by her devotees are questions that do not have clear or easy answers. In almost every sense, Kālī is *not* portrayed as a mother in the Hindu tradition prior to her central role in Bengali devotion beginning in the eighteenth century. Except in some contexts when she is associated or identified with Pārvatī as Śiva's consort, Kālī is rarely pictured in motherly scenes in Hindu mythology or iconography. Even in Bengali devotion to her, her appearance and habits change very little. Indeed, Kālī's appearance and habits strike one as conveying truths opposed to those conveyed by such archetypal mother goddesses as Pṛthivī, Annapūrṇā, Jagaddhātrī, Śatākṣī, and other Hindu goddesses associated with fertility, growth, abundance, and well-being.[29] These goddesses appear as inexhaustible sources of nourishment and creativity. When depicted iconographically they are heavy-hipped and heavy-breasted. Kālī, especially in her early history, is often depicted or described as emaciated, lean, and gaunt. It is not her breasts or hips that attract attention. It is her mouth, her lolling tongue, and her bloody cleaver. These other goddesses, "mother goddesses" in the obvious sense, give life. Kālī takes life, insatiably. She lives in the cremation ground, haunts the battlefield, sits upon a corpse, and adorns herself with pieces of corpses. If mother goddesses are described as ever fecund, Kālī is described as ever hungry. Her lolling tongue, grotesquely long and oversized, her sunken stomach, emaciated appearance, and sharp fangs convey a presence that is the direct opposite of a fertile, protective mother goddess. If mother goddesses give life, Kālī feeds on life. What they give, she takes away.

Although the attitude of the devotee to Kālī is different from that of the Tantric hero, although their paths appear very different, the attitude and approach of the devotee who insists upon approaching Kālī as his mother may reveal a logic similar to that of the Tantric hero's. The truths about reality that Kālī conveys—namely, that life feeds on death, that death is inevitable for all beings, that time wears all things down, and so on[30]—are just as apparent to the devotee as they are to the Tantric hero. The fearfulness of these truths, however, is mitigated, indeed is transformed into liberating wisdom, if these truths can be accepted. The Tantric hero seeks to appropriate these truths by confronting Kālī, by seeking her in the cremation ground in the dead of night, and by heroically demonstrating courage equal to her terrible presence. The devotee, in contrast, appropriates the truths Kālī reveals by adopting the attitude of a child, whose essential nature toward its mother is that of acceptance, no matter how awful, how indifferent, how fearsome she is. The devotee, then, by making the apparently unlikely assertion that Kālī is his mother, enables himself to approach and appropriate the forbidding truths that Kālī reveals; in appropriating these truths the devotee, like the Tantric adept, is liberated from the fear these truths impose on people who deny or ignore them.

Through devotion to Kālī, the devotee becomes reconciled to death and achieves an acceptance of the way things are, an equilibrium that remains unperturbed in Kālī's presence. These themes are expressed well in this song of Rāmprasād's:

O Mother! Thou has great dissolution in Thy hand;
Śiva lies at Thy feet, absorbed in bliss.
Thou laughest aloud (striking terror); streams of blood flow from Thy limbs.
O Tārā, doer of good, the good of all, grantor of safety, O Mother, grant me safety.
O Mother Kālī! take me in Thy arms; O Mother Kālī! take me in Thy arms.
O Mother! come now as Tārā with a smiling face and clad in white;
As dawn descends on dense darkness of the night.
O Mother! terrific Kālī! I have worshiped Thee alone so long.
My worship is finished; now, O Mother, bring down Thy sword.[31]

Rāmprasād complains in many of his songs that Kālī is indifferent to his well-being, that she makes him suffer and brings his worldly desires to naught and his worldly goods to ruin.

> Mother who art the joy of Hara's [Śiva's] heart, and who dost bring to naught the hopes of men, thou hast made void what hope was left to me.
>
> Though I place my soul an offering at thy feet, some calamity befalls. Though I think upon thy loveliness, unceasing death is mine.
>
> Thou dost frustrate my desires, thou art the spoiler of my fortunes. Well do I know thy mercy, Mother of mine.
>
> Great were my desires, and I spread them all out as a salesman does his wares. Thou didst see the display, I suppose, and didst bring confusion upon me. . . .
>
> My wealth, my honour, kith and kin, all have gone, and I have nothing now to call my own.

> What further use is there for me? Wretched indeed am I.
> I have sought my own ends, and now there is no limit to my grief.
> Thou who dost take away sorrow, to me most wretched hast thou given sorrow. And I must all this unhappy lot endure.[32]

He complains that she does not behave in the ways mothers are supposed to behave, that she does not hearken to his pleas.

> Can mercy be found in the heart of her who was born of the stone [a reference to her being the daughter of Himālaya]?
> Were she not merciless, would she kick the breast of her lord?
> Men call you merciful, but there is no trace of mercy in you, Mother.
> You have cut off the heads of the children of others, and these you wear as a garland around your neck.
> It matters not how much I call you "Mother, Mother." You hear me, but you will not listen.[33]

To be Kālī's child, Rāmprasād often asserts, is to suffer, to be disappointed in terms of worldly desires and pleasures. Kālī does not give what is normally expected. She does allow her devotee/child, however, to glimpse a vision of himself that is not circumscribed by physical and material limitations. As Rāmprasād says succinctly: "He who has made Kālī . . . his only goal easily forgets worldly pleasures."[34] Indeed, that person has little choice, for Kālī does not indulge her devotees in worldly pleasures. It is her very refusal to do so that enables her devotees to reflect on dimensions of themselves and of reality that go beyond bodily comfort and world security.

An analysis of the significance of Kālī to the Hindu tradition reveals certain constants in her mythology and imagery. She is almost always associated with blood and death, and it is difficult to imagine two more polluting realities in the context of the purity-minded culture of Hinduism. As such, Kālī is a very dangerous being. She vividly and dramatically thrusts upon the observer things that he or she would rather not think about. Within the civilized order of Hinduism, within the order of dharma, blood and death are acknowledged—it is impossible not to acknowledge their existence in human life—but they are acknowledged within the context of a highly ritualized, patterned, and complex social structure that takes great pains to handle them in "safe" ways, usually through rituals of purification. These rituals (called *saṁskāras,* "refinements") allow individuals to pass in an orderly way through times when contact with blood and death are unavoidable. The order of dharma is not entirely naive and has incorporated into its refined version of human existence the recognition of these human inevitabilities.

But the Hindu *saṁskāras* are patterned on wishful thinking. Blood and death have a way of cropping up unexpectedly, accidentally, tragically, and dangerously. The periodic flow of menstrual blood or the death of an aged and loved old woman (whose husband has cooperatively died before her) are manageable within the normal order of human events. But the death of an infant or a hemorrhage, for instance, are a threat to the neat vision of the order of dharma.[35] They can never be avoided with certainty, no matter how well protected one thinks one is.

Kālī may be one way in which the Hindu tradition has sought to come to terms, at least in part, with the built-in shortcomings of its own refined view of the world. It is perhaps best and even redemptive to recognize that the system does not work in every case. Reflecting on the ways in which people must negate certain realities in their attempts to create social order, the anthropologist Mary Douglas writes:

> Whenever a strict pattern of purity is imposed on our lives it is either highly uncomfortable or it leads into contradiction if closely followed, or it leads to hypocrisy. That which is negated is not thereby removed. The rest of life, which does not tidily fit the accepted categories, is still there and demands attention. The body, as we have tried to show, provides a basic scheme for all symbolism. There is hardly any pollution which does not have some primary physiological reference. As life is in the body it cannot be rejected outright. And as life must be affirmed, the most complete philosophies . . . must find some ultimate way of affirming that which has been rejected.[36]

Kālī puts the order of dharma in perspective, perhaps puts it in its place, by reminding Hindus that certain aspects of reality are untamable, unpurifiable, unpredictable, and always a threat to society's feeble attempts to order what is essentially disorderly: life itself.

Kālī's shocking appearance and unconventional behavior confront one with an alternative to normal society. To meditate on the dark goddess, or to devote oneself to her, is to step out of the everyday world of predictable dharmic order and enter a world of reversals, opposites, and contrasts and in doing so to wake up to new possibilities and new frames of reference. In her differentness, strangeness, indeed, in her perverseness, Kālī is the kind of figure who is capable of shaking one's comforting and naive assumptions about the world. In doing this, she allows a clearer perception of how things really are.[37]

Kālī allows (or perhaps forces) better perception by enabling one to see the complete picture. She allows one to see behind the bounteousness of the other goddesses who appear in benign forms. Kālī reveals the insatiable hunger that logically must lie behind their amazing fecundity and liberality. Similarly, Kālī permits individuals to see their overall roles in the cosmic drama. She invites a wider, more mature, more realistic reflection on where one has come from and where one is going. She allows the individual to see himself or herself as merely one being in an endless series of permutations arising from the ever-recurring cycles of life and death that constitute the inner rhythms of the divine mother. As cycling and recycled energy, as both the creation and the food of the goddess, the individual is permitted to glimpse social roles and identities in perspective, to see them as often confining and as obscuring a clear perception of how things really are and who he or she really is. Kālī reveals that ultimately all creatures are her children and also her food and that no social role or identity can remove the individual from this sacrificial give and take. While this truth may appear grim, its realization may be just what is needed to push one over the threshold into the liberating quest for release from bondage to *saṁsāra*.

The extent to which Kālī invites or provokes one over the threshold from order to antistructure is seen in the roles she requires of those who would establish any intimacy with her.[38] Iconographically, it is Śiva who participates in the most intimate relations with Kālī. In probably her most famous pose, as Dakṣiṇakālī, she stands or dances upon Śiva's prone body in the cremation ground. His eyes are closed in bliss, sleep, trance, or death—it is difficult to say which. His attitude is utterly passive and, whether he is dead or not, his appearance corpselike. The myth that explains the origin of this pose says that once upon a time, Kālī began to dance out of control on the battlefield after having become drunk on the blood of her victims. To stop her rampage, Śiva lay down on the battlefield like a corpse, so that when she danced on his body she would stop, recognizing him as her husband. It is thus as a corpse, as one of her victims, that Śiva calms Kālī and elicits her grace.[39]

In another myth, it is the infant Śiva who calms Kālī and stops her rampage by eliciting motherly emotions from her. In this story, Kālī again has defeated her enemies on the battlefield and begun to dance out of control, drunk on the blood of those she has slain. To calm her and protect the stability of the world, Śiva appears in the midst of the battlefield as an infant, crying out loudly. Seeing the child's distress, Kālī stops her dancing, picks him up, and kisses him on the head. Then she suckles him at her breasts.[40]

Both the dead and infants have a liminal nature. Neither has a complete social identity. Neither fits neatly or at all into the niches and structures of normal society. To approach Kālī, it is well to assume the identity of a corpse or an infant. Having no stake in the orderly structures of society, the devotee as corpse or infant is free to step out of society into the liminal environment of the goddess. The corpse is mere food for her insatiable fires, the infant, mere energy, as yet raw and unrefined. Reduced to either extreme, one who approaches Kālī in these roles is awakened to a perception of reality that is difficult to grasp within the confines of the order of dharma and a socialized ego.

NOTES

1. *Agni-purāṇa* 133, 134, 136; *Garuḍa-purāṇa* 38.

2. Śaśibhūsan Dāsgupta, *Bhārater Śakti-sādhana o Śākta Sāhitya* (Calcutta: Sāhitya Saṅgsad, 1367 B.S. [1961]), pp. 66–67.

3. D. C. Sircar, The *Śākta Pīṭhas* (Delhi: Motilal Banarsidass, 1973), p. 20.

4. *Bhavabhūti's Mālatīmādhava with the Commentary of Jagaddhara,* ed. and trans. M. R. Kale (Delhi: Motilal Banarsidass, 1967), pp. 44–48.

5. Krishna Kanta Handiqui, *Yaśastilaka and Indian Culture* (Sholapur: Jaina Saṁskṛiti Saṁrakshaka Sangha, 1949), p. 56.

6. Ibid., p. 22.

7. See chapter 10, "The Mātṛkās," in David Kinsley, *Hindu Goddesses: Visions of the Divine Feminine in the Hindu Religious Tradition* (Berkeley and Los Angeles: University of California Press, 1986).

8. *Skanda-purāṇa* 5.82.1–21.

9. Summarized in *Principles of Tantra: The Tantratattva of Śrīyukta Śiva Candra Vidyārnava Bhattācārya Mahodaya,* ed. Arthur Avalon (Madras: Ganesh, 1960), pp. 208–13.

10. *Adbhūta Rāmāyaṇa,* Sāralā Dāsa's Oriyan *Rāmāyaṇa,* and the Bengali *Jaimini-bhārata Rāmāyaṇa;* Narendra Nath Bhattacharyya, *History of the Śākta Religion* (New Delhi: Munshiram Manoharlal Publishers, 1974), p. 149.

11. C. Sivaramamurti, *Nataraja in Art, Thought and Literature* (New Delhi: National Museum, 1974), pp. 378–79, 384; M. A. Dorai Rangaswamy, *The Religion and Philosophy of Tēvāram,* 2 books (Madras: University of Madras, 1958), 1:442, 444–45; R. K. Das, *Temples of Tamilnad* (Bombay: Bharatiya Vidya Bhavan, 1964), p. 195.

12. Some renditions of Śiva's dance, in which the entire Hindu pantheon are shown as spectators or musicians, do include Kālī standing passively by: for example, the painting at the sixteenth-century Śiva temple at Ettumanur (Sivaramamurti, *Nataraja in Art,* fig. 150, p. 282) and the scene from a seventeenth-century temple at Triprayār, Kerala (ibid., fig. 152, p. 284). In both scenes, Kālī rides a *preta* (ghost), and her appearance is unchanged.

13. That Śiva should have to resort to his *tāṇḍava* dance to defeat Kālī suggests the theme of Kālī's inciting Śiva to destructive activity. Śiva's *tāṇḍava* dance is typically performed at the end of the cosmic age and destroys the universe. Descriptions of it often dwell on its destructive aspects. The chaotic dancing of Śiva, who wields a broken battle-ax, must be tempered by the soft glances of Pārvatī (Sivaramamurti, *Nataraja in Art,* p. 138). Śiva tends to get out of control in his *tāṇḍava* dance, and in the legend of the dance contest with Kālī, it is she who provokes him to it.

14. *Bhavabhūti's Mālatīmādhava,* pp. 44–48.

15. M., *The Gospel of Sri Ramakrishna,* trans. Swami Nikhilananda (New York: Ramakrishna-Vivekananda Center, 1942), p. 961.

16. The theme of Pārvatī's acting as a restraining influence on Śiva is mentioned by Glen Yocum, "The Goddess in a Tamil Śaiva Devotional Text, Māṇikkavācakar's *Tiruvācakam,*" *Journal of the American Academy of Religion* 45, no. 1, supplement (March 1977): K, 372.

17. *Principles of Tantra: The Tantratattva of Śrīyukta Śiva Candra Vidyārnava Bhattācārya Mahodaya,* ed. Arthur Avalon (Madras: Ganesh, 1960), pp. 327–28.

18. *Hymn to Kālī (Karpūrādi-stotra),* ed. and trans. Arthur Avalon (Madras: Ganesh, 1965), p. 34.

19. Ibid.

20. Ibid.

21. For example, *Mahānirvāṇa-tantra* 5.140–41; 6.68–76; 10.102.

22. *Tantra of the Great Liberation (Mahānirvāna Tantra),* trans. Arthur Avalon (Madras: Ganesh, 1972), pp. 49–50.

23. For the *pañcatattva* ritual, see *Mahānirvāṇa-tantra* 5–6; Agehananda Bharati, *The Tantric Tradition* (London: Rider, 1965), pp. 228–78; Mircea Eliade, *Yoga: Immortality and Freedom* (New York: Pantheon Books, 1958), pp. 254–62; Heinrich Zimmer, *Philosophies of India* (Cleveland: World Publishing, 1956), pp. 572–80.

24. *Hymn to Kālī,* pp. 84, 86.

25. In at least one Tantric text Kālī is identified with Lakṣmī and, by implication, Viṣṇu (*Lakṣmī-tantra* 8.13).

26. Throughout North India, Kālī is associated with Bengal, where she is most popular. Outside Bengal, for example, her temples will be established by Bengalis, Bengalis will often act as her temple priests, or the image of Kālī in the temple will be said to have some connection with Bengal.

27. *Rama Prasada's Devotional Songs: The Cult of Shakti,* trans. Jadunath Sinha (Calcutta: Sinha Publishing House, 1966), no. 181, p. 97.

28. Edward J. Thompson and Arthur Marshman Spencer, trans., *Bengali Religious Lyrics, Śākta* (Calcutta: Association Press, 1923), p. 22.

29. For Annapūrṇā, Jagaddhātrī, and Satākṣī, see chapter 9, "The Mahādevī, in Kinsley, *Hindu Goddesses.*

30. David Kinsley, *The Sword and the Flute—Kṛṣṇa and Kālī* (Berkeley and Los Angeles: University of California Press, 1975), pp. 133–45.

31. *Rama Prasada's Devotional Songs,* no. 221, pp. 118–19.

32. Thompson and Spencer, trans., *Bengali Religious Lyrics,* pp. 85–86.

33. Ibid., p. 84.

34. *Rama Prasada's Devotional Songs,* p. 106.

35. In *Purity and Danger: An Analysis of Concepts of Pollution and Taboo* (Harmondsworth, U.K.: Penguin Books, 1970), Mary Douglas locates taboo in the idea of dirt out of place. In a sense, Kālī may be regarded as taboo, a dangerous being out of place in the civilized sphere.

36. Ibid., p. 193.

37. "The unusual, the paradoxical, the illogical, even the perverse, stimulate thought and pose problems, 'cleanse the Doors of Perception,' as Blake put it"; Victor Turner, *Dramas, Fields, and Metaphors: Symbolic Action in Human Society* (Ithaca, N.Y.: Cornell University Press, 1974), p. 256.

38. The term "antistructure" is used here in the way Turner uses it, as a positive phenomenon that enables a culture to step outside itself in order to perceive itself more clearly. Antistructure is not necessarily chaotic or destructive.

39. The story is told in the *Adbhūta Rāmāyaṇa,* the Oriyan *Rāmāyaṇa* of Sāralā Dāsa, and the Bengali *Jaiminibhārata Rāmāyaṇa;* Narendra Nath Bhattacharyya, *History of the Śākta Religion* (New Delhi: Munshiram Manoharlal Publishers, 1974), p. 149.

40. *Liṅga-purāṇa* 1.106.20–28.

CHAPTER 2

Kālī the Terrific and Her Tests

The Śākta Devotionalism of the Mahābhāgavata Purāṇa

Patricia Dold

The *Mahābhāgavata Purāṇa* is a late medieval text[1] that develops a devotionalism centered on Mahādevī, the Great Goddess. While the Purāṇa describes the Goddess's births as Satī, Pārvatī, Gaṅgā, and others, Kālī is presented as her preeminent embodied form, and the text's devotionalism mutes but also redirects Kālī's extremes. Kālī in the *Mahābhāgavata* is "terrific": terrifying *and* magnificent. Her truest devotees are those who pass Kālī's test; they have the wisdom to recognize her supremacy and so find inspiration for tremendous devotion in the Terrific Goddess.

The *Mahābhāgavata*'s portrayal of Śiva's relationship with the Goddess and his passage through her test culminates in a myth of origin for the Dakṣiṇākālī image, in which Kālī stands on Śiva's chest. According to this interpretation, the image expresses Śiva's devotion to Kālī; in his ecstasy at encountering the Goddess once again, he places her feet on his chest and lies beneath her like a corpse. The *Mahābhāgavata*'s interpretation of the image as devotional is historically significant, for it reappears in Bengali Śākta poetry of the eighteenth and nineteenth centuries. Indeed, the *Mahābhāgavata* might have been a source for this and other aspects of the *bhakti* expressed by later Bengali poets.

THE *MAHĀBHĀGAVATA PURĀṆA* AND ITS VISION OF KĀLĪ

As a Śākta work, the *Mahābhāgavata* understands the Mahādevī, the Great Goddess, as the supreme deity of the cosmos. She is ultimately responsible for the creation, preservation, and destruction of the universe. As *vidyā,* liberating knowledge, she releases beings from *saṃsāra,* the world, while as *māyā,* an enchanting and delusive force, she traps them in it. She is the ultimate, qualityless, incorporeal *brahman.* She is *ādya prakṛti,* primordial matter, and *puruṣa,* spirit. She is *śakti,* cosmic energy. She is the source of and the power behind all deities, male and female. She is the most appropriate focus for devotional sentiment, the ultimate object of meditation, the source of dharma and the motive for dharmic behavior. As the Goddess herself explains to Himālaya, her father and devotee:

> Know that I am the supreme *śakti,* whose seat is made of the great lord [Śiva]; my form is eternal sovereignty and wisdom. I am the impeller of all, the genatrix of Brahmā, Viṣṇu, Śiva, and so on. I am she who bestows liberation to all, who orchestrates creation, preservation, and destruction, the matriarch of the world. I am that which abides in all, and I am she who enables [beings] to cross the ocean that is *saṃsāra.* I consist of eternal bliss, and I myself am the eternal one whose form is *brahman,* father.[2]

The *Mahābhāgavata* is almost entirely composed of narratives about the Great Goddess. It begins with the story of her embodiment[3] as Satī, her marriage to Śiva, and her conflicts with her father Dakṣa and her husband (chapters 1–12). The second narrative, called the *Gaṅgā Upākhyāna* (13–14), tells of the Goddess's embodiment as Gaṅgā. The third narrative, or *Śiva Upākhyāna* (15–35), narrates the birth of the Goddess as Pārvatī, daughter of Himālaya, and includes a *Bhagavatī Gītā* (16–19) and a hymn of one thousand names of the Goddess (*Mahākālīsahasranāmastotra*).[4] These stories, which are the focus of this chapter, comprise only about half of the text, that is, approximately two thousand verses. The second half of the *Mahābhāgavata* includes Śākta versions of the *Rāmāyaṇa,* the Kṛṣṇa cycle of myths (where Kṛṣṇa is an embodiment of the Goddess), and the story of Indra's defeat of Vṛtra.

A recurring feature of the *Mahābhāgavata*'s narratives is the devotional relationship between Kālī and her devotees. The Goddess is devoutly worshipped by her husband Śiva, by her fathers Dakṣa, Himālaya, and Nanda, and by her mothers Prasūti, Menā, and Devakī. Major sections of the text consist of devotees' expressions of adoration for the Goddess—for example, Śiva's *Mahākālīsahasranāmastotra* and the *Bhagavatī Gītā,* a discourse between the Goddess and her father Himālaya. Throughout the entire text, and especially in the first three narratives, there are descriptions of the pain devotees experience when separated from the Goddess, their longing to experience her presence, and their joy when graced by it. These themes, the pain of separation and the joy of union with the deity, are typical of Hindu *bhakti* traditions, and their prominence in the *Mahābhāgavata* clearly demonstrates that devotion is a major aspect of this text's religious vision. That the

Mahābhāgavata centers its devotionalism on Kālī is unusual; indeed, it is surprising. According to current scholarly understandings of Hindu religious history, devotion to Kālī appears only with the Bengali *bhakti* poets of the eighteenth and nineteenth centuries.[5]

The Great Goddess of the *Mahābhāgavata* appears in many forms. However, the text neither establishes a clear hierarchy among them nor describes the Goddess's supreme form consistently: sometimes she "looks" like a classic Kālī, but at other times, she is more like a Durgā, or even like a conflation of the two. Nevertheless, characteristics typical of Kālī appear in many of the *Mahābhāgavata*'s descriptions of the Great Goddess or her supreme physical form, and Kālī (by name or by description) is central to most of its narratives.

The *Mahābāgavata*'s devotionalism entails a multifaceted vision of Kālī, one that preserves some of her extremes while muting and ignoring others. To be sure, the *Mahābhāgavata*'s Kālī is not a personification of death, as in the *Mahābhārata.*[6] She is not the emaciated Kālī of the "Devī-Māhātmya," an emanation of Durgā's wrath, whose thirst for blood and lust for battle seem unquenchable.[7] Nor is this Kālī the angry and wantonly destructive alter ego of auspicious, benign goddesses of Purāṇic tales.[8] Moreover, no particular connection with thieves is attributed to this Kālī,[9] and neither is she linked with peoples outside or on the margins of Brāhmaṇical society. This Kālī does not haunt cremation grounds. Although she is omnipotent, the exercise of her power is not incomprehensible, and while she receives blood sacrifice,[10] her appetite for flesh and blood is not emphasized.

In the *Mahābhāgavata,* Kālī's attire and ornaments still include a lolling tongue, disheveled hair, and a garland of heads, but these are euphemistically called lovely, charming, and beautiful, and are said to complement her "sparkling tiara" and "full high breasts." That she becomes embodied as Satī, Gaṅgā, and Pārvatī renders her character more complex and inclusive of the auspiciousness associated with such goddesses, and so she becomes less extreme. Such embodiments also exalt Kālī, for she is no longer merely the dark side of auspicious goddesses; she is their very essence.

Has the *Mahābhāgavata* "tamed" Kālī? Yes, at least in part. I agree, in general, with the current scholarly view that many relatively late depictions of Kālī are less horrific than earlier ones. But I question the scholarly assumptions that prompt us to speak of a tamed Goddess. Do we imply that we prefer the untamed Kālī? Do we then look for the wild one, and call all others "tame"? I suggest that—to a degree—scholars have imposed their preference for the wild Kālī on their study of the Goddess. Proceeding from this initial bias, scholarship has at times emphasized the early Kālī's violent extremes by ignoring or omitting the respectable, balanced aspects of early portrayals.

In addition, the extreme early Kālī is sometimes the result of scholars' selective reading. For instance, a story from the *Bhāgavata Purāṇa* (5.9.12–20) is cited as evidence of her association with thieves and wild and unpredictable behavior. But a closer inspection of the Purāṇic verses reveals a more genteel side of the Goddess.

The story describes a band of thieves, worshippers of Bhadrakālī, who intend to perform human sacrifice to the Goddess to ensure the birth of a son to their leader. Bhārata, the intended sacrificial victim, is a saintly Brahman and an exemplary devotee of Viṣṇu. At the sacrifice, his fiery energy (*tejas*) burns the image of Bhadrakālī, causing the Goddess herself to emerge from it. She and her attendants slaughter the thieves, drink their blood, and, dancing wildly, play ball with their heads. The text then explicitly states that such sacrificial rites "have been laid down for men of fierce nature" facing "dangerous situations." The thieves' crime, their "act of unpardonable and intolerable cruelty," is equated not with the fact of sacrifice but with their choice of victim—a holy man who "had become one with Brahman."[11] In light of this evaluation, Kālī is a defender of Brāhmaṇical law, not a capricious, disloyal deity of thieves. Kinsley summarizes the story but does not mention the *Bhāgavata*'s evaluation of the thieves' crime. He thus creates the impression, perhaps unintentionally, that Kālī is a goddess so unpredictable that she destroys her own worshippers.[12] Cheever Mackenzie Brown also interprets the story without reference to the *Bhāgavata*'s self-understanding. For Brown, the story presents Kālī as a "mistress of life and death," since she is worshipped here to guarantee the birth of a child. She is violent but endowed with compassion, since she rescues the saintly Brahman.[13] A more complex Kālī emerges from Brown's interpretation, but still missing is any sense that she is enforcing Brāhmaṇical ritual norms by turning on the thieves.

Historical accounts of textual characterizations of Kālī also tend to exclude the Kālī of the *Mahābhārata*'s hymns to "Durgā."[14] According to these hymns, which are roughly contemporary with the "Devī-Māhātmya," the Goddess is compassionate and auspicious, a cosmic protectress who slays demons and rescues beings from danger. One of her many names is Kālī, as seen in a hymn by Yudhiṣṭhira: "O Kālī, Kālī, O great Kālī, fond of liquor, flesh, and beasts / Wandering where you wish, of spirits is your retinue composed, you a giver of boons."[15] Such hymns depict a complex goddess whose identity as Kālī should not be ignored in scholarly histories.

My intent here is to call for greater balance in scholarly assessments of Kālī's early portrayals.[16] Her extremes, even in some of the classic early texts, are mitigated by the cosmic or dharmic contexts of her behavior and by the relatively early but quite complex characterizations of Kālī as the Great Goddess.

Just as the early Kālī is not all violence and caprice, so the later Kālī is not completely "tamed." Because of her complexity and the muting of her rough edges, almost required by the *Mahābhāgavata*'s devotional religiosity, Kālī is Mahādevī, the object of worship and devotion for all beings, including the gods. Still, she remains the terrific—that is, terror-inspiring *and* wondrous—the essence of all goddesses rather than a personification of their anger or destructive powers. Accordingly, the *Mahābhāgavata*'s Kālī uses her awesome presence and appearance to test her worshippers and prospective devotees.

THE GODDESS TESTS HER PARENTS

The *Mahābhāgavata* consistently places the Goddess's (various) parents in devotional relationship with her. For example, her parents' joy over their daughter's birth and passage through youth are described, as is their sorrow over the prospect of separation from her when she marries and leaves them to reside with her husband. The Goddess's relationships with Prasūti and Dakṣa are depicted in great detail and have particular importance for the testing motif. Prasūti, Satī's mother, passes Kālī's test with flying colors. Dakṣa fails miserably.

Dakṣa, informed that the Goddess will become embodied as Śiva's wife, performs austerities for three thousand divine years before she appears to him. Though the text does not use the name Kālī here, its description of the Goddess suggests this identity: she is naked and has four "beautiful arms," the "luster of shiny collyrium," hands that dispel fear and hold a sword and lotus, a garland of "lovely heads," and loose hair (4.10–12). The Goddess grants Dakṣa his boon: she will become embodied as his daughter, "with limbs as pale as glittering gold, beautiful and charming," and she will marry Śiva. But, she also warns him that if he is disrespectful (*mandādara*) toward her, "I, assuming a body such as this again, after going to your city, will go to my own abode, having deluded the whole world with *māyā*" (4.15–20a).[17]

Kālī is born as Satī to Prasūti and Dakṣa. When she attains a marriageable age, Dakṣa arranges for her to choose her husband from an assembled crowd of guests (*svayaṃvara*), but he does not invite Śiva, whose appearance, behavior, and lineage are unacceptable in Dakṣa's opinion. Nevertheless, Satī chooses Śiva. All celebrate the marriage except Dakṣa, who grieves the loss of his daughter (5.21–23). But Dakṣa's reaction goes far beyond grief: he becomes "insane and, seeing in his mind the master of all whose ornaments are matted locks and ashes, he even revile[s] Satī" (4.59).

Later, Dakṣa arranges a sacrifice, to which he invites all the gods and goddesses except Satī and Śiva. The Goddess, aware of Dakṣa's disrespect (*mandādara*), decides that she will now abandon him. When the Goddess and Śiva argue over attending Dakṣa's sacrifice, Śiva insults her, and she takes this opportunity to reveal herself as Kālī and proceed to her natal home.

On her arrival, she first meets and is greeted with respect (*saṃmāna*) by her mother Prasūti, who embraces her, wipes "her lotus face with her dress," and kisses her again and again, weeping with joy (9.30b–31a). The text is explicit: the Goddess appears as Kālī before her mother and Prasūti recognizes her as her daughter and as the Great Goddess: "You are the Primal, supreme *śakti,* yourself the genatrix of the three worlds. You were born from my womb; this is my greatest fortune. Today, my grief, which I have had for a long time, is far away,[18] Satī" (9.4b–5).

Prasūti goes on to contrast her attitude with Dakṣa's: "I lovingly witness your arrival at my house, but your father is silly, having become ignorant regarding the supreme Śiva. Hating that very one, he performs a great sacrifice out of delusion [*moha*]" (9.6–8). In a nightmare, Prasūti has foreseen the "violent catastrophe, unbearably horrifying" that will be the result of Dakṣa's foolishness, following the arrival of "a certain goddess, a great Queen, black like a great cloud, her hair loose, naked, four armed, smiling broadly, blazing with her three flaming eyes." After a confrontation with Dakṣa, this goddess kills herself in the sacrificial fire, and chaos ensues: the sacrifice is destroyed, and Dakṣa is beheaded. Prasūti understands that what she has seen in the dream will come to pass, and that this is why she now sees her daughter as Kālī: "What I saw happen to you in the dream will actually happen. . . . . Hence, I see you exactly as you appeared in the dream" (9.25).

The Goddess's mother passes Kālī's test: she does not flee from Kālī in fear or disgust. Far from it. Prasūti immediately recognizes and lovingly greets her daughter. She fully acknowledges her status as Great Goddess. She also recognizes Dakṣa's foolishness and appreciates the Goddess's marriage to Śiva. Indeed, Prasūti emphasizes her bond with the Goddess: she is her daughter, "born from her womb," and insists that they shall never be separated.[19] Prasūti's dream and her reaction to it also suggest the intimate bond between the two and contrast drastically with Dakṣa's response to Kālī.

At the sacrificial arena, Dakṣa sees "Kālī, her eyes flaming with wrath, her hair loose, naked." He does not recognize her: "Who are you? Whose daughter, wife, are you, a naked, shameless woman? Why have you come here? You look like Satī, but how can you be my daughter Satī come here from Śiva's home?" She responds (ingenuously, but) with the respect of a dharmic daughter: "Father, why do you not know me, your own daughter, your Satī? You are my father, I am your daughter. I bow to you, my father" (9.43–46a). Dakṣa rejects her present appearance, which he blames on her marriage to Śiva:

> Why, Mother, is it so? Why are you black? O Satī! As she whose limbs were pale as brilliant gold, who resembled the autumnal moon, whose garment was a divine dress, you lived formerly in my house. Today she is you, a naked, shameless woman. Why have you come to this assembly? And why is your hair loose? Why are your eyes horrible? Have you, after obtaining an unfit husband, ac-

quired ten such qualities? . . . After obtaining the unworthy Śambhu as a husband, you are suffering, pretty-eyed one! (9.46b–49 and 51a)

The Goddess is enraged by his words but refrains from destroying him because of her role as dharmic daughter. Instead, she creates a shadow (*chāyā*), "whose form is the same as hers" (9.55). The Goddess tells her shadow to confront her father and to kill herself in the sacrificial fire in order to punish Dakṣa for insulting Śiva out of his fatherly pride: "I am his daughter. On account of that, that conceited one reviles Śiva. Therefore, crush his pride immediately!" (9.56–59).

The shadow accosts Dakṣa, who proceeds to insult both Śiva and his daughter, whom he calls foolish and orders to stop praising Śiva (9.68b–71a). When the shadow defies Dakṣa by defending Śiva, Dakṣa disowns his daughter: "Evil daughter! You are wicked! Be gone from my sight! When you obtained Śambhu as your husband, right then you were dead to me! . . . At the sight of you, my body burns with the fire of grief. You who are she, be gone from my sight now!" (9.73b–76). The shadow then enters the fire, saying, "Not only will I be out of your sight, but soon here I will be out of the body born of you!" (9.80–81).

Dakṣa fails Kālī's test because of "pride over the body" (*dehābhimāna*).[20] Although he had initially been blessed with *darśana* of Kālī, and although he had asked her to become his daughter, his pride causes him to revile Satī for her marriage to the "unworthy" Śiva, whose lineage and physical deportment are unacceptable from his body-conscious perspective.[21] Finally, his pride blinds him to his daughter's true divine identity and leads him to reject her in her form as Kālī. The devotional paradigm is inverted: Dakṣa burns with *grief in* the Goddess's presence. He is punished with the loss not only of his life and head but also of his daughter. Indeed, the Goddess (via her shadow) rejects the body born of him—a fitting punishment for one who bases his pride on bodily characteristics. Having failed the test miserably, Dakṣa's relationship with the Goddess is severed and never fully restored.[22]

In subsequent narratives, great care is taken by the Goddess herself to ensure that her future fathers do not repeat Dakṣa's mistakes. In general, the Goddess's relationships with males are characterized by tension, if not outright conflict. This tension always relates to her marriages to Śiva. Even in Śaiva mythology, Śiva is often criticized by his in-laws for the same reasons Dakṣa deems him unworthy here.[23] But there is more in the *Mahābhāgavata.* The Goddess's fathers know, on the one hand, that her marriage severs her ties to her natal family and therefore ends their own relationship with her. On the other hand, these fathers remain emotionally bonded to their daughter. Even Dakṣa feels the "loss" of his daughter that "cast[s] him into an ocean of grief" (4.21–23b). Yet he acts as if she were no longer part of his family when he fails to invite her to his sacrifice. When Himālaya, the father of Gaṅgā, learns that she is to marry Śiva, he says: "The permanent residence of a daughter is not in the father's house. A daughter exists for the sake of another, never for oneself" (13.90). But, Himālaya feels a contradiction between virilocality and fatherhood. He continues his lament: "Well do I know this, yet in my mind there will be unbearable suffering born of separation from Gaṅgā" (13.91). The Goddess herself reassures her father that she will "certainly be in [his] presence forever" (13.94).

UNDERSTANDING PRASŪTI AND DAKṢA

What accounts for the difference between the Goddess's relationship with her mother and father? Why is Prasūti so wise and Dakṣa so confused? Answers to these questions emerge from ethnographic studies of married women's family ties and connections between these and goddess mythology.

William Sax documents different understandings of married women's familial ties in his study of a goddess pilgrimage tradition in Garhwal (Uttarakhand). According to Sanskrit texts, Brahman authorities from North India generally, and local males speaking as husbands, a married woman is no longer part of her natal family but belongs to her husband's family (her *sauryās*). Marriage entails a change in residence but also "a complete transformation not only of her primary kin relationships and social obligations but also of her very nature and substance."[24] But this official male perspective is not the only one. As fathers, "[t]he men of Uttarakhand feel affection for their daughters just as much as fathers do anywhere, and they are not reluctant to acknowledge a continuing relationship to them."[25]

Himālaya's lament reflects such conflicting perspectives.[26] He well understands the "official truth" that a married woman belongs to her husband's family, but as a father he grieves over the loss of his daughter. The *Mahābhāgavata*'s characterization of Dakṣa expresses the same tension. However, the solution presented in Dakṣa's case, to disown his daughter, is not viable according to the *Mahābhāgavata*'s narrative, even though it would be consistent with the Sanskritic opinion that a married daughter no longer belongs to her natal family. The different male perspectives documented by Sax offer an explanation for the strain that characterizes the Goddess's relationships with her fathers.

Women of Garhwal have their own perspective. Married women "maintain enduring and substantial links to" their natal family and village (their *mait*).[27] They visit their natal homes for a variety of rituals and celebrations, they grieve over their own departure from their families, and they eagerly anticipate their periodic return. Indeed, there is general agreement that a married woman's ties to her natal family cannot be denied.[28]

Prasūti's insistence on her connection with her daughter, her joyous celebration of her daughter's return, and her conviction that they shall never be parted are perfectly understandable in light of Sax's ethnographic evidence.[29] The parallels are even more compelling inasmuch as the pilgrimage tradition studied by Sax celebrates the Goddess's return to her own natal village where her human devotee-parents duly welcome the divine daughter. This divine pilgrimage is also an occasion when daughters are received into their *mait*s. Social realities are projected onto mythology, here as well as in Bengal, where daughters' ongoing ties to their natal families are reflected in popular understandings of Durgā's annual visit to her birthplace during Durgā Pūjā.[30]

The *Mahābhāgavata* (which originated in or near Bengal and was known there) incorporates such social realities within its devotionalism and its testing motif. But one question remains: why are Kālī's mothers more inclined to recognize her? Why are they not subject to the pride that hinders male devotees such as Dakṣa? Are women granted a privileged spiritual position here? Is the text suggesting that males have more to learn to be devotees of the Goddess? So it would seem. Such an exalted view of women possibly derives from Tantra, which is also a likely source for this text's testing motif.

THE GODDESS TESTS ŚIVA

Śiva's relationship with Kālī is the focus of the first three narratives. Initially, he acknowledges her as the Great Goddess, but later, when married to her in the form of Satī, suffers from pride in his status and no longer recognizes Satī or Kālī as the supreme deity. By the end of the text's third narrative, Śiva overcomes his pride and becomes the Goddess's greatest devotee, humbling himself before the terrific Kālī.

According to the text's creation account, the Goddess creates the gods Brahmā, Viṣṇu, and Śiva, each of whom then undertakes austerities to win her as his wife. She appears before each in "a horrible form that shook the universe to test their austerities" (3.41a). Brahmā and Viṣṇu turn away from her in fear. Śiva alone perseveres in his austerities: "realizing that Prakṛti had come to test him with a horrifying form, Hara remained in absorbed meditation [*samādhi*]" (3.48). The testing motif is explicit here.[31] Brahmā and Viṣṇu lose their composure when faced with the Goddess's horrifying form. The text explains: "Brahmā and Viṣṇu were both attached to the senses [*viṣayāsaktau*]. Śiva was truly the supreme yogi desiring the great Prakṛti for his wife with his whole heart" (3.70–71). Thus Śiva is rewarded with the boon of marrying a full rather than a partial embodiment of the Goddess: "Indeed, I, the full Prakṛti, will be your wife, after being born, through *māyā,* as the beautiful daughter of Dakṣa" (3.76).

Once Satī and Śiva are married and Dakṣa has excluded them from his sacrifice, both Nārada and Satī try to persuade Śiva to go. When he refuses,

Satī dutifully asks him for permission to go by herself, insisting that, as a daughter who has heard about the celebration of a great sacrifice at her father's house, she cannot bear to remain at her marital home (8.25a–26b).[32] They argue at length, and finally Śiva insults her: "Although you are forbidden, Great Goddess, you do not hear my words! Having himself done an evil deed, the evil one corrupts another. I know that words do not get through to you, daughter of Dakṣa. Do as you please! Why do you await my permission?" (8.43–44) The argument ends, for this is more than the Goddess will take:

> Satī, the daughter of Dakṣa, was angry, red-eyed. At that moment, she thought, "After requesting and obtaining me as his wife, today Śaṅkara insults me. Therefore, I will demonstrate my supernatural power [*prabhāva*]." On seeing her, the Goddess, her lower lip trembling with rage, the pupils of her eyes resembling the doomsday fire, Śambhu then shut his eyes. Then she immediately laughed loudly, her mouth full of terrible fangs. Hearing that, the Great God was bewildered, exceedingly afraid. Forcing his eyes open, he saw her, the terrible one. . . . Removing her golden dress, she appeared old, naked, her hair flying, her tongue lolling, she had four arms. Her body was brilliant as the doomsday fire because of the sweat on the hairs of her body. That most horrible one, whose roar was dreadful, was adorned with a garland of human heads. Brilliant like a great multitude [*koṭi*] of stars, with a crown made of a half moon, her head blazing with its tiara, she looked like a rising star. Thus, after assuming her horrible form, Satī was burning violently by means of her own *tejas*. Then, smiling broadly, rising up with a great roar, she shone in front of him. (8.45–53)

Śiva flees from her "out of fear." The Goddess "compassionately" manifests herself as the ten Mahāvidyās, who surround Śiva, so that, wherever he runs, he comes face to face with another terrifying goddess, from whom he flees, only to run into goddess after goddess in every direction. Finally, he stops before Kālī and asks, "Why are you black? Where has Satī, dear as life itself, gone?" (8.61). The Goddess reminds him that she is, of course, Satī. Śiva, now calm, recognizes Kālī as the supreme deity, asks her forgiveness for the "displeasing words he spoke as her husband," and tells her to do as she pleases.[33]

Śiva, who once passed the test and was rewarded with the promise of becoming the Goddess's husband, forgets who Satī really is and so runs, terrified, away from Kālī, no longer recognizing her as the deity he himself had worshipped.[34] The Goddess states that his offense is pride over high rank or lordship (*prabhutvābhimāna*), a pride that led him, her husband, to speak disrespectfully to her. Like the attachment to sensuality of Brahmā and Viṣṇu, and Dakṣa's bodily pride, Śiva's hubris prevents him from duly appreciating Satī and Kālī.

Kālī proceeds to her natal home, greets her parents, and creates the shadow Kālī, who enters the fire. Chaos follows. Śiva, mad with grief on receiving the news of the Goddess's death, creates Vīrabhadra and a host of Pramathas, who destroy the sacrifice and massacre all in attendance. Śiva later restores the sacrifice and revives Dakṣa, who now humbly worships him (10.1–101).

Śiva then begins a long period of mourning, "weeping like a common man." Even after Brahmā and Viṣṇu inform him that only a shadow of the Goddess entered the fire, Śiva is inconsolable (11.4–5). The gods then sing a hymn to the Goddess so that she will grant them *darśana* with "precisely the form [she] had at Dakṣa's sacrifice" (11.30). She appears as requested and informs Śiva that she will become embodied as Pārvatī and marry him again. She assures him that she will never abandon him for, as she says, "the supreme refuge of Mahākālī is in your very own heart" (11.36). However, for insulting her through "pride in his lordship," Śiva must perform a penance: he must carry the corpse of the shadow Satī on his head until pieces of it fall to earth, thus creating the *pīṭhas,* or seats of the Goddess (11.37–42).

Śiva, weeping again, begins his penance but finds greatest joy while carrying the corpse and so begins to dance (11.51b–52a). However, his steps cause the earth to tremble so violently that the gods fear an untimely destruction of the universe. But Śiva is oblivious to this havoc: "supremely joyous," he thinks to himself, "Satī, you are my wife. Abandoning worldly shame [*lokalajjā*] I carry your shadow on my head. This is my very great blessing!" (11.60b–61). Śiva shows genuine insight here, for he defies the conventional thinking that would find shame where he finds bliss.

To save the world from destruction, the gods assign to Viṣṇu the task of removing the corpse from Śiva. Viṣṇu cuts it up and the pieces fall to the earth. Śiva remains at Kamarupa, where the female genitals (*yoni*) fell, performing austerities (*tapas*) so that the Goddess will become his wife again. She appears and explains that she will become embodied as Gaṅgā who will dwell on Śiva's head since he derived so much joy from dancing with Satī's corpse on his head (12.19b–21). Śiva, it would seem, may once again enjoy a physical subordination to the Goddess, now beneath her in liquid form rather than as a mere shadow. But his passage through the test is not completed until he places himself under the Goddess in all her terrific glory.

Even after Gaṅgā's descent, Śiva endures a lengthy and painful separation from the Great Goddess, whom he still misses in her form as Satī. Once again, he performs austerities to end his separation. Kāma, sent by the gods, induces lust for Pārvatī in Śiva, only to have Śiva reduce him to ashes. Pārvatī criticizes this act, reminding Śiva that the purpose of his austerities was to win her as his wife (23.6). Pārvatī assures Śiva that she was Satī who went to Dakṣa's sacrifice as "the terrible Kālī, Enchantress of the Triple World." Śiva asks for proof: "[I]f you are my Satī, of lovely eyes, equal to life itself, then show yourself to me with that appearance she had when, to destroy

Dakṣa's sacrifice, she was Kālī, resembling a great cloud, terrifying, naked" (23.15–16). Pārvatī then appears before Śiva as Kālī, "naked, dripping with blood, her long eyes horrible, her chest lovely and beautiful with its two full, high breasts. . . . She was most glorious with her garland of a string of heads, which hung down to her knees. Like flashing lightning in a row of thunderclouds, she shone, her four arms raised high" (23.17–22b). Śiva is delighted:

> Looking at her, the Great God, his soul ecstatic, the hairs on his body bristling with joy, his voice stammering with devotion, spoke to her. "My heart burned because of separation from you for such a long time. You are the inner controller [*antaryāminī*], the Power [*śakti*] abiding in the heart, the great queen. Worshipping [you], placing your lotus feet on the lotus that is my heart, I will make my heart, which was burnt by separation from you, very cool." (23.22b–25)

The text is clear: it is Kālī Śiva sees here, and it is as Kālī that the Goddess inspires greatest devotion from him, for he assumes his position beneath her feet and praises her with a hymn of one thousand names:

> After saying this, the Great God, established in supreme yoga, lay down. He then placed her lotus feet on his heart. Blissfully meditating, he remained [thus] in the form of a motionless corpse. His eyes darting back and forth, he gazed at her with utmost respect. With one part of [himself] he rose up in front of her, his palms pressed together reverently; the five-mouthed one praised the great queen Kālī with one thousand names. (23.26–28)

Pleased, Kālī promises him her eternal presence and offers him any boon he desires. Śiva asks for the boon of always appearing under her feet: "Wherever this, your captivating form that is Kālī, appears, it is to be established by you on the heart of me in the form of a corpse, and you, Kālī the great, will be known in the world as She Whose Vehicle Is a Corpse. Be pleased, matriarch of the world!" (23.186–87). The text then states that anyone who recites Śiva's hymn of one thousand names will become "equal to the Goddess" and will "obtain the supreme state" (23.190).[35]

By the time he places himself beneath her feet, Śiva has overcome his pride over his rank as husband of the Goddess. He has completed and completely transformed his penance—to carry the corpse of the Goddess's shadow, to subordinate himself physically to her—into his blessing, that is, to carry her on his chest while he adopts the attitude of a corpse. Rather than flee from Kālī, he welcomes her and asks the boon of always appearing beneath her. Now he passes her test.

EXPLAINING ŚIVA'S TEST

Tests similar to that faced by Śiva in the *Mahābhāgavata* occur in Śaiva mythology. There, Śiva tests Pārvatī's devotion to him by appearing in dis-guise before her and ridiculing his own outrageous habits and appearance, arguing, in effect, that he is not worthy of her devotion.[36] The myths of Śiva in the Pine Forest also include tests. Śiva flouts Brāhmaṇical conventions of beauty and asceticism when, adopting a particularly loathsome appearance, he dances seductively before the wives of sages living as forest hermits. The rage of these "ascetics" demonstrates their failure as ascetics—for they should not be attached to their wives—and their ignorance of Śiva's supreme status. In some versions, the ascetics curse Śiva with the loss of his *liṅga* and are punished when cosmic chaos ensues, a chaos reversed when they duly worship the *liṅga*.[37]

The *Mahābhāgavata*'s testing motif might be indebted to Śaiva mythology where the "disgusting" and unconventional are used to criticize ignorance and pride. But the most compelling parallels to the *Mahābhāgavata*'s tests come from the Tantras. Śiva's journey has specifically Tantric undertones because it is a journey from pride to joyous and humble appreciation of the goddess Kālī and because he transforms his penance into his blessing.

According to the Śākta Buddhist Tantras studied by Miranda Shaw, women teachers and enlightening goddesses (the two are often the same) frequently confront prospective male initiates with their unconventional—one might say "Kaliesque"—appearance and behavior. When prospective initiates pass the test by heroically facing the anomalous or repulsive (thereby demonstrating insight into the true nature of that which typically evokes attachment and repulsion), they are accepted as initiates. When they fail and flee from or reject the teacher, it is often due to pride in themselves or in their status.

The Buddhist missionary Atiśa passes such a "test." On meeting a woman who wears only a necklace of bones and skulls, who looks "like a skeleton" and behaves strangely, laughing at one moment and weeping the next, he thinks she might be a good teacher. He requests instruction and then follows her to East Bengal, where they reach a cremation ground. "There she suddenly turned back and asked Atiśa, 'How did you guess that I had some special instruction to impart? Do I look like [*sic*] I have any?' 'Yes,' replied Atiśa, 'you certainly do!' Pleased, she initiated him."[38]

Luipa, a yogi of royal birth, fails a test arranged by a *yoginī* because of "royal pride." She serves him a bowl of moldy leftovers, which he throws into the street in disgust, shouting at her, "How dare you serve garbage to a yogi?" She shoots back, "How can an epicure attain enlightenment?"[39] Luipa then takes up practice on a riverbank and eventually attains freedom from pride, "a state of continual bliss in which fish entrails tasted just like ambrosial nectar."[40]

To assist male adepts in recognizing such teachers and avoiding offense, some Tantric texts provide descriptions of *yoginī*s—their skin has a reddish or bluish hue, they laugh at one moment, weep the next, and their behavior is aggressive. Male adepts are warned that the appearance of a *yoginī/ḍakinī* can be intimidating. She "may try to repel an approaching hero with frightening cries and wrathful guise, as a test of his bravery and discernment."[41] But along with the warning comes the promise that the hero who is not frightened will be accepted as the *ḍākinī*'s consort and live with her in "paradise."[42]

The *Mahābhāgavata* is not a Tantric text. But considering its provenance, medieval northeast India, which is the same as that of many of Shaw's texts, and considering its exaltation of Kālī, Tantric themes might be expected. Indeed, the *Mahābhāgavata*'s testing motif, in which Kālī tests pride and attachment, is Tantric. Like the female teachers in Tantra, the *Mahābhāgavata*'s Great Goddess uses her terrific form as Kālī to teach devotees to overcome false pride. Those who pass her test acknowledge her supreme status in spite of, or perhaps *because of,* her terrifying appearance, just as Atiśa had no doubt that the bizarre-looking woman he encountered had something to teach him. Like Tantric *yoginī*s browbeating undiscerning adepts, Kālī and the rest of the Mahāvidyās intimidate Śiva into a fearful panic. But he then transforms the worldly or conventional shame of his penance into a blessing, just as Luipa learns to appreciate fish entrails as if they were nectar.

The privileged religious status of women devotees in the *Mahābhāgavata* might also be indebted to Tantric ideology. According to Shaw's analysis, women are ideal adepts in part because, with less of a personal investment in social status, they do not need to overcome pride as males do, and because they readily identify with female divine models.[43] To be sure, the *Mahābhāgavata* subsumes its testing motif and its understanding of women's religious abilities within a devotional and dharmic framework: the Goddess observes the dharmic requirements of a wife and daughter when she subjects her devotees to the test.

To the extent that the *Mahābhāgavata* expresses specifically Tantric themes in a clearly devotional context, the text blurs the distinction between Tantra and *bhakti.* But perhaps this distinction has been overemphasized.[44] Even Tantric adepts sometimes behave like devotees. A pertinent example here is from the biography of Rechungpa (1084–1161), a Tibetan adept sent to India by Milarepa. Worried that he will die before fulfilling his mission to bring teachings back to Tibet, Rechungpa goes to Siddharājnī, "Queen of Adepts," an expert in longevity techniques. Shaw summarizes the account of their meeting: "When Rechungpa first set eyes on Siddharājnī, her presence was so powerful that his hairs stood on end. Devotion so overwhelmed him that he trembled, wept, threw himself on the ground at her feet, and placed her feet on his head in a gesture of supreme respect."[45] Rechungpa, behaving exactly as Śiva does at the end of his test in the *Mahābhāgavata,* is accepted as her disciple. Siddharājnī is "enchantingly beautiful," "wears jewels and ornaments of bone," and "holds a curved knife and a skull cup,"[46] much like Kālī of the *Mahābhāgavata.* Rechungpa's devotional Tantrism, like the *Mahābhāgavata*'s Tantric devotionalism,[47] returns the present discussion to the image of Kālī upon Śiva. It is this image that marks the end of Śiva's test in the *Mahābhāgavata.*

DAKṢIṆĀKĀLĪ: CONCLUSION

I have argued that a testing motif is central to the *Mahābhāgavata*'s portrayal of Kālī. This motif renders Kālī benign and approachable, while preserving her awesome, fear-inspiring character. The kinship politics at work between the Goddess and her parents implies that social realities have influenced both the text and Kālī's tests. The Tantric themes of Śiva's tests in particular point to Tantric influence in the text's devotionalism. But where does the text stand on Kālī's extremes? Where is the Kālī of death? Where is the bloodthirsty Kālī? Is the *Mahābhāgavata*'s Kālī tamed? I want to suggest answers to these more general questions by comparing various interpretations of Dakṣiṇākālī's image with that offered by the *Mahābhāgavata.*

The name Dakṣiṇākālī indicates an association with cremation grounds and death. One meaning of *dakṣiṇa* is south or southern, the direction presided over by Yama, ruler of the dead. Cremation grounds are to be located to the south of villages or cities. Since Kālī is typically characterized as a goddess of death who stands upon a corpse, Dakṣiṇākālī is an appropriate appellation for her.[48] However, the *Mahābhāgavata* largely ignores this extreme interpretation of her iconography. Śiva here is merely "motionless *like* a corpse" and requests to be depicted *as* a corpse beneath her wherever she appears. But the two deities are not in a cremation ground, nor is one specified as the setting for subsequent appearances of the image.

A second exegesis of the iconographic depiction of Kālī and Śiva, this one metaphysical, is based on the principles of Sāṃkhya. Śiva is the inert soul, *puruṣa,* whereas Kālī is the active, creative *prakṛti,* stimulated into manifest condition by the presence of *puruṣa.* The *Mahābhāgavata* frequently refers to the Goddess as Prakṛti and often pairs her with Śiva as Puruṣa. Furthermore, Śiva himself calls her Ādya Prakṛti when placing himself beneath her.[49] The *Mahābhāgavata* thus invokes a Sāṃkhyan interpretation that tends to mute Kālī's extremes by rationalizing her into an abstract principle.

Tantra offers a similar metaphysical interpretation of the image. According to some Tantric texts, the two basic realities are *śiva,* spirit or consciousness, and *śakti,* power or energy. The two are interdependent, since *śiva* depends on *śakti* for the ability to orchestrate creation, preservation, and destruction. Tantric texts insist that without *śakti,* Śiva is a corpse (*śava*)—lifeless, powerless, incapable of action.[50] The *Mahābhāgavata* alludes to this interpretation: Śiva calls Kālī "Śakti" and then lies beneath her, "motionless like a corpse."

Tantric analyses also emphasize the "erotic" (that is, the simultaneously sexual and religious)[51] symbolism of the image. In defiance of conventional sexual mores, Kālī engages in intercourse with Śiva in the "reverse position." Hence their physical union symbolizes the Tantric goal of uniting Śiva and Śakti, and their sexual union, often set in a cremation ground, models the Tantric ritual practice of sacralized intercourse (*maithuna*).[52] However, in contrast to the more philosophical Sāṃkhyan and Tantric interpretations that the *Mahābhāgavata* does adopt, it does not develop any such erotic meanings.

There are other contrasts as well. Typical mythic settings for the Dakṣiṇākālī image include the battleground. For example, according to the *Adbhuta Rāmāyaṇa* (ca. 1600), Sītā becomes Kālī to defeat a demon for her husband, but after killing the demon and "tossing his heads and limbs about," she embarks on a destructive rampage that threatens to destroy the earth. The gods appeal to Śiva for assistance. He arrives at the battlefield and throws himself down among the corpses beneath her feet. When she sees that she is dancing on her husband, Kālī "is astonished and embarrassed and stops her dance."[53] The *Mahābhāgavata,* however, completely ignores any association of this image with battles. Indeed, this Purāṇa situates the action in Śiva's ascetic hermitage on a mountaintop. Could one be farther from a battlefield than this?

Again, many interpretations focus on Kālī's outstretched tongue. The research of Usha Menon and Richard Shweder among Oriya Hindus documents a prevalent interpretation of Kālī's outstretched tongue as an expression of her modesty and shame (*lajya*) when she realizes that she is standing on her husband.[54] Similarly, the seventeenth-century Bengali Tāntrika Kṛṣṇānanda Āgamavāgīśa is sometimes credited with introducing and popularizing the Dakṣiṇākālī image in Bengal. In his account, the tongue is also seen as a symbol of shame. Kālī appears to Kṛṣṇānanda in a dream and orders him to popularize the particular image of her that will be revealed to him the next day. In the morning, he sees a young woman preparing cow dung cakes. As she raises her right hand to set a cake on the wall, she stands "in the *ālīḍha* pose," her right knee thrown forward and her left slanted behind her. Noticing that she is being observed by Kṛṣṇānanda, "the woman felt very much ashamed and pressed her tongue, that lolled, with her teeth."[55]

The *Mahābhāgavata* does not attribute modesty or embarrassment to Kālī herself. It describes the Goddess's lolling tongue as a bodily adornment,[56] not an expression of shame. The text also shifts the focus of interpretation from Kālī to Śiva; it is not her recognition of her husband that gives the image its meaning; rather, it is Śiva's recognition of his wife. Any shame involved in the story is the "worldly shame" Śiva rejects as he blissfully carries Satī's shadow corpse (11.61).[57]

Eighteenth- and nineteenth-century Bengali poet-devotees of Kālī like Rāmprasād Sen incorporate several different interpretations of the Dakṣiṇākālī pose, including those derived from battle and metaphysics. However, Rachel Fell McDermott states that the most common interpretation offered by these poets is devotional: Śiva is most frequently portrayed "as the devotee who falls at [Kālī's] feet in devotion, or in surrender of his ego, or in hopes of gaining *mokṣa* by her touch. In fact, Śiva is said to have become so enchanted by Kālī that he performed austerities to win her, and having received the treasure of her feet, held them against his heart in reverence."[58]

Of course, the Bengali poets' devotional stance is precisely the interpretation offered by the *Mahābhāgavata.* In both the poetry and the Purāṇa, Śiva undertakes austerities to win the Goddess; once he gains her, he falls under her feet as the ideal devotee. Again, both texts detail the joy and grief of the Goddess's parents and envision Kālī as terrifying and benign—the inspiration for greatest devotion.[59]

It is highly probable that the *Mahābhāgavata* was known in Bengal before the eighteenth century.[60] Although the historical antecedents to the Bengali poets' vision remain something of a mystery to scholars,[61] the *Mahābhāgavata*'s influence on Bengali Śākta poets is clear. The similarity noted here between the visions of the two types of text suggests that further comparison would contribute significantly to scholarly understanding of this part of Kālī's history.

In sum, the *Mahābhāgavata*'s interpretation of the Dakṣiṇākālī image does seem to imply that she has been "tamed," for the text omits the Goddess's extreme physical associations with death, battle, cremation grounds, and even eroticism, preferring more abstract, philosophical understandings. On a literal narrative level, the image of Kālī atop Śiva expresses Śiva's joy at being reunited with the Goddess who was his wife as Satī and who will, in her full embodiment as Pārvatī, be his wife again. Religiously, the image expresses *bhakti:* not only does Śiva humble himself, but he also exalts her, recognizing her supremacy and transcendent nature. As he responds to Pārvatī/Kālī, Śiva also voices two prominent devotional themes: the devotee's pain when separated from the deity and joy when brought into her presence. In desiring always to appear beneath the Goddess's feet, Śiva is asking for the honor of being visible to the world as her greatest devotee. His hymn of praise to the one thousand names of the Goddess establishes a paradigmatic expression of devotion. Far from the battlefield and the cremation ground, therefore, this image conveys not shame, violence, or eroticism but love between Kālī and Śiva, her devotee. However, while her extremities thus may have been muted, her magnificent, even terrifying, power, has not. Her place is by the side, or in the hearts, of those devotees who know her and appreciate her terrific presence—those who pass her tests.

NOTES

1. R. C. Hazra dates the *Mahābhāgavata* to the tenth or eleventh centuries (see *Śākta and Non-sectarian Upapurāṇas,* vol. 2 of *Studies in the Upapurāṇas* [1963; Calcutta: Sanskrit College, 1979], p. 347. However, D. C. Sircar's work on related Śākta texts suggests a seventeenth-century dating. See his *The Śākta Pīṭhas* (Delhi: Motilal Banarasidass, 1973), p. 106 n. 2. In my dissertation on the *Mahābhāgavata* (forthcoming, McMaster University), I argue that a major period for the composition of the text was ca. 1400 to 1600.

2. *Mahābhāgavata Purāṇa* 15.16–18. This work is hereafter cited as *MbhP* in notes, and by chapter and verse number in the body of the essay. I have relied primarily on the printed edition of the text in Pushpendra Kumar, *The Mahābhāgavata Purāṇa (An Ancient Treatise on Śakti* [*sic*] *Cult)* (Delhi: Eastern Book Linkers, 1983). All translations are my own (no complete English translation exists). On occasion, I have adopted a preferable reading from one of three sources: an unpublished manuscript entitled "Mahābhāgavata by Kavira, Son of Dāmodhara Bhaṭṭa" (Banaras Hindu University # 12/7202 C1010), hereafter cited as BHU MS; the printed edition published by the Gujarati Printing Press of Bombay, 1913, hereafter cited as Bombay; or the printed version edited by Pandit Pañcānan Tarkaratna (Calcutta: Vaṅgavāsī Press, 1914), hereafter cited as Calcutta.

3. I have deliberately avoided the language of incarnation because it is commonly used to render *ava√tṛ* and its derivatives, especially *avatāra,* in Vaiṣṇava contexts. The *Mahābhāgavata* does not use these terms. Instead, it describes the Goddess "becoming born" as Satī, Pārvatī, and so on, using the verb *√bhu* with the noun *janman.*

4. See BHU MS and Calcutta; Kumar and Bombay refer to it as the "Hymn to Mahādevī."

5. For example, the devotional themes of joy, union, and pain in separation are said to appear in Kālī's cult beginning only with the Bengali poet Rāmprasād Sen (ca. 1718–75). See David R. Kinsley, *The Sword and the Flute: Kālī and Kṛṣṇa: Dark Visions of the Terrible and the Sublime in Hindu Mythology* (Berkeley and Los Angeles: University of California Press, 1975; reprinted 2000), pp. 115–24.

6. See *Mahābhāarata, Sauptika Parva* 8.65–68, where Kālī leads away Pāṇḍava warriors slain by the Kauravas in a night raid.

7. See, for example, the descriptions of Kālī's battles with the demons Caṇḍa and Muṇḍa and with the demon Raktabīja, from the "Devī-Māhātmya," chs. 7 and 8: 39–62, respectively. It is important to note that even the "Devī-Māhātmya"'s Kālī, with her bloodthirsty ways, serves cosmic order, as does Durgā, her source.

8. See the summaries of such stories in David R. Kinsley, "Kālī," in *Hindu Goddesses: Visions of the Divine Feminine in the Hindu Religious Tradition* (Berkeley and Los Angeles: University of California Press, 1986), pp. 118–19, reprinted as chapter 1 in this volume.

9. *Bhāgavata Purāṇa* 5.9.12–20.

10. In the *Rāma-Upākhyāna,* the Goddess accepts blood sacrifice (*bali*) and so ensures Rāma's victory over Rāvaṇa. In commemoration of this event, *bali* is to be offered to her during her autumnal festival (see *MbhP* 45.31–33 and 46.18–33).

11. *Bhāgavata Purāṇa* 5.9.17, quoted from *Srimad Bhagavata,* trans. Swami Tapas-

yananda, 4 vols. (Madras: Sri Ramakrishna Math, 1982), 2: 39. See also the translation of the same passage in *The Bhāgavata Purāṇa, Ancient Indian Tradition and Mythology,* trans. G. V. Tagare, 8 vols. (Delhi: Motilal Banarsidass, 1976), 8: 678–79.

12. Kinsley, "Kālī," p. 117.

13. Cheever Mackenzie Brown, "Kālī, the Mad Mother," in *The Book of the Goddess, Past and Present: An Introduction to Her Religion,* ed. Carl Olson (New York: Crossroad, 1983), p. 113.

14. *Bhīṣma Parva* 23 and *Virāṭa Parva* 6. For a translation of these hymns, see Thomas B. Coburn, *The Devī-Māhātmya: The Crystallization of the Goddess Tradition* (Delhi: Motilal Banarsidass, 1984), pp. 267–75.

15. Ibid., p. 270. There is no discussion of these hymns' portrayals of Durgā or Kālī in either Kinsley's chapter or Brown's essay, as mentioned above, although both include a historical overview. In *The Sword and the Flute,* which contains a more detailed history, Kinsley indicates that he did not incorporate a discussion of the *Mahābhārata* hymns in his account because they are later additions to the epic (p. 89 n. 12). Fair enough. But he does not discuss the hymns at any point, and this omission helps to create the impression of a clear, linear development from the extreme Kālī of early depictions to the tame Kālī of more recent ones.

16. For a balanced assessment of Kālī's epic and Purāṇic appearances, see Rachel Fell McDermott, "Evidence for the Transformation of the Goddess Kālī: Kamalākānta Bhaṭṭācārya and the Śākta Padāvalī Tradition" (Ph.D. diss, Harvard University, 1993), pp. 192–94. This dissertation has been published as *Mother of My Heart, Daughter of My Dreams: Kālī and Umā in the Devotional Poetry of Bengal* (New York: Oxford University Press, 2001).

17. The goddess who goes to Dakṣa's city later in the narrative is explicitly called Kālī. Thus, while the text does not name her here, her identity as Kālī becomes clear as the story unfolds.

18. Reading (with Bombay) *dūrībhuto* rather than (with Kumar) *dūrābhuto.*

19. See *MbhP* 9.30a.

20. These are the Goddess's words when she promises Dakṣa that she will become Satī (*MbhP* 3.77).

21. His *dehābhimāna* is evident throughout the story. See, for instance, *MbhP* 7.52–69.

22. According to the *Kṛṣṇa Upākhyāna,* Prasūti and Dakṣa propitiate the Goddess, who agrees to be born as their daughter when they take birth as Yaśodā and Nanda. But she informs them that she will not remain in Nanda's house long because of Dakṣa's behavior when she was Satī. See *MbhP* 52.6–23.

23. See Wendy Doniger O'Flaherty, *Śiva, the Erotic Ascetic* (Oxford: Oxford University Press, 1973), pp. 213–18.

24. William Sax, *Mountain Goddess: Gender and Politics in a Himalayan Pilgrimage* (New York: Oxford University Press, 1991), p. 115.

25. Ibid., pp. 117–25.

26. My use of Sax's work here is indebted to David Kinsley's application of Sax's ethnographic data to the Satī story. See David R. Kinsley, *Tantric Visions of the Divine Feminine: The Ten Mahāvidyās* (Berkeley and Los Angeles: University of California Press, 1997), pp. 26–27.

27. Sax, *Mountain Goddess,* p. 118.

28. Ibid., pp. 117–25.

29. Similar maternal perspectives are expressed in Bengali Śākta Padāvalī (Kamalākānta Bhaṭṭācārya, for example, depicts Menakā's intense longing to be reunited with Umā), and in sixteenth- to nineteenth-century Maṅgalakāvyas. See McDermott, "Evidence for the Transformation of the Goddess Kālī," pp. 225 and 253–59.

30. See Manisha Roy, *Bengali Women* (Chicago: University of Chicago Press, 1975), pp. 88–89, 120; and Lina Fruzzetti, *The Gift of a Virgin: Women, Marriage, and Ritual in a Bengali Society* (New Brunswick, N.J.: Rutgers University Press, 1982), pp. 155–56.

31. O'Flaherty's analysis of this passage also notes the explicit test. See *Śiva, the Erotic Ascetic,* pp. 154–55.

32. Satī's plea is a direct appeal to a married woman's right or duty to return to her natal home on festive occasions. Kinsley connects Satī's resistance to male control to her recognition of this right to visit and be honored in her *mait;* see *Tantric Visions of the Divine Feminine,* pp. 26–27.

33. *MbhP* 8.89–92.

34. By surrounding Śiva as the Mahāvidyās, the Goddess seems to treat him as an enemy, since, as the *Mahābhāgavata*'s own description of the worship of the Mahāvidyās says, they are invoked against enemies to paralyze, kill, stupefy, or cause flight. Kinsley makes the same point, noting that the Mahāvidyās typically act against enemies of their devotees. See his "Tārā, Chinnamastā, and the Mahāvidyās," in *Hindu Goddesses,* p. 164. However, and consistent with my analysis of the testing motif, the *Mahābhāgavata* specifies that the Goddess is acting out of compassion and not to inspire fear.

35. *MbhP* 23.90. *Pada* here means both foot and state.

36. For a discussion of such accounts, see Kinsley, "Pārvatī," in *Hindu Goddesses,* pp. 42–43, and O'Flaherty, *Śiva, the Erotic Ascetic,* pp. 196–97.

37. O'Flaherty, *Śiva, the Erotic Ascetic,* pp. 192–96.

38. Miranda Shaw, *Passionate Enlightenment: Women in Tantric Buddhism* (Princeton: Princeton University Press, 1994), p. 56.

39. Ibid., p. 57.

40. Ibid. The Hindu mystic Ramakrishna also failed Tantric tests, including "heroic" confrontations with female "teachers." Because he was unable to overcome "disgust, shame, and fear," the obstacles to realization of the Tantric goal, he also failed to become a Tantric hero and lover of Kālī, thereby remaining a child. I rely here on the work of Jeffrey Kripal, *Kālī's Child: The Mystical and the Erotic in the Life and Teachings of Ramakrishna,* 2d ed. (1995; Chicago: University of Chicago Press, 1998), pp. 121–32.

41. Shaw, *Passionate Enlightenment,* p. 55. *Yoginīs* are witches, and *ḍākinīs* are flesh-eating demons. Both are traditional companions of Kālī.

42. Ibid.

43. Ibid., pp. 69–70.

44. This caution was voiced by David Kinsley at the Kālī Conference, Barnard College, New York, September 1996.

45. Shaw, *Passionate Enlightenment,* p. 118.

46. Ibid., p. 119.

47. The phrase "Tantric devotionalism" was the inspiration of Rachel Fell McDermott (private communication, May 16, 2000).

48. For a more detailed analysis of the image's connection with death and death rituals, see Frédérique Apffel Marglin, "Types of Sexual Union and Their Implicit Meanings," in *The Divine Consort: Rādhā and the Goddesses of India,* ed. John Stratton Hawley and Donna Marie Wulff (Boston: Beacon Press, 1982), pp. 307–13.

49. *MbhP* 23.8 and 10.

50. This plays both on Tantric symbolic systems and on the characteristics of the Sanskrit script. In *devanāgarī,* the default vowel is "a." That is, unless the sign for a vowel other than "a" follows a consonant, "a" is implied. The letter "i" in Tantric symbolism represents *śakti.* So Śiva without *śakti,* i.e., minus the sign for the vowel "i," is *śava,* "corpse."

51. I am following Kripal's definition of the erotic. See *Kālī's Child,* p. 23.

52. For a detailed discussion of these erotic interpretations, see ibid., pp. 89–90.

53. Quoted from Kinsley, *Sword and the Flute,* p. 108.

54. See Usha Menon and Richard Shweder, "Dominating Kālī: Hindu Family Values and Tantric Power," chapter 4 in this volume.

55. Sircar, *Śākta Pīṭhas,* p. 74 n. 1. Sircar, who cites a narrative recorded by N. N. Vasu, provides the Bengali here: *lajjāya jiva kāṭā.* The biting of the outstretched tongue lends a note of authenticity to the account. Kripal explains that a slightly protruding tongue clenched or "cut" (*kāṭā*) by the teeth is the gesture Bengalis use when embarrassed.

56. *MbhP* 23.19.

57. In Kripal's analysis, Ramakrishna disavowed Tantra not only because of his own Tantric failures but also because of a "broader cultural rejection." Kripal suggests that Bengali shame over Tantra is projected especially onto Kālī's tongue. See *Kālī's Child,* pp. 243–45.

58. Rachel Fell McDermott, "Kālī at the Crossroads: New Directions in the Eighteenth to Nineteenth Century Śākta Padāvalī of Bengal," in *Bulletin: Center for the Study of World Religions* (Harvard University) 16, no. 1 (1989/1990): 22–42, 62. For Śiva as ideal devotee, see also her "Evidence for the Transformation of the Goddess Kālī," pp. 217–18.

59. McDermott, "Evidence," pp. 217–18, 251–59.

60. Manuscripts in Bengali scripts, dated to the late eighteenth and early nineteenth centuries, have been found in or near Bengal and Bangladesh. The *Mahābhāgavata* is quoted in ritual texts of eighteenth-century Bengali authors, as also in the *Bṛhaddharma Purāṇa,* a nonsectarian text known and probably composed in Bengali no later than ca. 1700. See Hazra, *Śākta and Non-sectarian Upapurāṇas,* pp. 346–47, 564, and Sircar, *Śākta Pīṭhas,* p. 106 n. 2.

61. See Kinsley, "Kālī," p. 126, and Brown, "Kālī, the Mad Mother," pp. 110–23, for two attempts to resolve the history behind Bengali devotion to "Mother Kālī."

CHAPTER 3

The Domestication of a Goddess

Caraṇa-tīrtha *Kālīghāṭ, the* Mahāpīṭha *of Kālī*

Sanjukta Gupta

From her [Ambikā's] broad forehead, clouded by frowning eyebrows, there sprang out at great speed Kālī of ferocious face, brandishing her sword and noose and the strange skull-staff. A garland of severed heads ornamented her body. She wore a tiger hide, and her emaciated form looked terrifying. From her wide-open mouth protruded an awful, lolling tongue. Her eyes red and sunken, she emitted screams that filled up all directions.

"DEVĪ-MĀHĀTMYA" 7: 5–7

Kālīghāṭ, the landing stage sacred to Kālī on the old course of the river Ganga at Calcutta, is regarded as an important seat of the Goddess (*mahāpīṭha* or *śaktipīṭha*) and is visited by thousands of pilgrims every day. As a major Indian pilgrim center, it is limited neither by the Bengali language nor by the cultural specialization of the local priests, for the temple authorities hire many non-Bengali priests to accommodate pilgrims hailing from other parts of India.[1] In this breadth of appeal, Kālīghāṭ clearly reflects the changing character of Calcutta itself, which was established in 1690 by Job Charnock of the East India Company. From the early nineteenth century, when it was the capital of the Indian empire as envisaged by Lord Wellesley, Calcutta gradually became the most important city of the Raj. Even when the capital was moved to Delhi in 1911, Calcutta, with its large, busy port, remained the trading and economic center of northern and eastern India. This naturally brought great numbers of people from other regions of the country, who in turn became woven into the rich fabric of Calcutta's socioeconomic life.

In spite of this rich mixture, however, Calcutta retained its highly specific, Bengali social and cultural identity, and the visitors who pursued their own business interests there also tended to adopt local traditions. This cultural interplay has been and continues to be noticeable in several arenas, including religion.

One particular feature of Bengali religiosity is a deep-seated devotion to mother goddesses. The most important public religious festivals in Bengal are connected with two goddesses, Durgā and Kālī, the goddess of war and victory and the goddess of death and regeneration, respectively. Even today, West Bengal is dotted with traditional temples of the Goddess, such as the Yogādyā Mā Temple in the Burdwan district.[2] Many of these temples were at one time patronized by local zamindars or sanctified by the presence of some famous holy man, as was the case with the Tārāpīṭh Temple and its great Tāntrika, Vāmākhyāpā. The most recent such center is the temple of Kālī at Dakṣiṇeśvar in north Calcutta, where Sri Ramakrishna taught his own interpretation of the traditional religion of India and nurtured the religious personality of his greatest disciple, Swami Vivekananda.

The concept of the Goddess, mainly identified with Kālī, is full of contradiction and ambiguity. On the one hand, she is seen all over India as the epitome of demonic ferocity and cannibalism, as is clearly depicted in her iconography: corpse-earrings; the long necklace of freshly severed heads and the belt made of amputated forearms; her nakedness or tiger's skin loincloth; her dress and ornaments dripping blood; and her grotesque habit of tearing apart the live bodies of her victims, lapping up their gushing blood with her lolling tongue and getting drunk on it. In other words, she is death and destruction. On the other hand, she is also the life-giving and life-protecting cosmic mother whose breast milk sustains the world and regenerates her creatures, weakened by the process of life and death and wearied by suffering.[3]

Partly in support of this second, life-affirming aspect of the Goddess, her wild and demonic iconography is toned down in favor of a dark but beautiful form for the benefit of Bengali religious sensitivities. Her red, round, bulging, unfocused eyes are made large, elongated, and serene; her disheveled, matted hair is changed into abundant, long, black, wavy tresses; and her greedy, lolling tongue and blood-smeared mouth are hidden behind cosmetic unguents, flower decorations, and ear and nose ornaments. Her nakedness is often covered, as at the Kālīghāṭ Temple, with an expensive sari. She is the perfection of youthful, charming, and feminine beauty.[4] At the same time, she is the active, sovereign, divine power controlling the universe. As both Kālī the Reaper and Kālī the Supreme Savior,[5] she is a cosmic mother, who may punish wrongdoers but in her infinite kindness is ever ready to forgive them and to save them from misery and transience.[6] According to her devotees, all other goddesses, worshipped at different places under different names and on various festive occasions (for instance, Tārā, Durgā, Sarasvatī, Lakṣmī, Pārvatī, and even village goddesses) are but facets of this unique mother goddess Kālī.

The thousands of pilgrims who flock daily to the Kālīghāṭ Temple treat Kālī very much like a human mother, bringing her their domestic problems and prayers for prosperity, and returning when their prayers are fulfilled to express their gratitude. Their attitude to the Goddess is guided by their religious traditions and training, their spiritual and intellectual capacities, and the guidance of their temple priests. I myself have witnessed such a priest guiding a group of pilgrims and worshipping the Goddess on their behalf with mantras meant for the worship of Sarasvatī, the goddess of learning and arts. The day in question was Sarasvatī Pūjā, and no one had any problem worshipping a nonvegetarian Tantric goddess with mantras intended for a vegetarian goddess, who, notwithstanding her identification with Kālī at the highest philosophical level and in other parts of India,[7] is treated in Bengal as one of her minor aspects.

CALCUTTA AND THE HOUSE OF KĀLĪ BY THE RIVER

Over the past hundred years, railroads and the publicity provided by newspapers and other periodicals have greatly enhanced the importance of the Kālīghāṭ *mahāpīṭha.*[8] The small Kālī Temple used to be served by one priest, allegedly a Tantric practitioner as well, who personally managed every aspect of the temple's activities. Because of the increased prestige of the temple, largely owing to modern communications, the numerous descendants of the early priestly line have gained enormous power and prosperity. This raises the interesting question of the relationship between the religious sensitivity of the members of this priestly lineage and that of their pilgrim-clients. Do their religious attitudes clash, or have they been peacefully integrated? As we shall see, the variety of religious attitudes toward Kālī seems not to be a problem, either for the priests, hereditary or temporary, or for the pilgrims, with their various cultural backgrounds.

In West Bengal, the great sacred centers dedicated to the Goddess as the divine active power (Śākta *pīṭha*s) have a different character from the religious temple centers of pan-Indian reputation. Unlike the temple of Jagannātha at Puri or of Mīṇākṣī at Madurai, for instance, Kālīghāṭ allows pilgrims to worship in a relaxed, informal way. Yet it is easy to detect the ever-present managerial influence of the temple's priestly clan. Here we encounter two streams of Hinduism: the domestic religious sphere of the temple priests, who consider the deity in the temple to belong to their family tradition; and

Figure 3.1 The Kālīghāṭ Temple. Photo by Jayanta Roy, February 2001.

the Hindu tradition of the Purāṇas and Tantras, however that may be understood by Hindu pilgrims from far and wide.

In the course of several visits to the Kālīghāṭ Temple (fig. 3.1) during a stay in Calcutta in 1995, I was able to witness the "domestication" of Kālī by the family and kinsmen of the Hāldārs, the priestly clan who enjoy ownership of this famous temple and manage its affairs with complete authority. In the process of such domestication, which follows the household religious ethos of the original forefathers who started the lineage some two hundred and fifty years ago, several important innovations have been made. Two points strike me as essential for understanding the religious attitudes of the temple priests and pilgrims. The first is the fusion at this religious center between two religious streams: the nonvegetarian Śākta (Tantric) tradition and the vegetarian Vaiṣṇava (Kṛṣṇaite) tradition. Since the seventeenth century, both have been strong in Bengal, and they have spawned a syncretistic religious attitude that ignores sectarian boundaries. The second point is the fact that the religion of a family that owns or manages a revered Kālī temple may differ from that of most of her devotees, and may consequently influence the cult. Here at Kālīghāṭ, the family religious tradition of the Hāldār *sevāyets* is Vaiṣṇava, and this impinges on the temple's own ancient tradition, the Tantric cult of Dakṣiṇākālī.

MOTHER KĀLĪ (MĀ KĀLĪ) AND THE IMPACT OF VAIṢṆAVA RELIGIOSITY

Let me now elaborate the first point. By the eighteenth century, largely under the influence of the Vaiṣṇava tradition, the religious attitude of Bengalis toward the supreme Goddess had completely changed. One can see this by comparing Kālī as she appears in the early sixth-century "Devī-Māhātmya" section of the *Mārkaṇḍeya Purāṇa* with Kālī as she is transformed in texts postdating the famous tenth-century *Bhāgavata Purāṇa,* which celebrates the youthful Kṛṣṇa. The "Devī-Māhātmya" describes the goddess Ambikā as the supreme *māyā* (delusive power) who appears in various manifestations to deliver gods and others from threatening demons. Kālī here assumes a subordinate form, as she emanates from the Goddess only to help her in fighting demons (ch. 7). The eleventh- to twelfth-century *Devībhāgavata Purāṇa,* however, clearly modeled after the popular Vaiṣṇava *Bhāgavata Purāṇa,* records a different legend (5.23.1 ff.). In this case, the supreme Goddess is Pārvatī. In order to slay the demon kings Śumbha and Niśumbha and their demonic hosts, she emanates an exquisitely beautiful goddess, the Mother (Ambikā), also called Kauśīkī. As if exhausted of all positive feminine beauty, Pārvatī then turns completely black and becomes terrifyingly menacing, like the night of world destruction (*kālarātrī*). In this dark form, she is called Kālī. Ambikā and Kālī go to where the demons reign and start singing delightfully, attracting their enemies' attention. A great battle ensues. Eventually, the goddesses slay all the terrible demons, freeing the universe from evil. In this Purāṇa, therefore, Kālī as Pārvatī, Śiva's spouse, is Kauśīkī's equal; this allows her to have a leading role in the battles fought and makes a clear theological point: the two goddesses are but one single divine power, subsuming all other forces and gods (5.23–29). Indeed, most of the late Purāṇas popular in Bengal show the blurring of sectarian boundaries; other popular deities are presented in their legends in such a way as to be taken as aspects of the supreme Goddess. For instance, the goddesses Ṣaṣṭhī (the protectress of children), Śītalā (the goddess of smallpox and other epidemics), and Manasā (the snake goddess) are all incorporated into the fifteenth-century Śākta *Brahmavaivarta Purāṇa.* Even Rādhikā, the cowherd woman beloved of Kṛṣṇa, is elevated to the status of the divine power, the cosmic mother, in Śākta Purāṇas such as the *Devībhāgavata* and *Brahmavaivarta Purāṇas.*[9] Seen from this perspective, then, there is nothing incongruous in being a devotee of Kṛṣṇa/Viṣṇu and Kālī at the same time, or in finding Ṣaṣṭhī, Śītalā, and Manasā integrated into the temple worship of Kālī. We shall presently see both phenomena in our temple at Kālīghāṭ.

The Vaiṣṇava tradition of the medieval Purāṇas was not the only influence upon Śākta sensibilities. Starting from the fifteenth century, Śrī Kṛṣṇa Caitanya's ecstatic Kṛṣṇa *bhakti* also had a tremendous impact upon conceptions of Śākta deities. As a result of both such Vaiṣṇava influences, by the eighteenth century in Bengal Kālī was transformed from a wild, ferocious deity of death to a benign youthful mother, albeit capricious and crazy,[10] who charmed her devotees. One famous example is Rāmprasād Sen, who poured out his ecstatic adoration in excellent lyrics that, sung by popular singers, conveyed this regeneration of Kālī to every corner of Bengal.

The new attitude was charged with emotion, an ecstasy of tenderness such as exists between friends, lovers, husband and wife, parents and children, and even master and servant. Such loving bonds of closeness made devotees overlook the Goddess's divine sternness and suppressed all awareness of her fearful aspects. While continuing to maintain that Kālī was the supreme deity, the cosmic controller of creation, omnipotent to save and to nurture, her traditional violence was converted into playfulness, and her blood-curdling, roaring laughter into the sweet, amused laughter of a teenage girl. Similar to the image of the teenage Kṛṣṇa in the *Bhāgavata Purāṇa,* Kālī was viewed as a beautiful, tender, youthful mother, like that idealized in the mind of a very young child. From the eighteenth century on, her cult attracted vast numbers of goddess worshippers, and both the "Devī-Māhātmya" and the *Devībhāgavata Purāṇa* became very popular.

VAIṢṆAVA INNOVATIONS AT A ŚĀKTA TEMPLE

The close association of the Vaiṣṇava and Śākta traditions in Bengal is illustrated by six innovations instituted in the ritual regime by the Hāldār *sevāyets* at the Kālīghāṭ Temple, presumably since the time of Bhavānīdās, the founder of their lineage. (1) An icon of Vāsudeva (Kṛṣṇa/Viṣṇu) has been placed in a niche in the inner sanctum where the Kālī image stands. All of my informants told me that Vāsudeva is the *gṛhadevatā* or *kuladevatā* (family or lineage deity) of the Hāldārs, and that it was their ancestor Bhavānīdās who installed the icon in the temple. Its role in the temple ritual is very important even today. (2) Kālī is daily decorated with a clear Vaiṣṇava mark on the ridge of her nose. (3) During the most famous and important Bengali festival to Kālī, Kālī Pūjā, the Goddess in the temple is worshipped as Lakṣmī, and no animal sacrifice is offered to her on that day. (4) The temple bursary does not pay for the daily animal sacrifice at the temple. (5) Animals are taken inside the temple to be sacrificed only twice a year. After their beheading, the heads are allowed to stay inside the inner sanctum overnight and are then immersed in the Ganga the next morning. (6) No animal is allowed to be sacrificed during the daily *bhoga-pūjā* when Kālī is offered food. I shall elaborate on each of these innovations in describing the layout of the temple and the ritual schedule. All of them indicate that a gradual synthesis of Vaiṣṇava and Śākta traditions must have changed the original (Tantric?) character of this *mahāpīṭha*.

Kālīghāṭ is situated on the bank of the Ganga in southern Calcutta and is a busy trading center. It is one of the famous fifty-one *pīṭhas* (seats, or sacred centers) dedicated to the Goddess, and has been mentioned in various Bengali religious texts from the sixteenth century on.[11] Each of these fifty-one *pīṭhas* is sacred because a part of the lifeless body of Satī, an ancient manifestation of the Goddess, fell on that spot. The well-known Satī myth of Indian antiquity appears in different forms in various texts. One recent version recounts the story as follows: In ancient times the Goddess was born as a daughter of Dakṣa Prajāpati and married to Śiva. Dakṣa considered Śiva to be unacceptable to the celestial community, and so when he organized a great sacrifice, he pointedly refrained from inviting Śiva and Satī. On hearing the news of this sacrifice, Satī went to her father and demanded to know why Śiva was the only god not invited. Dakṣa launched into a diatribe against Śiva in front of all the assembled gods. At this insult, Satī fell dead on the spot. In terrible anger and grief, Śiva destroyed Dakṣa's sacrifice and beheaded Dakṣa. Then, in desperate sorrow, he carried Satī's corpse on his shoulder and roamed the universe, desolate and disconsolate, oblivious of all his duties. On the decision of the council of the gods, Viṣṇu finally relieved Śiva of his gruesome burden by cutting Satī's body into fifty-one pieces, which fell to earth bit by bit and were scattered over a wide area. Wherever a piece of this sacred body landed, a Satī center grew up to commemorate her great power and fidelity.[12]

As legend would have it, four toes from Satī's right foot fell at Kālīghāṭ.[13] The image of Kālī in the temple does indeed consist of what the devotees call the face and the feet; hence the name *caraṇa-tīrtha* (pilgrimage place of the feet) became popular. The image is decorated with splendid jewelry and a costly sari that completely conceals the image, showing just the face and hands with their attributes and parts of the feet firmly set on a pedestal (fig. 3.2). Even the head is encircled by a sari in the Bengali style. The face is mounted with three large golden eyes and a large, lolling golden tongue, on top of which the Goddess's upper lip and upper set of teeth are en-

Figure 3.2 The Kālī image of Kālīghāṭ Temple. Photo by Jayanta Roy, February 2001.

graved. No other facial features are visible. No blood-dripping corners of her mouth or fangs are shown. Four silver arms are also mounted on the sides of the image; one holds a sword, one a severed head, and two make the usual gestures of granting safety and fulfilling the devotees' wishes. One of the main desires of every pilgrim is to touch the Goddess's feet and occasionally to offer a votive object like a miniature sword or, if the pilgrim has come in gratitude for the cure of some disease, a small replica of the healed part of his or her body. More generous gifts include money, jewelry, an expensive sari, or even a royal canopy made of gold or silver, in recognition of Kālī's supreme sovereignty and compassion.

The main temple is a simple rectangular building, consisting of one large room, the inner sanctum, surrounded by an elevated, circumambulatory, open balcony (fig. 3.3). Two doors open from this balcony, one in front of the image for a full view of the Goddess as one is circumambulating her, and one at the side, opening onto a flight of steps leading down to the inner sanctum. The pedestal rock on which the Goddess stands is situated almost in the middle of this room, facilitating a second circumambulatory passage. Devotees touch the Goddess's feet after presenting her with their ritual offerings (*pūjā*). On the wall of the inner sanctum, in a niche, an image of Vāsudeva is kept. Recently, this image has been covered with metal latticework doors, so I could not see it.

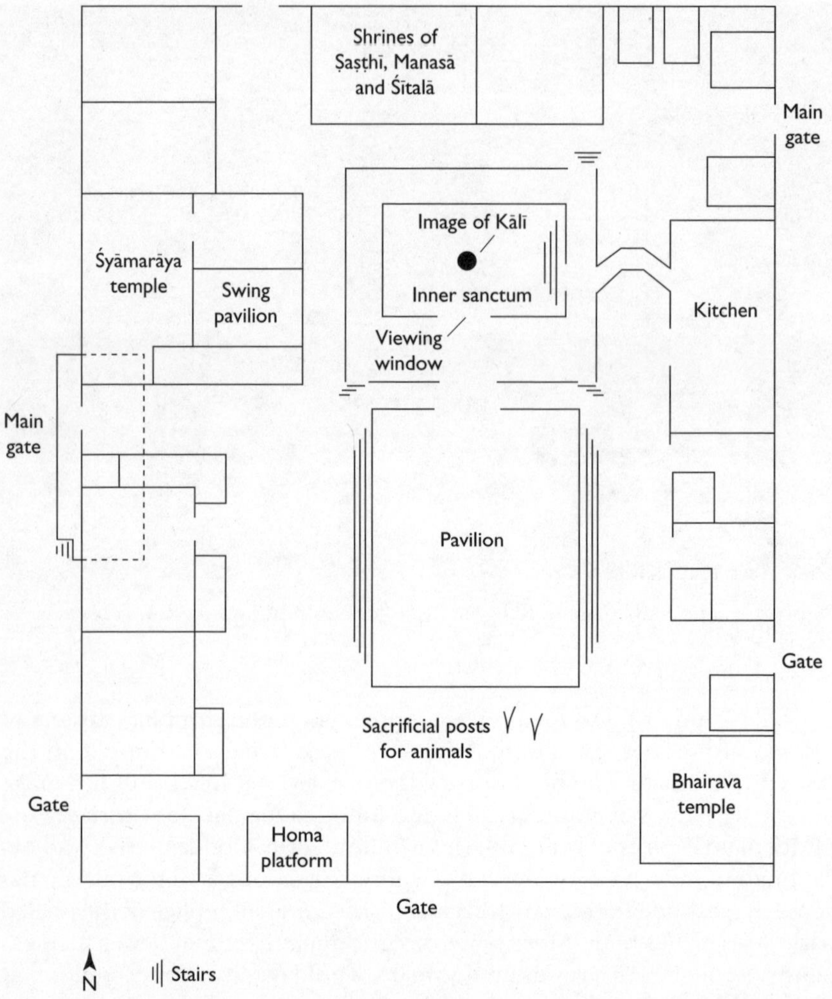

Figure 3.3 The floor plan of the Kālīghāṭ Temple, created by Sanjukta Gupta. Figure not drawn to scale.

On one side of the main temple, there is a smaller temple to Śyāmarāya (the Dark King), containing images of Rādhā and Kṛṣṇa. This is flanked by two storerooms and a small kitchen. Adjacent to the Rādhā-Kṛṣṇa Temple is the swing pavilion (*dolmañca*) kept for their annual festival. On another side of the main Kālī Temple, there are shrines of the goddesses Ṣaṣṭhī, Manasā, and Śītalā. The cults of all these minor temples and shrines are integrated within the Kālī Temple's special annual ritual events and are managed by the *sevāyet* Hāldārs and their appointed priests. The *pīṭha*'s actual Bhairava, or ferocious form of Śiva, is Nakuleśvara.[14] But his temple, built long after the temples of Kālī Mā and even Śyāmarāya, stands a little way outside the present-day main temple complex and its encircling wall, and is much more easily accessible to the public. Although the management of the Nakuleśvara Temple is also in the hands of the Hāldārs, its priests are from Orissa and follow their own program, independent of the main temple routine. It is not clear to me why the Hāldārs have not appointed a Bengali priest for this temple.

The sacrificial post (Bengali, *hāḍikāṭh,* Sanskrit, *yūpa*) for the main temple stands at present on one side of the temple pavilion (*nāṭamañca*) near a side door at the far end of the precinct, neatly enclosed by a low wall. The temple in front of this area is that of a Bhairava who is not Nakuleśvara Śiva, and whose identity I failed to determine. He is related to the actual ritual of animal sacrifice, and the severed heads of the animals are offered to him. Opposite this Bhairava Temple is the pavilion for the ritual fire sacrifice (*homavedī*). This area, containing the enclosures of the fire sacrifice, the animal sacrifice, and the Bhairava Temple, is accessible through three doors set in the temple enclosure walls, and it appears to be slightly distinct from the main temple area that is the center of the pilgrimage, which is served by two main gates. One of these gates leads to the small water tank called the Kālīkuṇḍa, into which the fossilized part of Satī's body is alleged to have originally fallen. The other leads to the temple of Nakuleśvara Śiva. A huge rectangular pavilion (*nāṭamandira*) stands between the main temple and the sacrificial area, with flights of marble stairs on each of its long sides, and its short sides facing the main temple and the sacrificial area, respectively. Its marble floor is level with the balcony of the main temple, and a devotee sitting there can see the image through the temple door facing it. This pavilion is not structurally connected with the temple and was erected thirty years later. The temple kitchen, with a wide verandah in front of it, sits across a small yard from the side of the main temple. The cooked food is transported across this yard to the inner sanctum by means of a bridged corridor.

From the layout of the additional temples and other utility structures, it seems to me that there has been a conscious effort both to incorporate local deities like Ṣaṣṭhī, Śītalā, and Manasā, as well as Kṛṣṇa and Rādhā from Bengali Vaiṣṇavism, and to downplay Kālī's connection with blood sacrifice and even with ferocious Bhairavas. This is an ongoing process and is still continuing. As far as I can remember, the only part of the temple to have been "tidied up" in the past thirty years is the sacrificial area; this is so as to shield it slightly from the prying eyes of pilgrims and visitors. In other Kālī temples, the beheading of the animal is performed right in front of the temple's main door, or near to it, symbolizing that the sacrifice is being made in the Goddess's full sight.[15]

The daily cycle of Mā Kālī's ritual worship begins at 4 A.M., when the Hāldār priest responsible for the day's worship enters the inner sanctum with an assistant priest, who cleans up and removes all previous offerings, garlands, and so on.[16] Special care is taken to clean the feet of the image, which is then decorated with fresh garlands before the temple door in front of it is opened to the public, although people are not allowed inside the inner sanctum. A simple ceremony of worship is followed by *ārati* (waving of various objects, including, at the end, lamps). This is always performed by the same member of the Hāldār family and is done grandly, with great devotional emotion.[17] At 6 A.M., the main ritual worship commences inside the sanctum to the right of the image. This is known as Mā Kālī's daily morning worship (*nitya-pūjā*). So far as I could check, the worship follows a handbook, which could very well be the famous *Purohit-Darpaṇ* (*Mirror for Priests*), compiled and edited by the late Surendramohan Bhaṭṭācārya. This handbook describes various rituals and mantras in Bengali, quoting Tantric sources as authorities, and it has run into more than thirty-five editions since it first appeared in 1891.[18] At this early morning worship no *homa* (fire sacrifice) is performed. Nor is a *yantra* (a mystic diagram representing the deity) drawn, but a *yantra* flower is placed on the body of the image—a substitution recommended by the *Purohit-Darpaṇ*.[19] Mr. Śānti Bhaṭṭācārya told me that the ritual program is based on the *Toḍala Tantra,* a fairly late text that describes the rituals of the ten Mahāvidyās. Interestingly enough, this text equates the ten Mahāvidyās with the ten *avatāra*s of Viṣṇu.[20]

This worship of Kālī takes about two and a half hours. Vāsudeva is also worshipped, and his icon is brought down and placed inside the sacred ritual area. As far as I could see, it was more a Purāṇic than a Tantric rite, as there is no sequence involving a fire ritual. After the priests have finished the formal ceremony, the public is allowed to come down into the inner sanctum and touch the Goddess's feet; in this, they are aided by ordinary ritualist Brahmans who are not temple priests but who are allowed into the temple to officiate for pilgrims. The latter give their offerings to such priests, who then offer them to Kālī. The officiating priests get a small fee for their services from their pilgrim clients, while the Hāldārs receive whatever is offered to Kālī. These officiating priests hail from various parts of India and are appointed by the Hāldārs to serve the pilgrims, who also come from all over India.

At 2 P.M., the inner sanctum is closed to the public, and the early afternoon worship starts. As I have not witnessed this, I can only state that my informants told me that it is much the same as the morning worship, except that in the afternoon, cooked food is offered, whereas in the morning, the Goddess only eats fruit and sweets. I did see the cooked meal offerings as they were being conveyed from the kitchen to the temple and to the sanctum. The meal appeared to be simple, resembling the normal midday meal any affluent traditional Bengali would eat: a couple of rice dishes, a few vegetable curries, fish and goat-meat curries, some fried items, and rice pudding. After the food is offered, the priest shuts both doors of the main sanctum for about forty-five minutes. I must add an interesting detail here. I was told by the priest that the temple cook first prepares all the vegetarian and sweet dishes and offers these to Vāsudeva in the kitchen. Only then are the meat dishes cooked and transferred, with the vegetarian and sweet ones, to the inner sanctum for the ritual offering to Kālī. After the Goddess's meal is complete, the priest goes in and finishes the rituals that follow the food offering.[21] The temple servants then convey the food back to a room next to the kitchen, where the chief *sevāyet* of the day stands. He not only receives all the day's gifts offered to the Goddess by the pilgrims but also bears the cost of the daily food ritual and other offerings furnished by the regular temple suppliers. In addition, he supervises the process of cooking and offering the food, and thereafter distributes it—now known as *prasāda* (deity's grace)—amongst the other *sevāyet*s, priests, servants, cooks, caretakers, and some special pilgrims, like myself. Finally, he oversees the feeding of a large number of beggars who are already gathered in the enclosed quadrangle. This is ritually called *daridra-nārāyaṇa-sevā* (serving Nārāyaṇa manifest as the poor) and has an obvious Vaiṣṇava overtone; the beggars are given only vegetarian food.

From 4 P.M. on, the public is allowed in again, and their offerings are administered by the *sevāyet*s or their agents. The temple priest can now go home and take the *prasāda* as his midday meal and breakfast rolled into one. He then rests or attends to his private affairs, returning to the temple later for the Goddess's evening rituals. These commence with another *ārati,* which is much more elaborate than that performed in the early morning. Then a cold supper (*śītal*) consisting of fruit and sweets is offered to the Goddess, and the public can once again approach her. After about 11 P.M., the public is excluded. Finally, Kālī's bed is made ready, and she is freshly clothed and decorated with flower garlands, preparatory for sleep. One feature of these nighttime rituals is the restoration of her Vaiṣṇava mark (*rasakali* or *tilaka*), which is made of special sandalwood paste and consists of a dot between her eyes above a vertical line where the ridge of the nose would be. It is an interesting ritual point that in the afternoon, when Kālī is about to be offered food that includes cooked fish and meat, the priest wipes out her Vaiṣṇava mark; it remains absent until she retires at night. When the Goddess is ready for bed, the priest and temple attendants close the temple doors, lock up all the other rooms of the temple enclosure, and finally lock the gates.

Not only has the Vaiṣṇavism of the Hāldārs impinged on the Goddess's Tantric tradition—making her, at least in their eyes, a Vaiṣṇavite Kālī—but popular cults have been merged into hers, and special *pūjā*s (*naimittika pūjā* or *utsava*) are performed at the temple for other deities who are somehow related to the ritual program of the main temple, whose shrines are accommodated in the temple complex.

For example, on every new moon day, Kālī is worshipped in the dead of night according to a special Tantric system, and one hundred offerings of clarified butter (*āhūti*) are poured onto the sacred fire that follows the Tantric *pūjā*.[22] Yet it is not clear to me whether any animal is sacrificed from the temple side. Many devotees visit the temple on that day and offer animals to the Goddess, but this always occurs in the morning, and their offerings are treated as something not belonging to the inner Kālī worship. There are other interesting *naimittika pūjā*s performed in the temple. For instance, I am informed that on the annual Kālī Pūjā day, which coincides with the pan-Indian Hindu festival of lamps and fireworks (Dīpāvalī) on the autumnal new moon day, the image at the Kālī Temple receives special worship, but as Lakṣmī, not Kālī. No special Kālī *pūjā* is offered to her that day, although countless pilgrims make it a point to visit her, preferably in the evening, since it is a specially auspicious day for Kālī. In addition, many animals are sacrificed by the pilgrims. It is well known that this Bengali Kālī Pūjā was inaugurated in the eighteenth century by the famous Rāja Kṛṣṇacandra of Navadvipa; thus it is not an ancient tradition.[23] It is also true that in the rest of India, Hindus worship Lakṣmī, not Kālī, on this day. But Bengalis have their own special annual festival for Lakṣmī, on the full moon day preceding Kālī Pūjā. The tradition at Kālīghāṭ of substituting Lakṣmī for Kālī worship on this occasion was probably introduced by Bhavānīdās. Is this evidence for Kālī's Vaiṣṇavī form as she is envisaged by the Hāldārs?[24] Even more strange, the most important festival of the temple community is observed on Rāmanavamī, the birthday of Rāma, when all the employees of the temple serving Mā Kālī get gifts of new clothes and money. The evening before, the swing festival of Kṛṣṇa, Dol-Yātrā or Cāñcar, is held with great pomp and grandeur at the swing pavilion. The next day, the images of Rādhā and Kṛṣṇa are taken out of their temple and are placed on a vehicle, which is conveyed in procession, to the accompaniment of a band, along a special route within the temple complex. The Hāldārs celebrate the festive day by playing the color-throwing game. The very oddity of not performing these rites on the usual vernal full moon day also indicates that this is an old family tradition.[25] The temple also celebrates the birthday of Kṛṣṇa, Janmāṣṭamī, and, on the previous day, the festival of Nanda, Kṛṣṇa's father.

It should be noted, too, that the temple bursary does not pay for any daily sacrifice of goats. These are brought by private devotees and pilgrims to offer, but neither blood nor raw meat enters the temple. After the beheading, the *sevāyet* of the day receives the head, and the body is given back to the donor. There is only one exception: the first goat offered as a sacrifice to Kālī is retained by the *sevāyet* for Kālī's food offering. I have been vaguely told that the *sevāyet* pays the donor money as the price of the goat meat. If no one agrees to give up his or her claim to the carcass, the *sevāyet* of the day has to buy a live goat and offer it himself.

Only twice annually does the temple fund pay for a goat sacrifice: once on the annual festival day for the goddess Manasā, who shares a shrine behind the main temple with the goddess Ṣaṣṭī; and once on the ninth or Navamī day of the annual Durgā Pūjā festival, when three goats are offered to the Goddess. The lineage norm of the Hāldārs allows animal sacrifices only on these two occasions. On Durgā Navamī, three goats are taken into the temple, where the preliminary rites are performed. One is offered in the name of the lineage guru (*kulaguru*) of the Hāldārs, who initiated them into Kālī worship, and the other two are offered in the name of the main Hāldār lineage. After the goats have been ritually beheaded, the heads are carried inside the main sanctum, where they are kept overnight; they are immersed in the Ganga the next day.[26] Another point brought to my attention by Mr. Vidyut Hāldār is that no animal sacrifice is allowed to take place while food is being offered to Kālī. This attitude toward animal sacrifice is very unusual for a Kālī worshipper and shows a certain uneasiness on the part of the Hāldārs about animal sacrifice. Sometimes, this feeling can be very intense. For example, I encountered total hostility to my taking a photograph of the temple precinct, lest I try to capture with my camera the cruel custom of decapitating a poor goat.

PILGRIMS' PERSPECTIVES ON KĀLĪ

The importance accorded to Vāsudeva, the application of a Vaiṣṇava *tilaka* on the Goddess's forehead, and the special observances of the temple ritual calendar all show the influence of the Hāldārs' Vaiṣṇava tradition. In contrast, the general public view of Kālī at Kālīghāṭ is reflected in the legends about the temple and its image. Since the image is the great goddess Kālī, and since the temple encompasses one of her famed seats, Kālīghāṭ is considered a great Tantric power center.[27] The earliest legends about the temple concern two Brahman Tāntrikas named Brahmānanda Svāmī and Ātmārāma Brahmacārī. The former was not a Bengali. Once, while he was deep in meditation, the rock on which he was sitting floated down the river Ganga, eventually arriving at Kālīghāṭ, where it came to rest on the riverbank. Meanwhile, Ātmārāma Brahmacārī—sometimes presented as Brahmānanda's disciple in Tantric practices (*sādhanā*) and sometimes treated independently —learned in a meditative vision that part of Satī's body was lying at the bottom of a nearby pond. When it was brought up, it looked like a piece of black rock. For various complex reasons, the sculptor who was using it to carve Kālī's image could not finish the job. Hence the image consists of the Goddess's face and feet, while other parts remain unfashioned.[28] This incomplete image was then placed on the rock that Brahmānanda had used as his meditation seat.

Ātmārāma is involved in many other legends as well. One of these claims that he was highly honored by Rājā Vasanta Rāy, uncle of Rājā Pratāpāditya Rāy of Jessore and a courtier of the Mughal emperor, in the seventeenth century.[29] Mr. Śānti Bhaṭṭācārya, the chief temple priest and author of a popular article on the history of the Kālīghāṭ Temple, maintains that Brahmānanda came from the Nilagiri mountain range in Tamilnadu and that he and his pupil Ātmārāma established a Tantric pupillary lineage at Kālīghāṭ. The last of this lineage was a certain Bhuvaneśvar Brahmacārī, a Tantric Kaula practitioner.[30] He had one daughter, named Umā, born of his union with his partner in Tantric practice, a woman whom he later married.

The final phase of the history of the Kālī Temple concerns Bhavānīdās Cakravartī, founder of the Hāldār lineage. I mention one version of how he became temple priest and beneficiary. For some reason, young Bhavānīdās, already married and the father of a son, made a pilgrimage to Kālīghāṭ. Bhuvaneśvar liked him and tried to persuade him to marry his daughter Umā as a second wife and to settle down at Kālīghāṭ as the *sevāyet* of the temple. By this time, the temple possessed a sizeable landed property and, being situated on the route to the East India Company's prosperous trading port of Calcutta, was a flourishing pilgrim center. Bhavānīdās found the proposal attractive and agreed. He married Umā and then, having brought his first wife and her son to Kālīghāṭ, took the position of *sevāyet.* This started the last phase of the priestly lineage at the Kālī Temple.

During the early period of the prosperity of Calcutta under the East India Company, the Kālī Temple became famous and flourished so much that the Hāldār family members felt that they could not handle all the affairs of the temple. About two hundred years ago, the Hāldārs employed a certain Śrīpada Bhaṭṭācārya from Somra, a village in the Hoogly District, to perform the actual daily worship of the image in the temple as the temple priest. The present chief priest, Mr. Śānti Bhaṭṭācārya, is the eighth generation descending from this Brahman. He explained that as the duties are very onerous, involving fasting every day until about 4 P.M. and working almost nonstop from 3:30 A.M., none of his children, brothers, cousins, or other male members of his clan want to do the job. He has therefore hired additional priests and is training them to help him execute the many long and complex ritual acts carried out daily in the temple. The day I witnessed the early 6 A.M. ritual worship of the Goddess, the officiating priest was Mr. Kārtik Mukherjee. He had been recruited just a few years ago. It was interesting to notice in this quiet young man (in his mid twenties) a sober and humble kind of devotion for the Goddess and to his duties.

For years, the Hāldārs enjoyed full authority over the temple management and evolved a self-regulating, kin-based association to run the temple affairs and to make an equal distribution of its assets and income. Recently, however, they came into legal conflict with the Sābarṇa Caudhurīs, who suddenly claimed ownership of the temple lands.[31] This led to government interference and to the establishment of a legal executive committee, formed democratically from members of the Hāldār lineage but also including nominees from Calcutta University and Calcutta Corporation, with the supreme authority held by a high government administrator. Yet the Hāldārs still retain their full authority over the day-to-day running of the temple's businesses and its considerable daily income, so they face no problem in introducing subtle changes and innovations into the temple's ritual services.

The aforementioned peculiar ritual practices at the Kālī Temple complex, as introduced by the Hāldārs, derive from Bhavānīdās's Vaiṣṇava background. There is nothing to suggest that he had any Tantric leanings (he was certainly neither a Kāpālika[32] nor a Kaula), or even that he showed any propensity to ecstatic adoration of Kālī. He was a traditional orthodox Brahman householder with strong Vaiṣṇava inclinations, and it is evident that his and his descendants' loyalty to Vāsudeva as their lineage deity has remained unchanged. It is even conceivable that the Vāsudeva icon in the niche of the inner sanctum is the very image that once belonged to Bhavānīdās. Although he applied himself to his duties as the caretaker, manager, and priest of the temple, in all probability being initiated into the Kālī mantra by his father-in-law when the latter handed over the proprietorship of the temple to him, he took measures to play down the Tantric aspects of the Goddess's worship, notably the blood sacrifice. The same is true for the rest of the Hāldār family, even though they acquired a hereditary Śākta lineage guru not long after Bhavānīdās's time.[33]

Mr. Vidyut Hāldār and other informants told me that they worship the Goddess in her Vaiṣṇavī form. One can see this both in the six ritual innovations described above and in the lack of attention paid to the obvious Śākta monuments associated with the main temple. The Hāldārs appear to have very little to do with the day-to-day functions at the shrine of Nakuleśvara Śiva, the main Bhairava of Kālīghāṭ, and the Kālī-kuṇḍa, or temple pond sacred to Kālī, has only recently been renovated after a long period of neglect. The obvious lack of interest on the part of earlier generations of Hāldārs in these older goddess-centered parts of the Kālī Temple complex is thus noteworthy.

What emerges from these small but very specific traditional variations in the ritual patterns of this Kālī Temple is that the Vaiṣṇava leanings of Bhavānīdās and his descendants have influenced their method of Kālī worship. Although the thousands of pilgrims daily visiting the temple definitely do not think her so, to the Hāldārs she is one and the same as Lakṣmī or Śrī or Ambikā—or indeed Kālī as recorded in the *Devībhāgavata Purāṇa.*

The ancient, strict, Tantric Kāpālika associations of the temple, revealed in the legends concerning Brahmānanda Svāmī, Ātmārāma Brahmacārī, and Bhuvaneśvara Brahmacārī, and in other legends about highway robbers performing human sacrifice at the temple, appear to have been completely wiped out both from the present-day temple rituals and from the arrangements of the various shrines within the Kālīghāṭ complex. However, for pilgrims visiting the temple, Mother Kālī is both compassionate and fierce. Contradiction is inherent in her, and she is easily prone to take offense. Declaring their total dependence on her mercy, pilgrims entering the temple loudly call on her, "Mother! O Mother!" The majority of these devotees believe that she is satisfied by receiving blood sacrifice, and a great number of goats are sacrificed every day by devotees seeking her favor. Some devotees even offer their own blood to show their loyalty and devotion. To them, she is neither vegetarian nor connected with Viṣṇu, but is the great Goddess extolled in the Tantric and Purāṇic tradition.

NOTES

For providing me with much of the information on the Kālī Temple at Kālīghāṭ to follow, I am indebted to several members of the Hāldār family, the hereditary owner-managers (*sevāyets*) of the temple. *Sevāyet* literally means "servicing man," but technically it refers to a temple priest who has the right to enjoy the temple's income. Such a person therefore has the responsibility for the management of the temple property, as well as its day-to-day running, including all associated rituals. The title *hāldār* or *hāolādār* (land custodian) was awarded to a descendant of the first *sevāyet* at the temple by Nawāb 'Alīvardī Khān of Murshidabad (1740–56). At present the Hāldārs are divided into five lines according to the ages of the five grandsons of Bhavānīdās Cakravartī (Hāldār), the first of the family to become associated with the temple. I am especially grateful to Mr. Vidyut Hāldār, who hails from the primary line, is the most important *sevāyet* of the Goddess at Kālīghāṭ, and is one of the few *sevāyet*s to work full-time, and to his uncle Mr. Aruṇkumār Mukherjee, now the secretary of the Kālī Temple Trust Committee. In addition, I thank Mr. Śānti Bhaṭṭācārya and Mr. Kārtik Mukherjee, the chief priest and his assistant at the temple, who gave me a lot of their time and allowed me to sit inside the temple during the main morning ritual worship of the Goddess.

EPIGRAPH: For the Sanskrit original, see *Devī-Māhātmyam: The Glorification of the Great Goddess,* ed. and trans. Vasudeva S. Agrawala (Ramnagar: All India Kashiraj Trust, 1963), p. 96. The more familiar form of Kālī is described in a late hymn called the Karpūrādistava, attributed to Mahākāla, or Lord Śiva. In this text, Dakṣiṇākālī, which is also the name of the Goddess in the temple at Kālīghāṭ, is naked and wears a girdle of severed arms; babies' corpses serve as her two earrings; and blood flows from the corners of her mouth. She resides in a terrible cremation ground and is seated on a corpse (Śiva). See *Karpurādistava,* as translated in Sir John Woodroffe's *Hymns to the Goddess and Hymn to Kali* (1913; Wilmot, Wis.: Lotus Light Publications, 1981), pp. 288–335.

1. See Indrani Basu Roy, *Kālighāt: Its Impact on Socio-Cultural Life of Hindus* (New

Delhi: Gyan Publishing House, 1993); and Surajit Sinha, "Kali Temple at Kalighat and the City of Calcutta," in *Cultural Profile of Calcutta,* ed. id. (Calcutta: Indian Anthropological Society, 1972), pp. 61–72.

2. This is another ancient Kālī-*pīṭha.* See *Paścimbaṅger Pūjā-pārvan o Melā,* ed. Aśok Mitra (Indian Census, 1961), vol. 16, pt. 7-B, no. 5, pp. 258–67.

3. See E. Alan Morinis, *Pilgrimage in the Hindu Tradition: A Case Study of West Bengal* (Delhi: Oxford University Press, 1984), pp. 174–75. It is said that the secret image of Tārā inside the outer wooden image at the Tārāpīṭh Temple shows the Goddess suckling Śiva her husband to restore his life and to annul the effect of the cosmic poison he drank to save creation.

4. Sanjukta Gupta, "Tantric Śākta Literature in Modern Indian Languages," in Teun Goudriaan and Sanjukta Gupta, *Hindu Tantric and Śākta Literature,* vol. 2, fasc. 2 of *A History of Indian Literature,* ed. Jan Gonda (Wiesbaden: Otto Harrassowitz, 1981), pp. 178–80.

5. *Lakṣmī Tantra: A Pāñcrātra Text,* trans. with notes by Sanjukta Gupta (Leiden: E. J. Brill, 1972), Introduction, p. xxvi.

6. Kālī is said to exercise the fivefold cosmic functions of creating (*sṛṣṭi*), sustaining (*sthiti*), and destroying (*laya*) the world, deluding or punishing (*tirodhāna* or *nigraha*), and granting the reward of her grace (*anugraha*). See ibid., pp. 69–72.

7. For example, the Lalitā cult of Kanci and the Śāradā cult of Sringeri in Tamilnadu.

8. See Sinha, "Kali Temple at Kalighat," and D. C. Sirkar, *The Śākta Pīṭhas,* 2d ed. (Delhi: Motilal Banarsidass, 1973), pp. 24 and 87, for the development of Kālīghāṭ's reputation as a great seat of the Goddess.

9. For further discussion of the parallel treatment of the Goddess in medieval Śākta texts and of Kṛṣṇa in the *Bhāgavata Purāṇa,* see studies by Cheever Mackenzie Brown: *God as Mother: A Feminine Theology in India* (Hartford, Vt.: Claude Stark, 1974); and *The Triumph of the Goddess: The Canonical Models and Theological Visions of the Devībhāgavata Purāṇa* (Albany: State University of New York Press, 1990).

10. "In the marketplace of this world, the dark mother sits flying her kites. One or two in a hundred thousand snap the string and fly away bondless, and how she laughs, clapping her hands!" Rāmprasād Sen, in Śivaprasād Bhaṭṭācārya, *Bhāratcandra o Rāmprasād,* 2d ed. (Calcutta: Modern Book Agency, 1967), p. 297. See also C. Mackenzie Brown, "Kālī, the Mad Mother," in *The Book of the Goddess Past and Present: An Introduction to Her Religion,* ed. Carl Olson (New York: Crossroad, 1987), pp. 110–23.

11. See the *Manasāmaṅgala* by Bipradās (1495), the *Caṇḍīmaṅgala* by Mukundarām Cakravartī (1590), and the *Pīṭhanirṇaya/Mahāpīṭhanirūpaṇa* and *Gaṅgābhaktitaraṅginī* (both eighteenth century). These are discussed by Sinha, "Kali Temple at Kalighat," p. 62, and Sirkar, *Śākta Pīṭhas,* pp. 4, 32–41.

12. See Sirkar, *Śākta Pīṭhas,* pp. 5–7. In earlier texts like the *Tantrasāra* of Kṛṣṇānanda Āgamavāgīśa, the number of *pīṭha*s is said to be fifty. Ibid., pp. 17–24.

13. There are different views on this point. According to some informants, these limbs are still kept in a silver box hidden in the body of the image in the inner sanctum. Once a year, on Kālī's sacred bathing day, known as her *snāna-yātrā,* a direct descendant of Bhavānīdās's eldest family line changes the dress and decoration of

this body part, the nature of which is a family secret. See Apūrba Caṭṭopādhyāy, "Kālīghāṭer Kālīpūjo," *Sāptāhik Bartamān,* November 9, 1996, pp. 8–11.

14. Every goddess-*pīṭha* has a special Bhairava as a guardian (*kṣetrapāla*) of the sacred area. See Sirkar, *Śākta Pīṭhas,* pp. 39–41.

15. Morinis's description of goat sacrifice as performed at the Tārāpīṭh Temple is interesting. The priests wave the animal toward the temple of Tārā to emphasize that it is being sacrificed to the Goddess. See *Pilgrimage in the Hindu Tradition,* pp. 184–85.

16. I mainly obtained this information from Mr. Vidyut Hāldār and Mr. Śānti Bhaṭṭācārya.

17. This gentleman, known as Kānāi Hāldār, is not compelled to perform the *ārati,* but does so willingly and meticulously. Probably, Kālī is his chosen personal deity (*iṣṭadevatā*). In "Kālīghāṭer Kālīpūjo," p. 9, Apūrba Caṭṭopādhyāy states that this *ārati* practice had been introduced only about twenty-five years earlier.

18. The first edition appeared in parts; it took eleven years, until 1311 [1904], before the manual was completed. A good edition, which, however, includes only a portion of the *Purohit-Darpaṇ,* is the *Sarva-deva-devī-pūjā-paddhati* (*Method of Worshipping All Gods and Goddesses*), ed. Vāmadeva Bhaṭṭācārya and corrected by Prabhākar Kāvyasmṛtimīmāṃsatīrtha, 4th ed. (Calcutta: Calcutta Town Library, 1355 [1948]). Bengali Era publication dates, which are 593 years fewer than those of the Gregorian calendar, are used in most Bengali books, and the Gregorian year is given in square brackets following the Bengali date in the notes that follow.

19. See the 38th edition of the *Purohit-Darpaṇ* (Calcutta: Satyanārāyaṇ Library, 1393 [1986]), p. 384.

20. For a detailed discussion of Tantras from eastern and northeastern India that contain Vaiṣṇava themes, see Teun Goudriaan, "Hindu Tantric Literature in Sanskrit," in Goudriaan and Gupta, *Hindu Tantric and Śākta Literature,* pp. 82–84.

21. See Sanjukta Gupta, Dirk Jan Hoens, and Teun Goudriaan, *Hindu Tantrism* (Leiden: E. J. Brill, 1979), p. 156. Mr. Kārtik Mukherjee told me that Ucchiṣṭacaṇḍālī, the goddess who is always invoked at the end of a Tantric Kālī *pūjā* as the first to accept the offered food (*prasāda*), so as to safeguard it from harmful spirits, is never called upon in the daily *pūjā* of Kālī.

22. See ibid., pp. 152–53.

23. Chintaharan Chakravarti, *Tantras: Studies on their Religion and Literature* (Calcutta: Punthi Pustak, 1963), pp. 89–93.

24. See Caṭṭopādhyāy, "Kālīghāṭer Kālīpūjo," p. 10.

25. Ibid., pp. 8–11. In addition to their devotion to Vāsudeva, the Hāldārs have probably long been worshippers of Rāma. Holi, or the festival of colors that accompanies Rādhā and Kṛṣṇa's swing festival, is normally held on the full moon day previous to the ninth day of the bright fortnight in Caitra (March–April), when Rāma was born.

26. Goat sacrifice on the occasion of Durgā Pūjā is a very common custom among Bengali upper-caste landowners, and the Hāldārs as the *sevāyets* of Kālī did at one time own much land. This holding has somehow dwindled to just the land on which the temple complex stands, plus a few hundred square meters outside it.

27. See Dīptimay Rāy, *Paścimbaṅger Kālī o Kālīkṣetra* (Calcutta: Maṇḍal Book House, 1391 [1984]), pp. 38–54.

28. I must quote a popular local Bengali verse reporting the unusualness of the image: "Kālīghāṭer kathā; āge beḍoy hāt pā, pare beḍoy māthā" ("The strange thing about Kālīghāṭ is that first emerge her hands and feet, and then emerges her head").

29. In some legends, Vasanta Rāy is replaced by Mansingh, the great general of the Mughals.

30. Kaula refers to a particular mode of esoteric Tantric ritual practices wherein certain objects held to be impure by orthodox Hindus are offered to the deity. These include impure foods like meat and alcohol. In addition, ritual sexual intercourse with a woman outside one's own caste is practiced in order to collect and offer to the deity the resulting sexual fluids. Such Kaula practitioners are mainly worshippers of the Goddess as the supreme divine Power, Śakti.

31. Job Charnock of the East India Company bought three villages from the Sābarṇa Caudhurīs that together formed the nucleus of modern Calcutta.

32. Kāpālikas belong to an ancient Śaiva ascetic sect. A Kāpālika must always carry his begging bowl made of human skulls, or *kapāla*s; hence the name. From the inception of this sect, its followers have practiced antinomian religious rites.

33. It is said that Bhavānīdās's grandsons appointed three hereditary types of Brahman ritualist: a *kulaguru* (lineage preceptor), a *bhaṭṭācārya ṭhākur* (temple priest), and two *miśra* assistants (Brahmans acting as aides to the temple priests). See Basu Roy, *Kālighāt,* p. 21.

CHAPTER 4

Dominating Kālī

Hindu Family Values and Tantric Power

Usha Menon and Richard A. Shweder

A few years ago, in 1991, we investigated the meanings that Oriya Hindus living in the temple town of Bhubaneswar attach to a particular Tantric icon of the goddess Kālī—the one in which the Goddess is depicted with her eyes bulging and tongue out, equipped with the weapons and emblems of all the male gods, grasping a bloody decapitated head, and with her foot placed squarely on the chest of a supine Śiva (fig. 4.1). In this earlier study, we were able to describe the systematic character of storytelling norms about the icon. Across storytellers, the elements of meaning form a "Guttman scale," in which one can predict which meanings are narrated. Expert storytellers differ from novice storytellers in an orderly way; they elaborate on the significance of the scene depicted in the icon by adding particular modules of meanings, which we recorded and analyzed. We also discovered that the particular constellation of elements that forms the contemporary Oriya story is not found in its entirety in any Sanskrit or Oriya text.

In this chapter, we suggest that this unmistakably Tantric icon with its emphatic, extreme representation of female power has been almost completely assimilated into mainstream Hinduism as it is practiced today in the temple town of Bhubaneswar. More important, the meanings of the icon appear to have undergone radical reconstruction. Far from highlighting the potency of the female and her power to create and destroy with impunity,

Figure 4.1 Calendar art depiction of Kālī as worshipped in Orissa, purchased in Bhubaneswar by Usha Menon.

the icon is used to uphold Hindu family values, especially those encouraging female self-control and self-restraint.

We further suggest that a particular Oriya text, dating back to the fifteenth century—the *Caṇḍī Purāṇa*—provided the conceptual framework for a creative interpretation of this Tantric icon, an interpretation that has today become a powerful way of persuading listeners of the importance of respectful self-restraint in maintaining social relations and preserving harmony within the family.

In asserting that this is the predominant way of interpreting the icon today, it needs to be emphasized that a more "authentic" Tantric understanding of the icon continues to have its adherents, few though they may admittedly be. And to demonstrate the creative distance that lies between these two interpretations, both will be presented: the one normative in the temple town; and the other a rather esoteric version propounded by only a couple of knowledgeable specialists.

Research for this study was done in the neighborhood around the Liṅgarāj temple in Bhubaneswar.[1] This medieval temple, dedicated to the god Śiva and dating back to the eleventh to twelfth centuries, is a fairly important pilgrimage site. Hindu pilgrims making their way to Jagannātha at Puri invariably stop and worship here before proceeding south.

For the Oriya Hindus who live here, this particular iconic representation of the Goddess has become a core cultural symbol—practically everyone recognizes this icon and identifies the Goddess correctly. Perhaps this is hardly surprising when one considers that on the main road leading to the Liṅgarāj temple, there is a small temple, the Kāpālī Mandir, dedicated to the Goddess, in which the object of worship is a granite representation of Kālī in precisely this divine posture.

However, only two men out of the ninety-two men and women who participated in the earlier study were able to identify the origin of the icon as Tantric; the rest simply said that this is the typical way Kālī is portrayed, her distinguishing mark (*lakṣaṇa*) being the protruding tongue displaying the emotion *lajjā* (shame) at having stepped on her husband, Śiva.

THE ESOTERIC VERSUS THE NORMATIVE

Not surprisingly, the two men who were aware of the Tantric meanings of the icon produced stories that diverged sharply from those narrated by the others. Both men were close to seventy years of age, both were married, both were the heads of large extended families, and both had been priests at Liṅgarāj for most of their adult lives. Both admitted to having attended some Tantric ceremonies, although neither claimed to be a true worshipper of the Goddess. One of their accounts, which broadly resembles the description of the Goddess in the *Mahānirvāṇa Tantra* (4.34),[2] is given below:

Q. *Do you recognize this picture?*

A. This is the Tantric depiction of Kālī. Kālī here is naked, she has thrown Śiva to the ground and is standing on him. She displays here absolute, overwhelming power. She is in a terrible rage—wearing her garland of skulls and in each arm a weapon of destruction: look, in this hand, the *triśūla* [trident], in this the *cakra* [disc], in this the sword, in this the sickle, in this the bow and arrow—this is how Kālī is shown in Tantric *pūjās* where the devotee is praying to the Goddess for perfect knowledge and awareness. All this kind of worship goes on in the Ramakrishna Mission—the monks there are all Tāntrikas and they know all about it. Sri Ramakrishna and Swami Vivekananda, both great sages, knew about such *śakti pūjās* and Tantric rites.

Q. *Can you tell me the story that is associated with this picture?*

A. In all these Tantric *pūjās*, the goal is to acquire perfect knowledge and ultimate power. The naked devotee worships Mother on a dark, moonless night in a cremation ground. The offerings are meat and alcohol. Ordinary people cannot participate in such worship—if they were even to witness it, they would go mad. I attended such worship once, but I am not a true worshipper, and I have no special knowledge of Tantric worship.

Q. *How would you describe Kālī's expression here?*

A. She is the image of fury.

Q. *You mean she is angry? She is in a rage?*

A. Yes . . . yes. You must understand that this is how she appears to her devotee—he has to have the strength of mind to withstand her fierceness—she is not mild or tender but cruel and demanding and frightening.

Q. *Do you think that she has put out her tongue in anger?*

A. Yes, she has put out her tongue in anger. Kālī is always angry, she is always creating and at the same time destroying life. Here you see her standing with her foot placed squarely on Śiva's chest—when the time comes for the universe to be destroyed entirely, no one will be spared, not even the gods; whether Viṣṇu or Śiva, everyone will be destroyed.

Q. *Some people say that she is feeling deeply ashamed at having stepped on her husband and that is why she has bitten her tongue. You don't agree?*

A. People have different views—people believe whatever makes them feel comfortable, and if they like to think that Kālī is ashamed, then let them. What I have told you is what the special devotees of Kālī believe. They believe that Mother is supreme; even Brahmā, Viṣṇu, and Śiva are her servants.

Q. *Have you seen this expression—that is, Kālī's here—in daily life?*

A. No, if one were to see this expression on an ordinary human being's face, he would have to be mad—to have lost all his senses. Kālī, in fact, is mad with rage but her rage has nothing that is remotely human about it; it is a divine rage, which only a human being who has completely lost his mind can duplicate.

Q. *Can you tell me why Śiva is lying on the ground?*

A. Kālī has thrown him to the ground, and she puts her foot on him to make clear that she is supreme.

Q. So you don't think that he is lying on the ground to subdue Kālī?
A. No, that is beyond Śiva's capacity. If Kālī becomes calm, it is because she wishes to, not because she is persuaded to be so. Even to her most faithful devotee, Kālī's actions sometimes don't make sense, but life itself often doesn't make sense, so what can one say?

Q. Who would you say is dominant in this picture—is it Kālī or Śiva?
A. Obviously, Kālī. But it is also important to realize that while Śakti is absolutely necessary for the creation and evolution of the universe, by itself even Śakti cannot achieve anything—Śakti has to combine with consciousness for the process of creation to take place, and so consciousness as symbolized by Śiva has a unique position. Just as it is only through the union of a man and a woman that a child can be conceived, so too, only when Śakti and Cit (consciousness) come together does creation occur.

For this narrator, the meaning of the icon centers unequivocally on the supreme and awesome power of the Goddess. His interpretation makes no concessions to commonly held notions about traditional hierarchy and social relations, and he explicitly denies the notion that Kālī bites her tongue to express the *lajjā* she feels when she realizes the degree to which she has forgotten herself and her duty toward her husband, Śiva.

A comparison between this understanding of the icon, known and shared by only two of our narrators, with the story that is far more commonly shared in this neighborhood enables one to appreciate the many divergences that separate these two interpretations. In sharp contrast to the Tantric narration, consider the most elaborate version of the story as it is typically told.

This particular narrator was a 74-year-old Brahman man, the father of three sons and two daughters. He used to run a small hotel near Bhubaneswar railway station, but he retired a few years ago, handing over his business to his second son. At the time of the interview, he lived with his wife, his son, and his son's family, spending his days keeping an eye on his grandchildren and going regularly to the Liṅgarāj Temple.

Q. Do you recognize this picture?
A. Kālī.

Q. Can you describe the incident that is portrayed in this picture?
A. This is about the time when Mahiṣāsura became so powerful that he tortured everyone on earth and heaven. He had obtained a boon from the gods according to which no male could kill him. All the gods then went to Nārāyaṇa and they pondered on ways to destroy Mahiṣāsura. Each contributed the strength and energy of his consciousness—his *bindu*—and from that Durgā was created. But when Durgā was told that she had to kill Mahiṣāsura, she said that she needed weapons to

do so, and so all the gods gave her their weapons. Armed thus, Durgā went into battle. She fought bravely, but she found it impossible to kill the demon—he was too strong and clever. You see, the gods had forgotten to tell her that the boon Mahiṣāsura had obtained from Brahmā was that he would only die at the hands of a naked female. Durgā finally became desperate, and she appealed to Maṅgalā to suggest some way to kill Mahiṣāsura. Maṅgalā then told her that the only way was to take off her clothes, that the demon would only lose strength when confronted by a naked woman. So Durgā did as she was advised to. She stripped, and within seconds of seeing her, Mahiṣāsura's strength waned, and he died under her sword. After killing him, a terrible rage entered Durgā's mind, and she asked herself, "What kind of gods are these that give to demons such boons, and apart from that, what kind of gods are these that they do not have the honesty to tell me the truth before sending me into battle?" She decided that such a world with such gods did not deserve to survive and she took on the form of Kālī and went on a mad rampage, devouring every living creature that came in her way. Now, the gods were in a terrible quandary—they had all given her their weapons—they were helpless, without any weapons, while she had a weapon in each one of her ten arms: how could Kālī be checked and who would check her in her mad dance of destruction? Again, the gods all gathered and Nārāyaṇa decided that only Mahādeva (Śiva) could check Kālī, and so he advised the gods to appeal to him. Now, Śiva is an ascetic, a yogi who has no interest in what happens in the world. But when all the gods begged him to intervene, he agreed to do his best—he went and lay in her path. Kālī, absorbed in her dance of destruction, was unaware that Śiva lay in her path, and so she stepped on him all unknowing. When she put her foot on Śiva's chest, she bit her tongue, saying, "Oh! my husband!" There is in Mahādeva a *tejas,* a special quality of his body that penetrated hers, that made her look down, that made her see reason. She had been so angry that she had gone beyond reason, but once she recognized him, she became still and calm. This is the story about that time.

Q. How would you describe the expression on her face?

A. She had been extremely angry but when her foot fell on Mahādeva's chest—after all, he is her own husband—she bit her tongue and became still; gradually her anger went down.

Q. So is there still any anger in her expression?

A. Oh yes, in her eyes you can still see the light of anger shining.

Q. And her tongue? What is she feeling when she bites it?

A. What else but *lajjā? Lajjā* . . . because she did something unforgivable, she is feeling *lajjā.*

Q. So would you say that her expression is a blend of both anger and shame?
A. Yes, that is right.

Q. Have you ever seen this expression in daily life?
A. Is that possible? Can humans mimic gods? I don't think so.

Q. Is Kālī merely stepping on Śiva or is she actually dancing on him?
A. As I told you earlier on, Kālī was dancing when her foot fell on Śiva, but just a touch was enough for her to recognize that this was not just anyone lying under her foot, which is why she looked down and to her deep *lajjā* saw that she had stamped on her own husband's chest.

Q. So you were saying that Śiva was lying on the ground because . . . ?
A. He had been asked by all the gods to do something to cool Kālī down.

Q. He was, in a sense, trying to subdue her?
A. No, no, help her check herself, help her understand that what she was doing was wrong and harmful, even disgraceful.

Q. Who do you see as dominant in this picture—Kālī or Śiva?
A. Let me talk about this in terms of Śakti—Śakti is indivisible, Śiva has no *śakti* of his own, it is all Devī's, and who is Devī? She is Kālī, she is Durgā, she is Pārvatī. She is self-creating, self-generating; while he is born of her, he takes his strength from her. And yet, he does have something that is uniquely his—he is pure consciousness—if he is the fire, then she is the energy with which the fire burns, and so it is foolish to talk of him being stronger or her being stronger; they need each other, and we can't talk of one without talking of the other.

This more popular interpretation of Kālī's icon appears to elaborate somewhat ambivalent views regarding female power. At one level, the prevailing notion seems to be that female power is, in and of itself, essentially dangerous, since it is always in imminent danger of slipping out of control. At another level, there is the sense that men are often so treacherous and exploitative that women would be justified in destroying the world. But the main message appears to be that the world survives and the flow of life proceeds as it ought to when women regulate, control, and hold *lajjā* in their power, when they cultivate their capacity to experience *lajjā,* and when they display that emotion appropriately.

COMMON UNDERSTANDINGS OF THE KĀLĪ ICON

The story given above was the kind produced by our more competent informants. In all, we collected ninety-two stories told us by twenty-six men and sixty-six women. Obviously, not all of our informants were equally expert or equally familiar with the cultural norms necessary for interpreting the icon. However, for the majority of them (seventy-one out of ninety), it symbolized the following: it is female power that energizes the world, but such power when unchecked has disastrous consequences; furthermore, such power can only be effectively checked and regulated from within oneself, through developing a sensitivity to the emotion of *lajjā*. According to these Oriya Hindus, to be full of *lajjā* is to be refined, to be civilized, to be a moral being. Clearly, the narrator of the first "Tantric" story, by explicitly rejecting these local values in his narration, was operating under the influence of a very different canon of storytelling, one that is not normative in the temple town of Bhubaneswar.

Before attempting to suggest how it is that an icon that invokes images of supreme female power is used today to exemplify the idea that respectful self-restraint and a heightened consciousness of one's social and domestic obligations are essential attributes of female virtue, we need to recapitulate some of the findings that emerged from our earlier study.

An analysis and Guttman scaling of the narrations suggested that the stories produced by our ninety-two informants could be decomposed into twenty-five elements of meaning, which could be grouped into three modules, each telling an internally consistent, self-sufficient mini-story (table 4.1).[3] Interestingly enough, the simplest story provided the background for a more detailed version at a higher level of complexity, and this version in turn set the stage for the most detailed interpretation of the icon, at the highest level of complexity.

The first module, "Kālī's *Lajjā* as the Antidote to Her Anger," involves eleven elements of meaning, in which narrators talk about Kālī and Śiva, their marital relationship, and the received hierarchy of domestic relationships in which the husband is superior to his wife. They mentioned that Kālī experienced acute *lajjā* at having been so outrageous and disrespectful as to step on her husband (displayed by her biting of the tongue), thereby restraining herself and cooling her anger by holding it in. The dominant theme of this first module of eleven meanings is therefore Kālī's *lajjā* as an antidote to her anger.

The second module, "The Destructive Nature of Female Anger," involves nine elements of meaning, in which narrators elaborate on the magnitude and destructive nature of the Goddess's anger. They describe the Goddess as a tremendously powerful force, created by the male gods to kill demons, in particular, a demon named Mahiṣāsura, and recount that after destroying Mahiṣāsura, she went on a murderous rampage, indiscriminately destroying everything that came in her way, threatening the very survival of the world. In order to bring her back to her nurturing sensibilities, the gods enlisted Śiva to lie in her path deliberately so that she would step on him and experience *lajjā*. The dominant theme of this second module of nine meanings is therefore the destructive nature of female anger.

The third module, "Men Humiliate Women and So Cause Their Anger,"

TABLE 4.1 The Twenty-Five Elements of Meaning and Their Origin

Elements of Meaning	*Is This an Element Found in the* Sanskrit Purāṇas?	*Is This Element Found in the Oriya* Caṇḍī Purāṇa?
Module 1. Kālī's *Lajjā* as the Antidote to Her Anger		
1. That is the goddess Kālī.	Yes	Yes
2. All goddesses are one, incarnations of the Great Goddess.	Yes	Yes
3. That is the god Śiva.	Yes	Yes
4. Śiva is Kālī's husband.	?	Yes
5. Kālī stepped on Śiva accidentally.	No	No
6. Males are superior to women in social status.	Yes	Yes
7. Kālī is more dominant and powerful than Śiva.	No	Yes
8. Kālī's expression is one of anger.	No	Yes
9. Kālī's expression is one of shame.	No	No
10. Kālī exercises self-control/self-restraint.	No	Yes
11. To "bite the tongue" is an expression of Kālī's shame.	No	No
Module 2. The Destructive Nature of Female Anger		
12. There once was a demon called Mahiṣāsura.	Yes	Yes
13. Durgā was created by the male gods to help them fight the demon.	Yes	Yes
14. In her rage the Great Goddess transformed herself into Kālī.	No	Yes
15. Rage is a loss in the capacity to discriminate/a loss of awareness of one's surroundings.	?	?
16. As Kālī, the Great Goddess threatened the survival of the world.	Yes	Yes
17. Kālī destroys the world with her dance.	No	Yes
18. Śiva lay in Kālī's path at the request of the male gods and/or mortal men.	No	No
19. Śiva lay in Kālī's path deliberately.	No	No
20. When she stepped on Śiva, Kālī became calm/still/statuesque.	No	No

TABLE 4.1 (*continued*)

Elements of Meaning	*Is This an Element Found in the* Sanskrit Purāṇas?	*Is This Element Found in the Oriya* Caṇḍī Purāṇa?
Module 3. Men Humiliate Women and So Cause Their Anger		
21. A boon was given by the male gods to the demon that he could never be killed except by a naked woman.	No	Yes
22. When the male gods were challenged by the demon, they were helpless and could not defend themselves.	Yes	Yes
23. Durgā was helpless against the demon until she stripped naked.	No	Yes
24. Durgā felt humiliated at having to strip.	No	Yes
25. Durgā's humiliation was followed by uncontrollable rage.	No	Yes

involves five elements of meaning in which the narrator explains the source of Kālī's anger. These elements of meaning link Kālī's rage to a boon given by the gods to Mahiṣāsura and to the ultimate humiliation experienced by the Goddess when she had to take off her clothes and stand naked before the demon in order to rescue the male gods from the powers they themselves had bestowed on him. The dominant theme of this third module of five meanings is therefore that men humiliate women, and that this humiliation is the cause of their anger.

Three levels of cultural knowledge can thus be discerned. The result is a nested hierarchy in which a small group of cultural experts tell the most complex story, drawing upon meanings from all three modules, while a somewhat larger group tell a less elaborate version, often using only meanings from modules 1 and 2, and the majority tell the simplest tale, involving meanings from module 1 alone.[4]

While the most detailed story that is told in the temple town about the Goddess and the buffalo demon fascinates listeners because of its vivid detail and provocative imagery, the less suggestive, less detailed story contained in the eleven meanings of module 1 has equal, if not greater, significance—at least from the perspective of this chapter. Its significance lies in the fact that this set of meanings is the one that is known and recognized by most people. The most common meaning of the icon, the one that has the widest currency, elaborates the view that Kālī's ability to experience *lajjā* is the most effective antidote to her destructive anger. For more than three-quarters of the narrators (and this includes the expert, the less expert, and the least expert), this icon of Kālī exemplifies the need to cultivate and experience *lajjā*. They describe *lajjā* as a highly refining emotion characterized by respectful self-restraint and deference, essential for the maintenance of social order. Furthermore, local understanding has it that women more than men need to develop their capacity to experience *lajjā* because they rather than men embody natural power, power that if not contained and if not controlled from within could spill into socially destructive emotions. And it is in this, the most common meaning, that we find the interpretation appears to have traveled the furthest from its beginnings. This creative distance exists whether the icon is seen as a Tantric symbol that elaborates meanings about uncontrolled female power or as an illustration of a contemporary local story with Purāṇic roots that tells about the buffalo demon's death at the hands of the Goddess, the dharmic consequence of overweening arrogance.

THE *CAṆḌĪ PURĀṆA*: GIVING NEW MEANING TO A TANTRIC ICON

The question then arises, how did this quite unmistakably Tantric icon of the Goddess get to be used in contemporary Oriya Hindu discourse to uphold family values, especially those encouraging and advocating female self-control and restraint? We suggest that the *Caṇḍī Purāṇa*,[5] a popular Oriya text on the Goddess and her various salvific activities, made possible this creative leap. This religious work is attributed to Sāralā Dāsa,[6] a devotee of the Goddess who is thought to have lived around the fifteenth century. We believe that by examining the various versions of the story of Mahiṣāsura's death as they occur in the "Devī-Māhātmya" section of the *Mārkaṇḍeya Purāṇa*,[7] the *Devībhāgavata Purāṇa*,[8] and the *Caṇḍī Purāṇa*, it is possible to trace its contours as they shifted over time till the story achieved its present form.

That the Oriya Hindus of the temple town have assimilated and integrated the icon almost completely into their everyday practice of Hinduism can be deduced from the ready confidence with which twenty-six of our informants, spread evenly across the various levels of cultural competence, claimed authority for their stories by citing the Purāṇas as the source of their knowledge, especially the two Sanskritic Purāṇas—the *Mārkaṇḍeya* and *Devībhāgavata Purāṇas*—and the Oriya *Caṇḍī Purāṇa*.

In tracing the transformations and elaborations that have occurred in the story about the encounter between the Goddess and the buffalo demon, we begin with the account in the "Devī-Māhātmya." Here, the battle between the Goddess and the demon is dealt with fairly straightforwardly—the gods led by Indra are put to flight by the demon, and they seek refuge with Brahmā, Viṣṇu, and Śiva. Anger at this defeat at the hands of a demon, however powerful, causes energy to emerge from all the assembled gods, energy that coalesces to form the Goddess, who then rides off to do battle armed with their weapons and emblems. The demon, although a brave warrior, is no match for the Goddess and is soon decapitated by her. Mahiṣāsura appears in this story, but there is no boon, no humiliation of the Goddess, and her energy is not transformed into destructive rage.

The retelling of this story in the *Devībhāgavata Purāṇa* has several new themes. The most relevant to our study are the following. Mahiṣāsura obtains a boon from Brahmā that makes him invulnerable to death, except at the hands of a female. He then becomes completely enamored of the Goddess, and when she rebuffs him unequivocally, he grows angry and attacks her. However, she never strips naked, there is no indiscriminate destructive rage, Śiva does not appear, and he is not needed to rescue the world.

Some of the most salient elements of the story—the idea that Durgā was helpless against the demon until she stripped naked, or that Kālī stepped on Śiva accidentally, or that Kālī's expression is one of *lajjā*—do not appear in either the "Devī-Māhātmya" or the *Devībhāgavata Purāṇa.* However, several key elements of the contemporary Oriya story seem to have been extant in the *Caṇḍī Purāṇa,*[9] although no text includes them all. In this Oriya text, the demon receives a boon that he can only be killed by a naked female, the Goddess strips naked, she becomes enraged at this humiliation, and she goes on a rampage, indiscriminately destroying everything in her path.

For instance, in chapter 4 of the *Caṇḍī Purāṇa,* entitled "Mahiṣāsura's Penance and Boon," the demon receives the boon that he can only be killed by a naked female:

Mahiṣāsura to Brahmā:

> "This boon that I crave from thee
> That I shall be slain neither by Nārāyaṇa,
> Nor killed by Viṣṇu's *sudarśan cakra,*
> And by vanquishing Śiva, let me attain my soul's desire
> And let me also not die at the hands of any man."

And Brahmā replied:

> "So be it. Let all you desire come true.
> But remember, no one born into this world
> Can remain immortal forever,
> No! Not even the gods!
> For they must also die one day,
> Mark my words, you too shall die,
> And you shall die at the hands of a woman."

And then Mahiṣāsura said:

> "If that be so, grant me another boon,
> That I shall not die even at the hands of a woman
> Till I have beheld her naked breasts, her bare *yoni* [genitals]."

Brahmā:

"So be it! So be it!"

And as sunset approached, he granted the boon and disappeared.

Another key element—the Goddess's disrobing—can be found in chapter 29 of the *Caṇḍī Purāṇa*—"Mahiṣāsura's Killing." In this chapter, the Goddess learns of the boon, that the only way to destroy the demon is to take off her clothes:

When Mahiṣāsura withstood the full fury of the Devī's onslaught,
She sought Sarvamaṅgalā's advice.
Sarvamaṅgalā:

"Do not be despondent, Devī,
Hear the secret of Mahiṣāsura's invulnerability,
After 80,000 years of penance, he sought a boon from Brahmā,
That no man could kill him,
That Viṣṇu would not be able to equal him in battle,
That only a woman could kill him.
But as he was sitting, after eating, his minister advised him,
That Viṣṇu could also take the female form.
Whereupon Mahiṣāsura had asked,
'What shall I do? What boon should I ask to protect myself from an apparent woman?'
The minister said that such things have been known to happen [done by Viṣṇu].
Having thought it over, Mahiṣāsura sought another boon
From Brahmā, who was willing to grant him all the boons he asked before sunset.
Mahiṣāsura then asked Brahmā, 'Grant me the boon that the woman who defeats me in battle,
Can only kill me after I have beheld her naked breasts, her bare *yoni.*'
Such is the strength of the one you now fight," said Maṅgalā.
"Until you show him your breasts and your *yoni,* Mahiṣāsura shall not die!
Unless you abandon your present state, unveil your naked form!
Let Mahiṣāsura see your *yoni!*
Let him desire you!
Till you do that, you cannot kill him."

Durgā, dismayed by Maṅgalā's words, heeding her advice,
Took the form of Cāmuṇḍī,
Discarding her clothes, unbinding her hair, wearing but a strip of cloth around her waist,
Exposing her thighs, her *yoni,* her breasts,
A sight at which even the 330,000,000 gods in heaven quailed,
Mahiṣāsura, beholding this form, stared in wonder with both his eyes,
Thus did he attain the vision of Devī's *yoni,* not beheld even by the gods.
. . . .
Thus did Mahiṣāsura remain, gazing at Durgā in wonder,

So on the banks of the river Tarini,
Mahiṣāsura gazed at Devī, in a trance.
And then, Devī, taking the opportunity,
Pierced his chest with the trident.
Looking up at her, looking at her *yoni,*
With no help left, Mahiṣāsura lay in a trance,
Seeing the demon fallen and as still as in death,
Durgā Devī was satisfied and killed Mahiṣāsura.

Finally, Sāralā Dāsa elaborates on the Goddess's rage at being betrayed by the gods, her sense of outrage at having to strip naked so as to kill the demon. In the same chapter as the one excerpted from above, in the section entitled, "After Mahiṣāsura's Death, as Kālī," he writes:

The gods in heaven were overjoyed and decided to go to Durgā
With offerings [*arghya*] in their hands;
They wanted to propitiate Devī.
In humility and joy, they came to the mountain of Ratnagiri,
Bedecked in colorful clothes, with their armies, bearing precious metals,
And there they beheld Devī, lying and resting, naked, without any clothes.
Overcome with *lajjā,* they could not draw near her.
Seeing the gods, Mahādevī exclaimed in rage,

> "There shall be no male gods left in heaven, none shall remain unslain today!
> You give the *asuras* such boons that they destroy the three worlds!
> Would I have had to disrobe myself if there had not been such gods in heaven?"

Seeing Durgā's anger, all the gods fled to the heavens, in fear,
And Devī, taking on the form of Kālī, bestrode the three worlds.
Mahakālī, Mahābetālī, Suneha Svarūpa
Assuming this terrible form, holding a skull in one hand,
The sword in another, with open hair tossing wildly, as Cāmuṇḍī.
Even the gods could not look upon this terrible form,
Glowing in such fiery radiance.
All the gods then hid,
Except Śiva, who could not flee.

But the solution that Sāralā Dāsa provides to the quandary in which the gods find themselves is suggestively different from that which the narrators of the temple town find suitable today. Far from the Goddess being the wife of Śiva and her husband's servant, the marriage between Śiva and the Goddess is yet to take place. Rather, Śiva worships the Goddess, accepting her as his particular deity (*iṣṭadevatā*) without reservation. Soothed by his worship and enchanted by the seductive power of his dancing, the Goddess offers Śiva the boon of his choice, and he asks her to be his wife. And since a boon once offered cannot be retracted, she accepts his proposal; her domestication saves the world from destruction. The *Caṇḍī Purāṇa* describes this interchange between Śiva and the Goddess in the following way:

The long-haired one with the top-knot [*jaṭā*],
Could not flee, he broke into dance, and thought:

> "Let her see this dance, let terrible Devī do whatever she desires
> Kill me or preserve me, perhaps she will be beguiled, attracted."

He danced on, wondering what would happen.
The greatest of the gods, the fearless lord of the universe,
Essence of the world, strength of the demons,
Fascinating the gods with his dance
Beating his *nabālakhā ḍamaru* [Śiva's drum] in the air,
Gazing at Devī with his fifteen eyes.
She, who lives in the cremation grounds, the holder of the trident,
Stared at him dance, fascinated, and said:

> "Remember your gods, Jaṭiā!
> How dared you give such boons to demons!
> That they destroy the very earth!
> Only by swallowing such gods can I quench my thirst for vengeance,
> I shall eat you as well."

As Cāmuṇḍī, bestriding the three worlds!
Sadāśiva, folding his hands in prayer,
Looked up at her and said:

> "You are my *iṣṭadevatā*, Śākambharī,
> Durgā Devī is my savior, Devī of my clan,
> Durgā alone dispels my sorrows."

And so he sang her praises.
As Paśupati bowed in such humility, Devī felt a calm descend upon her,
She said:

> "You gods are without wisdom,
> Why do you grant such boons to demons without any reason?
> Who, then, can slay or destroy them?
> Because of you, I had to lose my honor, and you put my might to the test.
> Today, we will know your greatness,
> Who will protect you? Tell me, Īśvara.
> I will kill you and all the other gods as well,
> So that there are no gods left in heaven.
> Remember your family gods, your father, your mother,
> Remember your friends!"

Prostrating himself at her feet in fear, and then rising,
Śiva said:

> "You are cruel,
> You are my family god,
> You are my father, you are my mother,

> You alone are my friend.
> I have no one but you in this world.
> Whether I live or die, it is as you desire."

Saying this, he danced and danced.
Seeing the dance that had fascinated the gods,
Durgā Devī was pleased and said:

> "Ask, Jaṭiā, ask your boon, ask what your heart desires,
> I shall grant you that boon.
> I am pleased with you, ask your boon."

Īśvara replied:

> "Promise, Devī, promise that you will grant me any boon that I crave!"
> "I promise, I promise!" exclaimed Devī,
> "Ask what you desire."

Thus she kept asking what he desired,
Īśvara then asked her to become his wife.
Kātyāyanī then agreed, and he embraced her and took her to his bosom.

Perhaps because Sāralā Dāsa was himself a Śākta, a worshipper of the Goddess who unquestioningly accepted the supremacy of the female principle, he has no difficulty in portraying Śiva as the devoted servant of the Goddess. In terms of divine hierarchy, Śiva ranks way below Devī and apparently has no hesitation in acknowledging his lowly position, in accepting her as his personal deity, and in seeking to engage her attention through entertaining her (see Patricia Dold's central thesis in this volume regarding Śiva adopting the position of the inferior when he approaches the Goddess).

However, the contemporary Oriya story weighs the relationship between Kālī and Śiva quite differently. It presumes upon the marital relationship between the Goddess and Śiva. It is awareness of that unequal domestic relationship that compels Kālī to bite her tongue and hold in her anger. In the current version, the domestication of Kālī is complete; not only is she Śiva's wife, but she experiences herself as his wife. The image of Kālī stepping on Śiva, the idea that she is experiencing *lajjā* when she bites her tongue, the notion that *lajjā* is a refining emotion essential for the maintaining of social order—all these elements of meaning are absent from the "Devī-Māhātmya," the *Devībhāgavata Purāṇa* and the *Caṇḍī Purāṇa.* But these are the core elements of the contemporary story, the most common perception of the icon today.

On examining the twenty-five elements of meaning described earlier (table 4.1),[10] we find that only eight of these meanings can be traced to the Sanskritic Purāṇas. Eighteen of these elements of meaning can be found in the *Caṇḍī Purāṇa,* and these include the eight present in the "Devī-Māhātmya" and the *Devībhāgavata Purāṇa* versions. But six elements of meaning—those having to do either with the ruse the gods and Śiva plotted, or with Kālī's sense of *lajjā* at having stepped on Śiva accidentally—are particular to the story as it is told today in the temple town of Bhubaneswar. And of these six elements, the three that describe Kālī's experience of *lajjā* are part of module 1 and, therefore, the most widely known.

THE POWER OF THE ICON

This icon, although of heterodox origin, appears to exercise a powerful hold over the Oriya imagination because it provides ways to discuss, organize, and better understand several issues important to Oriya Hindu culture: the disjunction between a male-dominated social order and the potential power of women, the nature of male-female relations, the role played by self-control and self-restraint in effectively regulating destructive power, and the ways in which a human being evolves morally. And so although the icon challenges the received hierarchy of the patriarchal Oriya Hindu world, the narrative experts choose not to reject it outright. Rather, they reconstruct its meaning, integrating elements from the *Devībhāgavata Purāṇa* and the *Caṇḍī Purāṇa* with substantive original contributions of their own to create a new and compelling narrative.

Two of the most striking features of the icon that the narrators feel the need to explain are the Goddess's nakedness and her stepping on Śiva's chest. The *Caṇḍī Purāṇa,* by modifying the classical Purāṇic idea of the boon and by making the conditions for the demon's death even more stringent, provides them with a satisfying explanation for the first feature, the Goddess's nakedness: Mahiṣāsura can only be killed by a *naked* female. With respect to the second feature, narrators resort to their own ingenuity. They explain her stepping on Śiva as a mistake, the result of a ruse planned by Śiva and the other gods to enable her to hold in her anger and become calm. Thus, the Goddess's nakedness and her stepping on her husband, her personal god, become parts of the logic of the story and are used to make sense of the sequence of narrated events.

And the final crowning element in the contemporary story—the idea that Kālī's protruding tongue is the distinguishing mark of her *lajjā*—appears to be an entirely local creation,[11] although the germ for this idea of *lajjā* can be found in the *Caṇḍī Purāṇa.* Inappropriate behavior, any kind of overstepping of the bounds of propriety, invariably results in the experience of *lajjā.* When the obsequious and grateful gods intrude on the Goddess resting after her exertions, bearing gifts, ready to praise and worship her, they, rather than she, are overcome with *lajjā* at seeing her naked, and they withdraw, painfully conscious of having encroached, of having forgotten their rightful place in the hierarchy of the heavens.

RECONSTRUCTING NARRATIVES: THE ROLE PLAYED BY LOCAL "EXPERTS"

We have no way of assessing the creative historical role played by local experts in synthesizing or transforming local narrative norms. R. G. D'Andrade has suggested that cultural experts both know a great deal about their own particular domains and—more important—are adept at integrating esoteric knowledge with meanings and understandings that are more commonly shared.[12] Perhaps this is what the narrative experts in the temple town have done: they have appropriated the Tantric icon, an item of esoteric knowledge, and reinterpreted it to suit the more commonly shared moral requirements of their world. In so doing, they have fashioned a narrative that harmonizes with notions of male superiority inherent in the patriarchal Oriya Hindu social order, while acknowledging simultaneously that female power when self-contained and self-regulated is the supreme force in the world.

It is possible that social recognition of the "expertise" of experts gives them a special authority to introduce new elements of meanings into their narratives and generate fresh interpretations of cultural symbols, which then become normative. Sāralā Dāsa was clearly such an expert. A Śākta with a powerfully persuasive pen, he not only reinvented the story about the Goddess and the buffalo demon in the *Caṇḍī Purāṇa* but also reinterpreted the *Rāmāyaṇa,* calling his version *Bilaṅkā Rāmāyaṇa.* Today, these two religious works have great mass appeal, being the most widely read of such texts in the temple town of Bhubaneswar.

What merits reiteration is that the story in its entirety, with its complete logical sequence of events, is not widely known. The final element that has to do with Kālī's realization of the transgression she has committed is known by most people, but it has, as we have shown, nothing to do with any textual version or with the original Tantric meaning of the icon. The experts who tell the most detailed stories build up to this climax—Kālī's biting of her tongue when she realizes the seriousness of her transgression—using elements from the various texts as well as contributing original ideas of their own. But their listeners appear to remember only this last crucial detail, and that is what they repeat when asked to recount the story. Hardly any of the details, and almost none of the events that preceded this climax, survive in their accounts.

We believe that this is perhaps the historical process that produced the story told today in the neighborhood of the Liṅgarāj temple. Sāralā Dāsa pointed the way and a later generation of experts integrated the image of Kālī in the Tantric icon, the boon, and the battle (as described in the *Caṇḍī Purāṇa*), together with socially meaningful details, to create a powerful new narrative, one that resonated with ordinary, everyday experience.

Thus, it seems plausible to suggest that this contemporary way of telling the story of Kālī represents a local Brāhmaṇical synthesis of a Tantric icon with the moral requirements of a patriarchal social world. In trying to integrate the images of female power invoked by the Tantric icon with the idea that *lajjā*—respectful restraint, deference—is an essential attribute of female virtue, the local imagination has invented a new and different story, one that has only the most tenuous links to classical Purāṇic versions of Goddess narratives.

NOTES

1. For more on this community, see Manamohan Mahapatra, *Traditional Structure and Change in an Orissan Temple* (Calcutta: Punthi Pustak, 1981); Susan Seymour, "Household Structures and Status and Expressions of Affect in India," *Ethos* 11 (1983): 263–77; Richard A. Shweder, *Thinking through Cultures* (Cambridge, Mass.: Harvard University Press, 1991); and Richard A. Shweder, Manamohan Mahapatra, and Joan G. Miller, "Culture and Moral Development," in *Cultural Psychology: Essays in Human Development,* ed. James Stigler, Gilbert Herdt, and Richard A. Shweder (Cambridge: Cambridge University Press, 1990), pp. 130–204.

2. This particular Tantric text describes Kālī as black-skinned because she encompasses everything in the universe: "just as all colors disappear in black, so all names and forms disappear in her." She is also said to be naked, clothed in space alone, because Mahāśakti is unlimited; to have a red, lolling tongue representing the passion and creativity of nature; and to stand on a pale, lifeless corpse of Śiva, whom she awakens in her capacity as giver and destroyer of life.

3. See Usha Menon and Richard A. Shweder, "Kali's Tongue: Cultural Psychology and the Power of 'Shame' in Orissa, India," in *Emotion and Culture: Empirical Studies of Mutual Influence,* ed. Shinobu Kitayama and Hazel Markus (Eugene: University of Oregon Press, 1994), pp. 241–84.

4. There were also a few who knew a little about storytelling norms as they related to this icon.

5. Sāralā Dāsa, *Caṇḍī Purāṇa* (Cuttack: Dharma Grantha, n.d.). Usha Menon has translated the excerpts of the *Caṇḍī Purāṇa* presented in this chapter.

6. Sāralā Dāsa is the name taken by Siddheśvar Parīḍā, a Śākta who lived out his days as the Goddess's servant at the temple dedicated to the goddess Sāralā at Chattia in Cuttack district in Orissa. Two other texts are attributed to him—the *Adhbhuta Rāmāyaṇa* and the *Bilaṅkā Rāmāyaṇa.* As a Śākta, Sāralā Dāsa's work elaborates a highly female-oriented perspective. For instance, in the *Bilaṅkā Rāmāyaṇa,* Sītā becomes Mahādevī, the Great Goddess, and kills the thousand-headed Rāvaṇa, while Rāma stands by in the shadows and watches.

7. This text has recently been translated by Thomas B. Coburn in *Encountering the Goddess: A Translation of the Devī-Māhātmya and a Study of Its Interpretation* (Albany: State University of New York Press, 1991).

8. See Cheever Mackenzie Brown, *The Triumph of the Goddess: The Canonical Models and Theological Visions of the Devī-Bhāgavata Purāṇa* (Albany: State University of New York Press, 1990).

9. In searching for an Oriya text that tells the story about Kālī's icon that is cur-

rent today in the temple town, we have conducted several exhaustive enquiries. Professor K. C. Sahoo, formerly of Utkal University, one of the two living authorities on Sāralā Dāsa and his work, told Usha Menon quite categorically in June 1995 that neither Sāralā Dāsa nor, to the best of his knowledge, any other Oriya litterateur had ever written any story about this particular representation of Kālī that included all the elements found in the story then told orally in the temple town.

10. Element 15, which refers to local perception about the nature of rage, can hardly be attributed to any of the concerned texts and so is ignored in the present discussion.

11. We should perhaps qualify this by saying that the contemporary story that speaks of Kālī's shame is current over a much larger area than just the town of Bhubaneswar. We know, for instance, that almost identical stories about the icon are told in the rest of coastal Orissa, eastern Madhya Pradesh, eastern Bihar, Bengal, and Assam. But we can speak with authority only with respect to the temple town, because our research has been limited to this region.

12. See R. G. D'Andrade, "Some Propositions about the Relations between Culture and Human Cognition," in *Cultural Psychology: Essays in Comparative Human Development,* ed. James Stigler, Gilbert Herdt, and Richard A. Shweder (Cambridge: Cambridge University Press, 1990), pp. 65–129.

CHAPTER 5

Kāḷi in a Context of Terror

The Tasks of a Goddess in Sri Lanka's Civil War

Patricia Lawrence

While the goddess Kāḷi travels into the unknown territory of the Internet's electronic highways, publicizing Indian-American temple activities and inspiring feminists and New Age seekers,[1] the Goddess is, at the same time, deeply engaged in tasks of another sort in Sri Lanka. On the east coast of the island, the number of participants in devotionalism to local, territorial forms of the Goddess has increased dramatically during recent years. Kāḷi's magnetism is, however, expanding in a narrowing landscape. The war-torn east coast is undergoing stifling isolation from the wider world as separatist fighters sever telephone lines and destroy electrical transformers with explosives. Moreover, the government has periodically discontinued rail and air transport, and a plethora of military barriers manned by heavily armed Sri Lankan security forces punctuates roads and highways, cordoning off the Tamil-speaking region from the rest of the island. The primarily Hindu Tamil minority living in the eastern coastal plain, the locus of this research, has suffered two decades of civil war. Tamil families caught in the region are turning to Kāḷi, more than to any other local Hindu deity, for help in coping with the terrible personal tragedy and chaos of this historical moment.[2] These pages examine the reworking of local religious life surrounding Kāḷi in conditions of civil war.

INTRODUCTION

Today, the majority of the island's people (approximately 74 percent) are Sinhalese, and Buddhism is the commonest religious orientation. The Tamil population, located in the north, the east, and the hill country, is the island's largest minority (approximately 18 percent). Most Tamils are Hindu, although some are Christian, just as there are Christian Sinhalese. Smaller minority groups include Muslims (approximately 7 percent) and Christian Burghers. Under British Rule, until independence in 1948, Tamil graduates of Christian missionary schools, located primarily in the northern Tamil-speaking region, received employment and economic opportunities. This favoritism ceased when the island became a sovereign state, whereafter the Tamil-speaking population was drastically marginalized.

In the interior Tamil villages and hamlets of the eastern paddy-cultivating plain, where there is a marked historical absence of Brāhmaṇical values and where local Hindu religiosity was not as disrupted by the colonial presence as in the northern peninsula, matriclan organization is still linked to local goddess cults.[3] Membership in specific matriclans is mandatory for the duty or privilege of serving as a temple trustee or non-Brahman priest (*pūjāri* [Tamil: *pūcari*]), to perform certain inside duties at the temple, to participate in the *pūjā* (Tamil: *pūcai*) of worshipping and ritually pounding newly harvested rice, and to be in the select group of prepubescent girls (*kaṉṉimār, kaṉṉipiḷḷai,* or *tollimār*) who serve the Goddess inside the temple for the duration of the annual propitiation. In many temples, specific matriclan rights also apply to those who serve the Goddess by offering their physical body for the ritual embodiment of the living presence of deities (in states of possession-trance) during temple *pūjā*s.

In eastern Sri Lanka, institutionalized possession is incorporated into the structure of *pūjā* ritual at temples for all local goddesses.[4] Possessed individuals are commonly known as deity-dancers (*teyvam āṭumākkaḷ*), and the deities who most frequently "come upon" them and speak through them include Kāḷi in the forms of Pattirakāḷiyammaṉ, Vīrakāḷiyammaṉ, and Vīramahākāḷi; the other local goddesses Māriyammaṉ, Pēcciyammaṉ, Tirōpataiyammaṉ, Nagakaṇṇiyammaṉ, Kaṭalacciyammaṉ; the god Murugaṉ; and the guardian deities Narasingha Vairavaṉ or Vairavar, Vīrapattiraṉ, and Nagathāmbiraṉ. During my research at temples on the east coast (1991–96), there were growing numbers of deity-dancers practicing institutionalized possession, and possession by forms of Kāḷi were most common. During a period of possession, the identity of the deity speaking through the deity-dancer may change, a process referred to as "changing face" (*mukam māṟrummāṟutal*). During pujas at different temples, I observed the priest instigating this transformation by summoning the goddess Māriyammaṉ when he thought the force of Kāḷi's presence had become too dangerous for the possessed individual.[5]

Tamil people still living on the east coast of Sri Lanka are enmeshed in the strangeness of the ordinary in a world altered by violence, and these traumatic changes are clearly reflected in the reworking of their local religious life. Ritual activities of local goddess cults, in particular rituals for Kāḷi, now draw an increased number of participants, focus on possession-states and the enactment of personal vows to the Goddess, and may incorporate practices of blood sacrifice of goats and chickens or, when these have been discontinued, ash pumpkins.

Importance is placed on the enactment of duties by selected prepubescent girls, the *kaṉṉimār,* and these rituals satisfy Kāḷi when they are conducted properly. The primary duties performed by the *kaṉṉimār* include waving of lamps and receiving a ritually cooked meal of "cooling" foods inside the temple. As the *kaṉṉimār* eat this meal, served by the *pūjāri* and his assistants, they are not only virginal servants of the Goddess but represent the Goddess herself, and are treated with the utmost care. This ritual meal is said to be vital for the protection and well-being of the *ūr* (the immediate area under the protection of the particular local goddess). I was told that the *kaṉṉimār* rituals keep "the troubles" out of the *ūr.* Said one *pūjāri:* "If any mistake is made in this ritual, large numbers of people might die in the *ūr.*"

The periodic influx of displaced people from vulnerable Tamil villages of the interior, where Sri Lankan Army ground operations and Air Force bombings occur, has contributed to growing cross-caste participation at some east coast Kāḷi temples. The numbers of devotees flocking to small temples where the goddess Kāḷi is propitiated have grown to thousands (rather than hundreds, as in earlier years), and many come to fulfill promises to Kāḷi in acts of intense devotion. Devotees who enact the vow to cross a long, deep bed of hot coals on the last day of Kāḷi's annual propitiation have increased from 12 in 1983 to more than 3,350 in 1999 at one of the Kāḷi temples I regularly visited in the Vaṇṇar ("Washerman") settlement. The number of devotees crossing the fire pit rose drastically in 1991, following the 1989–90 period of intense violence, during which the annual festival for Kāḷi could not be publicly performed.

Tamil refugees from the Vanni region have established temples for Kāḷi in encampments for displaced persons. At such temples, as well as in east coast temples generally, the performance of a vow known as *muḷḷukāvaṭi,* in which the devotee's back is pierced with iron fishhooks, has become popular. Moreover, the still more difficult vow of *paravaikāvaṭi* (suspension from hooks) is a spectacle appearing at more temples each year, although usually enacted by only one devotee, or perhaps two, at each temple.

In 1993, I was present when more than two hundred young Tamil men underwent piercing of the skin below their shoulder blades at a small Kāḷi temple in Paduvankarai ("Sunset Shore"), an isolated, interior area of Batticaloa District. People explained the popularity of this difficult *muḷḷukāvaṭi* vow to me by stressing that it brings the grace (*varam*) and protection (*kāppu*) of the Goddess and instills the devotee with courage (*vīram*). Tamil males from the late teens to the early forties form the largest category of civilian deaths. In some cases, the young men's mothers (who stood by as their sons underwent the piercing) explained that they were the ones who had initially promised Kāḷi that their sons would keep this vow, and once the vow had been made, the young men had agreed to perform it. In some other cases, to be encountered below, the *muḷḷukāvaṭi* vow was made by young Tamil men as a plea to Kāḷi while enduring severe ill-treatment and torture in government interrogation and detention camps.

Under the prevailing conditions of terror and intractable dilemmas created by the injury of prolonged war, the reworking of ritual for the goddess Kāḷi on the east coast has differed from religious change reported by Richard Gombrich and Gananath Obeyesekere for rapidly urbanizing areas of Sri Lanka.[6] Military repression, population displacement, continuing peripheralization, extremely high rates of "disappearance," and the shadow of unnatural death upon everyday life are important aspects in the devotional revitalization of Kāḷi worship in the eastern war zone.

THE BACKGROUND OF THE ISLAND'S VIOLENT CONFLICT

The causes of the violent conflict in Sri Lanka are deeply contested, and my background comments here are necessarily incomplete. The struggle between the Liberation Tigers of Tamil Eelam (LTTE), the dominant armed group fighting for the establishment of a separate state, and Sri Lankan government security forces drawn from the Sinhalese majority population has forced ordinary Tamil minority families trapped in the eastern coastal plain to face violence and death as a part of their everyday existence. The LTTE's fight for self-determination is based on a history of discrimination by successive Sri Lankan governments against the Tamil minority on issues of language, land allocation, education, employment, and politico-economic rights.[7]

Following independence from the British in 1948, those who secured political power came primarily from the upper echelons of society, and little was done in the way of radical social reforms to redress the grinding poverty and suffering of the disadvantaged.[8] Under Sri Lanka's constitution, modeled on the British democratic parliamentary system, the Sinhalese majority population acquired most legislative and executive power. The alienation of the Tamil-speaking population increased with the establishment of Sinhalese as the sole official language of the state in 1956. Buddhism was given primacy in the 1972 constitution, and at the same time state-sponsored development schemes colonized areas perceived by the Tamils as their traditional "homelands." Loss of faith in the unitary state system increased as changes to the university entrance system reduced Tamil access to university education, and negotiations for regional devolution of power failed. As separatist sentiment grew, armed Tamil militancy began to form in small groups in the northern Jaffna peninsula in the 1970s.[9] In July 1983, Sinhala-Tamil politics confronted unprecedented violence when anti-Tamil riots erupted in Colombo and continued without interference for days. The 1983 pogrom, noted for the complicity of the police and government forces, resulted in the deaths of hundreds of Tamils and the destruction of thousands of Tamil homes and businesses.[10]

Struggling to maintain Sri Lanka as a unitary state, the government enlarged and strengthened its armed forces as a countermeasure. Sri Lankan security forces committed large-scale massacres of Tamil noncombatants in eastern villages—the location of this research—in the late 1980s and early 1990s. This period of summary and extrajudicial executions is locally known as the "troubled times"—times when Tamil bodies were found floating in lagoons or along the sea beaches, or were burned on roadsides, in paddy fields, and inside government detention camps. The troubled times are not yet perceived as belonging to the past, and during each period of renewed offensives, the phrase is used again to speak of continuing internecine strife and consequent suffering. Middle-aged members of the families with whom I lived generally expect the violence to continue for the rest of their lifetimes. I have often heard people say that they hoped that their youngest children would not live in conditions of war.

When referring to numbers of deaths in the civil war, political analysts and human rights advocates often resort to the phrase "tens of thousands," while journalists currently report the loss of "more than 60,000 lives." Many executions were effaced from "official" public acknowledgment by the government military apparatus under the United National Party, although families in the east will carry the memory of their immense loss and diminishment for generations.[11]

ETHNOGRAPHIC LOCATION IN A LANDSCAPE OF VIOLENCE

My anthropological field research (1991–99), conducted in this least-reported eastern region of the island, concentrates on the consequences of extreme political violence for families still living in Batticaloa District, and the manner in which they cope. I conducted much of my research in temples during annual propitiation rituals for local goddesses primarily because there are severe constraints on movement and sociality inside the war zone, and they provided the only well-attended collective social events in the early 1990s. When I began my work in 1991, household members were careful to be inside their houses before dusk, as shooting between the Sri Lankan security forces and the LTTE frequently began in the fading light of the evening.

During events at local temples, the networks of families with whom I lived in the 1990s expanded, increasingly providing exposure to the way in which violence is carried into the family; thus I gained an understanding of personal tragedies, the intensity of emotion, and the shattering of the Tamil kinship nexus in this region. My ethnographic project became twofold: (1) to describe the entry of violence into everyday lived experience and Tamil religious imagination at work in these conditions of desperation, and (2) to offer an ethnographic perspective on political violence that reveals the consequences of the civil war at a historical moment when dissent is impossible for families caught in the region.

VIOLENT REPRESSION AND THE RESURGENCE OF RELIGIOSITY

The injury of war has so shattered Batticaloa's social infrastructure that 80 percent of the population was displaced in 1990.[12] Approximately 14,000 "disappearances" are estimated to have occurred in this eastern district in the late 1980s and 1990s, and by far the majority of these were perpetrated by government security forces. While the regular occurrence of mass killings has lessened, disappearances continue today.[13] Batticaloa is a region vulnerable to annihilation, where the psychological effects of political oppression manifest themselves in "silencing," in learning not to speak and to know what not to know—coping methods reported elsewhere in the world where there have been large numbers of disappearances and extrajudicial executions.[14]

In this political milieu threatening to dignity and life, families of the eastern region have been faced with a new learning of their social habitat. No single armed group has maintained stable control of the eastern war zone—apart from government security forces, Rohan Gunaratna has documented thirty-six different armed Tamil rebel groups on the island in the 1980s, prior to the rise of the LTTE as the dominant separatist group,[15]—so they have been unable to work out a modus vivendi with the forces of oppression. Confronted with impossible circumstances of life-threatening demands and broken trust, many families in the eastern region have distanced themselves from all armed groups and focus their attention instead upon local religious practices.

As social concentration has shifted toward religious resources, local practices are being profoundly reworked. In a passage that describes present conditions in eastern Sri Lanka well, Arthur and Joan Kleinman summarize such a response to systematic trauma :

> Studies of dissociation show that when individuals and small groups are under great pressure of traumatizing occurrence or other deeply disturbing events,

> there is a focusing of attention and narrowing of the field of awareness away from what is menacing toward absorption in a safer place. That place may be one's imaginings, an alternative self, or concentration of a highly focused part of the social field. Perception, imagination, and memory are absorbed into that particular focus.[16]

In Batticaloa, local people often frame narratives of their experiences of violence and suffering in religious terms. Sri Lanka's religious history suggests that the island's communities more than merely tolerate popular religiosity, and it continues to flourish.[17]

THE CHANGING AGENCY OF KĀḶI AND OTHER EAST COAST GODDESSES

If concentration on Kāḷi is flourishing in the popular religiosity of the Tamil-speaking people of the island, why haven't the Liberation Tigers of Tamil Eelam appropriated her image in their struggle for a separate Tamil state? I learned through attendance at many local temple events in the first half of the 1990s that LTTE fighters occasionally burned camphor and prayed at temples for Kāḷi, and enacted religious vows, such as crossing a deep pit of hot coals or piercing the skin, but it was carefully explained to me that in such instances, they were viewed as "local boys" and not as members of the dominant armed organization fighting for Tamil self-determination. Since the question of the relationship between Hindu religion and separatist politics was repeatedly asked when I first presented papers on my field research, I asked LTTE members why they didn't appropriate Kāḷi for their goal—as she has been appropriated as a political symbol in other regions of South Asia. The first opinion shared with me was, "Religion is not part of the consciousness of the struggle." While the majority of Tamils in Sri Lanka are Hindus, there are also Catholic and Protestant Tamils on the island, and the LTTE is extremely careful to avoid divisiveness within the Tamil populace that would weaken their movement. This stance on religion is required precisely because emotional outpourings are common in temples and churches in Tamil towns, villages, and neighborhoods throughout the war zone. In my field research, I found that people were often torn between protective silence and unconstrained expression of horror, and that sacred space was imbued with value as ground for unshielded expressiveness.

Such restraint is not, however, expected of noncombatants. Caktirāṇi is one of many local oracles of Kāḷi living on Sri Lanka's eastern coastal plain who has gained popularity through her expression of unshielded truth and her ability to feel the pain of others. Today, as before the war, the gift of uttering oracles (*vākku solluṟatu*) with the voice of the Goddess confers considerable respect upon an individual in the community. The guidance Caktirāṇi offers to those who are deeply disturbed by arrests or abductions of loved ones and her assistance in articulating grief and mourning the "disappeared" are recent developments in her work as an oracle. Two decades ago, before the war, her gift of seeing the unseen was sometimes called on by the local police, who dressed her in a uniform and requested that she locate stolen valuables. During my field research, I often found her on her veranda advising Tamil parents who were struggling with the difficult decision of whether to send their children out of the war to the expanding Tamil diaspora, or providing counsel and local medical remedies for survivors of torture.

In June 1996, the fifth year of our friendship, Caktirāṇi shared some of the motivation behind her vows of devotion at a temple of Kāḷi by stating her wish: "To solve the problems in this country, to solve the 'ethnic problem' [she used the English phrase]. No danger should fall on the children, the relatives, on the neighborhood. For this I walk the fire. *Arōharā! Ammākku Arōharā! Parācaktikku Arōharā!*" Having made this pronouncement, Caktirāṇi and a *pūjāri* approached each other, the latter piercing her cheeks with a single, long silver needle with a three-pronged *sulam* (trident) on one end. The *sulam* is often referred to in this region as an instrument of Kāḷi's protection. As she explains it, this vow, known as *vāyalaku* (mouth arrow), helps Caktirāṇi concentrate fully on the local presence of the goddess Kāḷi, Pattirakāḷiyamma<u>n</u>. Moments later, she led more than three thousand Tamil women, children, and men over a long bed of hot coals on the final day of Kāḷi's annual rituals of propitiation at the small Vaṇṇar temple facing the Bay of Bengal.

On the east coast of Sri Lanka, it is understood that "every goddess is very powerful" (*ovvoru amma<u>n</u>num mikavum vallamai uṭaiyavarkaḷ*). Local territorial Hindu goddesses are believed to ensure the well-being of devotees and their families and to protect the boundaries of household compounds, neighborhoods, and villages from negative influences—including the army, special task force, and countersubversive units. The identity of each local Tamil goddess, or Amma<u>n</u> ("Mother"), is defined in terms of place, and people state that neglect of any goddess may arouse her furious "face" and result in withdrawal of her protection.[18]

Among local goddesses, Kāḷi's rise in popularity is especially visible through dramatic propitiatory ritual. Some devotees say that only Kāḷi has the power to "change the position" (*nilamai ma<u>r</u><u>r</u>utal*) of those experiencing immediate vulnerability to annihilation. In today's desperate circumstances, she is considered one of the most responsive and powerful local goddesses in Batticaloa District. In fishing villages where there have been repeated retaliatory killings of noncombatants, people say Kāḷi can be "rough like the sea" and that only she can deal with the "ferocious activities of the people." The resurgence of her popularity is linked to beliefs about Kāḷi's *caktivalimai* (empowerment of *śakti,* the hot, active, and unlimited female energy of the Hindu cosmos). In the present circumstances of maiming, shooting, and indiscriminate shelling, many devotees' stories about the moment in which they made a vow to Kāḷi focused on a request that required immediate intervention. Devotees also expressed the belief that Kāḷi and other Ammaṉs have the capacity to return to safety family members who have disappeared, or to procure their release from Sri Lankan prisons and detention camps.

A characteristic of the Ammaṉs enshrined in east coast temples is referred to as *mukam māṟṟummāṟutal,* or "changing face." Every Ammaṉ has the capacity to change from a pleasing or protective attitude to an angry or offended state in which protection is withdrawn. For example, after a second massacre by government forces in the vicinity of the village of Kokkadichcholai, people who were devotees of Kannakaiyammaṉ said they realized that they must now finish the long incomplete reconstruction of their temple, because their goddess was so offended by her neglected state that "her peaceful face actually changed to the furious face of Kāḷi." Vows are often said to be made at the request of a local Ammaṉ, in dreams or during the telling of oracles. Promises may also be made to the Goddess during moments of heightened emotion—when a land mine explodes close by, when a cordon and search operation is taking place in the neighborhood, or in an overwhelming state of unresolved grief related to the abduction, arrest, or disappearance of a loved one. Today, people's narratives about enactment of vows for a local Ammaṉ emphasize both her protection (*kāppu, kāval*) and her grace (*varam*).

KUMĀRAVĒLU'S VOW

Kumāravēlu connects the *muḷḷukāvaṭi* vow he performed in June 1996 to a dream he had during detention. When I met Kumāravēlu at a local temple, he was nineteen years old, with a very wide smile and bright eyes, and he was the most slender of the group of twenty-one young men undergoing piercing of their backs for Kāḷiyammaṉ. His village is in Paduvankarai, on the western side of the Batticaloa lagoon. His skin is burnt dark by the sun under which he labors. The clustered houses of his village are surrounded by rice fields, although the cultivation of rice has become fraught with extreme difficulty in the war years. The area has been under control of the LTTE with the exception of the years 1992–94, when government military "clearing" operations resulted in the Sri Lankan army gaining a temporary foothold in Paduvankarai. In 1995, army and special task force camps established there were vacated under pressure of LTTE attacks. Slogans and sayings of famous LTTE members were painted on walls and at junctions on the way to Kumāravēlu's village in 1995: "I accept death with pleasure, therefore our people will be liberated"; "Unless the Tamil people are alert, their future is bleak"; and "Courage, cunning, and hard practice will lead us to victory." Kumāravēlu has not joined the LTTE, because he is the only able-bodied man in his family, and losing him would be a severe hardship.

Kumāravēlu was arrested in the outskirts of Batticaloa town in 1996 and interrogated by an army intelligence unit at the notorious Palpody camp, situated by the edge of the lagoon behind the main Batticaloa prison and hospital. Like many young Tamil men who are arrested on suspicion of being members of the LTTE, Kumāravēlu comes from a poor family and was not able to continue his schooling. During his week inside the Palpody camp, he vowed to a local form of Kāḷi that he would perform *muḷḷukāvaṭi* for her if she would release him from detention. Frequently promised to the Goddess during arrest and interrogation, piercing the body in this vow is believed to instill grace and courage, and also to ensure protection. Such a vow marks a relationship with a local goddess and a place, unlike the wounds of torture inflicted in detention camps—which mark the boundary between violator and victim.

The following dialogue occurred in front of Kāḷi's inner temple sanctum immediately after he completed the promised *muḷḷukāvaṭi* vow. This was the first time in his life that he had performed this very difficult religious act. Kumāravēlu was short of breath and clearly lacked the usual hesitancy and fear of speaking forthrightly about ill-treatment during detention:

Kumāravēlu: We made a vow for our release. They [the army] arrested me. Ammāḷ released me.

Q: *Where did they take you?*

K: Behind the hospital; to the Palpody camp. My family went to see many people [for help], but they did not release me. The people who are taken there normally get killed. Our Mother [Kāḷi] released me. She appeared in a dream.

Q: *Were you ill-treated?*

K: They did not beat me on the day I was arrested. I cried. The next day they beat me with a large stick. I could not bear it. I shouted "Kāḷiyamma!" Then they stopped. The next day they tied my hands and put chili powder on my face. They asked me how many months I went for [combat] training. I said I did not go. Four of them beat me badly on my back. I cried loudly. They poured water on my face. After making the vow, Kāḷiyammāḷ released me. My mother went to the temple many times and prayed for my release.

Q: *Are you studying?*

K: As a result of family hardships, I left school at third standard. Father is sick. There is Mother, three elder sisters, and one younger sister. I am the only male.

Q: *Was this muḷḷukāvaṭi vow painful?*

K: Does not feel. Does not feel even after the hooks are removed. It's not difficult. This is the grace of Amman̲.

Kumāravēlu's story is typical in a number of ways. His mother's many visits to the temple to pray to Kāḷi for his release, and his act of calling out to Kāḷi while being beaten in the detention camp resonate with the narratives of many other Tamils who have suffered arrest and ill treatment on the east coast.[19] When I had occasion to meet and assist detainees who had just been released from detention, sometimes one of their first requests was to visit a temple of Kāḷi. Kumāravēlu's dark skin, his age group, the fact that he was not enrolled in school, his apparent poverty, and his low-caste status all contributed to his vulnerability to arrest. He also does not have the resources to bribe soldiers into letting him pass through checkpoints freely.

For Kumāravēlu, and also Al̲akamma, to whom we next turn, grace is perceived to result from belief (*nampikai*) in and enactment of vows to Kāḷi. She is perceived as a close rather than distanced deity, her presence felt in the body. Al̲akamma explains her propitiatory rituals as help or toil for Kāḷi, in return for which Kāḷi will assist her in solving problems.

AL̲AKAMMA'S RELATIONSHIP WITH KĀḶIYAMMAN̲

I first saw Al̲akamma reading in the shade of a tree in a corner of the temple compound of one of the washerman settlements near Batticaloa town. The temple enshrines Pattirakāḷi (Bhadrakāḷi). In the heat of mid-afternoon, we chatted and struck up a friendship. Al̲akamma, her father and mother, her young son, and her younger sister live in a modest house very close to the temple, and this temple was one I frequently visited. Al̲akamma has a strong faith in Kāḷi and has performed many forms of vows for Kāḷi at the request of oracles at the temple. She walks across the long, deep bed of hot coals in front of Kāḷi's shrine every year.

When I asked Al̲akamma how she developed devotion (*bhakti;* Tamil *pakti*) to Kāḷi, she explained that from childhood, she and her sisters used to sweep and clean the temple and worship her. Their parents also worshipped at the temple. So, "from the beginning," devotion to the local goddess (*amman̲pakti*) was there. Before puberty, she was chosen by the deity-dancers to be one of the young girls who wave auspicious lamps and serve the Goddess during her annual propitiation. Her father, sisters, younger brother, and five-year-old son also walk the fire.

The temple of Kāḷi near Al̲akamma's family's house was only a small hut in the early 1980s. This particular Kāḷi has gained tremendous popularity in recent years, drawing thousands of devotees during the annual propitiation rituals. On the final day of those rituals in June 1992, I counted 560 devotees crossing the fire. In June 1993 and 1994, the number of devotees enacting fire-walking vows rose to 2,000; in 1999, we counted 3,556. Some of them now come from as far as forty miles to the south and thirty miles to the north, even though they must travel through many military checkpoints on the roads. Many of the "fire walkers" are very young children, for parents often promise Kāḷi that their children will walk the fire in return for her protection during periods of shooting or shelling in their neighborhoods. (In A̱lakamma's son's case, however, it was his decision to cross the fire.)

The rise in popularity of Kāḷi in this small settlement of about 150 Vaṇṇar families was so striking that I set about learning how local people would explain it to me. The temple *pūjāri,* the *talateyvam* (the most important deity-dancer), and A̱lakamma all had a similar explanation. The protective powers attributed to this local goddess are affirmed by local knowledge that not even one person has died within her temple grounds, while outside her sacred space there has been an uncountable number of violent deaths during years of chaos and destruction. A tragic fact of the civil war is that some Hindu temples have been bombed from the air at times when civilians have taken refuge there. Said A̱lakamma, "She guards us during troubles. So far during the troubled times, no one was shot here [inside the temple grounds] by the military. Many things happen in other places. Not in this area. So we have faith in Kāḷiyamma."

A̱lakamma's son was born in 1990 a few months after her husband disappeared. Her husband was among thousands of other disappeared Tamils that year in Sri Lanka. Her elder brother, who has been arrested twice, tortured, and held in the Kallady detention camp, was recently transferred to Kalutara prison, in a distant, difficult-to-reach Sinhalese area of the island. He suffers hearing impairment as a result of torture during his first detention and interrogation. Many males in the Vaṇṇar settlement have been arrested more than once, and some said they had lost count of the numerous times they had been arrested in the years of military occupation.

A few days before keeping her vow in 1996, A̱lakamma expressed her motivation in the words: "I walk the fire with devotion on Kāḷiyamma. I hope for the release of my brother, and I hope I will get my husband back." This year A̱lakamma was commanded by Caktirāṇi, one of the well-known local oracles through whom Kāḷi speaks, to enact other vows as well.

A̱lakamma and I went to visit Caktirāṇi at her house near the sea, and when Caktirāṇi saw A̱lakamma at the entrance to the veranda, she muttered:

> If one gets arrested twice and thrice, what is the end of this? To live or die? Don't be afraid. We can get him out. We can get him out of Kaluthurai. You search for that one [her husband]. We can get this one out [A̱lakamma's brother]. [*Then, in a more commanding voice:*] On the name of the Amma̱n, Vīramākāḷiyamma̱n, on the deity of Punnaicholai, I will get him released between the eighth month and the tenth month for sure. This year with the other women, you take the *ka̱rpūraccati* [a clay pot filled with burning camphor] and help the other women pounding the rice.

The *kaṟpūraccati* vow, circumambulating the temple while holding a clay pot of burning camphor, is enacted only by women. The oracle's last command of our morning visit was that A̱lakamma should give an offering of a "life for a life" at the temple. This offering refers to a ritual act of presenting a young sprouted coconut, a buffalo calf, a goat, or a fowl. The next day, A̱lakamma's family presented a white rooster to the temple.[20]

Then we learned that at Kalutara prison, where A̱lakamma's brother was detained, Tamil prisoners had organized a hunger strike for their release. In a moment of intense emotion at the small household shrine, A̱lakamma's mother summoned the Goddess, addressing her as "Parācakti, Kāḷi, Tāyār" and promised tearfully that her son would perform *muḷḷukāvaṭi* and that she would wear the *vāyalaku* (mouth arrow) in return for the release and protection of her son.

After crossing the fire for Kāḷiyammaṉ in 1996, the vow A̱lakamma had promised for the return of her husband and the release of her brother, she described an experience of profound identification with the Ammaṉ: "I thought about Kāḷi—everything is you—nothing else. I did not think about anything. . . . I only thought about Kāḷi that she is everything for me."

THE BODY RESIGNIFIED

Cittiravēl, a Tamil father of one son and one adopted daughter, once earned his living by carrying loads of merchandise on his back for delivery to shops. He is locally well known as a devotee of Kāḷiyammaṉ and Murugaṉ. Following twenty-six months of imprisonment under the Prevention of Terrorism Act and Emergency Regulations in one unlisted and four listed sites of detention, Cittiravēl was released in 1993, no longer physically able to support his family as a porter. During his experience of interrogation and ill-treatment in detention, he suffered bilateral fractures of both hips. Scarring from these fractures resulted in a permanently frozen pelvic girdle. Although Cittiravēl is permanently crippled as a result of torture, he enacts a vow to cross the bed of hot coals during the annual propitiation of his village goddess, Vīramākāḷi.

Cittiravēl has been walking the fire for thirteen years, with the exception of 1991–93, the years of his imprisonment. Like other devotees, he speaks of the Ammaṉ's "grace." He explains, in his gentle voice, that when promises of vows are kept every year, "The Ammaṉ will relieve you of suffering." Cittiravēl wears three wide white lines of sacred ash on his forehead, which are intersected by a mark of vermilion powder and sandal paste in the shape of Murugaṉ's *vēl* (sacred lance). He is a dark man, and he applies ash carefully on his forehead every morning, giving him a striking appearance. His work as a porter made him a familiar figure in the streets of Batticaloa town before the early 1990s, a period of intense violence in the Eelam wars.

I met Cittiravēl at the home of a family I knew well. When I first saw him he was napping on a narrow wooden bench on the veranda, tucked almost into a fetal position. When he arose, we sipped cups of tea while he talked about the rituals his father knew, for his father had been a *pūjāri* at the Vīramākāḷi temple, well known for conducting a ritual in which the god Hanumān (Tamil: Anumān) is summoned to answer questions. This ritual, known as *maipārttal* ("ink reading"), has become popular in the present context of extreme uncertainty and doubt. He told me about his wife and children, and then about his detention in four Sri Lankan prisons.

On July 4, 1991, Cittiravēl and several other porters were carrying heavy loads of sarongs in the afternoon heat. They were arrested by the police as suspected LTTE supporters. His wife searched everywhere for him, although her searching remained fruitless for months, until someone who had been inside the detention camp on Pioneer Road reported that Cittiravēl was there and alive. When he was first taken to the camp, he was forced to enter a large water tank, in which he was questioned and repeatedly dunked under water throughout the night. Finally, he was stabbed in the thigh and removed from the tank. Then his torturers packed the large knife wound with salt and chili powder and tied his thigh tightly. He was hung from a beam during continuing interrogation while his torturers burned the skin of his legs in many places with cigarettes. They had been drinking and repeatedly demanded, "You tell the names of the Tigers." Later, while his legs and arms were chained, one of the men knocked out four upper front teeth with a single blow of his fist. He also sustained a large wound on the left side of his skull.

Cittiravēl's thumbs were then tied together behind his back, and he was hoisted high off the floor, hanging again from the rafters. While suspended, he was severely beaten with a large *akappai* (a wooden utensil for stirring large pots of rice). As the beatings continued for a long time, the rope frayed and he fell to the floor: "When I regained consciousness they put each of my arms through a tire and ordered me to get up. But I couldn't." Cittiravēl suffered bilateral hip fractures. In the course of continuing years of detention, scarring of the fractured hip joints, which never healed properly, resulted in a chronically frozen pelvic girdle. After six months, Cittiravēl was transferred several times, and in the third year of incarceration, he was released from a fifth place of imprisonment. He was taken to the converted Piḷḷaiyār temple grounds, which served as a camp for the displaced in the capital. His wife sold her gold wedding earrings and made her first trip out of the peripheralized eastern region to bring her husband home. Cittiravēl credits her with intervening in his attempts to end his life several times during the following year.

When I asked him how he understood the purpose of his torturers' actions and what reasons were given for the systematic trauma he experienced, he simply answered, "They assumed that I was LTTE, and they were punishing me. They did this after drinking liquor."

I can think of no more powerful example of what Michel Foucault means when he states:

> the body is also directly involved in a political field; power relations have an immediate hold upon it; they invest it, mark it, train it, torture it, force it to carry out tasks, to perform ceremonies, to emit signs. This political investment of the body is bound up, in accordance with complex reciprocal relations, with its economic use; it is largely as a force of production that the body is invested with relations of power and domination; but, on the other hand, its constitution as labour power is possible only if it is caught up in a system of subjection (in which need is also a political instrument meticulously prepared, calculated and used); the body becomes a useful force only if it is both a productive body and a subjected body.[21]

Here, the power of the state is inscribed on the body through torture, its discipline written into Cittiravēl's now permanently scarred body. On the day he was arrested, he was only carrying sarongs, although after his arrest, there was a rumor that he carried tiger-striped camouflage T-shirts for the LTTE. Cittiravēl's body is inscribed with rumor. As in every zone of war, "information that came in the form of rumor was often treated as knowledge and, in a sense, became knowledge."[22] But Cittiravēl says he did not do anything wrong. In his own words, "I was only carrying things."

Torture is used to control "punishable" people, to force them into submissiveness and obedience,[23] but through ritual ceremonies that dignify the violated body-self, Cittiravēl's body is resignified. Before the gathered collectivity at the temple, during his enactment of the vow of crossing a scorching trench of glowing embers, his body symbolizes the capacity to persevere. He has improvised a "pivoting" manner of walking with his body bent at the waist, swinging one foot at a time as far as he is able. In his slow sideways manner of mobility, he continues to keep his promise to the goddess Kāḷi to cross the hot coals of the fire pit during her annual propitiation at the local temple. Within the reality of the local context, this is an act of defiant survival. Large numbers of local observers collectively voice the religiously validating *mantra,* "Harō harā!" in unison as he slowly crosses the deep firepit for Kāḷi—Vīramākāḷi—the goddess of courage. At this moment, multiple and contradictory meanings are written onto this body.

TELLING ORACLES (*VĀKKU SOLLUṞATU*)

The propitiatory rituals we have been examining emphasize a dissolution of self and a profound identification with Kāḷi; and this is nowhere as evident as in the expressiveness of oracles. The work of "oracles" (*kaṭṭātikaḷ,* or *teyvam āṭumākkaḷ,* deity-dancers), changed in Batticaloa during the 1980s and early 1990s as their practices became more visible, rather than collapsing along with the health care infrastructure and the judiciary during the prolonged war. In the aftermath of military occupation and thousands of disappearances, people could not take their problems to government authorities and so turned to a different form of agency: local goddesses, earlier called upon to bestow health and prosperity, remove disease, increase the paddy harvest, and bring the cooling rains, who are now urgently asked to intercede in violent events and to provide information.

In local temple ritual, oracles merge with *śakti,* the active, female energy of the Hindu cosmos, receiving her empowerment in a close relationship with a particular local goddess. During oracular rituals, body and voice take on extraordinary significance. The moment in which the oracle's body is commingled with the presence of the Amma<u>n</u> is referred to in Tamil as *uruvarutal* (assuming form). As one oracle explained:

> Before the time when I am dancing, I come and stand at that place. When I come and stand in the middle of the third hall, I am just my name. Then the Amma<u>n</u> is coming. She enters the body by moving from the ground into the tip of the big toes and the Śakti then rises, coming into the hips. First the legs will tremble, and the knees will shake, trembling like flowers on a tree. Then the *pūjāri* tucks cooling margosa leaves at the waist and places *cilampu* [heavy brass anklets or bracelets, which are sacralized] on the wrists. After that, the *pūjāri* rubs sacred ash and turmeric powder on the center of our forehead while reciting mantras and the Śakti rises to the throat. There is a feeling of heat [*vekkatayirukkum*]. Then we sit before the entrance to the inner sanctum—that Śakti will be here between the hips. After that, only Teyvam speaks [*tēyvamtānē sollura*]. Śakti is speaking from here [the *matti,* the naval region]. When I am dancing, Śakti is giving some words that she is expressing out [*veḷiyē sollutu*]. This is the moment of expressing oracles. Through my body. Through my tongue.

Oracles describe *śakti* possession as a painful sacrifice of the body, reporting feelings of unbearable heat and a trembling like the "shivering when one suffers from fever." They may also, particularly if embodying the agency of Kāḷi, describe an overwhelming feeling of *āvēcam* ("uncontrollable emotion, fury, wrath"). Oracles' speech and body language are considered divine, not their own, and they are therefore not held responsible for their words and actions. At the point in ritual when the hot energy of *śakti* reaches the level of the throat and the ability to speak in their individual human voices is lost, oracles may burn camphor on their tongues. They say they cannot remember what transpires during possession experiences. Such "active forgetting" and mimesis[24] during *śakti* ritual enable them to reinforce a redemptive memory, and reconstitute collective identity.

One of the most dramatic scenes I witnessed in an Amma<u>n</u> temple was entirely lost to the memory of the oracle who performed it. At the Kallady

Kāḷi temple in 1992, several thousand people had gathered to witness fire-walking on the seventh evening of the annual propitiation. It was dark, and the crowds were kept clear of the wide sacred area around the fire pit by constant patrolling of the temple trustees. The fire pit was prepared for hundreds of devotees to walk over in a few minutes. The oracle who would lead the fire walk was wearing a red sari with white plumes of *kamukampū* at his waist. At this heightened moment of ritual, three tall army officers from the nearby camp strode boldly into the cleared space surrounding the long hot bed of coals. There were rumors that arrests were imminent. Suddenly, the oracle rushed from the shrine, tore furiously across the space, and, growling angrily at them in the unbearable rage of Kāḷi, chased them out. And the officers did move quickly out.

The lives of oracles I met in Batticaloa have touched death in some way—they have lost children, husbands, or wives, or have received the "grace" of the Goddess in surviving near-death illness. They are women and men of both high and low castes. In many instances, a close member of the oracles' kin group, often deceased, also experienced oracular possession. The oracles themselves, ordinary people living in extraordinary historical circumstance of violence, experience the additional trauma of bearing witness and affirming the terror of annihilation.

The following condensed case is a typical interaction between a devotee and an oracle concerning a disappearance. Daily gatherings of as many as ninety people seek the help of this particular oracle for Kāḷiyamman͟:

> An elderly mother with white hair, a faded blue cotton sari, and a striking air of grace rose from the crowd and took the place in front of the oracle for *vettila vaiccu kēkkiṟatu* ["putting betel and asking"]. Her natal home is beyond Kovilporativu, where people say the helicopters are strafing. This mother has lost eight members of her family, including her husband. Her surviving daughter and grandchildren have moved in with her. The army is occupying her home now—a common practice in the area—so they have moved to an abandoned house. The most recently "disappeared" family member is a son who went to sell paddy and never returned. She has come to ask if he is alive. The female oracle confirms his death through singing a verse of a Tamil song from an old popular film [*Pālum Paḻamum*] while looking into the mother's eyes:
>
> Let things gone be gone
> Who in this world is living eternally?
>
> Then the oracle advises the mother, "Now you are with your daughter and three grandchildren. It's your responsibility to take care of them now. Live for them." She placed the offering of betel leaves, areca nut, flower, and a ten-rupee note back into the mother's hands. Her practice is to return the *vettilaipāku* offering when the person asked about is dead. She may return as many as ten offerings a day.
>
> Others who have gathered, bringing their own problems, then ask the eld-

erly mother questions about the area where she has come from and about how she is managing, showing their concern. They also talk with her about rice rations that she is eligible to obtain. Before they depart, the mother is reminded by the oracle that earlier, before the problems, they had annually worshipped Kāḷi and Vīrapattira<u>n</u> in the house compound. In a commanding voice, the oracle tells her that this must be done where she is now living.

Oracular utterances are frequently closed either by insisting that the devotee enact a propitiatory ritual or perform a vow such as crossing the fire, or by giving the devotee something from the Amma<u>n</u> shrine. Elaine Scarry points out that the body and voice are the most elemental categories we have, which we use in moments of creativity. To lose speech, therefore, is a sign of death, of the unspeakable.[25] Torture, as both she and Valentine Daniel have so well described,[26] destroys the capacity of speech. Moreover, the language-destroying pain of torture disintegrates the content of one's world and self. In the following interaction, the pain of oracular possession stands in opposition to violence inscribed upon the body through torture—while the oracle brings into knowledge the most inaccessible Otherness of the tortured body of the "disappeared." A large part of the work of oracles today is acknowledgment of injury that is beyond language, and injury veiled in political unspeakability.

A father whose son was one of 158 persons arrested by the security forces at the Vantharumulai refugee camp on September 5, 1990, positions himself before the oracle. The entire camp witnessed the mass arrests, but not even one of the individuals arrested has been found. This father has come to the oracle after receiving an official letter from the Ministry of Defense informing him that a thorough check of their detention records has been completed, according to which his son had neither been arrested nor imprisoned. He holds the letter of the so-called final report on his son in his hand, which in effect denies his son's existence as a still-living prisoner, or as dead.

He has come to the oracle to ask about the fate of his son, who has now been missing for almost three years. In response, the oracle uses both body and voice as an instrument for reenacting the son's experience of torture, experiencing his pain, calling out incoherently for approximately fifteen minutes, sometimes voicing the word *erivu* ("burning"), then vomiting. She returns his *vettilaipāku* offering, and lapses into an unconscious state lying on the sand. She then stands half bent as though being beaten, and vomits again. She holds her head, arms, neck, back, and legs—saying that she feels pain all over. She complains that it is too difficult for her. The oracle crawls to the shrine room. We hear her retching. By the time she eventually returns, those gathered expect her pronouncement of the death of his son. She does not attribute his son's death to the army. She reveals that he was incarcerated in Boosa prison and survived to be released. She tells the father that his son is living in the south near Galle, and he has changed his identity by becoming a Muslim. The Father is crying. He asks helplessly, "Now how am I going to find him there?"

Voicing the incoherent sounds of the tortured, representing injury on behalf of those silenced, oracles transform absence into presence, giving pain a place in the world. It often seems that oracles are not attempting to make sense of unacceptable social suffering—but rather are trying to find a voice to express unresolved grief in an altered world where the rule is to "keep quiet" about broken connections in the closest circle of human relationships.

Places of oracular ritual have also become the trusted space for treatment of physical and emotional wounds of torture in a region where little of the larger world is allowed to enter. The following is a summary of an arrest in Batticaloa under the Emergency regulations:

> An agricultural laborer from paddy fields in the interior, accompanied by his wife, was brought in front of the oracle shaking uncontrollably: He had just been released from his third arrest. His home is Ayttiyamalai. He has four children, and he is *not* an LTTE fighter. He has lost the sight of one eye, and there are deep wounds in the top of his feet where he says his army interrogators ground and gouged wounds with their boots.
>
> The female oracle looked steadily at him. There was no alteration in his uncontrollable tremors. Still looking hard at him, she stated, "This will happen to you again." She told them to go and bring three *iḷanīr* to the shrine. Someone went off with the wife to get the coconuts. When they returned the oracle placed the three coconuts in front of the statue of Kāḷi and called *śakti* into them. He drank one *iḷanīr* in the shrine room, and she explained that this would heal the wounds.

It is difficult to know how to assess the immediate interpersonal experience in this case. It disturbed me that he was told just after his release that it would happen again. The laborer seemed to benefit simply from contact and connection with the oracle, whom he believed had Kāḷi in her. The oracle creates an opening for trauma to make its way into collective experience and memory.[27] Moreover, she does not differentiate herself from the suffering of others. I described this particular interaction to another oracle, a man known to speak as the temple deity of a nearby Amma<u>n</u> temple, with whom I had many long conversations. I asked for his reaction. He simply said, "Sometimes Kāḷi will speak out like that." The oracles' religious imagination incorporates and reflects the world of chaos in which both they and those who seek their help live—a world in which people do not enjoy a sense of control over events. Even in conditions of extreme hardship and terror, the oracles or deity-dancers allow speech to be born.

CONCLUSION

This chapter takes seriously the work of local oracles for Kāḷi in eastern Sri Lanka, who now embody and interpret the injury of war. It has become their work to address agonizing doubts about lost connections, memory that cannot be erased and wounds that cannot heal. In Batticaloa, oracular revelation is a cultural confluence where many possibilities meet—where suffering and death are acknowledged, where courage can be instilled, where information about the future and protection might be given. To speak of unspeakable violation, a safe witness is necessary,[28] and through their presencing of the local goddess, oracles presence this witness. Veena Das[29] and Lindsay French[30] ask whether making sense of suffering is necessarily the concern of people whose lives rest on power relations over which they perceive they have no control. Das has suggested that "making meaning of suffering" is a discourse of the powerful. In the cosmology of oracles, who are compelled to act as embodied agents of Kāḷi and who serve as witnesses to the painful histories of shattered families, suffering is considered an inevitable part of human experience.[31] However, in acting under the governance of Kāḷi's agency, they reframe their world altered by the intrusive configuration of military checkpoints, bunkers, and detention camps—and they undermine the power of the state inscribed on the Tamil body through torture by enacting vows to Kāḷi of fire-walking and piercing the body—vows in which bodily wounds miraculously vanish.

While the erasure from official history of summary executions and the use of systematic violence continue to be part of the work of the Ministry of Defence, it is the work of oracles to speak and, through moments of acknowledgment of pain and loss, to embody and interpret the profound injury of war. In the immediate aftermath of arrests and abductions, Kāḷi's oracles calm family members, and during *śakti* rituals, through the mimetic courage of oracles, local histories of violent events are expressed. In a historical moment when dissent is impossible, amid fear, displacement, and unnatural death, it has become part of Kāḷi's many tasks to overcome political silencing, to embody memory, and to reconstitute a diminished world.

NOTES

Tamil transliterations in this chapter follow the Tamil lexicon system, but words whose Sanskrit spellings are more commonly known follow Sanskrit conventions. For example, Kāḷi is given in the Tamil form, but *cakti*/Cakti is rendered as *śakti*/Śakti, Civa̲n̲ as Śiva, A̲n̲umā̲n̲ as Hanumān, *pakti* as *bhakti,* and *pūcai*/*pūcari* as *pūjā*/*pūjāri*—unless they are included in compound words or proper names, in which case they retain their Tamil forms (*amma̲n̲pakti, caktivalimai, parācakti,* and Caktirāṇi).

1. See Rachel Fell McDermott, "Kālī's New Frontiers: A Hindu Goddess on the Internet," chapter 12 in this volume.

2. This chapter is based upon my field research in Batticaloa District, eastern Sri Lanka, a significant period of which was made possible by the SSRC–MacArthur Foundation Program on Peace and Security in a Changing World. The ethnographic data represented here covered a period of thirty-nine months, which spanned the

years 1991–94 and included two return trips to the eastern coastal plain in 1996 and 1999, the latter supported by the American Philosophical Society. I have deemed it necessary to alter personal names, place-names, and in some cases time sequences in order to protect people whose experiences are part of the continuing suffering inside the eastern region under the Prevention of Terrorism Act and Emergency Rule. In a few cases, I have attributed the violence experienced in the life of one person to two different pseudonyms. The actual names of locations of massacres by the government's security forces and the place-names of prisons and camps are correctly given. The names of individuals who collaborated with this research have been withheld whenever I thought that anonymity was required and whenever confidentiality was requested. I bear sole responsibility for any shortcomings in the presentation of these ethnographic materials.

3. Localized sets of named matriclans (*kuṭi*) are a distinctive component of Hindu and Muslim social structure in eastern Sri Lanka, where male elders of the local matriclans serve as the trustees of village temples and mosques. Men and women acquire matriclan membership from their mothers, and marriages must conform to a rule of *kuṭi* exogamy (out-marriage). For analyses of the matrilineal clan system, see Dennis B. McGilvray, *Tamils and Moors: Ethnic Minorities in Sri Lanka's War Zone,* forthcoming, and "Mukkuvar Vannimai: Tamil Caste and Matriclan Ideology in Batticaloa, Sri Lanka," in *Caste Ideology and Interaction,* ed. id., Cambridge Papers in Social Anthropology 9 (Cambridge: Cambridge University Press, 1982), pp. 34–97. See also Patricia Lawrence, "Violence, Suffering, Amman: The Work of Oracles in Sri Lanka's Eastern War Zone," in *Violence and Subjectivity,* ed. Veena Das (Berkeley and Los Angeles: University of California Press, 2000), pp. 171–204, esp. p. 177.

4. Karen Kapadia, *Siva and Her Sisters* (Delhi: Oxford University Press, 1996), pp. 124–60.

5. In the ritual language used by possessed deity-dancers and priests, the deity-dancer is usually referred to as a flowering tree (*pūmaram*). When the presence of Kāḷi is overwhelming in the extreme, the priest may say, "This flowering tree is wilting" and summon a gentler form of Śakti (Tamil: Cakti) such as the goddess Māriyamma<u>n</u>, Kannakaiyamma<u>n</u>, or Pēcciyamma<u>n</u> as a replacement. Based on my research, Kannakaiyamma<u>n</u>, who represents the Tamil ideal of wifely loyalty, chastity, and self-control, seldom possesses individuals.

6. Richard Gombrich and Gananath Obeyesekere, *Buddhism Transformed: Religious Change in Sri Lanka* (Princeton: Princeton University Press, 1988).

7. Stanley Jeyaraja Tambiah, *Buddhism Betrayed? Religion, Politics, and Violence in Sri Lanka* (Chicago: University of Chicago Press, 1992); and A. Jeyaratnam Wilson, "Race, Religion, Language and Class in the Subnationalisms of Sri Lanka," in *Collective Identities, Nationalisms, and Protest in Modern Sri Lanka,* ed. Michael Roberts (2 vols.; Colombo: Marga Institute, 1997), 2: 347–55.

8. Rohan Gunaratna, *War and Peace in Sri Lanka* (Colombo: Institute of Fundamental Studies, 1987); and Chelvadurai Manogaran and Bryan Pfaffenberger, eds., *The Sri Lankan Tamils* (Boulder, Colo.: Westview Press, 1994).

9. Chandra Richard De Silva, "The Impact of Nationalism on Education: The Schools Take-Over (1961) and the University Admissions Crisis, 1970–1975," in *Collective Identities, Nationalisms, and Protest in Modern Sri Lanka,* ed. Michael Roberts (2 vols.; Colombo: Marga Institute, 1979), 2: 103–62; and Stanley Jeyaraja Tambiah,

Sri Lanka: Ethnic Fratricide and the Dismantling of Democracy (Chicago: University of Chicago Press, 1986).

10. Sunil Bastian, "Political Economy of Ethnic Violence in Sri Lanka," in *Mirrors of Violence: Communities, Riots and Survivors in South Asia,* ed. Veena Das (Delhi: Oxford University Press, 1990), pp. 299–303; E. Valentine Daniel, "The Individual in Terror," in *Embodiment and Experience: The Existential Ground of Culture and Self,* ed. Thomas J. Csordas, Cambridge Studies in Medical Anthropology (Cambridge: Cambridge University Press, 1994), p. 235; Tambiah, *Sri Lanka: Ethnic Fratricide and the Dismantling of Democracy,* pp. 13–93; and Serena Tennekoon, "Newspaper Nationalism," in *Sri Lanka: History and the Roots of Conflict,* ed. Jonathan Spencer (New York: Routledge, 1990), pp. 205–6.

11. Extrajudicial executions include the first of two massacres in the vicinity of Kokkadichcholai, the Sathurukondan massacre, the disappearances from the Vantharumulai refugee camp, the Mailanthanai killings, the retaliatory killings at the fishing village of Puthukudiruppu after the Kattankudy massacre, the massacre of Udumpankulam, and the many disappearances within Amparai washermen families that were not reported to the Presidential Commission of Inquiry. There have been other extrajudicial killings of Tamil people by various arms of the government forces and groups allied with them in Tirukovil, Komari, Karaitivu, Pandiruppu, Kalmunai, Maruthamunai, Thuraineelavanai, Kurumunveli, Mandur, Vellaveli, Thikkodai, Kakkachchiveddai, Palachcholai, Periyaporathivu, Kovilporativu, Palugamam, Kaluvanchikudy, Ampilanthurai, Nochchimunai, Punnaicholai, Koddaimunai, Puliantivu, Unnichchai, Karadiyanaru, Ayttiyamalai, Periyapulumalai, Pulipainchakal, Chenkalady, Kommaturai, Sittandy, Murukkottanchenai, Santhiveli, Valaichchenai, and Vakarai. This list is far from complete and is submitted primarily to offer a sense of the pervasiveness of extrajudicial killing ordinary Tamil people are exposed to.

12. Joseph Pararajasingham, "'Clearing' Batticaloa," *Northeastern Herald* 1, no. 2 (Colombo, Sri Lanka, 1992): 3–4.

13. For more than twenty-seven of the past forty-three years, Sri Lanka has been ruled under a declared state of emergency, and the security forces commit serious violations with impunity under the emergency powers and the Prevention of Terrorism Act (PTA), which "dispense with the normal safeguards against arbitrary detention, disappearance and torture that are found in the ordinary law, and thus facilitate abuse," Elizabeth Nissan writes in *Sri Lanka: A Bitter Harvest* (London: Minority Rights Group, 1996), p. 30. Following arbitrary arrest, a person can be detained for an unlimited period under the combined PTA and emergency regulations. People have sometimes been detained for more than five years without having a court order or even a charge filed against them. Information provided in 1995 by INFORM, Sri Lankan Information Monitor, 5 Jayaratne Avenue, Colombo 5, Sri Lanka.

14. Veena Das, "Sexual Violence, Discursive Formations and the State," and Ritu Menon and Kamla Bhasin, "'They Wanted to Die': Women, Kinsmen and Partition" (papers presented at the conference, "Violence against Women: Victims and Ideologies," Sri Lanka Foundation, Colombo, Sri Lanka, March 28–31, 1996); Diana R. Kordon, L. I. Edelman et al., *Psychological Effects of Political Repression* (Buenos Aires: Sudamericana/Planeta, 1988 [originally published in 1986 as *Efectos psicológicos de la represión política*]); Marcelo Suarez-Orozco, "A Grammar of Terror: Psycho-

cultural Responses to State Terrorism in Dirty War and Post-Dirty War Argentina," in *The Paths to Domination, Resistance, and Terror,* ed. Carolyn Nordstrom and JoAnn Martin (Berkeley and Los Angeles: University of California Press, 1992), pp. 219–59; and Michael T. Taussig, *The Nervous System* (New York: Routledge, 1992).

15. Gunaratna, *War and Peace in Sri Lanka,* pp. 18–27.

16. Arthur and Joan Kleinman, "How Bodies Remember: Social Memory and Bodily Experience of Criticism, Resistance, and Delegitimation Following China's Cultural Revolution," *New Literary History* 25 (1994): 707–23.

17. Obeyesekere and Gombrich, *Buddhism Transformed,* pp. 9, 11.

18. "Ammāḷ" and "Amma<u>n</u>" are interchangeable honorific terms of address meaning "Mother" that are employed for all local Hindu goddesses in eastern Sri Lanka; see Patricia Lawrence, "Violence, Suffering, Amman." "Tāyār," a third frequently used term of address in the region, also means "Mother." The most commonly enshrined forms of the Goddess along Sri Lanka's eastern littoral include Kāḷiyamma<u>n</u>, Kannakaiyamma<u>n</u>, Kaṭalacciyamma<u>n</u>, Māriyamma<u>n</u>, Pattirakāḷiyamma<u>n</u>, Pēcciyamma<u>n</u>, and Tirōpataiyamma<u>n</u>.

19. Torture of Tamil people is continuing in the region. Electroshock torture has been practiced in detention camps under the command of the Sri Lankan army, the government's special task force, and the countersubversive units. The special task force regularly sweeps through Tamil residential areas, sometimes arresting several hundred Tamil people at a time. In 1996, after speaking about a boy who was "put on a metal bed" for electroshock treatment and then describing the appearance of another young boy's back, which had been severely burned with a heavy washerman's iron following a roundup of about 300 youths in the village of Thuraineelavanai, an interviewee in the village stated, "The torture we are undergoing is very unbearable [*taṅkamuṭiyāta*]. These roundups are taking place here every month. We want an amicable settlement and peace in the country." The Human Rights Task Force and members of the International Committee of the Red Cross (ICRC) are not permitted to visit all detention centers in the east. Lawyers representing prisoners from the eastern region stress the fact that forced confessions are admissible as evidence, and the burden is upon the accused.

20. The majority of the animals offered at this temple are auctioned at the end of the annual festival. Several fowl or a goat may be sacrificed during an all-male nighttime ritual performed to ensure protection of the area (*ūr kāval*) for the coming year. With perseverance, I managed to bypass the gender barrier and have described this ritual based on firsthand observation elsewhere (Patricia Lawrence, forthcoming).

21. Michel Foucault, *Discipline and Punish: The Birth of the Prison* (New York: Vintage Books, 1979), pp. 25–26.

22. Anna Simmons, "The Beginning of the End," in *Fieldwork under Fire: Contemporary Studies of Violence and Survival,* ed. Carolyn Nordstrom and Antonius C. G. M. Robben (Berkeley and Los Angeles: University of California Press, 1994), p. 53.

23. Carole Nagengast, "Violence, Terror, and the Crisis of the State," *Annual Review of Anthropology* 23 (1994): 122.

24. Michael T. Taussig, *Mimesis and Alterity: A Particular History of the Senses* (New York: Routledge, 1993).

25. Elaine Scarry, *The Body in Pain: The Making and Unmaking of the World* (New York: Oxford University Press, 1985).

26. Daniel, "Individual in Terror, " pp. 237–38.

27. Jonathan Boyarin, ed., *Remapping Memory: The Politics of TimeSpace* (Minneapolis: University of Minnesota Press, 1994).

28. Shoshana Felman and Dori Laub, *Testimony: Crises of Witnessing in Literature, Psychoanalysis, and History* (New York: Routledge, 1992).

29. Veena Das, "Moral Orientations to Suffering: Legitimation, Power, and Healing," in *Health and Social Change in International Perspective,* ed. Lincoln C. Chen, Arthur Kleinman, and Norma Ware (Boston: Dept. of Population and International Health, Harvard School of Public Health, 1994), pp. 139–67.

30. Lindsay French, "The Political Economy of Injury and Compassion: Amputees on the Thai-Cambodia Border," in *Embodiment and Experience: The Existential Ground of Culture and Self,* ed. Thomas J. Csordas, Cambridge Studies in Medical Anthropology (Cambridge: Cambridge University Press, 1994), pp. 69–115.

31. For comparative ethnographic documentation of visitations from Tamil goddesses in which individuals are compelled to become healers and containers of *śakti* in Tamilnadu, South India, see Isabelle Nabokov, *Religion against the Self: An Ethnography of Tamil Rituals* (New York: Oxford University Press, 2000), pp. 19–30.

CHAPTER 6

Kālī Māyī

Myth and Reality in a Banaras Ghetto

Roxanne Kamayani Gupta

Kālī Māyī. I can still see her there behind the iron gate, well settled in the midst of all that noise, confusion and filth, her temple a small sanctuary of human frailty in the holy city of hardened decay.

Banaras, 1990. If it weren't for Mark Dyczkowski, I would have never known her. One night on the way back from the Chinese restaurant in Lanka, he casually stops his scooter in front of her place. It's autumn, not rainy season. Why is there a mud puddle in front of her gate? Water from the communal water tap must have spilled over—one spigot for the whole congested ghetto. "You don't know about Kālī Māyī? You should," he says before he drives off, leaving me on her doorstep just behind Durgā Kuṇḍ. There She has been living without my ever having heard of Her, just a stone's throw from my room at Gaṅgā Maṭh on the river, a ten-minute walk past the post office and theater, through the Assi crossing. This is strange to me since I've made it my business to investigate all the terrifying forms of the Goddess in these parts. For nearly a year I have been living in Banaras on a research grant, undertaking a study of the Aghorīs, one of the most enigmatic of all Hindu ascetic sects. Throughout North India, they are infamous for their extremely transgressive practices, which fly in the face of Brāhmaṇical Hinduism's obsessive concern with ritual purity. The Aghorīs act out their denial of the distinction between spirit and substance, purity and pollution, by ingesting any form of food or intoxicant, engaging in a variety of sexual practices, ritually or otherwise, and allegedly meditating on dead bodies in cremation ground rites.[1] Although they call themselves Śaivites, Aghorīs are nonetheless inextricably bound to the Goddess. It is no wonder the terrifying Daśamahāvidyās (the ten "great" forms of the Goddess), which include Kālī and Tārā, are the preferred tutelary deities invoked by these types of Tāntrikas. For just as the Aghorīs, in emulating Śiva in the form of Bhairava, are the most marginal of ascetics, marking the outer boundaries of the official Hindu world, Kālī likewise lives on the edge, enthroned in the center of heterodox practice.

In the process of my research, I have come to understand how the Aghorīs, deliberately embracing the status of outcastes among outcastes, play an important role for the society by literally "eating the sins" of their mainstream caste Hindu followers. In countless myths and hagiographies, the most famous Aghorīs of North India are attributed with having the power, not only to swallow polluted and poisonous substances, but to transform them into harmless or benign residues. In this regard, they emulate Śiva, whose throat is blue from having swallowed the poison that emerged from the churning of the milky ocean. But the Aghorīs draw this power from their invocation of the Goddess, who by Her very material nature encompasses all substance. As the embodiment of all creation, She negates the very possibility of purity or pollution. Hence the Aghorīs move far beyond standard Tantric ritual practice not only by invoking Her with the *pañcamakāra*—meat, fish, parched grain, wine, and sexual intercourse—but in addition by offering their feces and urine.[2]

For an anthropologist, hearing about these transgressive practices was one thing and witnessing or experiencing them was another. The larger universe of meaning in which such radical practices made perfect sense was shrinking in the face of modernity and its aftermath, even in Banaras. Hence it was not every day that one met a practicing Aghorī, or a devotee of Kālī, for that matter. I was beginning to discover that to wander into that confused intersection of hard-core fact and fantasy was to mess irrevocably, not only with the reality of the "other," but also with one's own sense of identity.

At first, as I enter her small, one-room shrine, the old woman doesn't know what to make of me, a thin, pale woman with long blonde hair, dressed in sari and *sindūr,* my large black bag (containing pen, notebook, video camera, and a bunch of bananas) under my arm. As I drink in the dimly lit room with my eyes, the old Māyī sits crouched at the feet of her precious Kālī Mā (fig. 6.1). A bent and shrunken woman, perhaps in her sixties, she stares at me through huge, little-girl eyes. While Māyī huddles, back bent, Mā stands there straight and regal on Her pedestal, black as coal, cool as night. A thin young thing, so pretty. A Bengali Mātā, for sure: three feet tall; lean and hungry; and endowed with two small, barely perceptible Dracula-sharp teeth protruding from between Her slightly parted lips; a bright red tongue po-

Figure 6.1 Kālī Māyī with her image of Kālī Mā. Photo by Roxanne Gupta, January 1992.

litely lolling out, and the faintest of all-knowing smiles. Long black hair hangs loose down Her back, all the way to Her knees. She is dressed in Her best skirt and blouse, the red one with the gold tinsel border, and has a painted brass crown on Her head.

Eyes full of calm and compassion. I want to stare into them for the longest time, but when my gaze wanders to Her feet, it gets caught up in each and every item that lies on Her cluttered altar. So many *things:* small pictures of terrifying goddesses in yellowed frames, soapstone incense holders, dry old pieces of fruit, human and animal skulls, faded marigold garlands, a bowl of ash, stones of various sizes, a few Śiva *liṅga*s, tin containers, a copper water vessel, a large seashell, some glass bangles, a *sindūr* pot, a bell, and a camphor lamp. Nothing worth any money, but precious goods nonetheless, these objects somehow look as if they have grown there, or at least belong there together, laden with life force, caked with prayers, dust, and ash.

Behind and above Her head, Māyī has decorated the smoke-blackened room with a now faded glittering shroud like those placed over dead bodies on their way to the cremation ground. Well-worn calendars of bygone years featuring Hindu deities now hardly recognizable collect dust on the wall. A string of small red lights mingles with the cobwebs that hang from the ceiling. A Carnival of the Soul. Holy Halloween.

A thin young man dressed in a faded white *luṅgi* sits playing a flute on the front porch. He and a few bedraggled friends move in close to me and start rubbing tobacco and *gāñjā* for a chillum.[3] "Bam Bole!" They fire it up, offer it to me. The cloth is crusty with resin and I put my hands together in a gesture that is half gratitude and half self-defense. Thanks but no thanks; I am already high. You see, She simply sends me into inner space. Then, of course, there is the obligatory, "Which country, where do you stay, what are you doing in Kashi, How do you like our city of Lord Śiva *Hara Hara Mahādev Pārvatī Pate?*"[4]

"Fine." I want to be alone. With Her.

A half-hour of my rude withdrawal passes and the boys in the band disperse. Māyī and I sit in silence for another hour, me in intermittent meditation and Māyī in comfortable quiet. Not staring, not inquiring, not expecting nor asking for anything. What a rare treat, a temple where one is actually left alone.

Meditating on Kālī, I realize that as Her title "the Black One" suggests, She extends infinitely in all directions—into the primordial past, with Her roots in pre-Aryan tribal cultures, and equally into the future. She played an important role in Indian nationalism, and in the postmodern era, Her influence is global; of all the Hindu goddesses, in the West, Kālī's name is arguably the most recognizable.[5] In space, She similarly marks the outer edge. As the deity of cremation grounds, She lives on the outskirts of settlement, with spirits and ghouls as companions, Her visitors primarily the bereft and bereaved, madmen, criminals, and Tāntrikas—holy seekers on the fast track to realization. If, in time, She embodies the first and the last, in space, as close as death, She represents the near and the far. Marking the limits of both time and space, She encompasses and contains all that lies within.

After some time, I begin my homeward stirrings. Wearing a torn and faded red cloth wrapped around her brown leather skin, with sturdy hands and blackened fingernails, Māyī reaches into an aluminum tin to offer me *prasāda,* the leavings of the Goddess, stale milk sweets discarded who knows how long ago from the rundown *miṭhāi* (sweet) shop across the street. Not wanting to hurt her feelings, I take a nibble. Rancid. Terrible and sweet, just like Mā.

Soon it becomes my evening ritual to go there. At the end of the day, I have nowhere else to go. A letter has come from home. My marriage is over —the same marriage that began full of faith, here in this city, by this same holy river, nearly twenty years ago. The same marriage, in a sense, that could never have taken place without Her grace. Way back then, we had arrived at a little understanding, She and I . . .

Hyderabad, April 1973. My first year in India. Living in the South, I was practicing my classical dance five hours a day. It was spring, when the weather turns from hot to hotter. In no time at all, I had contracted a fever. Utterly debilitating, it began as a slow fire that soon ravished my entire body. For days on end, I had 102 degrees of fever, and soon 105, but no one around me seemed to know what could be done about it. My kind landlady Lakṣmī sat beside me nights, tears in her eyes, reciting the *Lalitā Sahasranāma,* the thousand names of the Goddess. My doctor, more interested in pulling up my sari to look at my legs than in diagnosing my disease, could admit me to the hospital, but said I would be the worse for it. So I stayed home in my little room on the roof, which every day turned into an oven, vomiting and shitting until there was nothing left to come up or out. Eventually, I got to the point where even a sip of water caused violent retching. Delirious and beyond pain, I began somewhat perversely to enjoy the feverish haze of consciousness to which I was hanging by a thread. One night, lying on my back under the starry sky, I saw the entire cosmos begin to spin, slowly at first, then more rapidly, until it formed a vortex, a tunnel that began to draw me in. At the last moment, I realized what was happening and only by a supreme effort of will managed to pull myself back into my body and drag it inside to safety.

This went on for more than two weeks, to the point where I no longer knew, and hardly cared, whether I would survive. Tottering on the edge of life and death, it was then that She appeared to me, at sunrise, in a dream:

> I am walking down the street in Hyderabad. Old and bent, a beggar woman slowly approaches from the opposite direction. As our paths are about to cross, she looks up at me, and I casually glance at her face. Suddenly, she takes on a very ugly and threatening demeanor. As I watch in horror and fascination, she begins to grow into a huge, dark, and towering figure, sprouting hundreds of heads, mouths, protruding teeth, and tongues, breasts, legs, and arms bearing weapons of destruction. I feel panic grip me in the pit of my stomach, and instantly know that I have no time to waste. Indeed, I sense that time is literally "of the essence." In a split second, it comes to me that no matter how

> frightened I feel inside, I must not show it, for she will only feed off my weakness. If I am doomed, at least I'll go down with dignity. Struggling to control my reactions, I lock my eyes into hers. Without moving, we stare at each other for an excruciatingly long time. Then the words form in my mind: "As black as she is, that is how white I must become." My eyes still locked in hers, I feel a tremendous power rise from deep within me. Using every ounce of remaining strength, in that excruciatingly slow and dampened dream state, I will myself to grow into a form equal to hers, sprouting heads, arms, and legs, but without weapons, smiling with confidence, free from anger. I feel my feigned fearlessness transform itself into a deep and abiding calm, which radiates outward like a searing light, countering her terror with compassion, becoming the perfect opposite, the perfect complement, the perfect white reflection of Her, Her Royal Blackness, She, My Nemesis, My Mirror, My Shadow. We have reached an understanding. It is a crystal moment of true balance and identity. It is the turning point. Standing perfectly still, I do not blink as I watch her shrink in size and return to the form of an old woman who hobbles on past me. I then feel my power withdraw back into the center of my body.[6]

At that moment, I awoke with the morning's first ray of sunlight shining in my face. My body was drenched in sweat, the fever broken. I lay perfectly still as the dream came flooding back to me, for I was still enveloped by a strange sound that not only vibrated inside my head, but permeated my entire body. It was the sound of a thousand winds moving in all directions of eight-dimensional space, harmonized into a single vibration. I shall never forget that sound, although there is no description in language that can begin to capture its absolute fullness. I would never have believed it, even in my dreams, but within a week I would find myself in Banaras, about to be married.

Twenty years later, here I am back in Banaras, looking into the eyes of that same "beggar woman" and seeing my own reflection there. Feeling Her terrible form flare up in my face, I have no choice but to look straight into Her eyes and face my own worst fears. Yes, I am the destroyer of my own destiny—a faithless woman, unfit for the role of *pativratā,* the wife who sacrifices on behalf of her husband. There is nowhere to hide in the mirror. Tears stream down my face. "Mā, please. What is love in the face of our ultimate freedom? He has a right to a happier life, someone who won't disappoint him as I have, but I don't want all those years to end in hatred. Mother, I beg you to help me, undeserving as I am." Her eyes stare back at me in blank pity.

Exposed by the unforgiving sun each day, I wait for the night and the promise of Her cool dark mercy. After countless hours of staring into the bottomless void of Her eyes, I begin to understand why Mā has taken on Her terrifying persona. She too is wretched, having swallowed the accumulated sin, guilt, and senseless suffering of countless lifetimes. Could she swallow mine? One night, as I confess my sins once more, as always, fully expecting, perhaps even hoping to be struck down by lightning or some other fitting punishment, I prepare myself for the usual waves of self-recrimination. But instead, I am pleasantly surprised by a change in Her expression. Behind that unwavering gaze, do I detect a slightly wicked little smile? Then a voice resounds inside my head: "Honey, I've seen it all. Why do you think I never married? And one more thing, I'm no Mother Theresa." I burst out in hysterical laughter.

Through the whole emotional circus, as on all other nights, Māyī sits quietly. Doesn't she think I'm crazy coming here to cry, and now laugh, at Mā's feet? Maybe she too has seen it all. The cat sits in the corner, howling for the fish pieces Māyī has hidden from her. The cat has scabs on her leg but knows she has a home. I wish I did.

Several times I try to get Māyī to tell me about her life, but she simply shrugs it off. I understand that she doesn't live much in the past. Finally, one night, she shows me a faded picture of a tall woman with long, matted hair. Not so many years ago, she explains, this was the outskirts of the city and looked like a jungle. Bengali Mātā, the Tantric *yoginī* in the photo, had installed a simple shrine to Kālī Mā over a *pañcamuṇḍa* (a pile of five skulls, human and animal, such as monkey, goat, or vulture, in order to create a site for invoking power). I figured this to have been about sixty years earlier, when the area was, according to Brajamadhaba Bhattacharya, heavily overgrown with mango, jackfruit, toddy palm, jamuns, peepals, and banyan.[7] The temple building was built later, probably sometime in the late 1950s. In her old age, Bengali Mātā "adopted" Māyī and her husband, a childless couple, as her *celās* (disciples) to help look after her and the place. When she died, they stayed on to serve Kālī Mā. Māyī's husband had died more than twenty years ago, leaving her alone. Now it was Mā who was looking after her.

I try to ask if Māyī was ever initiated into any Tantric practices, but she hardly understands my question. What is "Tantra" to her? She doesn't know any mantras or rituals; I doubt if she even knows how to meditate. But she does know how to make the daily *pūjā* offerings, to bathe Mā once a week (with the doors closed!) and according to her humble means to celebrate the yearly festival for Kālī on Diwali (Dīpāvalī) night. Most of all, she knows Mā's story, which she loves to tell over and over again. She doesn't have any idea that it is "only" a myth:

> Once there was a great battle with blood everywhere. Durgā fought the Buffalo Demon and slew him, but so many more demons were there. Every time she would slay one, from each drop of blood that fell on the ground another demon would spring up. So in order to save the world, out of Durgā's third eye came Kālī, the queen of destruction. She went on a killing spree, killing everything in sight. Killing until the whole world began to look like a cremation ground. Gods became frightened that nothing in the world would be left.

> They knew that only Lord Śiva could stop her, so he went and lay down on the earth. In her mad dance of destruction she accidentally stepped on his chest. When she looked down and saw that her foot was on her consort, she stopped dead in her tracks and in embarrassment stuck out her tongue. AHHHHHHH. That is why Mā's tongue is hanging out.[8]

Māyī asks me to buy Mā a new dress for Diwali, which is fast approaching. She needs a black one to wear during Navarātrī, the nine-nights festival of the Goddess, when all over the country, devotees are singing Her praises. In North India, especially, hundreds of thousands of devotees will be fasting, performing *pūjā,* and reciting the "Devī-Māhātmya," the story of Durgā and Her victorious battles with various demons. Kālī too is worshipped during the same period. I go to the shop and buy enough black silk for a new dress for the Goddess and a sari blouse for myself. Māyī makes noises about a new hairpiece, which I ignore. Of course, I can easily afford it, but I like Her ratty dreads—why should She look like just another Barbie doll?

Every night, I leave Māyī a few rupees on the altar, and buy her tea from the chai shop next door, fetching it in her dented aluminum tin. Now and then I give her some of my saris, and I keep her stocked with *cyavanprāś,* an Ayurvedic tonic for elders. I can afford to take care of her now, but what about when I am gone? If she gets used to me supporting her, then what? I am afraid for her future; she is already old, vulnerable. One afternoon, passing in a rickshaw, I catch a glimpse of her, bent over and struggling to wash her hair in the street, under the communal tap. It breaks my heart.

While I worry about her, Māyī is only worried about who will look after Mā when she is gone. I get an idea. I'll take her to the ashram, introduce her to the Guru, the Avadhūt.[9] He is, after all, a miracle worker; maybe he will take an interest in the old woman's plight. Early one morning, I hire an auto-rickshaw and off we head across the pontoon bridge at Ramnagar, taking the less traveled route to Parao, past the maharaja's palace and through the crowded bazaar. It takes us about forty-five hair-raising, exhaust-laden minutes to reach, and soon we are in the presence of the Guru himself. Huddled at his feet now, she asks him only one thing—to take responsibility for the temple. "There is no one after me to look after Mā." The Guru, who must have had at least a hundred old women crying at his feet in the past few days, looks at me and says, "Why don't *you* do it?"

"Me?!" Suddenly I picture myself camping there, cleaning the place up a bit, maybe lining the room with deep red tiles, installing proper lighting. Why not? I could open a small school for the kids from the neighborhood, mobilize the ghetto dwellers to agitate for better facilities from the municipality, open a family planning clinic. . . . Wait a minute! What is this, "City of Joy *Redux?*" Or just a convenient way to avoid going home to face the music? On the way back, we stop for a cold drink. It is so hot, I think it will be a treat for Māyī. But the next day, she comes down with a cough and fever from either the icy cold drink or the strain of the whole adventure, no closer to having solved her problem.

Filled with guilt, I make another attempt. Kīnā Rām Sthāl, the headquarters of the Kīnā Rāmī Aghorīs, the notorious Kālī worshippers on whom I am conducting research, is just down the road. I go there and make my plea to the resident *bābās.* "Please look after Māyī. At least once in a while, send her some food, make sure she gets medicine when she is sick. She is all alone." They assure me that they will look into it, but months go by and nothing happens. It begins to dawn on me that no one cares, no one is going to care. All these men who sing the praises of the Goddess, who chant Her thousand names and beat their chests in front of Her image, couldn't care less about the way they treat living women, especially one as old and useless as Māyī.

Finally, like Māyī, I resign myself to the fact that only Mā knows what is in store for her. Preparing to return to America, I leave some money with a trusted friend who lives nearby, requesting him to give her a small allowance each month. It's not much, but it's better than nothing. When I come to say goodbye, she holds my hand and walks me to the gate. I ask, "Will you remember me when I come again?" She replies, "Why not? When our hearts are one, where is the question of remembering?"

It is four years before I see her again. In the meantime, two women friends of mine are going to Banaras to study, so I give them some money and her address, asking them to look after her if they can. When they return, they tell me that they too grew quite fond of the old lady and gave her saris, food, and small amounts of money, and that she seems to be doing well. I am relieved at the news.

Banaras, 1995. In November, I finally make it back to her during a brief visit to my beloved city. I arrive late one afternoon, breathe a sigh of relief when I see the familiar gate, the small courtyard and cluttered room. Looks as if someone has painted the place in the meantime; the old posters are gone and the place looks a bit brighter. I walk in slowly and prostrate in front of Mā. She is as beautiful and ageless as ever, and since Diwali has just passed, She is wearing Her black dress, the one I bought Her.

"Mā, I am so grateful to you. My life is so much better now; I could never have dreamed that things would work out the way they have. All by your grace. I never forget the comfort you gave me during those dark nights."

Māyī watches me, looks at me as if to say, "I know you from somewhere . . . " Finished with my prayers, I sit down directly facing her and ask in Hindi, "Do you remember me?" Puzzled, she replies somewhat shakily, "Why not?" But I am not convinced.

Surprisingly, Māyī hasn't changed much, but she looks a bit thin and, despite the unseasonably cold weather, sits without a sweater or shawl. In fact, her clothes are literally in tatters. "Don't you have a sweater?" I ask her. She shakes her head. I wasn't prepared for this. All I have with me is my favorite Gujarati shawl, a rustic weave, nothing too expensive, but after years of carting it around America, Europe, and India, I am quite attached to it. It is light, but warm, and the colors don't show the dirt. Oh well, that's what sacrifice is all about, giving up things that mean something to you. I can buy another one. If I give her money, she will only use it for Mā, not herself. I take off the shawl and place it around her shoulders. Her face lights up like a small child's at Christmas. "I am going to Delhi, but I'll be back in a few weeks," I tell her. "I'll see you then." She follows me to the gate. "Come soon, daughter."

In December, I only have about a week in Banaras, but I can't wait to see her again. I plan to give her a brown sweater woven like a short jacket, one of my longtime favorites, brought from America, when I leave this time. I still remember the compliments I invariably got when I wore it at the university. It had seen its day, but it would be perfect for her. The shade even matches her skin.

When I enter the courtyard, I see she has company: a few shady-looking characters, typical Banarsiwalas[10]—unemployed young men in their thirties or maybe twenties (they age fast here) with oiled hair, unkempt in dirty *luṅgis* and Western shirts, red *pān* (betel) juice leaking from the corners of their mouths. A familiar sight. Many of the poorer young men in this part of the city have monkeys on their backs. Last year, we watched Bhābhījī's nephew die of a heroin overdose. Like most of them, he used to smoke *gāñjā* or take *bhāṅg* (a paste of marijuana and spices, which is eaten) on a regular basis. It was, and still is, available at subsidized prices from a government shop. Then, overnight, it seems, sometime in the late 1970s, the pushers moved in. Under the sponsorship of high-level organized crime leaders from the major cities, they practically gave away brown sugar (raw heroin) to anyone who wanted it—young kids, sadhus, rowdies. Once they were hooked, the dealers upped the price. Now, everywhere you look you see the signs of hard drug use. Rickshaw drivers, washermen, boatmen, even shopkeepers and lawyers, but most of all those countless nameless, faceless men who just hang out all day on the streets chewing *pān* and drinking tea, show it in their bone-thin bodies and drawn faces, staring eyes. How they get the money to support their habit, God only knows.

As I enter the temple, one of these guys starts to talk to me as if he owns the place, welcoming me in, full of artificial smiles and uneasiness. I inquire after Māyī. She seems to be cowering next to him, in that typical and infuriating way in which so many Indian women change their personas simply because a man—any man—is present. She is also shivering. I ask her, "Why aren't you wearing the shawl I gave you?" She looks at him fearfully and says, "It's not here."

"Where is it?"

Fumbling, she says, "He borrowed it."

I confront him. "What's the matter? You don't have any sweater? It looks to me like you are warm enough." I walk over to a clothes line in the corner where a man's sweater is hanging. I throw it at Māyī. "Here, put this on." She looks at him with fear, and I order her to wear it. He is obviously angry at the idea of her even touching his clothes, but he is also afraid of me, so he says nothing.

"Why are his things here?" Māyī replies that he is staying with her for a while, looking after her. I turn back to the stranger. "I want that shawl back in this house by tomorrow, do you understand? And if I hear that you said one word to her about this, there will be trouble." With the thinnest of smiles, he says, "No problem." I walk out, knowing that as soon as I leave he will strip his sweater off her. No, on second thought, I know that she will hand it to him submissively.

Late the next morning I show up. From the road, I see him inside her room, drinking tea. When he spots me, he bolts out the back door and is gone. I ask her if he brought the shawl. She goes into a tall tale of how he sent it for mending. "Mending? Why? What happened to it?" It seems it accidentally ripped. I tell her to give him a message, that he either gets the shawl back by tomorrow or he will buy her a new one. Outside in the courtyard, her neighbors stop me to report, "He is a bad man. His father owns a shop near here, but he is thrown out from his family. He steals everything from Māyī. He sold the shawl. Whatever anybody gives her, he takes it and sells it. Even ten pice he will take. Only for drugs."

I wait a few days, and this time I am the one who is clever. A friend of mine at the university who has heard my story offers to help. "No use going to the police. They are too involved in the local community to start trouble with any of these types. Some of my friends are in the student union here. Take them with you." In my friend's van, we pull up to the gate. Seeing the fellow inside the room with his back to the door, I sneak up and grab him by the back of the neck. "Where is the shawl, bastard?" He struggles to get free. I tighten my grip on his neck, turn him around, and, grabbing him by the hair, give him a good slap across the face. He wants to fight back but then sees the two muscular young men standing behind me. Feeling my blood heat up, I shout a stream of abuse at him in his own language. "You dog, you want to run away now? Is that how you treat an old woman in this country? Taking food out of her mouth for your drugs? Moving into her house to steal from her? In Kālī Mā's house, you dare to behave like this? Don't you know Mother sees everything? Now you are going to pay."

Holding him by a fistful of his greasy hair, my other hand at his throat, years of anger slowly well up inside me. He begins to look more and more like the perfect human sacrifice, the stand-in for all those filthy sons of bitches who abuse women as a matter of routine—no, of birthright. A payback for all those aborted female fetuses, all those men sitting on their asses while their wives carry wood, water, start the fire, cook the food, wash the clothes, bear the children, take their beatings, and then bow down to them like living gods. For all those marriages, dowry schemes arranged in hell: "Rāju Weds Lakṣmī" reads the marriage sign. But I see "Rāju Burns Lakṣmī. Rāju Weds Gītā . . ." All those bald men with paunches who want to get me alone to lecture me on the moral superiority of Indian women, "because they know how to suffer." Chuckling idiots. "Madame, we Indian men are very bad." Drooling, "I believe in your country women are very free with sex?" My own mouth waters now at the feel of my fingernails sinking into the back of his throat, the prospect of my knee, hard and swift between his legs. I'm sure it would only take a single swift blow and he would be on the floor.

At some point, my gaze focuses on his pleading bloodshot eyes. All at once my stomach turns, and I am overtaken with shame. Look at me. I consider myself a scholar. Talk about keeping your distance from your subject! This poor slob is already impotent, already a victim. I let go and turn away in disgust. The two *guṇḍās* with me grab him and escort him to the van. We drive away toward the university. They ask me what I want them to do with him. "You want us to break his legs? We can even arrange for him to 'disappear.'" The very thought that I could hold his life in my hands nauseates me further. "No, please, don't hurt him. Just scare him enough to make sure he gets his things out of her house and stays away from her. He should understand that we mean it."

A few days later, it's time for me to leave again. I open the iron gate and enter. Māyī sits on the floor sorting her paltry things. I sit down and we talk about Mā. Yes, Her hairpiece is getting a bit ratty. Neither of us mentions the incident, but I no longer see any evidence of his clothes. It is time to give her the sweater. The night before, I had taken it out, tried it on one more time. Then I took a pair of scissors and cut long slits in the front and back, just in case. Who would want to buy a sweater with big holes in it? Māyī puts it on and gives me one of her huge grins. It is time for me to go. I prostrate myself in front of Mā and ask only one thing: "Please Mā, I don't need anything, but look after Māyī. Protect her from harm and these useless men. Let her live out the rest of her life in peace." Sadly, we walk to the gate a last time. The neighbors see me and gather around, assuring me that they will take care of her, but this is not my world. I don't know who can be trusted, who is friend or enemy. I announce to them in a loud voice, "Tell anyone who wants to give trouble to Māyī that she is not alone. She has her friends and we'll look after her."

"When will you come again, daughter?"

"Anytime." I shout so that they all could hear. "I could come next week or after a month or a year, you never know, but I'll be back." Despite the bravado, inside I am crying. I have no idea when I'll see her again, what will become of the old lady.

Banaras, 1997. Another short visit to my beloved city. In Gaṅgā Maṭh, I wake up in the middle of the night in a sweat. "Tomorrow I'll go to her. What if . . . ? No, I can't think about it." The next morning I walk up from the river, past the Assi crossing, past the theater and the post office. I spot the iron gate. I am practically running now. I open the gate and skip through the courtyard. The doors to the temple are open. I look in.

Oh no.

Mā stands there, stark and alone, wearing a new red *cunnī* (woman's scarf) and skirt, but looking naked. She has a new hairpiece, and some fool has repainted Her face. Stripped to the bone and freshly painted, the place is empty. No altar, no rags in the corner, no cat, no colored lights, no clothesline, no cobwebs, no Māyī. "No, Māyī, you *didn't.* I told you I would come again . . ." Unable to bear the sight of such emptiness, I stagger, sobbing, to the iron gate next to the communal water tap. A few of the locals walk up to me.

"When did it happen?"

"About a year back."

"How did it happen? No, wait, don't tell me. I don't want to know." I am aware that I am being selfish. I choose ignorance. But nothing can change the past, and at least this way, my faith will not be destroyed. I can always believe that my prayers were answered, that she lived out her last days peacefully, under the watchful protection of her precious Mā. As for that young lady, I have eventually come to feel grateful to whatever idiot messed up Her face with his gaudy paint job. Let them all take Her for just another cheap idol. Now that Māyī is no longer here, it is right that the Goddess's elegant beauty be safely hidden from thieves who would only seek to profit from it. Her true nature lies buried in my heart, clothed in the darkness of the past, collapsing into the infinity of the black hole of time and space.

I wrote this account in 1998, thinking that if my memory were to fail me when I grow old, I might read it and remember Māyī. I hardly expected that it would be published. Yet, looking back on this episode with a dispassionate gaze, several questions related to the study of Kālī rise to the surface of this narrative. Some of the most interesting center on the question of identity: Who was Māyī? As the primary devotee of this particular Goddess, the caretaker of the temple, how did she relate to her deity? Did her worship of Kālī define her sense of self in the world? If so, then why, despite worshipping such a powerful deity, was she in need of my protection and help? Or did she need it? Who was I, "the anthropologist," in relation to Māyī, or Mā for that matter?

The perceived contradiction between powerful female divinities and seemingly "oppressed" Indian women is repeatedly raised as an issue in courses I teach on Hinduism and Goddess worship here in America. But this is precisely where we must become most self-conscious, for this contradiction, so much taken for granted in this country, reveals less about Indian religious practice than it does about our own presumptions regarding both female deities and Indian women's lives. When the focus of our inquiry is turned back on ourselves, another set of questions comes up: Why was I not able to find out more about Māyī? And why, despite knowing so little about her, did I come to feel so emotionally attached and responsible for her? In attempting to answer these questions, I am influenced by the same (Jungian) psychoanalytic framework of understanding that I use to interpret religious meaning in my own life. In this regard, there is a continuity between my life and my scholarship, yet in neither arena do I allow this approach to reduce religious experience to psychological explanation.

Furthermore, I am not interested here in discussing the personal psychology of Māyī or myself. But I am intrigued with the shifting projections, identifications, and role reversals taking place between Mā, Māyī, and myself for what they say about the disjuncture between Western and indigenous Hindu understandings of Kālī. These seem not only to reveal the limitations of the categories with which a Western feminist anthropologist unknowingly armed herself for "battle" in the research field, but also might shed light on the way the majority of Hindus relate to this particular form of the Goddess.

To me there was no question that Māyī's relationship to Kālī defined her sense of self in the world. But what kind of identity did it offer her? Her devotion seemed to result in an erasure of self rather than any positive identification with either her own personal history or the qualities of her chosen deity. When I questioned Māyī about her biographical details, she remained mum, not out of any modesty, feigned or real, but simply because the details of her past were unimportant to her. Dates, of her birth, her marriage, her husband's death, were recorded not in years but in terms of "long ago," so long that when speaking of these events, she seemed to be totally detached. She owned no passport, birth certificate, or any other papers, apart from a few miniature prayer pamphlets (inexpensive books of verse associated with a particular deity, sold in the gullies of pilgrimage places like Banaras). I doubt she could read even those. When pressed by me about her past, she eventually pulled out a few yellowed photographs: of the Bengali Tantric woman who had established Kālī in this place, and of her husband and herself when young. Neither of these photos was on display or located in any place of prominence in her house or temple. They had been buried under other things lying on the shelf. In fact, the spatial arrangement of Māyī's living quarters said a great deal about her priorities: the temple was her living room, sitting room, and kitchen. She prepared her food on a small portable kerosene stove in the corner in front of the altar. She retired to a small back room, no more than five feet wide, only to sleep. She used a communal toilet in the back of the building, and the water spigot on the street was her bathing place.

She spent every waking hour in the temple, and every activity of her day revolved around Kālī Mā, whom she took care of like a mother. What is important to note is that Māyī played the role of mother, not the other way around. As our visit to the Avadhūt revealed, Māyī was worried about her own passing, not because she was afraid of what would happen to her at death (the issue of whether she would attain "liberation" or not, a typical concern of many of the more spiritually inclined devotees of the Avadhūt, did not arise), but because she didn't know who was going to look after Mā when she was gone.

Despite the Hindu ideal of the submersion of the ego in Brahman or God in the sense of highest truth or reality, the effacement of Māyī's personality in her role as a mother to Kālī did not strike me as any self-conscious quest for transcendence. Rather, it suggested something much more "down to earth," indicative of the cultural norms of Hindu India in which women sacrifice themselves for their children. Māyī had no children of her own, and so treating Mā like her little girl was one way in which she could fulfill her destiny as both a woman and a devotee. Furthermore, like a typical mother who lives vicariously through her children, compared to lackluster replies to my questions regarding her own past, Māyī really came alive when recounting the story of Kālī's exploits on the battleground. In telling it to me, she never framed the story as a myth; nor was there any indication in her manner or voice to indicate that she took this story to be anything other than the literal account of why Mā's tongue sticks out. It was as simple as that. In sensing her childlike acceptance of this account as reality, I felt extremely protective of Māyī and, at that moment, as in many others, fell into a motherly role with her.

Yet beneath my feelings of affection lies my own unconscious agenda. For me, as for many Western women, the role of mother is not without its conflicts. I suspect this might be true of most women who are drawn to the idea of a Mother Goddess, as if the psyche seeks to resolve on a "higher" plane the unfinished business of the earlier developmental stages. More to the point of this essay is the collective dimension, for women in the West are in an active struggle with the societal expectations placed on them as mothers. The questioning of all traditional notions of maternity is reflected in the attempt in the social sciences to deconstruct the idea of any innate, biologically based "maternal" instinct in women.[11] This is one reason why an angry deity like Kālī, at least on the surface, is often such an attractive image for women influenced by feminist ideals: She seems to embody the collective anger and rebelliousness of women who have been oppressed by their social roles. And yet the same women will also invest Kālī with the powers of the archetypal "Great Goddess," an image that invokes, and at the same time compensates for, a stage of infantile dependency upon an all-powerful mother.

As Rachel McDermott points out in "The Western Kālī," women in our culture attribute to Kālī a paradoxical nature embracing all opposites.[12] One of the most important aspects of this Western-constructed Kālī is Her explicit sexuality. As an image, She thus serves to resolve a central conflict: between the traditional role expectations of a mother (the "Virgin" Mary as the Western ideal of a chaste motherhood) who subordinates her desires to societal demands, and the free will of a sexually independent female. In contrast, for Indians, Kālī's dangerous character stems precisely from the fact that She is a "virgin"—that is, not under the control of any male deity—and, by implication, full of pent-up sexual heat and anger.[13] From this Indian perspective, I read into the story told by Māyī about Mā's tongue sticking out: with Śiva lying in prone position to stop Her dance of destruction, Kālī takes the active "male" role by being "on top." Hence, Her protruding tongue may be understood as a thinly disguised phallus. Only when She is allowed this dominant position is She propitiated and brought under control, never fully subdued, but at least contained. And this only happens due to the intervention of a more encompassing, even more transcendent *male* principle. Śiva, the Lord of Destruction, is the only one who can assume the role of Her "husband," the only power capable of holding Her intrusive, penetrating, and dangerous energy in check, a point hardly compatible with a radical feminist perspective. In short, for Hindus, the independent virgin (celibate) Kālī represents unbridled death and destruction, the intrusion of the timeless into time, and this becomes the basis for Her *propitiation,* which in the myth is symbolized by the cooling of Her anger by Śiva. In contrast, for Western feminists, the terrifying, sexual aspect is precisely what is sought to be *invoked.*

While we in the West interpret Kālī's fierceness as a symbol of empowerment for women, this turns out to be the projection of our own desire for power and independence. We seek a personal identification with Kālī in order to strengthen our egos, our sense of self, and our effectiveness in the world. I would submit that apart from Tāntrikas who purposely seek to invoke such terrifying goddesses as a means to *siddhi*s (occult powers) or a shortcut to liberation,[14] this is the opposite of how most Indians relate to Kālī. "Empowering" was certainly not the way in which Māyī understood her Mā. At no point did she identify herself with the Goddess, even though given Māyī's old-crone appearance, other devotees and visitors to the temple might well have done so.

Because, in the Indian context, Kālī is often worshipped by the outcast, oppressed members of the society, from a Western perspective, we are quick to presume that Kālī can most easily be understood as an expression of their repressed anger and rage. Certainly, it is tempting to interpret cases in which devotees become possessed by Kālī and other fierce deities in these terms. Yet even here we must distinguish between individual cases of uninvited possession, which in Hindu society are always fraught with danger—recognized as symptomatic of an individual or social imbalance—and ritualized possession, which frames the danger within a context of control. Even in the case of the latter, as Sarah Caldwell points out in connection with her fieldwork in Kerala, men are more likely to become possessed by Kālī than women. In her words, "male performers and spectators identify with female energy to gain more power, not to empower women. The performances and stories of Bhagavatī, rather than providing role models of female defiance and independence, serve rather to reinforce cultural ideas about the inherent danger a woman holds for men, which it is her responsibility to contain and control."[15]

This would indicate that instead of expressing the rage of the oppressed, possession might express the fear of those seemingly "in control." From a feminist perspective such as Caldwell's, this constitutes the "coopting of female suffering."[16]

And yet as my own experience has taught me, co-opted by men or not, Kālī is an attractive image for those who are suffering. Perhaps it is precisely Her terrifying appearance that bestows solace on deeper levels, as if Her wretchedness reflects the psychic condition of the sufferer, that reflection then becoming the opportunity to "hold" or abide in one's pain, or simply to survive in the face of it.

In my own case, by looking into the face of Kālī, I was able to face truthfully the imminent end of my marriage. At first I projected onto Her a wrathful, moralistic, and punishing deity that was probably the legacy of my upbringing as a Christian. But as time went on, because I had the courage to face Her (and my own fears), She began to reveal deeper layers by stripping away, layer by layer, all the illusions I had once held about myself. It was a profoundly humiliating process, but at the same time, at least when I was in Mā's presence, strangely consoling to find that I could survive in such a wretched condition, living day by day at rock bottom, grateful for the smallest acts of kindness, which I took to be small signs of Her grace.

Although it may seem contradictory or even ironic from a Western point of view, for Hindus, Kālī is the embodiment, not of rage, but of compassion. In order to assess whether this compassion is "empowering" or its opposite, we would have to become much more self-conscious about our own definitions of power: to ask whether by this term we refer to an external or internal agency, power as the ability to *do,* or power as the ability to *be,* to simply continue to exist in the face of potential annihilation, real or imagined.

I would like to suggest that Kālī might be better understood in a sense directly opposed to Western notions of empowerment as external agency. I would understand Her instead in terms of surrender, a total acceptance of the external conditions in the face of which one feels powerless. This invokes an ever-present awareness of the human's inevitable surrender to time itself. For in the form of death, time swallows all. In that case, Kālī's terrible ferocity represents, not an empowered agency *in* time, but the terror of a transcendent time *beyond* time, a time that envelops all temporality, past, present, and future. Within a Hindu framework, this surrender to transcendent inevitability, as in the case of Māyī, can look a lot like the egoless state needed to attain enlightenment. To the Westerner, it can look a lot like powerlessness.

This disjuncture of meaning between "Eastern" and "Western" readings of Kālī, between "surrender" and "empowerment," is what came to a head in the episode of the shawl. Surrender to time or fate is what characterized Māyī's response to life, extending even to being taken advantage of by the male intruder. And it was this aspect of Her that triggered a particularly "Western" rage in me, spurring me on to active intervention. There is no question that I was fueled in my self-righteous indignation by my "motherly" feelings toward Māyī, but I suspect that the form my affection took had a great deal to do with my need to take charge, to identify with the Goddess and make Her (myself) into what I wanted Her to be, the powerful protectress, offering youthful strength and independence as an antidote to Māyī's passive acceptance of the conditions of her old age and dependency. All of this was based on my unquestioned understanding of Kālī as a symbol of feminine "power." The price of this inflation could have been quite high: for a moment I was tempted to wreak vengeance on all Indian male oppressors by wringing that poor guy's neck.

My actions obviously offer a lesson regarding the limits one would be wise to respect when engaging in research and "participant observation." And yet my subject position within Indian culture as both a scholar and a practitioner of the traditions I study places me somewhere between safe categories. I have not often found it possible or even desirable to privilege my identity as an anthropologist over that of a friend or devotee. In retrospect, my analysis of what happened in Banaras causes me no regret and certainly does not in any way diminish the love I hold for Māyī in my memory. Furthermore, scholar or not, for me Mā Kālī will always be the "Great Mother," the timeless one, a deity so powerful that even *in* time, She is capable of resolving all conflicts—perhaps even the basic differences between indigenous and "Western" ways of relating to Her.

NOTES

1. My study of the Aghorīs, "The Politics of Heterodoxy and the Kina Rami Ascetics of Banaras" (Ph.D. diss., Syracuse University, 1993) sheds light on the traditional role of the Aghorīs as the most heterodox of all Hindu sects and discusses the reform of the Kīnā Rāmī sect of Aghorīs under the late contemporary Guru Avadhūt Bhagvān Rām, who appears later in this chapter.

2. Interview with Kālā Bābā, Vindhyachal, Spring Navarātrī, 1990, cited in Gupta, "Politics of Heterodoxy," p. 105.

3. A chillum is a clay pipe used for smoking marijuana (*gāñjā*).

4. This is the rallying cry of the Hindu masses in Banaras, which says, "Hail, Hail the Great God Śiva, husband of the Goddess Pārvatī!" This refrain is heard at communal festivals during religious ceremonies and is also used to greet the maharaja of Banaras during his public appearances.

5. See Rachel Fell McDermott, "The Western Kālī," in *Devi: Goddesses of India,* ed. John Stratton Hawley and Donna Marie Wulff (Berkeley and Los Angeles: University of California Press, 1996), pp. 281–313.

6. This account also appears in the autobiographical first chapter of my book *A Yoga of Indian Classical Dance: The Yogini's Mirror* (Rochester, Vt.: Inner Traditions, 2000), pp. 22–23.

7. See Brajamadhaba Bhattacharya, *The World of Tantra* (New Delhi: Munshiram Manoharlal, 1988), p. 223.

8. Recorded in Bhojpuri, translated by Professor Shukdev Singh, Banaras Hindu University.

9. The Avadhūt to whom I refer here is Aghoreśvar Bhagvān Rām, the late reformer of the Kīnā Rāmī Aghorī lineage.

10. Banaras dwellers. In Hindi, Banārsīvālās.

11. In stating this, I am neither for nor against such a position, not only because the scientific evidence itself is ambiguous, but also because, as an anthropologist, I am more interested in what cultures believe to be true than in any "objective" conclusions that might be offered by science. It is noteworthy, however, that the allocation of resources to studies that would seek to reach a definitive conclusion on such a matter is only a priority in the Western world.

12. McDermott, "Western Kālī," p. 285. Throughout this section, I am indebted to Rachel McDermott for her thorough research and insights into Western attitudes toward Kālī.

13. For more on the notion of pent-up heat stemming from unreleased sexuality, see Sarah Caldwell, "Bhagavati: Ball of Fire," in *Devi: Goddesses of India,* ed. John Stratton Hawley and Donna Marie Wulff (Berkeley and Los Angeles: University of California Press, 1996), pp. 195–226. In North India, as well, there is a prevalent notion that women who do not have sexual relations build up too much heat in their systems that begs to be released. See Gupta, "Politics of Heterodoxy," p. 108.

14. See ibid., ch. 3, pp. 72–119.

15. Caldwell, "Bhagavati: Ball of Fire," p. 218.

16. Ibid.

PART II

Kālī in Western Settings, Western Discourses

CHAPTER 7

Wrestling with Kālī

South Asian and British Constructions of the Dark Goddess

Cynthia Ann Humes

> *If we were to form a graduated scale of religions, that of Christ and that of Kalee would be the opposite extremes.*
>
> *The Edinburgh Review* (1837)

For over two thousand years, both South Asians and newcomers to the Indian subcontinent have had diverse encounters with Kālī. Their imaginings of her have enacted cultural and sometimes national dramas of imperialism and religious conflict and have figured in definitions of theological identities, ethnicity, and gender. When eighteenth- and nineteenth-century British merchants and colonialists encountered Kālī, they did not conjure up extreme tropes from an isolated Western background: there already existed a wealth of literary sources and historical incidents, as well as considerable ill-will—counterposed by dedication and devotion—toward Kālī. British encounters with "Kālī" thus meant grappling with overlapping, even contradictory indigenous stances on Kālī that had emerged from a long history of contentious debate. In this chapter, I articulate six such indigenous South Asian models of experiencing Kālī and illustrate five of them with examples drawn from both Indian and British writings on the Goddess.

INDIGENOUS CONSTRUCTIONS OF KĀLĪ: SIX MODELS

I identify the first interpretive stance of Kālī—which bears a tempered acceptance of a benevolent but potentially terrifying Goddess and her coterie of followers—as the *Devotional Model* of Kālī.[1] Following the earlier hymns of the *Mahābhārata* and its appendix *Harivaṁśa,* the most famous example of such a model is the sixth-century C.E. "Glorification of the Goddess" ("Devī-Māhātmya," found in the *Mārkaṇḍeya Purāṇa*), where Kālī appears from the skin of the enraged Great Goddess's furrowed brow (7.6–8). An embodiment of divine anger, Kālī bears a strange skull-tipped staff, wears a garland of skulls, and is clad in a tiger's skin. Her emaciated flesh, gaping mouth, lolling tongue, and deep-sunken reddish eyes are shocking, and filling the directions with gargantuan roars, she seizes her enemies and devours them whole.

Strands in the Hindu tradition have long asserted that the divine Other may be experienced as sheer power (*śakti,* or its feminine divine personification, Śakti), a confrontation with which stimulates fear and awe, foreboding yet attraction. All power, licit or illicit, and thus all reality is an expression of her being. Just as ancient Hindu seers imagined the universal deity, so might Kālī be conceived: she who extends several fingers beyond the expanse of space, occupying the center, yet constituting and extending beyond all boundaries.[2] Because devotional sources situate the Goddess within accepted parameters according to shared faith stances, their portraits of Kālī may differ markedly, reflecting regional and cultural variations.

A second mode of South Asian response to Kālī can be characterized as the *Apologist Model.* Apologist authors have accepted Vedic and Brāhmaṇical religion and can thus be called "Hindu" in our modern parlance. However, adopting a cautionary approach, apologists seek to distance themselves from certain features of Kālī worship. For instance, they themselves may be less sympathetic to her purported ferocity in battle or capriciousness and thus seek to emphasize her beauty, motherliness, or supportive and creative aspects. Others seem to be uncomfortable, not with Kālī's life history, but with practices of which they disapprove.

Outside what we call the "Śākta" fold, many South Asian sources portray the Goddess as well as her devotees in a negative light. I include in this group Christian folklore, Jain morality tales, Buddhist hagiographies, and other Hindu sects' propaganda. The hostility of their vision is expressed in four chief guises: she is denied altogether, demonized, ignored, or scandalized, sometimes in a highly sexualized manner. What can be called the *Disbelieving Model* alleges that the Kālī mythos is a fiction propagated by opportunists or fools and denies her any roots whatsoever in reality. Since even a fictional Kālī can have demonstrable effects, however, such as encouraging ignorance and vice in human devotees, "she" must be opposed. The *Demonizing Model* of Kālī posits that the Goddess does indeed exist and is evil. Kālī herself is beyond the boundaries of decent behavior; often relying for proof-texts on their rivals' devotional or apologist portrayals, the "Kālī as demonness" camp asserts that her domain of authority and morality is socially and religiously marginal and evil. *Dismissive* conceptualizations render Kālī qua goddess as innocuous; she is a mere nuisance, especially in contrast with what they pose as a more powerful Ultimate. A sixth model I characterize as *Sensationalizing* and *Scandalizing*. Although this interpretation draws on all of the other modes, its peculiar characteristic is the heightening of danger represented by the Goddess or her devotees. Such depictions acquire their power by appealing to sexual titillation, often resulting in a conflation of the Goddess and an essentialized enemy woman. Note that the four models of hostile representation can sometimes overlap. For example, a single source might deploy both demonizing and dismissive stances, characterizing Kālī as a minor demon, who, as a flirtatious female, is dismissed as inconsequential.

In this essay, I discuss British colonial responses to Kālī by relating them to five of these six indigenous South Asian models of experiencing Kālī—that is, all except the devotional.[3] I show how British authors—Orientalist, missionary, administrator, novelist, and voyeur—mirror and at times directly utilize prior indigenous sources' depictions to construct their own visions of Kālī. Indeed, precedents for virtually all major British reactions can be found in, and are in some cases directly linked to, South Asian Christian, Jain, Buddhist, and Hindu attitudes toward the Goddess. I also contend that the various constructions of Kālī and her cult served as important features in the historical discourse of imperialism, marking both how the British saw South Asians and how they justified their role and rule in the subcontinent.

A BRITISH APOLOGIST: ORIENTAL JONES AND THE TEMPLES OF DOOM

In 1789–90, Sir William Jones (1746–1794), president and founder of the Asiatic Society, published several articles in *Asiatick Researches* that reveal that he saw in Kālī a direct parallel to ancient European deities, envisioned as allegories of noble human ideals.[4] Jones was among the first to argue the shared cultural heritage of the Persians, Indians, Romans, Greeks, Goths, and Egyptians. This belief in a common history, coupled with his commitment to the primacy of Christianity, influenced his interpretations of Hinduism. "Oriental Jones," who was so named for his having brought so much of Oriental culture to the West, argued that Genesis was the origin of several Hindu myths, including those of Manu and the flood,[5] and he was so inspired by his own interpretations of Hindu mythology that he composed moving hymns to several Hindu goddesses, whom he likened to European deities. Padmā or Lakṣmī was the "Ceres of India," the preserving power of nature, or "in the language of allegory, the consort of Vishnu or Heri [Hari]."[6] The "Indian Isis" appears variously as Pārvatī, Kālī, Durgā, and Bhavānī, who respectively resemble Juno, Hecate, Pallas, and Venus.[7] Regarding Kālī in specific, Jones noted that although offerings of human sacrifices were enjoined in the Vedas, they were eventually replaced by less bloody rites in autumn, due to the happy coincidence that the festivals of Kālī and the more benevolent Lakṣmī were celebrated nearly at the same time. Such rhetoric mimics devotional and apologist discourse seeking to substitute more acceptable vegetarian for blood rituals, or to emphasize goddesses commonly said to be "wealth," "power," "thirst," and so on.[8]

Indeed, Jones's Orientalist discourse is similar in many respects to that of indigenous apologist models. Many South Asian apologists composed entertaining narratives that exploit Kālī's horrific symbolic ambiance, but—perhaps because they wrote for an audience who they anticipated would be less receptive or misunderstand—they adopted stock strategies in their portrayals meant to downplay her "negatives" and accentuate her "positives." For example, Daṇḍin (*Daśakumāracarita*), Bāṇabhaṭṭa (*Kadambarī* and *Caṇḍī Śataka*), Bhavabhūti (*Mālatīmādhava*), Vākpatirāja (*Gauḍavaho*), and Somadeva (*Kathāsaritsāgara*)[9] all tell exciting tales of a dangerous goddess whose devotees are from the margins of accepted society. Each author positions the Goddess in a generally favorable light, thus revealing the "misperceptions" and limited or deliberately selective understandings of the Goddess evinced by stock marginal characters. Playing on motifs of a ragamuffin clientele, such apologists seek to demonstrate that the Goddess is not in fact who or what her bad followers think she is. She does not respond favorably (if at all) to thieving and murdering villains who seek her assistance in their quests. In fact, rather than rewarding them, she is often portrayed as punishing their scurrilous violations of social norms. Also featured in these accounts are Kāpālika- or Tāntrika-wannabes, buffoons laughable for their attempts to inspire fear by transgressing social and religious boundaries.[10] Apologist authors thus acknowledge worship of Kālī by members of peripheral groups, but they vindicate religious faith in her—and prevailing social mores—even as they purposefully titillate and shock audiences with outrageous carnivalesque scenes.

Negative aspects of Kālī's cult could be blamed not only on her followers but also on her leaders. Resonant with his Protestant heritage, Jones compared the temples of Durgā, whom he equates with Kālī or Bhavānī, to the churches of Rome: the errors practiced there came not from the deity but from her human caretakers. Although human sacrifice was absolutely prohibited, Jones claimed, less noble priests persisted in presiding over offerings of buffaloes and goats. In a letter to Jonathan Duncan of 1790, he commented, "With all my admiration of the truly learned Brahmens, I abhor the sordid priestcraft of Durga's ministers, but such fraud no more affects the sound religion of the Hindus, than the lady of Loretto and the Romish impositions affect our own rational faith."[11] His criticism has numerous parallels to indigenous critiques of Kālī worship, which blame greedy priests for perpetuating sanguinary rites in her filthy temples.

CREEPING ACCRETIONS: KĀLĪ AS TANTRIC FICTION

The view that Kālī worship practices were a superstitious accretion not enjoined in the higher scriptures was common to many Hindus, particularly those of the reformist, "neo-Hindu" schools. The great Bengali "Father of Modern India," Ram Mohan Roy (1772–1833), rejected many "social ills" of Hinduism that were in his view wrongly accorded religious status by various individuals in pursuit of personal wealth or power. Like Jones and numerous other South Asians, Roy found animal sacrifice repugnant, and he even refused to perform his family's traditional Kālī worship. In addition to his staunch monotheism, partially informed by Islamic critiques of trinitarian Christianity, Roy evaluated Hindu doctrines and practices largely in terms of whether they seemed to improve human life. Kālī worship, for Roy, did not fall into this category; he disbelieved her importance to Indian cultural and spiritual life.

A similar stance was held by numerous Britons, notably Henry T. Colebrooke (1765–1837), one of Roy's contemporaries. Colebrooke's works represent a crucial departure from the favorable views of Kālī espoused by Jones. As David Kopf has noted, in contrast to Jones's sensitive, nuanced interpretations of Upaniṣadic monism, Colebrooke discerned a monotheism in the Vedas that had been "unnoticed" before.[12] True Hinduism was found here, in the shared monotheistic heritage of the Aryans. The Hinduism of his time was in decline, and he advocated investigating the history of Indian Aryan culture to ameliorate its decadence. Each discovery or rediscovery of Vedic India "was dramatically and metaphorically contrasted with the peculiarities of contemporary Hindu society."[13] Colebrooke's disbelieving view was subsequently popularized in British, European, and even many Indian circles.

In contrast with Jones, to whom Kālī was the Indian counterpart of one of the ancient goddesses of Europe, Colebrooke accepted a common Aryan past in the Vedas but did not see Kālī there at all: she was a recent invention, a fiction perpetrated on the gullible. The "evil personification of Kālī" was the horrific spawn of Tantric corruptions and pretenses—evidence of the eclipsing, not the continuation, of Aryan truths in the Vedas.[14] In 1805, Colebrooke stated, "Most of what is there [in the Vedas] taught, is now obsolete; and new forms of religious ceremonies have been established. Rituals founded in the Puranas and observances borrowed from a worse source, the Tantras, have in great measure . . . [replaced] the Vedas."[15] By the 1790s, a growing hostility to Hinduism began to extend beyond evangelical and missionary circles. The hardened stance reflected changed political circumstances. The British were no longer the representatives of a mercantile monopoly that required the goodwill of the people; they became increasingly the agents of a governing institution that took over the authority and functions of local and regional administration ad hoc and sought to impose a morality hitherto considered detrimental to the quest for profit. In 1813, Parliament repealed the ban on missionaries going to India, opening up to evangelism a vast territory populated by what many held to be heathens requiring conversion. Once the two divisions were official—colonizers and colonized—Kālī came to occupy a more critical position in the broader Orientalist project of imagining India, for she was commonly regarded as the most extreme, sexual, and irrational embodiment of the worst tendencies inherent in the essentialized Indian mind. Within this strategic reimagining, a different valence was at work than for most South Asians, for the British espied her from cultural as well as political stances. Kālī the uncontrolled South Asian came to be imagined as the consummate "Other" opposed to their imperialist goals, and her vilified cultural baggage helped justify British providential rule.

ONWARD, CHRISTIAN SOLDIERS: FIGHTING THE DEVIL AND HER MINIONS

In 1802, the missionary William Ward wrote, "Last week a deputation from the Government went in procession to Kallee Ghat & made a thank offering to this goddess . . . of the Hindoos, in the name of the Company, for the victories & successes which the English have lately obtained in this country. Five thousand rupees were offered. Several thousand natives witnessed the English presenting their offerings to this idol."[16] To Ward, Kālī was "truly horrid," exhibiting "drunken frantic fury," "on whose altars thousands of victims annually bleed, and whose temple . . . is the resort of Hindoos from all parts of India."[17] Missionaries believed that the payment of tribute to Hindu temples by ostensibly Christian Company officials would imply a Christian approval of sacrifice and polytheism. This might even keep Hindu souls from Christian teachings, thus setting them on a path to hell. In the 1820s and 1830s, missionaries criticized government offices for collecting pilgrim taxes that made the government co-conspirators in the expansion of superstitious, unproductive pilgrimage practices.

Like Jones, British and other European missionaries (e.g., William Carey, Claudius Buchanan, and the French Catholic Abbé Dubois) drew many parallels between Kālī and the pagan deities they were familiar with from Europe. Yet whereas Jones wrote for a rational but romantic audience of intellectuals and scholars, missionaries spoke to the devout and potential political representatives back home. Protestants and Catholics emphasized a similarity between the goddesses of sorcery, polytheism, and sexual licentiousness.[18] They criticized Kālī's cult as the most extreme and dangerous of all Hindu groups. In support, they turned to translations of Hindu texts, such as the *Kālikā Purāṇa*. Identifying Kālī as a demon, they often blamed (as had Jones as well) the creation of her sorry rituals on debased Brahmans who snared superstitious and ignorant natives through their horrible cult. Missionaries did not reject all Hindu officiants as charlatans, however; many spoke of the priests' frightening powers, which they implied had satanic origins. Such accounts betray fascinating parallels to an Indian Christian account in which the Goddess is portrayed as a demoness.[19]

Kālī figures prominently in the story of the great miracle-working Apostle Thomas, "Mar Thoma," who is believed by followers to have brought Christianity to South India. His advent, labors, and martyrdom constitute a living tradition, rich in folklore, songs, and dance. In the Mar Thoma account, Kālī's priests are opportunists who invent traditions for their own benefit, and her worshippers—doomed, of course, to an afterlife of perdition—are ignorant and base. The actual powers to be derived by the Goddess's magical rites are not denied, but they are denounced as satanic or demonic and are counteracted by the greater force of a Christian saint.

Consider this Malayalam poem by Maliakkel Thomas, compiled toward the close of the sixteenth century from older works and oral traditions of Malabar.[20] In this telling, Kālī, although recognized as an actual spirit, is depicted as far weaker than the saint, and her worship is said to be devil worship. This is Paul Thomas's free rendering of the relevant portion of the poem:

> Mar Thoma, who had established the Way in several countries and regions of the earth, and whose laws were faithfully followed by the leaders and followers of the communities he had founded, was, in the early hours of the 3rd day of July 72, going on a journey and happened to pass by the Mount in Mylapore. Here stood a temple of Kali, and the priests of the temple, bitter enemies of the Apostle, furiously issued forth from the temple and stopped the saint. "No man," said they, "shall pass this way without worshipping at the shrine; hence come with us and worship the goddess. If you do this, not only shall we let you pass this way undetected but shall feed you sumptuously on delicacies." "What?" replied Mar Thoma, "Am I to sell my soul for a morsel of rice, and worship the devil? But if you insist I shall do your bidding and you shall see how your goddess will run away from her shrine and the temple itself be destroyed by fire." "Do not utter blasphemy," cried the priests, and they forced him to go to the temple. As the saint approached the temple, a splendorous light shone forth and Kali ran out of the temple and the temple itself was consumed by fire. Thereupon, the infuriated priests fell upon Mar Thoma like mad animals. And one of them taking a long spear thrust it cruelly into the heart of the Apostle.[21]

This South Indian hagiography shares much of the drama of Christ's crucifixion. Just as Jesus is the target of jealous Jewish priests, the evil impulses of Brahman priests catalyze Mar Thoma's martyrdom. Both sets of priests demand obedience to barren ritual. Both saint and savior cause destruction at a temple site after being "tested" by their accusers, who are enraged by their saintly powers. And in both stories, the demonic Other is banished.

There are also obvious parallels between the Mar Thoma Christian account and the much later missionary diatribes of the British, wherein Christian saint or Christian preachers prove victorious over the demonic. Although there are differences between them—each is refracted through its own astigmatic gaze—it is clear that Ward and his contemporaries did not invent the rhetoric of demonization and critique, for the Christian religious structures of good versus evil, evidenced already in the Mar Thoma accounts, contributed much earlier to Kālī's default position as alien Other. And, as contemporary literature and website statements of missionary Christian groups amply testify, such portrayals are still invoked in Christian discourse today.

WHAT? ME WORRY? DISMISSIVE BUDDHIST, JAIN, AND HINDU ACCOUNTS OF KĀLĪ

Buddhism and Jainism share several key features that affect their responses to Kālī. They embrace an ethical commitment to *ahiṁsa,* or noninjury, and thus for over twenty-five centuries have criticized Vedic and then later Hindu ritual sacrifice of animals or people. Further, while boasting rich pantheons of salvific figures, heroes, and heroines, in general, both Buddhism and Jainism posit the necessity of self-effort and the conscious modeling of oneself on great human beings to achieve ultimate enlightenment. To assert their philosophical supremacy over the less enlightened theologies of Indic culture, Buddhist and Jain authors at times skillfully employed humor and inventive reimaginings of contemporary opponents, including spoofs of rival sects' deities. Given Kālī's well-known thirst for blood and association with violent, frightening devotees, she merited critique on both counts and was targeted in Buddhist and Jain literature. Hindu reformists who espoused *ahiṁsa* and elevated self-realization over adoration of the Other also criticized worship of idols and the bloody rites meant to appease them.

Aśvaghoṣa, a Buddhist who lived in the first century C.E., penned a polemical account of a humorously powerless demonic Kālī. The earliest classical Sanskrit poet whose works have survived to any extent, Aśvaghoṣa portrays the skull-bearing Kālī as an unsuccessful flirt in the thirteenth chapter of his *Buddhacarita,* "The Deeds of the Buddha." As a last resort in his attempts to shake Gautama from *samādhi,* the unshakable mental state that precedes nirvana, or enlightenment, the great demon Māra sends in "a woman named Meghakālī, bearing a skull in her hand," whose intent was "to infatuate the mind of the sage." Instead of shaking the Buddha, however, she herself "flitted about unsettled and stayed not in one spot, like the mind of the fickle student over the sacred texts."[22]

The poet here plays with a number of themes then current in Sanskrit literature. "Meghakālī" is the feminine personification of the "time [*kāla*] of clouds [*megha*]," that is, the rainy season. The rainy season—like spring in many Western cultures—is described as the most romantic time of the year and, particularly in Sanskrit poetry, the season evokes intense and protracted erotic symbolism. Here the Time of Clouds, or the Cloudy/Dark One, seeks to unnerve the Buddha by enthralling him with her weapon of sex appeal. But like the vapors her name symbolizes, she is sent whirling off, dispelled like an amorphous, ever-shifting cloud at the mercy of a mighty wind. She is no more powerful than a daydream, oozing up from the depths of a bored, undisciplined mind. Through strategically adding the phrase, "bearing a skull in her hand," Aśvaghoṣa succeeds in rooting this anthropomorphized, bewitching experience and emotional state in a greater mythological tradition: the Kāpālikā, or skull-bearing female, her deity, and the larger cult of followers. In this missionizing, gendered hagiography of the Buddha, our poet re-envisions the raw imagery of a skull-bearing and thus presumably frightening demon-goddess-woman, transforming her into a fickle, flitting, and even trivial female.

The theme of imperturbable, impassive resolve in the face of an external threat redolent with symbolism nestled deep in the Kālī mythos is replayed in a later Buddhist work, this time featuring a historical figure, Hiuen-Tsiang.[23] Hwui-li wrote a biography of Hiuen-Tsiang, who himself had composed *Si-yu-ki,* the "Record of Western Countries." Tsiang had spent sixteen years in India during the mid seventh century C.E. In many *jātaka* or prior "birth stories" of the Buddha, commonly dated before or around the time of Aśvaghoṣa, the then *bodhisattva* is portrayed as willfully and cheerfully giving up his own flesh—and even life—to benefit others. Such cheerful self-sacrifice is also attributed to Hiuen-Tsiang in Hwui-li's hagiography. Oddly, the veracity of this account is not generally questioned, yet nearly every single phrase has a direct parallel with selections from the *jātaka* stories. I think it meet to accept that the account is a reshaping of prior imaginings of the Buddha's former lives, in a fashion markedly similar to that which we have seen in the Malabar Christian account. Here, the great founder/saint of a particular region—Hiuen-Tsiang of China—is, like Mar Thoma of Malabar, provided with a mythological biography richly documented with miracles performed in dire circumstances posed by rival religious advocates, all reshaped from the life stories of his tradition's greatest savior.

According to the story, Hiuen-Tsiang is seized by river pirates in search of an offering to Durgā, a "spirit of heaven." They bind him upon an altar, and just as they are about to sacrifice him with their knives, a black tempest (typhoon) arises from the four quarters of heaven, smiting down the trees; clouds of sand fly on every side; and the lashing waves of the river toss boats to and fro. The terrified robbers repent of their faults, bow their heads in profound obeisance (or, *embrace the religion of Buddha*), and accept the five obligations of a lay believer.[24]

The powerless skull-bearing goddess menacing an immoveable hero first found in the *Buddhacarita* appears in a new guise in the tales of Hiuen-Tsiang. In both Buddhist accounts, Kālī and her devotees are defeated, even as the would-be victim's body lies unmoving and unprotected but for his inner resolve. In the Chinese retelling, the robbers are frightened and convert, a long-standing *jātaka* motif. As in the *Buddhacarita,* the virtue of the would-be victim sufficiently shields him from falling prey to the evil Goddess. In both, there is a miraculous whirlwind—a natural manifestation of personified power—but whereas in Aśvaghoṣa's telling, they are ineffective breezes of the Cloud-Black goddess, in the tales of Hiuen-Tsiang, the winds are transformed into the power of the Buddhist preceptor, taking form as a whirling black cloud. Both uses of the Black Cloud lead the audience to question the substantiality and significance of the supposed Goddess. Her devotees are powerless to harm the Buddhist, and they become frightened precisely when they realize that their intended victim is unafraid, unmoving.

The subsequent defeat, flight, or conversion of devotees of the Head-Coveting Goddess has also had enormous currency in Jain literature. Like their Buddhist and Hindu counterparts, Jain authors have also used Kāpālikas to provide exciting frame-stories and to serve as foils introducing didactic passages. Consider, for example, the many extant versions of "The Deeds of Maṇipati."[25] The *Maṇipati-carita* begins with King Maṇipati, who has become a Jain ascetic and assumed a motionless meditation posture in a park outside Ujjain. A Kāpālika seeking skulls takes the unmoving king for dead, lumps him together with two corpses, and proceeds to light a funeral fire. When the Jain's head involuntarily twitches because of the fire, the supposedly fearless Kāpālika is spooked and runs away. The hero is so focused on his ascetic practices that he remains literally "unmoved" by the Kāpālika's efforts to burn him in his gruesome religious devotions. In this account, the Jain ascetic is as imperturbable as the Buddha and Hiuen-Tsiang, while the Kāpālika is scared out of his own, as well as his intended trophy's, skull.

There are abundant scornful reactions to Kālī by Hindus as well. Many Hindu *bhakti* saints and reformers were unfazed by Kālī and highly critical of her priests and cohorts. Kabir, a poet-saint of the fifteenth century, "found the sacrifices that priests made to the goddess Kālī hideous"[26] and is said to have sung in his blunt fashion, "If you live near goddess-worshippers, move!"[27] In another poem, he lamented: "Saints, the Brahmin is a slicked-down butcher. He slaughters a goat and rushes for a buffalo without a twinge of pain in his heart. He lounges after his bath, slaps sandalpaste on his brow, does a song and dance for the Goddess, crushes souls in the wink of an eye —the river of blood flows on. How holy!"[28] Such anti-Śākta and anti-Kālī rhetoric was common among those who espoused a view of Hinduism that embraced *ahiṁsa.*

Centuries after Kabir, Ram Mohan Roy voices similarly dismissive attitudes toward Kālī. Perhaps most intriguing about the "Father of Modern India" for our purposes here is his near mirror reflection of William Jones's strategy of understanding Hinduism in relation to his revised version of Christianity: Roy interpreted Christianity in relation to his revised version of Hinduism. To Roy, Christ was a model social reformer and advocate for the oppressed, and his principal message was liberation. In their quest to make India a modern nation, reformist Indians drew on Christ's example to argue for multiple personal and national goals. Indeed, some Hindu reformists went so far as to argue that most Europeans, especially British missionaries, had misinterpreted Christ. They knew—better than their hypocrite colonizers, they said—his true meaning, his true Good News. They thus consciously sought to differentiate their Christ from the Christ misrepresented by evangelical orthodoxy: theirs was the Asiatic Christ, the Oriental Christ, the Beloved Son, their Brother, the same Being as Brāhmo, a complex term based on the word "Brahman," meaning the Ultimate, One Divinity, whose presence, mystery, and power they believed to have inspired the ancient Hindu scriptures. Roy used the same techniques as Oriental Jones in interpreting the links between Hindu and ancient European religion. But Roy claimed that, contrary to British imperialist and Orientalist interpretations, Hindu philosophy—that is, the true Hindu philosophy as he defined it—was the quintessential, most elevated religion, not "polytheistic" trinitarian Christianity, which was, in a neat trick, seen as a degenerate form of the ancient Aryan religion. In a word, in his excursions to meet the West, Roy left Kālī back home.

JUMBLED STANCES: THE SHOTGUN APPROACH OF "THUGGEE SLEEMAN"

Turning from demonizing and dismissive religious polemics, the British administrator William Sleeman adopts a more complex stance in his portrayals of Kālī and her devotees, who, thanks in large part to his efforts, have been immortalized in Western culture as the "Thugs," or "Deceivers."[29] Sleeman employs multiple negative portrayals: he is alternatively demonizing, dismissive, disbelieving, and sensationalizing. This latter stance soon escalates to scandalizing, particularly in later characterizations of the Thuggee Goddess in the popular press.

The period from 1790 to 1830 saw a great rise in interventionist documents penned by missionaries that exhorted the British to take decisive measures against many Indian social practices. These included infanticide, exposure on the ghats, Caḍak Pūjā[30] and self-flagellation rituals, *satī*, and animal and human sacrifice. To many British, the most infamous and sinister religious practice, however, was the "cult" known as "Thuggee." South Asian sources had long employed the word *ṭhag* to refer to a cheat or a thief.[31] The term "thug" was used in British government correspondence at least as early as 1810, where it is found in a letter by a Major General Sargent Leger,[32] and "thug" appears again in the *Madras Literary Gazette* of 1816; therein, Dr. Richard C. Sherwood published a report on a criminal group known as Phansigars, or "stranglers"—so designated because of their use of a noose (*phansi*)—who were a "distinct class of hereditary murderers and plunderers" devoted to "the goddess Cali, or Mariatta, who is also invoked under the name of Jayi, Ayi, or Tuljapuri."[33] The Phansigars were spread all over India, where they had different names; in the north, wrote Sherwood, they were called "T'hegs, signifying deceivers." The superstitious element of the Phansigars is noted to be symptomatic of "most—perhaps all—classes of Indian delinquents."[34] Dr. Sherwood claimed to have been privy to their distinct customs, which he narrates in detail, and in part to lend credence to his position as an insider, he provides a dictionary of technical Phansigar vocabulary. This Phansigar dictionary was eventually used as a resource for those attempting to penetrate the Thug cult, and in its sensational popularity among those seeking vicarious thrills in an Oriental netherworld, it served as a kind of early *Hobson-Jobson.*[35] Novelists began to adopt the vocabulary, and to show their writers' acculturation, letters home to Britain were rife with the now public "secret" Phansigar terminology.

In 1824, H. H. Wilson published the first five chapters of Somadeva's ca. 1100 C.E. *Kathāsaritsāgara* in the *Oriental Quarterly Magazine.* These passages characterize Durgā as dwelling in the Vindhya mountains, a site famous for its nefarious tribal inhabitants, which even today shelters more tribals than any other place in the subcontinent. In Somadeva's work, the Vindhya Dweller is revealed to have a voracious appetite for animal sacrifice and human head offerings. In a later portion of the epic, a party traveling in the Vindhya forest is surprised by an army of brigands, who rob them and then drag one of their victims to the awful temple of Durgā as an offering. In this apologist account, Vindhyavāsinī rejects the sacrifice and kills the robbers instead. Other texts that were available in translation included the highly colorful *Mālatīmādhava* of Bhavabhūti (ca. 700 C.E.) and the *Gauḍavaho* of Vākpatirāja (ca. 730 C.E.), both of which speak of a Vindhya-dwelling goddess who consumes animal and human sacrifices. Some of the portions of these resemble Sleeman's narrative so closely that an indebtedness is indubitable, particularly since Wilson explains that the worship of Devi "is one of considerable antiquity and popularity. Laying aside all uncertain and fabulous testimony, the adoration of Vindhy Vasini, near Mirzapur, has existed for more than seven centuries"; and in a note, Wilson explains that the site is frequently mentioned in the Vrihat Katha (the lost epic on which the *Kathāsaritsāgara* is based), which is at least seven centuries old.[36]

The facts that indigenous narratives portrayed Kālī/Durgā as somehow connected with the margins of behavior and often located her in the Vindhya mountains are particularly important in questioning the origins and veracity of British records of Thugs. The single most influential British document on Thugs was penned anonymously in 1830 by then Captain [William] Henry Sleeman.[37] He accused the "Thugs" of being a religious "cult of murder" especially devoted to the Vindhya mountain-dwelling goddess, also known at her shrine in Vindhyachal as Bhavānī, Durgā, or Kālī. By comparing his versions with sources that were available to him, it is apparent that he relied on translations of indigenous apologist descriptions of Kālī and the Vindhya Dweller to construct his accounts of the Thug phenomenon. He thereby successfully lent his assertions an air of authority and immediate recognition that was indisputable by Hindus who would oppose him. After all, he could turn to their own sources as "proof." Nor was he a lone voice crying in the wilderness. In later writings about the Thugs, Sleeman cites Leger and reproduces Sherwood's article in its entirety, amplifying the latter through footnotes drawing on "all the advantages of his subsequent investigations, personal and historical."[38]

The religious element of Thugs is deeply etched in Sleeman's works, after which authors who discuss Thuggee tend to repeat exhaustively what he claimed. There is a marked similarity between Sherwood's account and Sleeman's "findings," and both bear an uncanny likeness to Prakrit dramas and Sanskrit poetic descriptions of the Vindhya Dweller and her tribal followers. Lists of superstitions, for instance, are almost verbatim, leading me to infer that such constructions are based on literary rather than ethnographic sources. This feature necessarily raises the question of the historicity of narratives, including that penned by "Thuggee Sleeman." While relying on indigenous literature might be appropriate for certain purposes, it is extremely questionable in a quest to understand a modern group or groups of soldiers, all the more so since the valence of each source—devotional, apologetic, or polemical—gets overlooked.[39]

British officers battling Thugs emphasized again and again that the latter did not prey on unfortunate natives in order to undermine British law and order, which was yet to be established. Indeed, Sleeman said they were thriving under lax British policies, because officials deliberately ignored them. Eliminating Thugs was precisely the rationale for the British to enter new areas, demand cooperation from princely states, and countermand standard Muslim law, which required greater proof than mere accusations by cohorts. If one follows the trail of correspondence, an interesting pattern emerges. On August 7, 1830, Governor-General Lord William Bentinck sent a letter to Francis Curwen Smith requesting him to consult with Captain Sleeman and other functionaries to develop a plan for "the secret employment under due precautions of some of the witnesses and approvers, stimulated by the promise of a liberal reward on the conviction of the leaders in question, such a knowledge might be acquired of the place for their next annual excursion as might greatly facilitate their apprehension."[40] But soon thereafter, alarmed by a letter published on October 3, 1830, in the *Calcutta Literary Gazette,* government officials contacted Sleeman directly.[41] The letter, penned anonymously by Sleeman, was an amalgamation of multiple stances opposed to the Thuggee Goddess, her cult, and government intransigence, and it drew, without attribution, upon the prior works of Sherwood and Wilson. George Bruce explains, "Sleeman must at this time have become desperate with impatience in the belief that action would never be taken," and to further distance Sleeman from any criticism, the admiring biographer surmises that he may "perhaps have been urged by his determined wife into the uncharacteristic move he now made. He decided with a bold stroke—one that would have ruined him today—to try so to shock the feelings of educated opinion in India that swift and decisive anti-Thug action must follow."[42]

Sleeman's letter makes interesting reading, but I only quote and comment on portions relevant for our purposes. "Kali's temple at Bindachul (Vindhyachal) . . . is constantly filled with murderers from every quarter of India between the rivers Narbada, Ganges and Indus, who go there to offer up in person a share of the booty they have acquired from their victims strangled in their annual excursions," he wrote.[43] It is no doubt true that armed groups could have been seen going to Vindhyavāsinī's temple. Many did so in *digvijaya*—the quest for conquering the directions—whose aim was political legitimacy and martial success. The same is true today: political candidates come to Vindhyachal in droves at election time. So do violent upstarts whom the Indian press has characterized as "mafiosos" but who are getting elected to democratic offices and thereby becoming "legitimate" politicians. Such success is testimony, Hindus believe, to the Goddess's nature as giver of authority and power. According to an 1830 pilgrim narrative composed by a Hindu from South India, the goddess of Bindhachul temple (Vindhyavāsinī) accepted, not blood offerings, but sumptuous royal offerings given during victory rituals. Elsewhere, I have discussed the groups of people whom Sleeman essentialized as Thugs.[44] Some of them honored the Goddess who bestowed power and aided military ventures. They also murdered citizens of other provinces for profit to support their own province's mobilization efforts against the British. In short, they were soldiers, or anyone unlucky enough to be named by somebody being interrogated during the brutal Thuggee suppression campaigns launched by the British.

Another key feature of Sleeman's anonymous letter is its attack on the shrine's Brahman priests. It is interesting that he did not invoke this criticism in work submitted under his own name:

> The priests of this temple . . . suggest expeditions and promise the murderers in the name of their mistress immunity and wealth, provided a due share be offered up to their shrine, and none of the rites and ceremonies be neglected.

> If they die by the sword in the execution of these murderous duties by her assigned or sanctioned, she promises them paradise in its most exquisite delights; if they are taken and executed . . . it must arise from her displeasure, incurred by some neglect of the duties they owe to her.[45]

Sherwood had earlier surmised that Brahmans, although not assisting directly in "the actual perpetration of murder," nevertheless were "employed" in providing intelligence to Thugs.[46] Sleeman's claim that the priests were among those who profited from Thugism and that they directed Thuggee campaigns has no support whatsoever in the testimony he reputedly recorded of those accused of being Thugs. In fact, several explicitly denied it. In the responses of men said to be Thugs, the Islamic concept of fate, *iqbal,* is invoked the most often. The Hindu goddess Bhavānī is only rarely referred to, and almost always in response to Sleeman's leading questions.

At least in the initial years of the military campaigns against Thuggees, as also in Sherwood's earlier essay on the Phansigars,[47] Kālī as the Thuggee Goddess symbolized *what threatened Indians.* Sleeman, however, took this sentiment further, using the Thugs as justification for the expansion of British law and order. "If these people are led by the priests to expect great rewards in this world and the next we must oppose to it a greater dread of immediate punishment and if our present establishments are not suitable for the purpose we should employ others that are, till the evil be removed, for it is the imperious duty of the Supreme Government of this country to put an end in some way or other to this dreadful system of murder, by which thousands of human beings are now annually sacrificed upon every great road throughout India."[48] Sleeman accordingly advocated the benevolent extension of the rule of the Father: the rational, just, controlled, and male God as a substitute for the irrational, amoral, wild, and female Goddess. Execution of Thugs by the British was portrayed as grim but just and necessary, and it was contrasted with the immorality of the murders committed by Thugs.

Sleeman stressed that the reasons why compatriots had not been slain themselves or seen any evidence of Thug activity were because the Thugs only threatened natives and acted in secret at night. The only proof, aside from bodies buried along roads, was the "direct testimony" of the Thugs themselves. Thus he received approval to arrest those named by purported Thugs, prosecuting them without any substantiating evidence, recording over "several days" their "direct testimony," and producing the "Substance of Conversations held by Captain Sleeman, with different Thug Approvers, while preparing the Vocabulary."[49] Curiously, even people concerned with revisiting materials about Thugs have not called attention to the fact that the "direct testimony" of Thugs was not "direct" at all. There is no possible way that in a matter of days, Sleeman could have interviewed and transcribed all of the statements preserved in his writings.

What I find fascinating in these published accounts of Sleeman's testimony is the lack of any references to Vindhyachal by the men interviewed as Thugs. For instance, on page 150 of Sleeman's book *Ramaseeana,* Feringea, the "model Thug," was in Sleeman's recollection asked,

Q. *"Do you in the Duckun send any offerings to the Brahmans of the temple of Davey [Devi]?"*
A. His response was, "Never; we neither make offerings to her temples, nor do we ever consult any of her priests or those of any other temples. Our sages alone are consulted, and they consult omens alone as their guides."

Q. *. . . But you worship at Davey's temples?*
A. Yes, of course, all men worship at her temple.

Q. *No.—We sahib loge never do.*
A. I mean all Hindoos and Musulmans.

Then Sleeman adds, "Here my Mahommudun officers again interposed, and declared that they never did; that it was only the very lowest of Musulmans that did."

Sleeman's "discovery" of the Vindhyachal cult, as reported in the letter to the *Gazette,* is the earliest, indeed only source of information about a connection between that specific temple and the purported Thugs.

Bruce points to this curiosity, saying, "All the facts that he unearthed about the Thugs and their beliefs were presumably incorporated in the early reports he forwarded to the Government. But there is no evidence in the official records that their contents were circularized to magistrates and police in India; nor was anyone appointed to direct action against the Thugs. Sleeman's reports must have been pigeon-holed and destroyed, as were so many official records, by the white ants that infested Fort William, Calcutta."[50] While I do not dispute the notorious fondness of white ants for paper in India, surely the utter absence of any proof requires one to adopt a hermeneutic of suspicion. Were documents destroyed by someone on purpose? In my opinion, it is more likely that there were never any such documents in the first place, simply because the connection between the temple and the "Thugs" was imagined, not real, created to stigmatize warlike men in pursuit of authority and power. Indeed, Sleeman's entire literary production regarding the Thugs was built upon unsubstantiated, even patently false, prior publications, some his own: his anonymous letter of 1830 plagiarized the works of Sherwood and Wilson; his *Ramaseeana* of 1836 was based on Sherwood, Wilson, and his own misleading letter of 1830; and *The Thugs or Phansigars* of 1839 was a further drawing out of Sherwood, Wilson, his letter, and *Ramaseeana.* Relying on translations of centuries-old South Asian dramas, including apologist sources that, ironically, connected the Vindhya Dweller with robbing murderers in order to prove the triumphant conventional morality and salvific power of the Goddess, Sleeman succeeded in marginalizing, not just the men seeking her power, but the Goddess herself.

After only a few years, Sleeman declared "victory" over these devotees of Kālī. Providence had brought the British to power and the era of the Thuggee goddess to an end, he asserted, adopting numerous stances toward Kālī. Alternatively demonizing, dismissing, disbelieving, and blaming her priests, as well as scandalizing the Goddess and her devotees, he assured his countrymen that active British engagement against Kālī and her cohorts had made Thuggee a thing of the past.

By midcentury, however, the Thuggee Goddess and her minions had been reimagined as direct threats to the British themselves, and the tone was suffused with sexual and ethnic overtones. British accounts from the 1820s to the 1840s, ranging from government briefs, missionary tracts, and novels to scandalmongering magazines, objectify Kālī as a murderous, inhuman, sexualized she-devil and consort-attacker. This reflected developments in the 1840s, when more British women emigrated to serve as suitable mates for British men, thus preserving British males from cavorting with, if not marrying, Indian women. The darker Hindu woman was marginalized as a sex partner and imagined as the uncontrolled "native." This was in explicit contrast to an idealized Mem Sahib, the white "Madam Sir" whose chastity and patriotism were proof of her proper role as facilitator to the Sahib in the colonialist project.

Whereas Sleeman had portrayed them as an internal civilian threat to Indians, especially after the Indian uprisings in 1857–58, the reimagining of the Thugs typified them quite differently. Many sources now described them as members of a widespread subversive organization united under the patronage of a sadistic, sexualized Kālī and dedicated to undermining British law and order.

BARBARIANS AT THE GATE

Once again, there are indigenous sources that directly parallel fearful British projections of Kālī as a scandalously sexual enemy and woman out of control, and the elevation of a female ideal whose sexuality remains in check. The highly evocative first episode of the *Maṇipati-carita*'s sixteen parables bears a telling resemblance to Hindu myth models of Kālī as the angry wife of Śiva. The scenarios outlined there, however, subvert the Hindu moral. The *Maṇipati* asserts Jain truths about male-female relations, and in its efforts to titillate and entertain, it operates in a manner akin to many British novels that exalt the superiority of Protestant Christian gender relations and the Empire even while seeking to keep readers squirming on the edge of their seats.[51]

The Jain story begins with the ascetic Dhanada, who recalls that in a former life he came to a cemetery named "Mahākāla" on the way to his father-in-law's house. There he saw a weeping woman, who asked him to boost her up so she could give food and drink to her husband, who had been impaled on a tall spear by the evil king's soldiers. She specifically asked Dhanada not to look up. The man agreed and let her climb atop his shoulders. He felt something dripping down and, curious, looked up only to see her carving the poor man up and throwing chunks of him into her pot. Dhanada dropped his sword in alarm and fled toward the city gate, followed at his heels by the bloody woman holding aloft his own sword. There, the benevolent guardian of the gate protected him, but the demonic female nonetheless sliced off one of his buttocks, which unfortunately was outside the gate.

In one version, the benevolent deity who guards the gate is simply called *duvāra-jakkhiṇi,* or *yakṣinī* of the gate, but in others she is "Durgā." She calms him—in one episode calling him "son"—and in some accounts she even restores his buttock.[52] He worships her. Arriving at his destination, however, he finds his in-laws' door locked. Looking through a peephole, he discovers to his final horror that the *śākinī* who has attacked him is in reality his own wife: there she sits, happily sharing his cooked flesh with her mother.[53] When her mother asks her why she killed him, the daughter replies that it was not her fault, because although she had warned him not to, he had nevertheless looked up.

At first glance, this episode does not seem to bear much connection with Kālī. Yet interpreting it from a structuralist vantage point reveals critical Jain reformations of indigenous South Asian, particularly Śaiva/Śākta, motifs. The story begins in Mahākāla cemetery, named after Kālī's husband Śiva, Great Lord of Time. The woman transforms from a weeping, helpless damsel in distress into an aggressive, sexually voracious woman who stands atop Dhanada with her sexual organs potentially exposed. The impaled man is still breathing, but stuck on the pole, he is helpless and vulnerable, like Śiva's "corpse," which Kālī pins by taking control of his phallus/stake. In some Purāṇic myths, Śiva's *liṅga* falls off when he inappropriately "looks" at the wives in the Pine Forest, just as Dhanada looks up at the woman in our story after promising not to do so. In other Purāṇic tellings, Śiva purposefully cuts off his own member to prove his sexual disinterest, which Dhanada accomplishes through asceticism in a later life.

But the story takes place within a historical context as well, raising a fascinating second set of associations. An infamous—and horrifying—contemporary means of punishment inflicted on practicing Jains by Hindu kings was impaling them. N. K. Sastri reports that even today, Madurai Śaivite temples celebrate the impalement of eight thousand Jains by a lapsed Śaivite king in the seventh century. The king was reconverted from Jainism by the boy-saint Sambandhar and was subsequently urged to take proper measures against Jains.[54] Our episode thus portrays the wife/Kālī as a collaborator of the evil king, perpetuating the suffering of a man who has been unjustly impaled; she is the imagined fearful Other.

When the woman chases the terrified Dhanada, she is portrayed by the author as acting in a manner a South Asian audience would recognize as fury. According to the Nātya Śāstra (12. 50–51), "In the Furious sentiment the body should be dripping in blood, mouth should be moistened with it and pieces of flesh in the hands."[55] She also appears uncannily like the furious Kālī of the "Glorification of the Goddess," who is engaged in righteous battle: running from a funeral ground, sword in hand, bloody from severed male body parts, and threatening a frightened male victim. This Jain telling inverts the story's characterization from that of the devotional Hindu model: here the woman is decidedly evil, and the man Dhanada whom she wishes to consume is the future saintly monk, not the demon Raktabīja.

After a slapstick scene of comic relief, with the slashing of Dhanada's exposed buttock, and the divine intervention by the nonsexual and hence unthreatening woman "at the gate," or Durgā, Dhanada attains final realization at the peephole. What he understands, however, is not the inherent divinity of women or the merits of remaining married, both possibilities preserved in Hindu accounts of Kālī. Nor is his conclusion particularly Buddhist, although the obvious misogynist projection of Kālī/*śākinī*/"powerful woman" recalls the Buddhist Meghakālī—fickle and lustful. In the Buddhist accounts, Woman as Other is not overwhelming; the *bodhisattva,* being enlightened (or nearly so), is able to control his fears and repel her mentally. By contrast, the Jain is not religiously accomplished. He thus experiences this Woman as Other and is so shaken that he runs off in fear. The encounter leads to revulsion, and although it is a female who ultimately protects him, the parable's moral denies the ultimate salvific or even moral abilities of any female. The man must undergo austerities, by which he will become totally unmoved.

These selected Jain and Buddhist characterizations of a dangerously sexual, dark, female Other prefigure and contribute to the dangerous, erotically imagined Other of the British, who centuries later relied on many of these very same indigenous narratives and themes to reformulate, understand, and communicate their own encounters with Kālī in a remarkably similar situation and with extremely similar religious and political intentions.

AFTERTHOUGHTS

What Orientalists saw in Kālī reflected their own presumptions, religious attitudes, and historical interpretations. To early British traders settling in South Asia, Kālī was merely one part of an immensely rich landscape, accepted without much inquiry or trivialized as another "picturesque" item to be observed and possibly tokenized in a keepsake statue. Although some British are reputed to have truly worshipped her with genuine devotion, for the most part, their "worship" of her was initially simple convention, self-conscious mimesis of South Asian rulers and lordly men. To Jones, however, Kālī was a lovely divine allegory exalting the vicissitudes of nature. Later Orientalists would fixate, as Colebrooke did, on presumed historical changes in her cult by "Romish" Brahman priests bent on exploiting the masses' depraved instincts. Missionaries encountered Kālī and reported that they had met the devil: she was an evil, black, naked woman, completely debauched and capable of offering nothing to her devotees but evil power rooted in Satan's dominion.

Sleeman's encounter with Kālī was far more complicated. In his anonymous letter, he adopted the language and moral tenor of a devout Christian, yet in his signed works, he portrayed himself as neither devout nor even religious, preferring instead the persona of the idealized modern, utilitarian man: rational, but moral. This reasoned stance, arguing for the complete uprooting of her cult for the good of all other South Asians, albeit constructed from indigenous narratives about Kālī, is a unique strategic twist to prior apologists and rival accounts.

Finally, after British rule was established by the brutal suppression of the "Thugs" through unprecedented disemboweling of all protective rights of the accused, Kālī and her cult become increasingly scandalized. In fantastic, lurid British novels, titillating public ruminations, and voyeuristic glimpses in the aftermath of her exposure as the Thuggee Goddess, Kālī underwent a quick succession of personality changes. Eventually, the many competing shapings merged into a less malleable reification; she hardened into an implacable, oversexualized female enemy. The painfully impoverished gender roles of British society rendered problematic their attempts to locate a sexualized Kālī. Women were either saintly and untainted by sex or decidedly otherwise. British women (at least of the proper class) came to occupy the first niche, and Asian women the latter. As woman out of control, Kālī symbolized the disorder and panic the British themselves felt when they found to their chagrin that South Asians were hitting back. Unlike the ascetic Jain reworkings of the woman-out-of-control, however, the suggested response was an embattled and sexually charged assault. Wrestling with Kālī, British imperialists sought to domesticate and colonize her and thereby to diffuse the dangerous and erotic tensions evoked from their illicit union. But, as this chapter has argued, they did so using the models, conceptions, and interpretive maneuvers of their Indian predecessors; that these reactions to Kālī had a history on the subcontinent may also account for the success of the British in promulgating such views.

NOTES

EPIGRAPH: "The Thugs; or, Secret Murderers of India," *Edinburgh Review* 84 (January 1837): 394.

1. Representations of something other are inherently subjective. Thus each of my models is framed to reflect the perceiver's stance, not the nature of the object(s) perceived.

2. Rig Veda 10.90 begins with this evocative imagery describing the Puruṣa, "Man," who pervades and yet extends beyond the limits of the known world: "The Man has a thousand heads, a thousand eyes, a thousand feet. He pervaded the earth on all sides and extended beyond it as far as ten fingers. It is the Man who is all this, whatever has been and whatever is to be." Translated by Wendy Doniger O'Flaherty in *The Rig Veda* (New York: Penguin Books, 1994), p. 30.

3. A wealth of materials already exists that describes indigenous and British constructions of Kālī from devotional stances. To give just one example, Sir John Woodroffe (1865–1936) was among the most famous British converts to the Goddess. Under the alias Arthur Avalon, Woodroffe translated and provided careful and critical editing of about twenty important Tantric texts. He also wrote commentaries and illuminating introductions. These include *The Serpent Power, The Great Liberation, Principles of Tantra, Kamakalavilasa, Garland of Letters (Varnamala), The World as Power,* and *Mahamaya (Cit-Shakti or Power as Consciousness).*

4. Sir William Jones and Lady Anna Maria Jones, *The Works of Sir William Jones,* 6 vols. (London: G. G. and J. Robinson and R. H. Evans, 1799), vol. 6.

5. Ibid., pp. 36–37.

6. Ibid., p. 355. The impulse to compare Hindu with European deities infused most later writings on Hinduism. Edward Moor's influential *The Hindu Pantheon* (London: Johnson, 1810) continued in this vein, for instance.

7. *The Works of Sir William Jones,* vol. 6. On Durga, see p. 323; Bhavani, p. 333; Lacshmi, p. 355; Sereswaty, p. 375; and Ganga, p. 383.

8. "The Glorification of the Goddess" also honors the Goddess as personified qualities—usually feminine nouns. In chapter 11, for example, the Great Goddess is exalted in a hymn as water, boundless power, intelligence, time, auspiciousness, wealth, shame, faith, growth, and great knowledge as well as great illusion.

9. Daṇḍin (fl. ca. sixth century C.E.), Bāṇabhaṭṭa (fl. ca. sixth century, C.E.), Bhavabhūti (fl. seventh-eighth century C.E.), Vākpatirāja (fl. eighth century C.E.), and Somadeva (fl. ca. 1000 C.E.).

10. See, for example, the portrayal of the female Kāpālikā in the *Mālatīmādhava* of Bhavabhūti. She is outraged when not taken seriously as a threat because of her gender. The *Kadambarī* of Bāṇabhaṭṭa details a hilarious spoof of the "Draviḍa," a South Indian Tāntrika-wannabe attempting to walk the walk and talk the talk in a temple of Caṇḍikā in Ujjain, only to be assaulted by onlookers once their laughter dies down.

11. The letter was dated February 7. The allusion is to Santa Casa, Mary's Nazareth house, which was said to have been miraculously transported by angels to a spot near Loreto in 1294, after the Virgin's appearance. See *The Letters of Sir William Jones,* ed. Garland Cannon, 6 vols. (Oxford: Clarendon Press, 1970), 2: 856.

12. David Kopf, *British Orientalism and the Bengal Renaissance: The Dynamics of Modernization, 1773–1835* (Berkeley and Los Angeles: University of California Press, 1969), p. 40.

13. Ibid.

14. Ibid., pp. 39–41.
15. Ibid., p. 41.
16. Quoted in E. Daniel Potts, *British Baptist Missionaries in India, 1793–1837: The History of Serampore and its Missions* (Cambridge: Cambridge University Press, 1967), p. 161.
17. William Ward, *History, Literature, and Mythology of the Hindoos,* 3d ed. (4 vols.; 1817–20; Delhi: Low Price Publications, 1990), 3: xxxvii.
18. For example, on Kālī specifically and her parallels in vice with Greco-Roman deities, see Abbé J. A. Dubois, *A Description of the Character, Manners, and Customs of the People of India; and of their Institutions, Religious and Civil,* 2d ed. (1817; Madras: Thacker Spink, 1862), pp. 127–28 and 252–53.
19. The Indian Christian accounts here are from Christian groups whose ancestors practiced their faith in South Asia since what many believe to be the first and second centuries.
20. In lauding their founding Apostle, the Malabar Christians reduplicate the cultural pattern of hagiographical origin stories in other South Asian religious sects, such as those preserved in the sixteenth century *Bhaktamāla* of Nabhadās, an account of Hindi *bhakta* poets.
21. Paul Thomas, *Christians and Christianity in India and Pakistan: A General Survey of the Progress of Christianity in India from Apostolic Times to the Present Day* (London: George Allen & Unwin, 1954), pp. 17–19. I have been unable to verify whether the name of the goddess described in the translation as "Kali" is actually in the original, because no title was given in the text, nor is any Malayalam source listed in the author's bibliography. As it stands, the author describes Kali as Mari Amma (Māriyamma<u>n</u>) elsewhere on p. 47, so it is possible that the specific name of the Goddess here is Mari Amma, the "terrible goddess of the south," rather than Kālī. In any case, the translator conflates them, as do most South Asians.
22. "The Buddha-karita of Asvaghosha" (13.49), trans. E. B. Cowell, in *Buddhist Mahayana Texts, Part I,* vol. 49 of *The Sacred Books of the East* (Oxford: Clarendon Press, 1894), p. 144. Other goddesses were not immune to the Buddha's charms either. In bk. 10, the Buddha crosses the Ganges and comes to the town of Rajagriha. The townspeople are charmed by his majesty, strength, and splendid beauty, and "having beheld him with the beautiful circle of hair between his brows and with long eyes, with his radiant body and his hands showing a graceful membrane between the fingers—so worthy of ruling the earth and yet wearing a mendicant's dress—the Goddess of [Rajagriha] was herself perturbed" (10.9). Ibid., p. 105.
23. *The Life of Hiuen-Tsiang* by the shaman Hwui Li, trans. Samuel Beal (London: Kegan Paul, Trench, Trubner, 1914).
24. Beal, *Life of Hiuen-Tsiang,* summarized from pp. 86–90. Italics in original.
25. Robert Williams lists eighteen extant manuscript versions and surmises that there are probably others. Names of this cycle of tales vary: *Muṇipati-carita, Muṇipati-rāsa, Muṇipati-kathā, Maṇivai-muṇi,* for example, and a Sanskrit version is titled *Sāroddhāra.* They are written in Prakrit, Gujarati, and Sanskrit, and appear as early as the eighth or ninth century. See *Two Prakrit Versions of the <u>Maṇipati-carita</u>,* ed. Robert Williams (London: Royal Asiatic Society, 1959), p. xi.
26. John S. Hawley and Mark Juergensmeyer, *Songs of the Saints of India* (New York: Oxford University Press, 1988), p. 43.

27. Ibid., p. 60.

28. *The Bījak of Kabir,* trans. Linda Hess and Shukdev Singh (San Francisco: North Point Press, 1983), pp. 46–47.

29. The nickname "Thuggee Sleeman" stuck to William Sleeman throughout his life.

30. Caḍak Pūjā is an annual festival in which one expresses devotion to a deity by swinging on hooks imbedded in one's flesh. The Pūjā is usually associated with Śiva, although devotees swing on hooks and pierce themselves with long lances in honor of Vindhyavāsinī, the goddess of the Vindhyas at Mirzapur, Uttar Pradesh, during annual spring festivals.

31. Both the English words *thug* and *loot* are derived from Hindi, the former from *ṭhagnā,* to cheat or deceive, the latter from *lūṭnā,* to plunder. Paul Dundas summarizes a story appearing in the *Upadeśamālā* by the twelfth-century Jain monk Hemacandra Maladhārin that specifically mentions the term *ṭhagavidyā,* "thug wisdom/magic spell." In this allegory, a horde of thieves attempts to loot (*luṇṭayitum*) a city. Their *ṭhagavidyā* is overpowered by a Jain superman (*mahāpuruṣa*) named Lord of Ascetic Convention (Samayarāja), who is summoned by a Jain woman named Fate (Bhavitavyatā). Such thieves are portrayed with attributes of pride, egoism, greed, and craftiness, and they demonstrate the ability to adopt various outward shapes, habitual stealing of vast quantities of wealth, lack of concern for military strength used against them, contempt for divine and temporal power, and skill in burglary. However, "there is no particular stress in the story on murderous activities carried out by these Ṭhags nor any hint of religious motivation behind their activities." See "Some Jain References to the Ṭhags and the Saṁsāramocaka," *Journal of the American Oriental Society* 115, 2 (1995): 281–84.

32. William Sleeman, *Ramaseeana* (Calcutta: G. H. Huttmann, 1836), p. 15.

33. "Of the Murderers Called Phansigars," reprinted in *Journal of Asiatick Researches* 16 (1816): 260. This was so despite Sherwood's observation that "the Phansigars are almost all mussalmans." The portrayal of the cheat, and the specific mention of the worship of Tuljapuri, makes me wonder whether Śivājī, the infamous Mārāṭhā warrior, could qualify as a "cheat" or a "Thug." He, too, was a marauder, with little authority prior to his victories. Tuljapuri was Śivājī's goddess, and in his notorious psuedo-surrender, he used deceptive methods, giving the enemy a false sense of security, and then returned their trust with murder. Also, from a preliminary study of the terms included in the "vocabulary" of Thugs, many appear to be from Marathi-based dialects. Sherwood claims, p. 271, that many of the Phansigars "have left the Company's territories and fled to those of the Nizam, and of the Mahrattas." I am grateful to Sanjukta Gupta for drawing my attention to the fact that Tuljapuri was Śivājī's patron goddess.

34. Ibid., p. 260.

35. The allusion is to Henry Yule and A. C. Burnell's great dictionary, *Hobson-Jobson: A Glossary of Colloquial Anglo-Indian Words and Phrases, and of Kindred Terms, Etymological, Historical, Geographical and Discursive* (1886, 1903; facsimile reprint of the 2d ed., London: Routledge & Kegan Paul, 1985).

36. H. H. Wilson, *Essays and Lectures on the Religions of the Hindus: Selected Works,* coll. and ed. Dr. Reinhold Rost (2 vols.; 1861–62; New Delhi: Asian Publication Services, 1976); see vol. 1: *Religious Sects of the Hindus,* p. 253.

37. Contributed to the *Calcutta Literary Gazette,* for Sunday, October 3, 1830. See discussion below.

38. Captain [William] Henry Sleeman, *The Thugs or Phansigars: Comprising a History of the Rise and Progress of that Extraordinary Fraternity of Assassins; and a description of the system which it pursues, and of the measures which have been adopted by the Supreme Government of India for its suppression* (Philadelphia: Carey & Hart, 1839).

39. The lack of awareness of, or inattention to, this strategic positioning of South Asian accounts of Kālī and her worshippers permeates most accounts of Thuggee. Even such eminent scholars as Wilhelm Halbfass are not immune to assuming an identity yet to be proven. In his "The Thags in Classical and Colonial India," Halbfass draws on references in Jain, Buddhist, Tibetan, and Vedic apologist works that use terms related to the verb *ṭhagnā* and speak of "deceivers." These then are taken as proof of a "tradition" of "deceivers" that can be historically linked for centuries and who can legitimately be called Thags. See his *Tradition and Reflection: Explorations in Indian Thought* (Albany: State University of New York Press, 1991), pp. 102–5.

40. George Bruce, *The Stranglers: The Cult of Thuggee and Its Overthrow in British India* (London: Longmans, 1968), p. 80.

41. Sleeman, *Thugs or Phansigars,* p. 67.

42. Bruce, *Stranglers,* p. 81. Sleeman later admitted that he had written the letter, but he did so only to Curwen Smith, whom he authorized to report the deception to George Swinton on November 19, 1830, weeks after the intense response of the British government.

43. Most of this is reproduced in the accessible book by Bruce, *Stranglers,* pp. 81–83.

44. See my "Rājās, Thugs, and Mafiosos: Religion and Politics in the Worship of Vindhyavāsinī," in *Render unto Caesar: Religion and Politics in Cross-Cultural Perspective,* ed. Sabrina Petra Ramet and Donald W. Treadgold (Washington, D.C.: American University Press, 1995), pp. 219–47.

45. Sleeman, quoted in Bruce, *Stranglers,* p. 82.

46. Sherwood, "Of the Murderers Called Phansigars," p. 253.

47. Ibid., p. 250.

48. Sleeman, quoted in Bruce, *Stranglers,* p. 83.

49. *Ramaseeana,* p. 141.

50. Bruce, *Stranglers,* p. 39.

51. For a tantalizingly brief comparison of some parallel accounts, see *Two Prakrit Versions of the Maṇipati-carita,* ed. Williams, pp. 25–27.

52. Our hero explains, "I fell down and cried piteously before the *yakṣiṇī* and that family deity, being moved to compassion, removed my pain and transferred to my leg the buttock and leg of the other man who had been impaled and was still alive." Ibid., p. 192.

53. Ibid., pp. 191–93.

54. N. K. Sastri, *The Culture and History of the Tamils* (Calcutta: Firma K. L. Mukhopadhyaya, 1964), p. 110.

55. G. H. Tarlekar, *Studies in the Nātya Śāstra* (Delhi: Motilal Banarsidass, 1975), p. 140.

CHAPTER 8

"India's Darkest Heart"

Kālī in the Colonial Imagination

Hugh B. Urban

To know the Hindoo idolatry, AS IT IS, *a person must wade through the filth of the thirty-six pooranŭs . . . he must follow the brahmun through his midnight orgies, before the image of Kalēē . . .*

WILLIAM WARD, *History, Literature, and Mythology of the Hindoos*

No one can tell in what age it was that divinity revealed itself to the vision of some aboriginal or Dravidian seer in the grotesque form of Mother Kali, nor does any record exist regarding the audacious hand that first modelled . . . those awful features . . . crudely embodying in visible form the very dread of femininity always working in the minds of a most sensuous people, too prone to fall before the subtle powers of the weaker sex. . . . The strange shapes of Kali . . . must have an immense antiquity . . . and may be regarded as only the fantastic shadows of divinity, seen . . . in the dim twilight of world's morning.

J. C. OMAN, *The Brahmans, Theists, and Muslims of India*

Since the beginnings of Western scholarship in India, the figure of the bloodthirsty, violent, and explicitly sexual goddess Kālī appears to have held an especially central, but also ambivalent and disturbing, place in the colonial imagination. In the eyes of the early British colonial authorities, missionaries, and scholars, Kālī was identified as the most depraved of all forms of modern popular Hinduism, the quintessence of the licentiousness and idolatry that had destroyed the noble, monotheistic spirit of the Vedas and Vedānta. If European scholars identified the "Golden Age" of India with the Vedas, they also identified its darkest and most perverse age with the worship of Kālī and her votaries, the secret cults of the Tantras.

At the same time, British colonial authorities began to find Kālī frightening. From the beginning of the nineteenth century on, she was believed to be closely associated with criminal and subversive groups, such as the infamous robber gangs, the Thuggee; and these fears would grow all the more intense with the rise of the revolutionary nationalist movement in Bengal, which was commonly thought to be led by mysterious secret societies under the patronage of the "terrible Goddess." Finally, by the dawn of the twentieth century, the image of Kālī also began to capture the imagination of Victorian popular culture. With her combination of lasciviousness and bloody violence, Kālī appears throughout Victorian novels as the quintessential symbol of the dark and terrifying—yet also strangely seductive and alluring—powers of the Orient.[1]

In this chapter, I examine the various ways in which Kālī was represented and perceived in the British colonial imagination of the nineteenth and early twentieth century. The powerful figure of Kālī, I submit, represents a crucial element in the history of colonialism and Orientalism, or European scholarship on Eastern cultures. Objectified under the "colonial gaze," she formed a part of the broader project of "imagining India" as an Other of the West. Indeed, Kālī might be said to embody the *extreme Orient,* the *most Other,* that inherently passionate, irrational tendency of the "Indian Mind" opposed to the rational, progressive, modern West.[2]

Yet as in the case of *satī* (widow burning) or the *devadāsī*s (temple courtesans), the image of Kālī has always been an ambivalent source of mixed horror and fascination, of simultaneous revulsion and lurid attraction.[3] She represents the allure of the forbidden Other, which threatens to seduce and corrupt the colonizers themselves. Indeed, Western representations of the violently sexual Kālī appear to be part of the more pervasive Victorian discourse on sexuality and perversion, which Michel Foucault has so insightfully analyzed. Rejecting the usual view of Victorian culture as puritanical and repressive, Foucault has shown that nineteenth-century British culture was suffused by a fascination with, and an unprecedented proliferation of discourse on, sexuality. "What is peculiar to modern societies . . . is not that they consigned sex to a shadow existence, but that they dedicated themselves to speaking of it *ad infinitum,* exploiting it as *the* secret."[4] A similar paradox surrounds the descriptions of Kālī.

However, like colonized peoples in all cultures, the Indian devotees of Kālī were by no means passively informed by Western representations of the Goddess. On the contrary, as Jean Comaroff, Michael Taussig, and others have shown, colonized peoples always remain creative agents, who retain the freedom to rethink, reshape, and redeploy their own mythic symbols in new ways, in response to or even subversion of the colonial order.[5] In some instances, as Rachel McDermott has argued in the case of Bengal, Kālī underwent a kind of "sweetening"; she was transformed from a violent, ugly

Tantric goddess into a benevolent maternal object of devotion.[6] Yet in other cases, during the nationalist struggle in Bengal the terrifying figure of Kālī was turned into a powerful weapon of the colonized, now used in the service of anti-colonial revolution; moreover, the nationalists seized upon the bloody, destructive figure of Kālī as a symbol of Mother India *precisely because* she represented threat and terror to the colonial imagination.

In my analysis of the colonial image of Kālī, I borrow some insights from Michael Taussig—specifically his notions of *mimesis* and the *dialectical image,* which he in turn adapts from Walter Benjamin. Mimesis, as Taussig defines it, is the fundamental human ability to imitate and mirror what is different from oneself, the capacity to represent and thereby control otherness. This faculty is common to all cultures and historical periods, from preindustrial to modern capitalist; however, it assumes new and particularly intense forms under the special circumstances of colonial contact, when different cultures are confronted with one another, often in unequal, exploitative, or violent circumstances. In the colonial situation, the mimesis or imagining of the Other becomes all the more politically charged. "Colonial history too must be understood as a spiritual politics in which image-power is an exceedingly valuable resource."[7] In order to master the native subject, the colonizer must imaginatively construct the native in terms that he can comprehend and control (as primitive, irrational, feminine, etc.). However, as Taussig also shows, the power of mimesis can just as well be employed by the native, as a means of mimicking, aping, and even magically appropriating the power of the colonizer himself.

Kālī, I hope to show, served as a very powerful kind of "dialectical image"—a crystallized fusion of ancient history and contemporary, political present; she lies at the nexus of a complex play of mimesis, imagining and counterimagining between colonizer and colonized in nineteenth- and twentieth-century India. If she could be imagined by her British viewers as the darkest, most savage heart of India, she could also be seized upon by her devotees as the most powerful and threatening image of India in revolt.

THE EXTREME ORIENT: THE IMAGE OF KĀLĪ IN THE ORIENTALIST AND COLONIAL IMAGINATION

When the British Orientalists and colonists first confronted the dark image of Kālī, this goddess already had a long and rich history in India. Although the word Kālī is mentioned as early as the *Atharva Veda,* it first appears as a proper name in the *Kāṭhaka Gṛhya Sūtra* (19.7). The first known account of Kālī as the wild, bloodthirsty, and frightening goddess that we find today appears in the Sauptika Parvan of the *Mahābhārata,* during Aśvatthāmā's night attack on the Pāṇḍavas (10.8.64).[8] In the early medieval Purāṇas, Kālī emerges as a goddess of battle and war, often associated with low-caste peoples and non-Aryan tribals. However, her most famous manifestation is found in the "Devī-Māhātmya" section of the *Mārkaṇḍeya Purāṇa,* where she appears as a wrathful projection of Durgā. Here she is a bloodthirsty, hideous, emaciated creature, raging about the field of battle and slaying the demons Caṇḍa and Muṇḍa.[9]

Despite these many early references to Kālī throughout greater India, her widespread public worship appears to have achieved its height of popularity only recently. The popular autumnal celebration of Kālī Pūjā as we find it in contemporary Bengal, for example, cannot be dated any earlier than the late eighteenth century. Yet rather strikingly, by the dawn of the nineteenth century, Kālī had become an enormously popular and, for many, quintessentially "Bengali" goddess, identified as the Mother and protectress of the land itself.[10] A variety of scholars have suggested a connection between the disastrous economic and political events in Bengal and the progressive rise of this violent, destructive, bloodthirsty goddess. As Payne argues, it was in large part the series of catastrophic events in the mid eighteenth century, beginning with the fall of the Muslim Nawāb, the Mārāṭhā invasions, the Dacoit gangs, the Sannyasi Rebellion, the famine of 1770, and the rise of the East India Company, that inspired the downtrodden Bengalis to turn to a powerful and terrible goddess such as Kālī.[11]

The early figure of Kālī that we see depicted in paintings from the eighteenth and nineteenth century is a horrific creature with long thin limbs, a distended belly, protruding ribs, long fangs, and a lolling tongue, who lurks in battlefields and cremation grounds consuming human flesh. She is, as a whole, an ambivalent fusion of death and sensuality, of terrifying violence and erotic power. When she is portrayed with her husband Śiva, she appears in the most explicitly "improper" form for a Hindu wife, as a woman who is not subservient to her husband but rather overwhelms and subdues him. As the supreme embodiment of disorder, chaos, and instability in the cosmos and in the social order, she is portrayed sometimes standing on Śiva's dead body and sometimes riding atop him, dominating him in sexual intercourse.[12]

In order to understand the representation of the goddess Kālī in the Western imagination, we must place it against the backdrop of the broader programs of colonial morality and British attitudes toward sexuality and gender in the nineteenth century. As great critics of Orientalism such as Edward Said have argued, imperialism as a whole was very often a "gendered" project. The colonial West was consistently imagined as the masculine, rational, active power that "penetrates," possesses, and rules the Orient, which is imagined as feminine, irrational, or passive: Edward Said has famously argued that "the sexual subjection of Oriental women to Western men 'fairly stands for the pattern of relative strength between East and West and the discourse about the Orient that it enabled.' . . . For Said, Orientalism takes perverse shape as a male power-fantasy that sexualizes a feminized Orient for Western power and possession."[13] As Robert Orme described the Indian as early as 1782, "Breathing in the softest climates, having so few real wants; and receiving even the luxuries of other nations with little labor . . . the Indian must become the most effeminate inhabitant of the globe."[14] Or, as Katherine Mayo put it in her widely read *Mother India,* the Indian character is characterized by a basic kind of effeminate "slave mentality," which is "the *flaccid subject of a foreign rule*"—"softly absorbing each current blow," due in large part to the "devitalizing character of the Hindu religion."[15] Not only was India commonly imagined to be an inherently "feminine" land, but, in the discourse of many British authors, India also came to be imagined as the quintessential realm of sexual perversions and abnormal carnal desires. "[A]nything and everything that deals with sex, procreation, union and human passion is worshipped and glorified," Sir George Fletcher MacMunn concluded in his book *The Underworld of India.*[16] Mayo described the Indian character as corrupted by premature sexual stimulation, excessive masturbation, the cult of the phallus, and other moral evils. At the very age "when the Anglo-Saxon is just coming into the full glory of manhood," the Indian is so drained and debilitated by sexual indulgences that he is left "poor and sick and his hands too weak to hold the reins of Government."[17] The Indian female, conversely, was commonly imagined to be excessively sexual, dark and seductive, insatiable in her carnal appetites, and possessed of a "draining and destructive" power—a power embodied in the aggressively sexual image of Kālī.[18]

The Victorian era witnessed a tremendous proliferation of medical and pseudo-medical treatises on sexuality, in both its proper and perverse forms. The British respectable classes of the nineteenth and early twentieth centuries came increasingly to regard only one form of sexual relation to be proper and healthy, namely, intercourse within the proper confines of heterosexual marriage, intended solely for the "useful" purpose of procreation. Viewing any deviation from "normal" marriage as morally suspect and socially destructive, Victorians were obsessed with the detailed scientific identification, classification, and enumeration of every imaginable perversion or sexual aberration. Among the most popular works in Victorian England was Richard von Krafft-Ebing's textbook *Psychopathia Sexualis* (1886), the most influential catalogue of deviations. Under the protective cover of medical nomenclature and moral outrage, Victorian readers "could indulge in this 'medicoforensic' peep-show of sexual hyperaesthesia, paresthesia, aspermia, polyspermia, spermatorrhea, sadism, masochism, fetishism, exhibitionism, psychic hermaphroditism, satyriasis, and nymphomania."[19] And among the most sinister perversions were those that, under the guise of transcendental ideals, confused religion and sensuality. As Miranda Shaw has shown, the British were both horrified and fascinated by the devotees of the

Goddess and the rituals of the Tantras, which seemed to embody the most unthinkable, even pathological, combination of sexuality and worship.[20]

Thus the India of the colonial imagination—seductive and mysterious, yet imbued with "debauchery, violence and death"[21]—was naturally embodied in the image of Kālī. Not only was she a goddess of disorder and aggressive sexuality, but she was a *wife who dominated her own husband, who stood on top of or straddled him in the most shocking form of intercourse.* As "India's darkest heart," she combined devotion, violence, and eroticism in a single form.

The first British authors to write about Kālī were not the early Orientalist scholars like William Jones or H. T. Colebrooke, who make only brief passing reference to the Goddess;[22] even the great European Orientalist Friedrich Max Müller gives only the slightest attention to Kālī, whom he regarded as a "decidedly non-Vedic" and non-Aryan pollution of the true Hindu tradition.[23] Rather, the first Europeans to take a serious interest in Kālī were early Christian missionaries. For instance, Reverend William Ward, a respected Baptist missionary, describes "the Hindoo system" as "the most PUERILE, IMPURE, AND BLOODY OF ANY SYSTEM OF IDOLATRY THAT WAS EVER ESTABLISHED ON EARTH."[24] A similar, even more vividly horrific perspective is that of the Reverend Alexander Duff, a Scottish missionary, who portrays Kālī's worship as the quintessence of hideous idolatry and superstition: "Of all the Hindu divinities, this goddess is the most cruel. . . . [Her] supreme delight . . . consists in cruelty and torture; her ambrosia is the flesh of living votaries and sacrificed victims; and her sweetest nectar, the copious effusion of their blood."[25]

As we see throughout the accounts of British authors of the nineteenth and early twentieth century, the image of Kālī seems to represent a kind of impenetrable, almost staggering and inconceivable mystery—a source of simultaneous horror and fascination, which the Western mind cannot fathom, but which it still feels compelled to try to describe in endless, almost obsessive detail (see figs. 8.1–3). As early as the mid nineteenth century, the image of Kālī had begun to be popularized through various travel narratives of British citizens in India, such as Fanny Parks's widely read *Wanderings of a Pilgrim in Search of the Picturesque* (1850).[26] As Sara Suleri comments on Parks's disturbing encounter with Kālī:

> Kali's excessive signification disrupts her narrative by embodying not only the dangers of divinity but . . . a colonial and a feminine sublime . . . [Parks's] obsession with the image of Kali signifies a moment of ideological self-questioning. . . . As an image of intense empowerment, she conjures up the Indian threat repetitively perceived as impinging on Anglo-Indian women's bodies. . . . The goddess's bodily demeanor suggests a frenzy beyond the heterosexual, converting her into an icon for the unlocatable aura of colonial threat.[27]

Figure 8.1 "Kali, the Dreaded Goddess of Destruction," from Augustus Somerville, *Crime and Religious Beliefs in India* (Calcutta: "The Criminologist," 1929), frontispiece.

Not only the Goddess's image but also her worship by Śākta and Tantric devotees caused a mix of fascination and revulsion. Esoterically, as Ward recounts, Kālī is worshipped in secret by the followers of the "Tŭntrŭs"—a sect "so singularly corrupt," so addicted to "unutterable abominations," that they even dare to make liquor and sexual intercourse their holy sacraments.[28] On the public level among her ignorant lower-class devotees, Kālī is worshipped with blood sacrifices in an orgy of killing and violence. Ward

Figure 8.2 "Kali," from Charles Coleman, *The Mythology of the Hindus* (London: Parbury, Allen, 1832), pl. 19, facing p. 91.

recounts his own experience at Kālīghāṭ: "Never did I see men so eagerly enter into the shedding of blood, nor do I think any butchers could slaughter animals more expertly. The place literally swam with blood. The bleating of the animals, the numbers slain, and the ferocity of the people employed, actually made me unwell, and I returned about midnight, filled with horror and indignation."[29] Similarly, as the widely read *Calcutta Review* described it in 1855, the Śākta worship of the cruel Kālī, with its union of sex, violence, and religion, "open[s] the way for gratification of all the sensual

Figure 8.3 "Procession for the Goddess Kali," from Sir Colin Campbell, *Narrative of the Indian Revolt from its Outbreak to the Capture of Lucknow* (London: G. Vickers, 1858), p. 258.

appetites, they hold out encouragement to drunkards, thieves and dacoits, they present the means of satisfying every lustful desire . . . and lead men to commit abominations which place them on a level with the beasts." Indeed, if one were unfortunate even to observe this worship, one's "morals are corrupted by . . . scenes of impurity which we cannot commit."[30]

By the early twentieth century, as we see in Mayo's *Mother India,* the gruesome worship of Kālī had not only become infamous in the colonial imagination as the most explicit example of the natural tendency toward violence and perversion that characterized the Indian mind; she was now conceived as the very soul of the lower-class and poverty-stricken Indian populace, for all "the lowest and most ignorant of Indians are Kali worshippers."[31] It is no accident that Mayo chooses to begin her general survey of Indian sexual and cultural life with the following extremely vivid and rather ghastly description of a goat sacrifice at Kālīghāṭ:

> Of a sudden, a piercing outburst of shrill bleating. . . . Here stand two priests, one with a cutlass in his hand, the other holding a young goat. The goat shrieks, for in the air is that smell that all beasts fear. A crash of sound as before the goddess drums thunder. The priest who holds the goat swings it up . . . its screaming head held fast in a cleft post. The second priest with a single blow

of his cutlass decapitates the little creature. The blood gushes forth on the pavement, the drums and the gongs burst out wildly. 'Kali, Kali, Kali!' shout all priests and the suppliants together, some flinging themselves face downward on the temple floor. Meantime . . . a woman who waited behind the killers . . . has rushed forward and fallen on all fours to lap up the blood with her tongue—'in the hope of having a child' . . . while half a dozen sick, sore dogs horribly misshapen by nameless diseases, stick their hungry muzzles in the lengthening pool of gore.[32]

THE PATHOS OF THE UNDERWORLD: "HUNGRY KALI" AND BRITISH COLONIAL AUTHORITIES' FEARS OF CRIMINAL OR REVOLUTIONARY POLITICAL ACTIVITY

[I]t is just this presence of some ancient horror, existing beneath the outer surface of perfectly reasonable political aspirations, which has been a source of trouble to many a kind Viceroy desiring only India's good.

LIEUTENANT GENERAL SIR GEORGE FLETCHER MACMUNN, *The Underworld of India*

[T]his divinity is the avowed patroness of all the most atrocious outrages against the peace of society.

CALEB WRIGHT, *India and Its Inhabitants*

Within the European colonial imagination of the nineteenth and early twentieth centuries, the fear of perverse, transgressive or immoral practices often went hand in hand with the fear of violent, subversive political activities among the natives under their rule.[33] As we see in the case of the Mau Mau in Kenya or in various native uprisings in South and North America, political rebellion was, in the colonial gaze, often associated with sexual transgression, perverse secret rituals, or the violation of social taboos. The rebellious colonial subject threatened not only to subvert the government but also to unravel the moral fabric of society itself. And nowhere was this believed to be more true than in the case of India, where "crime, religious belief, and magic are entangled . . . to a degree absolutely inconceivable to the western mind."[34]

Shortly after the dawn of British rule in India, Kālī's violently sexual image, together with the transgressive rites of her Tantric worshippers, became closely associated with fears of criminal activity, subversive politics, and whatever else might undermine British law (see fig. 8.1). Kālī embodies, in MacMunn's words, that "*ancient horror beneath the surface*" of British rule, always threatening to burst forth and subvert all just political order.

The most infamous of these groups, and the most sinister in the British imagination, were the robber gangs known as the "Thuggee." To what degree the Thugs were a real organization, and to what degree they were a fabrication of British imagination and colonial paranoia, is very difficult to say. As Cynthia Humes has shown in her contribution to this volume, early-nineteenth-century British authorities initially regarded the Thuggee as clear evidence of dangerous criminal elements on the subcontinent that threatened Indians themselves—and thus justified the need for extensive British rule and the strict imposition of colonial law and order. However, increasingly in the late nineteenth century, and above all after the Mutiny of 1857, the threat of the Thuggee began to intensify in the colonial imagination, growing into a sinister nationwide organization, dedicated to the subversion of British colonial rule itself.[35]

Indeed, to many officials, the Thuggee were far more than a simple gang of robbers—they were nothing less than a vast widespread subversive organization united under patronage of the sadistic goddess Kālī and dedicated to undermining British law and order:

> [T]his cult . . . was a vast secret society based perhaps on some hatred of the wealthy and fortunate as persons . . . and devoted to the conception of Kali . . . Kali is specially concerned with everything cruel and hard. Under her form of Bhowani, the Thugs rendered her homage. . . . [I]n the heart of every initiate there soon arose a sacred joy in depriving people of their lives for the mere sensual gratification—a form . . . of Sadism, and of that unholy joy with which Soviet female executioners have put their prisoners to death.[36]

Not only were they thought to engage in rampant violence in the name of Kālī, but the Thuggee were also believed to hold dark secret rituals dedicated to the Goddess. These sinister rites were described almost as a kind of "black mass," or inverted communion, consisting of blood sacrifice and sacramental consumption of wine and meat. A sheep was sacrificed in front of an image of the Goddess, a black-skinned, vampirelike figure, smeared with dried gore.[37]

However, the fears of the political and revolutionary role of Kālī would only reach their height of intensity in the early twentieth century, with increasing discontent and political resistance in Bengal. Beginning with the Swadeshi movement, which burst into violent agitation following the Partition of Bengal in 1905, the nationalist revolutionaries appeared to the British government to represent a very dangerous and disturbing combination of religion and politics (a confusion almost as dangerous as the perverse mingling of sex and religion).[38] In many official accounts, members of this "underground murder cult," consisting of a "strange mélange of masonic ritual and a festival of horrible furious Kali in her wilder aspects,"[39] were thought to engage in secret rituals in which they actually consecrated bombs to Kālī, so that they might gain the cruel goddess's favor and inflict the most destruction when hurled at British officials. "A '*bomb-parast*' is one who has put a bomb in the shrine of Kali that he may worship it and gloat with hungry Kali on the blood that may flow. . . . [T]he Hindu student depraved and often injured by too early eroticism, turns to the suggestiveness of the murder monger, and worships the nitro-glycerin bomb as the apotheosis of his goddess."[40]

All this was only natural, of course, since the "Indian mind" always had an inherent tendency toward the combination of sexual licentiousness and political violence. As Sir Valentine Chirol described the Swadeshi movement in his widely read *Indian Unrest,* this group was basically rooted in a mixture of religious mysticism, sexual perversion, and lawless violence, all centered around the horrific image of mother Kālī.[41] In fact, some, like MacMunn, attributed the prevalence of revolutionary activity among Bengali students to the unnatural, overstimulating sexual practices of this culture—specifically the exposure of young men to "early eroticisms" and young marriage:

> One of the most pitiful of all the manifestations of unrest . . . is the strange underground movement, which has produced a secret bomb and revolver cult. . . . [T]here is behind it a sinister tradition . . . of a peculiar aspect of the Hindu religion. Behind all the horror, cruelty and sudden death of the world lies . . . Kali, the goddess of all horrors . . . "I am hungry," is her cry, "I want blood, blood victims!" . . . The tragedy of this semi-religious murder . . . is but one instance of how the Kali cult may bear evil. . . . Not even the perverted imaginations of the Marquis de Sade could devise a more horrible nightmare. . . . To minds such as those of students . . . overstrained by the premature eroticism . . . the deity becomes a cult in which insensate and half-mystical murder may be a dominant thought.[42]

"THE MINGLED PERFUME OF LOVE AND WORSHIP, SEX AND RELIGION": KĀLĪ AND THE VICTORIAN LITERARY IMAGINATION

> *Kali-Ma . . . symbolizes the ultimate mystery in life—the mystery of sex.*
> FLORA ANNIE STEEL, *The Law of the Threshold*

The cruel and lascivious image of Kālī was not only a central preoccupation of colonial administrators and Orientalist scholars; she also entered the Victorian imagination in a more popular form, permeating British culture through newspapers, magazines, and, above all, Victorian novels.[43] As Benita Parry and Lewis Wurgaft have argued in their studies of Victorian novels between 1880 and 1930, English novelists like Flora Annie Steel, F. E. F. Penny, and I. A. R. Wylie were fascinated, perhaps obsessed, by what they had heard about the erotic, violent figure of Kālī. They filled their novels with lurid tales of the horrible, yet strangely seductive Tantric yogis and their Goddess, the naked, cruel Kālī.[44] Penny recounts these hideous rites in her novel *The Swami's Curse* (1929): "[T]he follower of the Tantric cult professes no austerities. He seeks to kill desire by an unlimited indulgence which brings satiety and extinction of emotion . . . his depravity is commended as a great virtue."[45] Worshipped in sexual orgies and gruesome, necrophagic rituals, the Death Goddess is the terrifying image of "something unknown—*horribly unknown*—that lay beyond that life."[46] She is "India's darkest heart." "To the Indian multitudes the mystery of sex is symbolized in Kali . . . Kali's shrines reek of the 'mingled perfume of love and worship, of sex and religion.' The desire for blood and the pursuit of promiscuous sex coalesce in the Tantric rites."[47]

Steel's tale "On the Second Story" explicitly portrays "Kâli" as the symbol of everything that is backward, regressive, primitive, and horrifying about India, all that is directly opposed to reform, modernity, and scientific advance. The protagonist, Ramanund, a science teacher and active member of reform societies, is scornful of religious superstitious and traditional customs. During an outbreak of cholera, while other men allow the women to intercede with Kālī on their behalf, Ramanund pleads for cleanliness and the use of filtered water. However, a naked old sannyasi—a "savage-looking figure"—warns him of Kālī's great strength, juxtaposing the ancient mystical power of the Goddess to the modern ways of the scientist: "Let it be Kâli, the Eternal Woman, against thee, Ramanund the Scholar."[48] Thus, Kālī, the symbol of old India and its ancient magic, triumphs against the futile challenge of the emancipated Ramanund.

Echoing government anxieties, the Victorian novelists also played upon the deep fear of Kālī as a potential source of criminal activity and political subversion—above all, for her role in the revolutionary violence of the nationalist movement. As we see in I. A. R. Wylie's novel *Daughter of Brahma* (1912), the goddesses Kālī and Durgā become the inspiration for the Indian revolt against colonial rule, thirsting for the sacrificial blood of the "white goats":

> Hindu fanaticism and the cults of Kali and Durga are directly related to sedition and revolt. A Brahminical secret sect issues a manifesto that rouses a native army to demoniacal fury. "Arise," the manifesto proclaims, "and in the name of Durga use your weapons until no single demon defiles our holy soil! . . . to every man who dips his hand in the blood of a white goat it shall be counted more than all the virtues."[49]

But perhaps the most vivid account of Kālī worship, Tantric immorality, and their associations with revolutionary violence appears in Steel's novel *The Law of the Threshold,* which aims to account for the terrorism in twentieth-century political movements. Dismissing any possibility of genuine political grievances as irrelevant to an Indian psyche dominated by inborn blood lust and religious fanaticism, Steel portrays the revolutionary as a kind of twisted religious fanatic: "Their care for freedom, for self-government, for all the shibboleths of the young India party was as naught to their care for the glory of their cult." At the very heart of this cult lies the black Goddess herself: "Kali-worship represents, even constitutes, the nationalist movement."[50]

Steel's novel recounts the story of an American convert to Tantrism named Nigel Blennerhasset. Accompanied by a lovely Indian girl, Maya Day, who has been brought up and educated in the United States, Nigel travels to India in order to convert Indians to his Tantric sect. Unbeknownst to Blennerhasset and his consort, however, his Tantric cult is being exploited by two Bolshevist-Jewish agents who are working with Indian nationalists in order to overthrow British rule. By appealing to Indians' inherent religious fanaticism and perversion, they hope to use Kālī worship to arouse widespread violence and hence to achieve (in words Steel puts into the mouth of the anarchist Bakunin) "*the destruction of law and Order and the unchaining of evil passions.*"[51]

Clearly, however, the terrifying and yet disturbingly seductive descriptions of Kālī and her devotees that we find throughout colonial writings and Victorian English literature reflect as much—and probably far more—of the British imagination as they do of the "Indian Mind." They are, in Taussig's sense, mimetic projections of the colonizer's simultaneous fear of and secret desire for the native Other, the mixed repulsion and attraction to his untamed savagery, sexuality, and animal violence. Likewise, as Wurgaft argues, these fanciful descriptions are a clear example of projection: the displacement of one's own deep-seated wishes and fears onto some external object. For Victorian novelists, the image of Kālī was a powerful projection of their own sexual desires and anxieties, objectified in the mirror of an exotic Other.[52]

SACRIFICING WHITE GOATS TO THE GODDESS: THE APPROPRIATION OF THE IMAGE OF KĀLĪ IN THE BENGAL NATIONALIST MOVEMENT

> *Rise up, O sons of India, arm yourselves with bombs, despatch the white Asuras to Yama's abode. Invoke the mother Kali. . . . The Mother asks for sacrificial offerings. What does the Mother want? . . . She wants many white Asuras. The Mother is thirsting after the blood of the Feringhees [foreigners] who have bled her profusely. . . . [C]hant this verse while slaying the Feringhee white goat . . . : With the close of a long era, the Feringhee Empire draws to an end, for behold! Kali rises in the East.*
>
> *Yugantar* (1905)

As in virtually every case of colonial domination, Indians were by no means content to remain passive and unreflective, merely accepting the imaginary representations imposed on them by Orientalists and colonial authorities.[53] On the contrary, like native peoples in all situations of colonial contact, they too had the potential to engage in a variety of appropriative and subversive strategies, often by turning colonial sources to anti-colonial uses.[54] Borrowing the terms of Taussig and Benjamin, we could say that Kālī is an ideal example of a "dialectical image"—a crystallized fusion of ancient religious myth and present historical and political context. Every community, Benjamin suggests, has a kind of "cultural memory" or a "reservoir of myths and utopian symbols from a more distant ur-past." These collective images can be used by established institutions in order to legitimate existing ideologies and hierarchies, but marginalized and oppressed classes may also claim them as sources of political awakening and "revolutionary rupture." "Where thought comes to a standstill in a constellation saturated with tensions, there appears the dialectical image. It is the caesura in the movement of thought."[55] In the dialectical image, mythic narratives of past traditions, utopian visions, and nostalgic longings for lost paradise can be seized and transformed into revolutionary visions of liberation.[56]

The dialectical image, in turn, lies at the nexus of a complex play of representations and imaginary projections—a play of mimesis. Mimesis, Taussig suggests, becomes especially intense in periods of colonial contact, when cultures are suddenly and dramatically confronted with a radical Otherness that brings domination and imperial control. The colonizing powers for their part construct a variety of imaginary representations of native peoples —as savage, primitive, feminine, emotional, or violent, rather than rational or scientific. Projecting their own deepest fears of disorder or subversion, together within their own repressed desires and fantasies, the colonizers project a kind of negative anti-type of themselves in the mirror of the colonized Other.[57]

And yet, particularly in cases of colonial contact, mimesis is always a "two-way street." Colonized peoples also have their own forms of mimesis, their own ways of imaginatively representing the colonial Other; through mimicry, parody, and satire they seize upon the imaginings of the colonizers themselves, often turning them on their heads and manipulating them as a source of "counter-hegemonic discourse." For example, Taussig examines the common European representation of America as a woman, typically a beautiful naked woman adorned with feathered headdress and holding a bow and arrows. This New World/Woman, however, could assume both benevolent and terrifying features, imagined either as an inviting maiden awaiting the European colonial powers, "languidly entertaining Discoverers from her hammock," or as a horrifying, rebellious demonness, "striding brazenly across the New World as castrator with her victim's bloody head in her grasp."[58] Yet as Taussig points out, the image of America as female was not only used by the European colonizers, but was also reappropriated by the Indians themselves, now transformed into a symbol of Indianness and anti-European revolutionary spirit (as we see in Pedro José Figueroa's painting of Bolivia as a woman in a feathered headdress, seated next to the liberator of the nation, Simón Bolívar).

It is precisely this kind of dialectical, double-edged role, this complex play of mimesis and imagery, that we find in the role of Kālī in early-twentieth-century Bengal. In the nationalist movement of that period, the violent image of Kālī was newly adapted and transformed into the supreme symbol of Mother India fighting against her foreign oppressors. Although the origins of the nationalist movement in Bengal lie with the more moderate ideals of the Indian National Congress of the last quarter of the nineteenth century, led by conservative figures such as R. C. Dutt and G. K. Gokhale, its second, most volatile period begins from 1904, with the Swadeshi movement and its direct challenge to the legitimacy of British rule. And it burst into open conflagration in 1905, with the British partition of western Bengal from eastern Bengal and Assam. Above all, in the period after 1907, the movement began to assume a far more violent form, abandoning the earlier doctrines of passive resistance and turning instead to the tactics of revolutionary secret societies and terrorism. Organized in underground groups like the Calcutta Anuśīlan Samiti or the Dacca Anuśīlan, and combining "neotantric rituals" with elements of European secret societies like the Carbonari, the terrorist groups made it their sworn duty "to effect a revolution and overthrow of British government."[59] Ironically, among the most active members of the violent strain of the movement was none other than Aurobindo Ghose—a man who would, in his later years, renounce the political life altogether in order to pursue spirituality, yoga, and art. In the years 1902–10, Aurobindo and his brother Barindrakumār worked among the revolutionary secret societies, such as Yugāntar and the Anuśīlan Samiti, and directed the most radical papers, such as the English-language *Yugantar* and *Bande Mataram.*

From the outset, the writings of the nationalist movement had made extensive use of traditional religious and mythic themes to legitimate their revolutionary activity. *Yugantar,* for example, calls upon the traditional Hindu model of the avatar or successive incarnations of Viṣṇu sent to right the world and combat evil: "the army of young men is the Nrisinha and the Varaha and the Kalki incarnations of God, saving the good and destroying the wicked."[60] Surely the most powerful religious symbol employed by the revolutionaries, however, was the goddess Śakti—power or strength—and above all, her most violent and frightening incarnation as Kālī (see fig. 8.1). As we have seen above, British Orientalist and colonial authors had consistently portrayed the Bengali male as an effeminate, flaccid, weak creature, naturally subdued and easily ruled by the more masculine and virile Europeans. Aurobindo himself is painfully aware of the figure of the "effete Babu," the fawning, submissive servant of the colonial administration. He too criticizes the "passivity" and weakness of modern Bengalis, who have been "emasculated" by foreign powers, and he calls upon them to adopt a virile, militant stance against their oppressors. He hopes to awaken an inner strength, a "hyper-masculinity": "India needs Shakti alone . . . what we must strive to acquire . . . is strength—strength physical, strength moral, but above all strength spiritual."[61] Hence, it is not surprising that the leaders of these revolutionary groups would turn to the imagery of the Kṣatriya, or warrior ideal, and to the cult of Śakti, or "Power." "The morality of the Kshatriya justifies violence in times of war," Aurobindo declares. "The sword of the warrior is as necessary to the fulfillment of justice and righteousness as the holiness of the saint. . . . Therefore, says Sri Krishna in the *Mahabharata,* God created battle and armour, the sword, the bow and the dagger."[62] As Ashis Nandy comments,

> [M]any nineteenth century Indian movements of social, religious and political reform . . . tried to make Kṣatriyahood . . . a new . . . indicator of authentic Indianness. . . . [T]he search for martial Indianness underwrote one of the most powerful collaborationist strands within Indian society, represented by . . . protest against colonialism (such as the immensely courageous but ineffective terrorism of Bengal . . . led by semi-Westernized middle-class urban youth).[63]

In short, the image of hypermasculine, militant Bengali was the counterpart to the image of Kālī or Śakti as the powerful, violent Goddess of the Motherland.[64]

The most famous and influential depiction of Kālī as the supreme symbol of the Motherland appears in Bankim Chandra Chatterjee's well-known novel *Ānanda Maṭh* ("Abbey of Bliss"), published in 1882. Set in the mid eighteenth century, the novel centers on a secret group of sannyasi rebels who oppose their Muslim rulers and fight to win back their Motherland. Rather ironically, Bankim's intention in writing the novel does not seem to have been to arouse anti-British sentiment, for its original thrust was more anti-Muslim than anti-British. Nevertheless, Bankim presents Kālī as the symbol of the Indian nation, the Motherland, who is both glorious in her original splendor and terrible in her present oppressed condition: "Kali was at once a symbol of the degradation of the society under alien rule and a reservoir of unlimited power."[65] In one of the most remarkable passages in Bankim's work, the Goddess appears as a kind of fusion of past, present, and future. Inside the temple at the Abbey of Bliss, we are successively introduced to three goddesses, representing Mother India in three historical periods. First we meet a beautiful noble image of Jagaddhātrī as the "Mother, what once was," symbolizing India's golden past. Then we encounter the dark, dreadful Kālī, the bloodthirsty image of India in the present age under foreign oppression: "Look what the mother has *now* become . . . Kali, covered with the blackest gloom, despoiled of all wealth, and without a cloth to wear. The whole of the country is a land of death and so the Mother has no better ornament than a garland of skulls."[66] Lastly, he sees a third image—a golden, radiant, ten-armed goddess who represents the future of India, the liberated form of the nation in its original glory. "This is the mother as she *would be.*"

During the first years of the Swadeshi movement, Bankim's novel and his politicized image of the Goddess became a favorite weapon of the revolutionaries. Newly appropriated by figures like Swami Vivekananda and Sister Nivedita, in her widely influential *Kali the Mother* (1907), and seized upon above all by the extremist Bengali periodicals, the image of Kālī suddenly assumed a markedly political form. The famous hymn from Bankim's novel, "Bande Mātāram," was rendered into English by Aurobindo himself, who made this the battle cry of the nationalist movement and "the gospel of fearless strength and force."[67] However, Aurobindo and the revolutionaries also profoundly reinterpreted Bankim's original story, transforming it from a piece of pro-British, anti-Muslim propaganda into a radically anti-colonialist, anti-British call to revolution. Moreover, Aurobindo forged an even more explicit fusion of the political and the religious domains in the image of the Goddess, drawing above all on the traditional Tantric imagery of the divine Mother as "power" on both the spiritual and revolutionary planes.

The most important work from Aurobindo's early political period, which fuses the religious and the revolutionary domains, is a brief pamphlet entitled "Bhawani Mandir"—the temple of the Goddess. Here, Aurobindo lays out his ideal of a secret religio-political organization, an order of young ascetics who would consecrate themselves to the liberation of the motherland. The ascetics would meet at a temple of the goddess "Bhawani," a manifestation of "Kali," "hidden in a secret place where the members of the order would acquire strength in preparation for the armed struggle for independence." In the following remarkable passage, Aurobindo identifies Śakti as the force underlying the industrialization, wealth, and power—including the West's growing military might—that characterizes the modern world:

> Wherever we turn our gaze, huge masses of strength rise before our vision, tremendous, swift, and inexorable forces . . . terrible sweeping columns of force. All is growing large and strong. The Shakti of war, the Shakti of wealth . . . are a thousand-fold more prolific in resources [and] weapons. . . . Everywhere the Mother is at work; from her mighty . . . hands enormous forms . . . are leaping forth into the . . . world. We have seen the . . . mighty rise of great empires in the West. . . . Some are Mleccha Shaktis . . . others are Arya Shaktis, bathed in . . . self-sacrifice; but all are the Mother in Her new phase. . . . She is whirling into life the new.[68]

But although she is at work everywhere in the modern world, Śakti is first and foremost the power of the Indian nation. While the forces of Westernization and industrialization manifest the demonic form of Śakti, harnessed toward destructive, selfish ends, the Indian nation reveals the true Aryan force of Śakti, turned toward spiritual ends. For Aurobindo, this divine Śakti is nothing other than the collective power of the souls of all India, the combined energy of each individual Indian. The nation of India "*is not a piece of earth nor a figure of speech*. . . . It is a mighty Shakti, composed of the Shakti of all the millions of units that make up the nation."[69]

Most important, Aurobindo and the other revolutionaries drew upon precisely those elements of Śakti in her terrible form of Kālī, and particularly those aspects that the British most feared and despised—the violent destructive Goddess who drinks human blood and wears severed heads. As early as 1905, the leaders of the Swadeshi movement began to administer swadeshi vows before Kālī at Kālīghāṭ; and soon many of the secret societies like the Dacca Anuśīlan followed suit, in order to cement the bonds of loyalty and inspire terrorist activities.[70] Indeed, one of the nationalists' most powerful images—one frequently commented upon by the British—was taken from a traditional Tantric image of the Goddess as Chinnamastā, standing naked on the corpse of Śiva, holding her own severed head and drinking the blood that flows from it. According to the accompanying caption, this represents the motherland, "decapitated by the English, but preserving her vitality unimpaired by drinking her own blood."[71]

However, Kālī's image was used not only to represent the humiliation of modern India. Since her first appearances in Hindu mythology, she has been linked to destruction, bloodshed, and war—and such resonances are effective resources in inciting political violence.

> The Mother is thirsty, and is pointing out to her sons the only thing that can quench that thirst. Nothing less than human blood and decapitated heads will satisfy her. Let her sons, therefore, worship her with these offerings. . . . On the day on which the Mother is worshipped in this way in every village, on that day the people of India will be inspired with a divine spirit and the crown of independence will fall into their hands.[72]
>
> Will the worshippers of Shakti shrink from the shedding of blood? The number of Englishmen in this country is not above one lakh and a half . . . you can in a single day bring English rule to an end. The worship of the goddess will not be consummated if you sacrifice your lives at the shrine of independence without shedding blood.[73]

Today, the revolutionaries declare, the soil of India itself has become a vast "cremation ground"—much like the cremation ground that is the ritual field of the Tāntrikas—upon which the violent and destructive Kālī unleashes her terrible power: "The cremation ground symbolizes cosmic dissolution. Mahakali is no doubt the symbol of destruction. . . . This form of Kali [is] . . . the motherland in the days of alien rule . . . the sole purpose was for preparing the nation for a 'revolution' that would . . . 'Aryanize a world.'"[74] But ironically, despite its powerful shock effect, the nationalists' use of the image of Kālī does not appear to have been entirely successful, because in many ways, it played right back into the colonial view of India as spiritually corrupt and morally depraved, as a land of barbarous violence and perverse irrationality. Similarly, Nandy has argued that the self-image created by the Bengali revolutionaries also backfired and worked against them: the "hyper-masculine" Kṣatriya ideal of the revolutionaries still played by the rules of the colonial views of sexuality and manhood, replicating the European ideal of the virile, active, superior male and the passive, submissive inferior female. Hence, it could not succeed in overthrowing colonial ideology, but ultimately reinforced it.[75] The solution that would finally win out, of course, was not the radical program of the extremists like Aurobindo and the revolutionaries, but the ideal of passive resistance and chastity promoted by Mahatma Gandhi. By 1910, in fact, Aurobindo himself would abandon the revolutionary project and instead turn inward to the life of the spirit.

EPILOGUE: IMAGINING AND REIMAGINING KĀLĪ IN THE TWENTIETH CENTURY

> *Kill for the love of killing! Kill lest ye be killed yourselves! Kill for the love of Kali! Kill, Kill, Kill!*
>
> PRIEST OF KĀLĪ (EDUARDO CIANNELLI) in the film version of *Gunga Din* (1939)

> *Kālī's reminder of the dark, avenging side of life, and the power of rage, . . . posed against the contemporary backdrop of a plundered and wounded earth, is a vision of spiritually emerging power far removed from the benevolent mercy and accepting patience of Lakṣmī or Mary."*
>
> LINDA E. OLDS, "The Neglected Feminine"

The figure of Kālī, it would seem, lies at a critical fulcrum between colonial and anti-colonial imaginations, emerging out of a dynamic process of mimicry, mirroring, and countermirroring.[76] On one hand, the image of Kālī in colonial discourse was in large part a mimetic reflection, a projection of everything that frightened British citizens in a foreign land, all the disorder, savagery, and unrest that threatened to unravel the fragile order of their rule. On the other hand, she was a highly ambivalent image, which could be turned around, seized by the colonized, and turned into a powerful—if ultimately unsuccessful—revolutionary instrument.

And, of course, the imagining and reimagining of Kālī has by no means ended with the collapse of imperial rule in this century. On the contrary, Kālī has been reappropriated and transformed—by both Indians and Westerners—in a variety of surprising new forms. Not only does Kālī continue to appear throughout literature and cinema—for example, in *Gunga Din,* in the Beatles' *Help,* and, more recently, in *Indiana Jones and the Temple of Doom* —as the quintessential symbol of the savagery and violence lying at India's darkest heart; but, rather strikingly, she has been appropriated in a variety of more positive ways in the modern imagination.

One of the earliest and most influential of the positive revalorizations of

Kālī has occurred among the romantic and idealistic scholars of the early twentieth century—such as Heinrich Zimmer and Mircea Eliade—and above all, among the Jungian tradition of archetypal psychology—as we see in Erich Neumann, Marie-Louise von Franz, and the great popularizer of world mythology, Joseph Campbell. For Zimmer, Kālī is still regarded as the darkest, most primordial heart of India as a whole—the very essence of the world process of unceasing life and death, which is the core of the Indian worldview: she is "destruction unending, wrought by the generating, life-bearing, *Ewig-Weibliche, le charme éternel.*" However, this has a positive spin: she is the dark side of primordial nature, the power of sexuality, death, and destruction, which has been neglected and repressed by overly rationalized, intellectual and "masculine" Western man. Hence, she is a figure from whom we "moderns" have much to learn.[77]

The various disciples of Carl Jung have taken this revalorization of Kālī further still. For depth psychologists like Neumann, Kālī represents one of the most archaic archetypes of the unconscious, which lies within the deepest recesses of every psyche and ultimately within the oldest layer of the human collective unconscious. She is the quintessential embodiment of the darker side of the "great Mother," the destructive and devouring half that complements the benign, nurturing positive Mother.[78] As such, the image of Kālī represents a much-needed therapy for the unbalanced psyche of Western man, who is "one-sidedly patriarchal" and has lost the archetypal power of the Feminine, particularly in its darker, more terrible aspects.[79]

The various reappropriations of Kālī in this century are virtually endless. One might also, as Rachel McDermott has done, examine various uses of Kālī among New Age enthusiasts, Goddess-worshippers and feminists in the West, where she appears throughout a wide array of popular forms—books, cassettes, tarot decks, posters, greeting cards, and now, as we see in vividly spectacular computer graphics, on the Internet itself. In contrast to the repressive male-dominated Western world, Kālī represents, in contemporary feminist and new age literature, a powerful celebration of the dark side of femininity and sexuality.[80] On the other hand, one might return to the Indian world, and examine the ways in which contemporary feminists such as "Kali for Women" have now positively valorized and reinterpreted the Goddess. Yet despite their wide diversity and seeming constant transformations, virtually all of these cases continue to reinforce the image of Kālī as the "extreme orient," the most Other, the most archaic or primordial heart of India. Whether attacked as the sign of the decadence of Indian civilization or hailed as the symbol of empowerment and liberation, Kālī remains a critical pivot in the ambivalent, often violent confrontation between the West and its Others.

NOTES

EPIGRAPHS: William Ward, *History, Literature, and Mythology of the Hindoos,* 3d ed. (4 vols.; 1817–20; reprint, Delhi: Low Price Publications, 1990), 3: xcv; John Campbell Oman, "Kalighat and Hinduism in Bengal," in id., *The Brahmins, Theists, and Muslims of India* (London: T. Fisher Unwin, 1907), p. 11.

1. See Benita Parry, *Delusions and Discoveries: Studies on India in the British Imagination, 1880–1930* (London: Allen Lane, 1972).

2. See Ronald B. Inden, *Imagining India* (Oxford: Blackwell, 1990).

3. See Lata Mani, "Cultural Theory, Colonial Texts: Reading Eyewitness Accounts of Widow Burning," in *Cultural Studies,* ed. Lawrence Grossberg, Cary Nelson, and Paula A. Treichler (New York: Routledge, 1992), pp. 392–408; and Frédérique Apffel Marglin, *Wives of the God-King: The Rituals of the Devadasis of Puri* (Delhi: Oxford University Press, 1985).

4. Michel Foucault, *The History of Sexuality,* vol. 1: *An Introduction,* trans. Robert Hurley (New York: Vintage Books, 1980), 1: 25.

5. Jean Comaroff and John Comaroff, eds., *Modernity and Its Malcontents: Ritual and Power in Postcolonial Africa* (Chicago: University of Chicago Press, 1993), pp. xi–xii; Jean Comaroff, *Body of Power, Spirit of Resistance: The Culture and History of a South African People* (Chicago: University of Chicago Press, 1985), pp. 131, 236; and Michael T. Taussig, *The Devil and Commodity Fetishism in South America* (Chapel Hill: University of North Carolina Press, 1980).

6. Rachel Fell McDermott, "Evidence for the Transformation of the Goddess Kālī: Kamalākānta Bhaṭṭācārya and the Bengali Śākta Padāvalī Tradition" (Ph.D. diss., Harvard University, 1993).

7. Michael T. Taussig, *Mimesis and Alterity: A Particular History of the Senses* (New York: Routledge, 1993) p. 177.

8. Thomas B. Coburn, *Devī-Māhātmya: The Crystallization of the Goddess Tradition* (Delhi: Motilal Banarsidass, 1984), pp. 110–13. On the evolution of the Goddess, see also Wendell Beane, *Myth, Cult, and Symbols in Śākta Hinduism: A Study of the Indian Mother Goddess* (Leiden: Brill, 1977), pp. 42–149.

9. David Kinsley, *Hindu Goddesses: Visions of the Divine Feminine in the Hindu Religious Tradition* (Berkeley and Los Angeles: University of California Press, 1988), p. 118.

10. In the Bengal area itself, there is no clear reference to Kālī until the sixteenth century. The first known mention of her in a Bengali text is a mid-sixteenth-century source on Caitanya, the *Caitanya-Maṅgala.* Here, in fact, the violent and warlike Kālī appears before the Muslim ruler of Bengal and terrifies him so much that he ceases to oppress Hindus. Jayānanda Miśra, *Caitanya Maṅgala,* ed. N. N. Basu (Calcutta: Baṅgīya Sāhitya Pariṣad, 1906), p. 11, cited in David R. Kinsley, *The Sword and the Flute. Kālī and Kṛṣṇa: Dark Visions of the Terrible and the Sublime in Hindu Mythology* (Berkeley and Los Angeles: University of California Press, 1975), p. 99 n. 33. According to Chintaharan Chakravarti, the oldest textual reference to the public annual worship of Kālī in Bengal is quite late indeed, appearing in the *Śyāmāsaparyāvidhi* of Kāśīnāth composed in 1777; see *Tantras: Studies on Their Religion and Literature* (Calcutta: Punthi Pustak, 1963), p. 92.

11. Ernest A. Payne, *The Śāktas: An Introductory and Comparative Study* (Calcutta: Y.M.C.A. Publishing House, 1933), p. 93.

12. See David R. Kinsley, "Kālī: Blood and Death Out of Place," in *Devī: Goddesses of India,* ed. John Stratton Hawley and Donna Marie Wulff (Berkeley and Los Angeles: University of California Press, 1996), p. 80. For illustrations of Kālī at this time, see Philip Rawson, *The Art of Tantra,* rev. ed. (1973; London: Thames & Hudson, 1978), pp. 114, 121, 122, 123.

13. Anne McClintock, *Imperial Leather: Race, Gender and Sexuality in the Colonial Conquest* (New York: Routledge, 1995), p. 14, quoting Edward Said, *Orientalism* (New York: Pantheon Books, 1978), p. 6. See also McClintock, *Imperial Leather,* p. 207, for a similar statement.

14. Robert Orme, *Historical Fragments of the Moghul Empire, of the Morattoes, and of the English Concerns in Indostan, from the Year MDCLIX* (1782; New Delhi: Associated Publishing House, 1974), p. 306.

15. Katherine Mayo, *Mother India* (1927; London: Jonathan Cape, 1930), p. 29. Emphasis added.

16. Sir George Fletcher MacMunn, *The Underworld of India* (London: Jarrolds, 1933), p. 96.

17. Mayo, *Mother India,* p. 38. For English views on Indian sexuality, see also Kenneth Ballhatchet, *Race, Sex, and Class under the Raj: Imperial Attitudes and Policies and Their Critics, 1793–1905* (New York: St. Martin's Press, 1980), p. 5.

18. Lewis Wurgaft, *The Imperial Imagination: Magic and Myth in Kipling's India* (Middletown, Conn.: Wesleyan University Press, 1983), p. 49.

19. Steven Kern, *The Culture of Love: Victorians to Moderns* (Cambridge, Mass.: Harvard University Press 1992), pp. 334–35.

20. Miranda Shaw, *Passionate Enlightenment: Women in Tantric Buddhism* (Princeton: Princeton University Press, 1994), pp. 8–9.

21. Wurgaft, *Imperial Imagination,* p. 49.

22. William Jones briefly discusses "Cali"—whom he seems to have viewed with a surprisingly benign attitude—when he compares her to the Greek Hecate and the Roman Diana (*The British Discovery of Hinduism in the Eighteenth Century,* ed. Peter J. Marshall [Cambridge: Cambridge University Press, 1970], p. 237). For Jones's other brief references to Kālī, see *The Works of Sir William Jones* (6 vols.; 1799; Delhi: Agam Prakashan, 1977), 4: 132–33. For Colebrooke's mention of the Goddess, see *Essays on History, Literature, and Religion of Ancient India: Miscellaneous Essays* (2 vols.; 1837; reprint, New Delhi: Cosmo Publications, 1977), 1: 111–12; 2: 185–86n.

23. In his Gifford Lectures of 1891, Max Müller said: "I cannot bring myself to believe that this modern . . . goddess represents a continuous development of the older Vedic . . . goddesses. There is . . . a decidedly non-Vedic spirit." See Friedrich Max Müller, *Anthropological Religion* (1891; reprint, New Delhi: Asian Educational Services, 1977), p. 163.

24. Ward, *History, Literature, and Mythology,* 3: ciii; Ward's emphasis.

25. Alexander Duff, *India and India Missions: Including Sketches of the Gigantic System of Hinduism, Both in Theory and Practice* (1839; reprint, Delhi: Swati Publications, 1988), p. 265. Also see Duff, *A Description of the Durga and Kali Festivals Celebrated in Calcutta, at an Expense of Three Millions of Dollars* (Troy, N.Y.: C. Wright, 1846), pp. 21, 31.

26. Fanny Parks, *Wanderings of a Pilgrim in Search of the Picturesque: Four and Twenty Years in the East; with Revelations of Life in the Zenana* (1850), 1: 165, cited in Sara Suleri, *The Rhetoric of English India* (Chicago: University of Chicago Press, 1992), p. 95.

27. Ibid., p. 96.

28. Ward, *History, Literature, and Mythology,* 3: li.

29. Ibid., p. 155.

30. "The Śāktas—Their Characteristics and Practical Influence in Society," *Calcutta Review* 24, no. 47 (1855): 67, 66.

31. Mayo, *Mother India,* p. 19.

32. Ibid., pp. 15–16.

33. Epigraphs to this section from MacMunn, *Underworld of India,* p. 218; Caleb Wright, *India and Its Inhabitants* (1854; St. Louis: J. A. Brainerd, 1860), p. 225.

34. M. Paul Dare, *Indian Underworld: A First-Hand Account of Hindu Saints, Sorcerers, and Superstitions* (New York: Dutton, 1940), p. 56. See also Augustus Somerville, *Crime and Religious Beliefs in India* (Calcutta: "The Criminologist," 1929).

35. See Cynthia Ann Humes, "Wrestling with Kālī: South Asian and British Constructions of the Dark Goddess," chapter 7 in this volume.

36. MacMunn, *Underworld of India,* p. 213.

37. Richard Sherwood, "Of the Murderers Called Phansigars," reprinted in George Bruce, *The Stranglers: The Cult of Thuggee and its Overthrow in British India* (London: Longmans, 1968), p. 20. According to another account, a "ritual feast . . . took place after every murder, sometimes upon the grave of the victim. The *goor* or coarse sugar took the place of the Christian communion bread and wine" (David Annan, "Thuggee," in *Secret Societies,* ed. Norman MacKenzie [New York: Holt, Rinehart & Winston, 1967], p. 76).

38. Earl of Ronaldshay [Lawrence John Lumley Dundas, marquis of Zetland], *The Heart of Âryâvarta: A Study of the Psychology of Indian Unrest* (London: Constable, 1925), p. 92.

39. MacMunn, *Underworld of India,* p. 239.

40. Ibid., p. 218.

41. Sir Valentine Chirol, *Indian Unrest* (London: Macmillan, 1910), pp. 83–84.

42. MacMunn, *Underworld of India,* pp. 209–10.

43. Epigraph to this section from Flora Annie Steel, *The Law of the Threshold* (New York: Macmillan, 1924), pp. 1–2. The title of the section is taken from id., "On the Second Story," in *Indian Scene: Collected Short Stories of Flora Annie Steel* (London: Edward Arnold, 1933), p. 309. On the depiction of India in Victorian novels, see Ralph J. Crane, *Inventing India: A History of India in English-Language Fiction* (New York: St. Martin's Press, 1992); Allen J. Greenberger, *The British Image of India* (Oxford: Oxford University Press, 1969); Avtar Singh Bhullar, *India, Myth and Reality: Images of India in the Fiction by English Writers* (Delhi: Ajanta Publications, 1985).

44. Parry, *Delusions and Discoveries,* p. 84; I. A. R. Wylie, *Daughter of Brahma* (Indianapolis: Bobbs-Merrill, 1913).

45. F. E. F. Penny, *The Swami's Curse* (1922; London: Heinemann, 1929), p. 48.

46. Flora Annie Steel, *On the Face of the Waters* (London: W. Heinemann, 1897), p. 102. Emphasis added. The goddess being referred to in this quotation is Durgā.

47. Parry, *Delusions and Discoveries,* p. 111.

48. Steel, "On the Second Story," pp. 303, 302. The full story is found on pp. 292–326.

49. Wurgaft, *Imperial Imagination,* p. 67, summarizing Wylie, *Daughter of Brahma,* pp. 305–6.

50. Steel, *Law of the Threshold,* p. 146; see Parry, *Delusions and Discoveries,* p. 120n.

51. Steel, *Law of the Threshold,* p. 37. Emphasis added.

52. Parry, *Delusions and Discoveries,* p. 99; also see Wurgaft, *Imperial Imagination,* p. 56. A more recent example of this fanciful representation of Kālī and political violence is John Masters's popular novel, *The Deceivers* (New York: Viking, 1952).

53. Epigraph to this section from the Bengali periodical *Yugantar* (1905), quoted in Chirol, *Indian Unrest,* p. 346.

54. See Bill Ashcroft, Gareth Griffiths, and Helen Tiffin, *The Empire Writes Back: Theory and Practice in Post-Colonial Literatures* (London: Routledge, 1989).

55. Walter Benjamin, *Das Passagen-Werk,* ed. Rolf Tiedemann, vol. 5, in Susan Buck-Morss, *The Dialectics of Seeing: Walter Benjamin and the Arcades Project* (Cambridge, Mass.: MIT Press, 1989), p. 219. "The true picture of the past flits by. The past can be seized only as an image which flashes up at the instant when it can be recognized and is never seen again"; Walter Benjamin, *Illuminations,* ed. Hannah Arendt and trans. Harry Zohn (New York: Schocken Books, 1969), p. 255.

56. Buck-Morss, *Dialectics of Seeing,* p. 116.

57. The colonizers, Taussig suggests, typically condemn non-Western cultures as savage or barbaric, and then mimic that very savagery in their own acts of violence: "[T]he imaginative range essential to the execution of colonial violence . . . was an imagining drawn from that which the civilized imputed to the Indians . . . and then mimicked. . . . This mimicry by the colonizer of the savagery imputed to the savage is what I call the colonial mirror of production and it is . . . identical to the mimetic structure that Horkheimer and Adorno single out when they discuss . . . the blow-up within modern European civilization itself, as orchestrated by anti-Semitism. This is what they mean when they write: 'They Cannot Stand the Jews But Imitate Them'" (*Mimesis and Alterity,* pp. 65–66).

58. Ibid., p. 177.

59. Sumit Sarkar, *The Swadeshi Movement in Bengal, 1903–8* (New Delhi: People's Publishing House, 1973), p. 400. Sarkar provides a nice outline of the Swadeshi movement, dividing it into four classes: (1) the moderates; (2) the trend toward self-development without inviting an immediate political clash (constructive swadeshi); (3) political extremism using extended boycott or passive resistance; and (4) terrorism (p. 33). Gradually, the revolutionary secret societies divided into two main forms: "The Yugantar groups . . . tried to conserve their resources and establish international contacts . . . The Dacca Anushilan . . . preferred to stick to the pattern of dacoity and individual terror" (p. 490).

60. *Yugantar,* cited in Chirol, *Indian Unrest,* p. 92. On the revolutionary wing of the Nationalists, see Leonard A. Gordon, *Bengal: The Nationalist Movement, 1876–1940* (New York: Columbia University Press, 1975); Nemai Sudhan Bose, *The Indian Awakening and Bengal* (Calcutta: Firma K. L. Mukhopadhyay, 1960); and Ramesh Chandra Majumdar, *History of the Freedom Movement in India* (Calcutta: Firma K. L. Mukhopadhyay, 1962).

61. *Bhawani Mandir,* cited in Arun Chandra Guha, *Aurobindo and Jugantar* (Calcutta: Sahitya Samsad, n.d.), p. 18. On Aurobindo's political life and work, see Gordon, *Bengal: The Nationalist Movement,* ch. 4; K. R. Srinivasa Iyengar, *Sri Aurobindo: A Biography and a History,* 3d rev. ed. (2 vols.; 1950; reprint, Pondicherry: Sri Aurobindo International Centre of Education, 1972); Sirsirkumar Mitra, *The Liberator, Sri*

Aurobindo, India and the World (Bombay: Jaico Publishing House, 1954); Haridas and Uma Mukherjee, *Sri Aurobindo's Political Thought, 1893–1908* (Calcutta: Firma K. L. Mukhopadhyay, 1958); and A. B. Purani, *The Life of Sri Aurobindo*, 4th rev. ed. (Pondicherry: Sri Aurobindo Ashram, 1978).

62. Aurobindo Ghose, *Doctrine of Passive Resistance* (Calcutta: Arya Publishing House, 1948), pp. 87–88.

63. Ashis Nandy, *The Intimate Enemy: Loss and Recovery of Self under Colonialism* (Delhi: Oxford University Press, 1983), p. 7.

64. These sexual images could perhaps be schematically represented as follows:

	MALE	FEMALE
Imperial imagination	effeminate, weak, degenerate, licentious	overly sexual, seductive, and draining
Nationalist imagination	strong, virile, militant, hypermasculine ksatriyahood	violent, strong, militant

65. Keshub Choudhuri, *The Mother and Passionate Politics* (Calcutta: Vidyodaya, 1979), p. 39; On Bankim's life and thought, see Rachel Rebecca Van Meter, "Bankimchandra and the Bengali Renaissance" (Ph.D. diss., University of Pennsylvania, 1966).

66. *The Abbey of Bliss* (*Ānandamaṭh*), trans. Nares Chandra Sen-Gupta (Calcutta: Cherry Press, n.d.), pp. 40–41. Emphases in the original.

67. Cited in Iyengar, *Sri Aurobindo*, 1: 134.

68. "Bhawani Mandir," cited in Purani, *Life of Sri Aurobindo*, pp. 67–68.

69. "Bhawani Mandir," cited in Guha, *Aurobindo and Jugantar*, p. 18. Emphasis in the original.

70. Sarkar, *Swadeshi Movement*, pp. 312–13. Aurobindo was among the first to introduce religious ritual elements as part of the secret societies, by administering a vow to Hemcandra Kānungo in 1902. Later, the Dacca Anuśīlan would develop an elaborate initiatory system in its secret organization, with a complicated system of vows, emphasizing total subordination and readiness to do anything for the group. The vows were taken before the image of Kālī, in some cases at a deserted Kālī Mandir in the suburbs of Dacca (ibid.).

71. Payne, *Śāktas*, p. 104.

72. *Yugantar*, quoted in Choudhuri, *Mother and Passionate Politics*, p. 46.

73. *Yugantar*, quoted in Chirol, *Indian Unrest*, p. 94. Similar calls to battle can be found in other Bengali papers: "What have we learnt from the Shakti Puja? . . . When the Hindus realize the true magnificence of the worship of the Mother, they will be roused from the slumber of ages, and the auspicious dawn of awakenment will light up the horizon" (*Hitaishi*, [Barisal]) (ibid., p. 18).

74. Choudhuri, *Mother and Passionate Politics*, pp. 49–50.

75. "[T]he colonial culture's ordering of sexual identities assumed that . . . manliness is superior to womanliness, and womanliness in turn to femininity in man. . . . [T]he first Indian response to this was to accept the ordering by giving a new salience to Kṣatriyahood as true Indianness. To beat the colonizers at their own game and to regain self-esteem . . . many . . . sought a hyper-masculinity . . . But . . . such

Dionysian games with the colonizers were doomed. This is what the Bengali . . . terrorists found out to their own cost" (Nandy, *Intimate Enemy,* p. 52).

76. Epigraphs to this section from *Gunga Din* (1939), directed by George Stevens (what is especially remarkable is that this film opens with a disclaimer stating that all of the scenes portraying worship of Kālī are based on historical fact [!]), and Linda E. Olds, "The Neglected Feminine: Promises and Perils," *Soundings* 69, no. 3 (1986): 234, cited in Rachel McDermott, "The Western Kālī," in *Devi: Goddesses of India,* ed. John Stratton Hawley and Donna Marie Wulff (Berkeley and Los Angeles: University of California Press, 1996), p. 289 n. 30.

77. Heinrich Zimmer, *Myths and Symbols in Indian Art and Civilization* (Princeton: Princeton University Press, 1974), p. 215.

78. Erich Neumann, *The Great Mother: An Analysis of an Archetype,* trans. Ralph Manheim (Princeton: Princeton University Press, 1955), p. 150. Neumann is quoting Heinrich Zimmer; see Zimmer, "The Indian World Mother," trans. Ralph Manheim in the *The Mystic Vision,* ed. Joseph Campbell, Papers from the Eranos Yearbooks, 6 (Princeton: Princeton University Press, 1968), p. 81.

79. Neumann, *Great Mother,* p. xlii.

80. McDermott, "Western Kālī," p. 288. "Hinduism does indeed contain a model and image that could be used to fit the needs of today's women. . . . The image centers on the goddess Kali . . . [T]his image must be extricated from patriarchal interpretations . . . that have clouded its essential meaning." Lina Gupta, "Kali the Savior," in *After Patriarchy: Feminist Transformations of World Religions,* ed. Paula M. Cooey, William R. Eakin, and Jay B. McDaniel (Maryknoll, N.Y.: Orbis Books, 1991), p. 16, as quoted by McDermott, "Western Kālī," p. 281 epigraph. For Kālī on the Internet, see McDermott, "Kālī's New Frontiers: A Hindu Goddess on the Internet," chapter 12 in this volume.

CHAPTER 9

Why the Tāntrika Is a Hero

Kālī in the Psychoanalytic Tradition

Jeffrey J. Kripal

> *There is an insistence in Hinduism that the world as it appears to us is a show, that there remains hidden from our normal view an aspect of reality that is different, perhaps shockingly different, from our ego-centered way of apprehending it. . . . Why would one wish to identify with, to actually become (in the logic of Tantra), a goddess such as Kālī . . . [who] dramatically embodies marginal, polluting, or socially subversive qualities? . . . The answer . . . probably lies in certain Hindu tantric emphases. These goddesses "fit" the logic of certain aspects of Tantra, especially left-handed Tantra, in which a central aim is to stretch one's consciousness beyond the conventional, to break away from approved social norms, roles, and expectations . . . To take on such a perspective, to become one of these goddesses, might very well involve or imply a transformation of identity in which hardened categories are jettisoned and the emotions, mind, and spirit are stretched in exhilarating fashion.*
>
> DAVID KINSLEY, *Tantric Visions of the Divine Feminine*

TOWARD A PSYCHOANALYTIC POETICS OF THE GODDESS

Śākta mystical practice, like psychoanalysis, is an exercise in excess, a ritualized confrontation with both universal and culturally constituted anxieties about death, sexuality, pollution, and the dissolution of the socialized self. In the famous *pañcamakāra* ritual or the Five M's, for example, the male Tāntrika secretly ingests substances or performs acts that are otherwise forbidden and considered highly polluting by his public Brāhmaṇical culture. He thus consumes meat, drinks wine, and engages in sexual intercourse with his Tantric consort precisely to transgress, ritually and emotionally, the orthodox categories of impurity, pollution, and taboo. It is as if his own culture deconstructs itself within this remarkable practice.

Without denying the very real and important differences between the two systems, I would like to suggest that psychoanalysis can poetically be described as a kind of Western Tantra, as a century-long meditation on the powers of sexuality, the body, life, death, and religion. Psychoanalysis, after all, gazes into zones of human experience that were previously off-limits, obscene, unthinkable. And it accesses altered states of consciousness—dreams, hypnosis, hysteria, trance states, fantasy, free association, and so on—to advance its claims about the nature of human being. Moreover, again not unlike the Tantra, psychoanalysis is something of a scandal to the larger culture, an embarrassment to many, a horror to more than a few. And why not? As Freud pointed out long ago, psychoanalysis is an offense to humanity's self-assured arrogance (the "third blow," as it were, after the Copernican and Darwinian revolutions), for it removes the ego from its pedestal and reveals it to be what it has been all along—a social construction always threatened by the instinctual forces of the id, an often overbearing superego, and the terrifying whirlpool of the unconscious . . . by no means a permanent condition.[1] Psychoanalysis even possesses a similar esoteric ritual structure, with analysts and analysands trained in closed private sessions, accessing a kind of personal *gnosis* or *jñāna* reserved for the few who can understand. It is not for nothing that Sudhir Kakar once wrote, "[o]f the many Indian mystical-spiritual cults, tantra is perhaps the most congenial to a psychoanalyst."[2]

I am certain that we can easily make too much of such analogies, but we also can too quickly ignore them and so miss an opportunity to think again about both psychoanalysis and Hindu mysticism. In what follows, then, I explore these Śākta-psychoanalytic correspondences through a kind of intellectual genealogy, in this case, a history of the twentieth-century psychoanalytic study of Kālī, the Tantric Goddess par excellence, in the hope that it might bring us a bit closer to what we might call a psychoanalytic poetics of the Goddess.

The literature of the psychoanalytic tradition is especially rich in meditations on this provocative being. It is also, however, quite diverse in its plural voices and passionate debates. Consequently, there is no way we can begin to understand it without a further focusing device. I have chosen to focus my own gaze through a seemingly simple question: Why is the male Tāntrika, who sexually engages Kālī either imaginally in meditation or ritually through an actual female consort, consistently described in the Tantric texts as a *vīra,* or "hero"? Or put more psychologically, what is specifically "heroic" about heterosexual contact with the Goddess?[3]

Familiarity with this psychoanalytic Kālī, I suggest, is central to any adequate Western understanding of Kālī (this chapter does not attempt to represent South Asian understandings), since psychoanalytic thought is one of the few places in Western theory where Kālī has come to play a significant role. If handled properly, such a theoretical tradition has much to offer, both positively and negatively, to scholars and believers alike who wish either to understand the Goddess in their South Asian cultural contexts or to reappropriate her in ways conducive to gender equality, social justice, and full embodiment in our modern and postmodern worlds.

KĀLĪ IN THE PSYCHOANALYTIC TRADITION (1923–1999)

This chapter in no way pretends to be exhaustive. Instead, I shall proceed chronologically, beginning with Freud's correspondence with Romain Rolland (1923–36) and ending with the recent publication of Sarah Caldwell's *Oh Terrifying Mother* (1999), stopping in between at a few of the most significant "markers" or "signposts" along the seventy-five-year path. As we shall see, the differences between such a beginning and such an end are quite striking.

Sigmund Freud and Romain Rolland: Analyzing the Maternal Ocean (1923–1936)

Although Freud himself never actually wrote about Kālī, he definitely knew more than a little about her through the work of C. D. Daly (discussed below) and what he playfully called the "twin-headed three-volume work"[4] of his dear friend and thirteen-year correspondent, the French novelist, playwright, and social activist Romain Rolland. Rolland admired Freud for his firm stand against the illusions of religion in his controversial, and, for many, deeply offensive, book *The Future of an Illusion*[5] (like Freud, Rolland believed in neither the immortality of the soul[6] nor the existence of a monotheistic God).[7] However, he also sought to convince Freud that there was another way of being religious, a mystical way that could dispense with the common man's immature projections and rest content with the innate beauty and pleasure of what he liked to call "an oceanic feeling" (*un sentiment oceanique*), which he linked with the biographies of Ramakrishna and Vivekananda that he was at that time (1927) writing. "I myself am familiar with this sensation," Rolland wrote to Freud. "All through my life, it has never failed me. . . . In that sense, I can say that I am profoundly 'religious' —without this constant state (like a sheet of water which I feel flushing under the bark) affecting in any way my critical faculties and my freedom to exercise them—even if that goes against the immediacy of the interior experience."[8] In a private letter to Rolland, Freud admitted, "I am not an out-and-out skeptic. Of one thing I am absolutely positive: there are certain things we cannot know now."[9] In another context, an exchange with the Swiss poet Bruno Goetz, Freud compared the mystic to a kind of "intuitive psychologist" or proto-analyst who dives into the terrifying whirlpool of the unconscious to return with genuine psychological, artistic, or therapeutic insight.[10] In his *New Introductory Lectures on Psycho-Analysis,* Freud went so far as to suggest that psychoanalysis and "certain mystical practices" share a common approach: to gaze into and appropriate the psyche's hidden depths by "upsetting the normal relations between the different regions of the mind."[11]

This dialogue had been going on for some time when, early in 1930, Rolland sent Freud his newly published biographies of the Hindu saints Ramakrishna and Vivekananda, his *Essai sur la mystique et l'action de l'Inde vivante: I. La Vie de Ramakrishna* (1929) and *II. La Vie de Vivekananda et l'évangile universel* (1930). What did Freud read about Kālī when he picked up Rolland's work? The first Ramakrishna volume, where Kālī appears, is as much about Rolland as it is about Ramakrishna, for Rolland's unique brand of perennialism, originating in his own mystical experiences and nurtured by political developments in a post–World War I Europe,[12] shines through almost every chapter and heavily colors the manner in which he reads both Ramakrishna's life and its significance for the world. So too with Rolland's oceanic feeling, which rolls and thunders behind his impassioned prose and occasional references to his own beliefs. When interpreting Ramakrishna's experience of Kālī as an Ocean of Light (happily, the metaphor was central to the Bengali texts and the tradition), for example, Rolland returns to his "oceanic" experiences and reads them—perhaps not inaccurately—into those of Ramakrishna. As for Kālī herself, Rolland begins with the usual romantic suggestions that she represents "the Nature Mother"[13] but quickly moves on from there to invoke the emergent psychology of mysticism—primarily in its American forms (Starbuck and James)—to read Ramakrishna's visions of Kālī as a contentless feeling state akin to dream consciousness.[14]

Shortly after Rolland's biographies appeared, Freud's *Civilization and Its Discontents* was published. It is doubtful whether anything in it refers to Rolland's discussion of Kālī (his book was already in press by the time he received Rolland's), but Rolland's "oceanic feeling" runs through much of it as a central subtext. Indeed, Freud begins with an analysis of Rolland's "oceanic" experiences, which he interprets as psychic regressions to the infant's primary narcissistic/unitive state.[15] In classical psychoanalytic fashion, he isolates the central content of such feelings, the idea of unity, and then traces it back to developmental patterns in the human maturation cycle: "An infant at the breast does not as yet distinguish his ego from the external world as the source of the sensations flowing in upon him." "[O]riginally the ego includes everything, later it separates off an external world from itself."[16] And then the central thesis:

> Our present ego-feeling is, therefore, only a shrunken residue of a much more inclusive—indeed, an all-embracing—feeling which corresponded to a more intimate bond between the ego and the world about it. If we may assume that there are many people in whose mental life this primary ego-feeling has

> persisted to a greater or less degree, it would exist in them side by side with the narrower and more sharply demarcated ego-feeling of maturity, like a counterpart to it. In that case, the ideational contents appropriate to it would be precisely those of limitlessness and of a bond with the universe—the same ideas with which my friend elucidated the "oceanic feeling."[17]

Later in the text, Freud suggests that further study might reveal "connections here with a number of obscure modifications of mental life, such as trances and ecstasies."[18] Here psychoanalytic studies of both mysticism and, indirectly, Kālī definitively begin. That "further study" of which Freud wrote in 1930 would proceed impressively over the years and is still progressing today.

C. D. Daly: Hindu Mythology and the Castration Complex (1927)

In 1927, C. D. Daly, an English psychoanalyst practicing in colonial India,[19] published a long essay dedicated largely to the mythology and iconography of Kālī, "Hindu-Mythologie und Kastrationskomplex."[20] Although much of his theorizing (most of it revolving around castration anxiety, penis envy, oedipal conflict, and the menstruation complex) must strike the modern reader as heavy-handed and rather primitive, not to mention colonizing,[21] the piece is important for a number of historical and hermeneutical reasons, foremost among them the facts that this is the first major psychoanalytic essay dedicated almost exclusively to Kālī, and, even more interesting, that in it Daly discusses Freud's own reading of an earlier draft of the same essay, clear proof that Freud was more than familiar with Kālī's mythology and iconography (Daly, p.177).

Also of significant methodological interest is the manner in which Daly used European materials in order to throw psychoanalytic light on Indian materials. In one place, for example, in order to decode the cut-off-arm motif (in both contexts) as a symbol of castration anxiety, he moves from Kālī's skirt of arms to an exegesis of a European's dream of a sculptor who had hung a collection of modeled arms (to complete a Venus statue) by a rope. A remarkably similar "free associative" method, I should add, would later be used with exquisite effect by Gananath Obeyesekere, who in July 1973 used his own free associations between the inexplicable anxiety he felt looking at a Sinhalese female ascetic's snakelike, matted hair and Freud's essay "Medusa's Head" (where Freud links the terror inspired by Medusa to the fear of castration) in order to trigger a chain of thoughts that would eventually produce his now classic *Medusa's Hair.*[22] Indeed, Daly himself discusses the Medusa myth in relationship to Kālī (Daly, p. 167) and later interprets hair- and snake-symbolism as related to castration anxieties through analysis of another European man's dream.[23] The latter dreamt that he was holding his phallus in his hand while it let loose a stream of liquid; as he watched, the end or tip of it became a threatening snake head, whose mouth seemed to emit streams of fire before he awoke and thought immediately of a "certain woman" (no doubt a reference to Medusa) whose hair consisted of snakes (pp. 172–73).

In terms of actual theorizing, Daly reads Kālī as "ein Weihnachtsbaum mit phallischen Symbolen bedeckt" (Daly, p. 174), that is, "a Christmas tree bedecked with phallic symbols"—surely one of the most remarkable, if not to say weirdest, lines in the literature. The garland of heads, the skirt of arms, the extended tongue—all of these features of Kālī's iconography take on phallic meanings for Daly. Hence Kālī is the "castrating mother" who dominates the father and produces anxiety in the son, even as she delays the son's anxiety about his own feared castration by directing her rage to the father. Hindu mythology is thus read as a product of elaborate processes of psychological "splitting" (*Spaltung*) in which the different features and attributes of the son's early object-libido are projected onto the screen of religious belief (p. 147). In terms of the goddesses, this splitting occurs between two contradictory types of mother figures: those of a gentle nature, such as Umā, Lakṣmī, and Sarasvatī, and those of a severe or dark nature, such as Durgā, Kālī, and Cāmuṇḍā.[24] Here also we find early psychoanalytic readings of Gaṇeśa and his decapitation (p. 155), the worship of Śakti as a veneration of libidinal energies (p. 165), symbolic analogues between milk, semen, and urine (p. 175), the extended tongue as a sexual symbol, and an interpretation of red hibiscus flowers (traditionally associated with Kālī) as symbols of menstruation and sexual fertility (p. 177): all motifs that would be picked up by later Indological writers, if often in a nonpsychoanalytic key.[25]

The Schjelderup Brothers: Typing the Religious Personality (1932)

David Wulff has pointed out that the mother-goddess of Freud's rare speculations on the subject is not the mother who enfolds, nourishes, or protects but "the mother in the context of the Oedipal crisis, whose son-lover dies an early death and whose priests are castrated for her protection, presumably at the instance of the father."[26] Indeed, Freud focused on the developmentally late oedipal stage and seldom ventured further back along the developmental arc. The British psychologist Ian Suttie states that Freud found the Great Mother cults "a mystery as repellent as they are insoluble," and this despite the fact that, according to Suttie, they are "perhaps the greatest problem for the archaeology of culture and the psychology of religion."[27] Fortunately, other thinkers developed Freud's ideas in precisely these directions and cast considerable light on the remarkable tendency of these cults to emphasize maternal merger, blood sacrifice, and decapitation/castration. Such approaches usually fall under the rubric of object-relations theory, developed especially by the British theorists Ian Suttie, Ronald Fairbairn, Harry Guntrip, and D. W. Winnicott, or the self psychology of the American Heinz Kohut, particularly in reference to his model of narcissism. As Wulff points out, however, the groundwork for all of these approaches was laid long before in the work of the Norwegian psychologist Harald Schjelderup and his brother Kristian, a theologian and psychotherapist.[28]

Specifically, the Schjelderup brothers' early German study *Über drei Haupttypen der religiösen Erlebnisformen* (1932)[29] drew on eighteen case studies of glossolalia to categorize the religious personality into three basic types (*Grundtypen*) along a tripartite developmental perspective—the oedipal, the pre-oedipal, and the narcissistic. Wulff summarizes the brothers' elegant model:

> In the first of these types [the oedipal], the preeminent feelings are those of guilt and fear, occurring in conjunction with longing for submission and atonement and occasionally with the experience of conversion. For this type, the relation to the father lies in the foreground. The second type [the pre-oedipal] is characterized by deep yearning for the divine, for closeness to or even union with God, for peace and rest in God. For this type the individual's relation to the mother is decisive. The third type [the narcissistic] is marked by fantasies of being oneself divine, an outcome of narcissistic withdrawal of libido from external objects and corresponding infantile self-grandiosity. The three types—father religion, mother religion, and self religion—thus correspond to three different stages of childhood development.[30]

Years later, Erik Erikson would describe the same three "objects" of the psyche in more poetic terms. As his invocation of specifically mystical idioms to communicate the beauty and power of such object-states will become significant for us below, it is worth quoting him at length here:

> One may say that man, when looking through a glass darkly, finds himself in an inner cosmos in which the outlines of three objects awaken dim nostalgias. One of these is the simple and fervent wish for a hallucinatory sense of unity with a maternal matrix; it is symbolized by the affirmative face of charity, graciously inclined, reassuring the faithful of the unconditional acceptance of those who will return to the bosom. . . . In the center of the second nostalgia is the paternal voice of guiding conscience, which puts an end to the simple paradise of childhood and provides a sanction for energetic action. It also warns of the inevitability of guilty entanglement, and threatens with the lightning of wrath. . . . Finally, the glass shows the pure self itself, the unborn core of creation, the—as it were, preparental—center where God is pure nothing: *ein lauter Nichts,* in the words of Angelus Silesius. God is so designated in many ways in Eastern mysticism. This pure self is the self no longer sick with a conflict between right and wrong, not dependent on providers, and not dependent on guides to reason and reality.[31]

Such a mystical reading of the three objects, however, was implicit in psychoanalytic discourse from the beginning. Hence, when the Schjelderups wanted to demonstrate each type of religion—mother religion, father religion and self religion—they turned to two famous Asian mystics and a Western reformer: the Hindu saint Ramakrishna, the Protestant founder Martin Luther, and the Buddhist monk Bodhidharma. Even in their choice of examples, the Schjelderup brothers were quite prescient, because the first two case-studies, those of Ramakrishna and Martin Luther, later became central reference points for the psychoanalytic study of religion. With reference to Kālī, they turned to Ramakrishna and the Goddess as powerful examples of a "mother-religion" free from guilt and sin. Unlike the father religions, which worked through the emotions of guilt, atonement, and sin so prominent in a later oedipal stage of conflict, the mother religions emphasize the bliss of physical intimacy, contentment, and union. Such emotional states in turn produce a specifically mystical type of religiosity, that is, one that emphasizes maternal merger: "Very often there appears here the fantasy of a return to the mother's womb as an expression of the wish to flee the world and make an innermost contact with the object. Where religious expression takes its form according to the mother complex, we find a type of religious experience with a tendency toward mystical unity with the divinity."[32]

Coming as it did before the Indological advances of the twentieth century, the Schjelderup brothers' study of Ramakrishna and Kālī was naturally superficial and brief (only eight pages, to be exact). It also failed to struggle with the "terrible" aspects of Kālī, emphasizing instead the warmth and security of the maternal object (which, to be fair, are also major components of the Kālī traditions). Still, even with these limitations, they laid the groundwork for what would follow, insisting on the developmental nature of human religiosity and its diverse grounding in the primordial experiences of childhood and human maturation.

Gananath Obeyesekere: Mother Goddess and Social Structure (1981–1990)

The early work of such figures as Freud, C. D. Daly, and the Schjelderups was developed further in the middle of the century by G. M. Carstairs and Philip Spratt before it came to a decisive consummation in the works of Sudhir Kakar and Gananath Obeyesekere, who took this half-century Indological tradition and bestowed on it a new sophistication, theoretical substance, and literary presentation (unlike that of most of their predecessors, their prose is often quite beautiful). Kakar's first major book on the subject was his now classic *The Inner World* (1978), which functioned as a true watershed in the discourse and was followed quickly by a second major monograph on India's healing traditions, *Shamans, Mystics and Doctors* (1982). Both books have much to say about Kālī and the Tantric traditions.[33] But since I have summarized Kakar's approach to Kālī in *The Inner World* elsewhere,[34] and since Obeyesekere tells us that the manuscript of his *The Cult of the Goddess Pattini,* which advances a remarkably similar hermeneutic, was completed in 1978—making 1978 an especially auspicious year for psychoanalytic Indology—I shall privilege Obeyesekere here, focusing primarily on two of his *Pattini* chapter-essays, "Mother Goddess and Social Structure" and "Virgin, Wife, and Mother."[35]

Obeyesekere approaches the question of mother goddesses anthropologically through a comparative study of multiple cultures across space and time (with Hindu India and Buddhist Sri Lanka as his primary points of reference, supplemented by an occasional insightful reference to Mediterranean Catholicism). What such comparison reveals is that mother goddesses, although quite common, are by no means universal and always display specific themes and patterns idiosyncratic to the cultures in question. One sensible conclusion to such an observation is that mother-goddess cults, like all religious traditions, are "projective systems," that is, "culturally constituted representations that permit the expression and channeling of nuclear infantile experiences," thus "giving the individual the psychological security to cope with his inner (unconscious) anxieties by projecting them outward into a preexisting cultural belief system."[36] But Obeyesekere's is not a simple reduction of cultural or religious forms to psychological processes. The notion of a projective system may help us explain why family relationships are almost universally projected onto the cosmos, but it cannot help us explain the equally consistent phenomena of philosophical, metaphysical, and mystical systems woven into these psychological projections. Religions are always more than projective systems (Obeyesekere, p. 428); a projective system is but a *partial* explanation. Moreover, Obeyesekere sees culture and psyche as mutually constitutive forces that interact across time to produce both individually unique psyches and publicly shared religious traditions. This interaction between personal unconscious fantasy and the creation of culture is the leitmotif of much of his remarkable psychoanalytic trilogy, *Medusa's Hair* (1981), *The Cult of the Goddess Pattini* (1984), and *The Work of Culture* (1990).[37]

Because of this same psyche-culture dialectic, neonatal experiences are necessary but not sufficient causes of projective systems. For such experiences to become mythology and religion, two conditions must be met: (1) the culture must encourage the expression/projection of ideas and emotions in religious terms; and (2) the nature of the psychological problem or dilemma that lies at the base of the projection must be intense and pronounced enough to warrant the creation and preservation of a symbolically salient system. For Obeyesekere, both conditions are more than met in South Asia, where "the child's attachment to the mother is extremely intense, and the religious projective system is both a cultural statement and an expression of these intense feelings" (Obeyesekere, p. 428). This is why India is "the locus classicus of the mother goddess" (p. 429).

But what creates this special intensity? Probably not the infant, since neonatal attitudes are biologically determined and can be treated as cultural constants. Obeyesekere thus turns to the mother and her culturally constructed female role in the Indian patrilocal family. Briefly, "we may say that in Indian society a woman's husband and in-laws are aloof; she cannot fulfill her need for love through them; she therefore fulfills it through her child" (Obeyesekere, p. 429). "[T]he Brahmanic scale of values" implies ideals for the Indian mother and particularly for the *pativrata* (literally, "the vow to or for the husband"), which encompasses such virtues as absolute loyalty, humility, submissiveness, and religious devotion. And this cultural ideal of "virginity in brides, chastity in wives, and continence in widows,"[38] like all ideals, has psychological consequences:

> *Since the Hindu female role ideal of pativrata pertains to sex and aggression control, implementing the ideal in the socialization process entails the radical proscription of sexual and aggressive activity, which on the personality level demands the radical and continued repression of sex and aggression drives.* . . . In Hindu society this control as it applies to female role learning is carried to an extreme, and certain psychological problems pertaining to the adult handling of sex and aggression must flow from it. On the personality level certain consequences are expectable: sexual frigidity, somatization of conflicts, propensity to hysteria, and masochistic tendencies owing to the internalization of aggression. (Obeyesekere, p. 431; italics in original)

Because of this same Brāhmaṇical concern with the virginity of the woman (but not the man), the girl is protected and given considerable attention from her family, such that her own emotional needs are usually met in her natal home. The mother disciplines and instills in her the proper values, whereas the father can take a purely loving and benevolent attitude. This generally happy situation, however, changes dramatically when the girl or woman must leave her natal home to move into the often-distant patrilocal home of her new husband, where her new in-laws, and especially her mother-in-law, can be quite critical. Numerous factors—the "institutionalized hostility" between a woman and her husband's sisters, the aloofness of the other males of the household (with the important exception of the husband's younger brothers), the lack of physical privacy in an extended family, the injunction against public shows of affection between husband and wife, the continued presence of the husband's mother as the husband's primary female relationship, and the evaluation of sex as polluting and physically harmful—create a situation for the young bride that is more than ready for an emotional outlet.

Fortunately, this situation is altered radically with the birth of the first child, especially if it is a son, a necessary event in Brāhmaṇic ideology, since it is believed that only a male heir can perform the postmortem rituals that ensure a man's salvation. The young wife's moral status now rises considerably, and she finally has an outlet for her frustrated emotional needs: "*With the birth of the child the female's starved affective needs are realized through her infant, so that she develops an intense symbiotic attachment to her child*" (Obeyesekere, p. 437; italics in original). Such an attachment possesses clear erotic dimensions for Obeyesekere (pp. 439–41), but there is more to express than sexuality. There is also repressed aggression in the form of rage, born from the young woman's subservient role in the joint family and the larger culture. Brāhmaṇic values, however, prohibit her expressing anger toward the objects who have engendered it. It is thus "likely that some of this rage will be expressed toward the child, whenever he frustrates the mother, since that is the only object in the sociological landscape toward whom this rage can be directed with impunity"; in addition, as G. M Carstairs observed, there are times when the mother, by virtue of her menses, is regarded as "polluted" and unapproachable, and although other members of the joint family may fill in for her during these times, "it is likely that the image of the untouchable, menstruating (bloody) mother conditions the child's maternal image" (Obeyesekere, p. 439).

Lest readers jump to unnecessary conclusions about the overly negative picture painted above, Obeyesekere himself points out that "it would be ridiculous to say that all Indian children, even those affected by Brahmanic values, experience the mother in the same manner" (Obeyesekere, p. 440). For some, maternal rage will be dominant; for others, the nurturing, loving mother; for still others, some combination of the two. "Yet these experiences of the mother would occur with sufficient frequency for them to be represented in various ways in the religious projective system."[39] Such broad yet consistent diversity among childhood experiences results in a tripartite model of the Hindu goddesses, consisting of three archetypal images: (1) the sacred cow, or the nurturant, totally good, undemanding, loving mother; (2) the Pārvatī image, the benevolent mother and model wife of the father; and (3) the Kālī image, "the cruel, unpredictable, smothering, or castrating aspect of the mother, based primarily on the unpredictable (hysterical) nature of maternal rage as perceived by the infant" (p. 44). In true structuralist style, the Pārvatī image mediates between the two polar extremes of the sacred cow and the Kālī image, which are in actuality two sides of the same maternal imago: "the totally loving and nurturant mother will smother her child, which then creates for the child the terrifying image of the mother" (p. 440).[40]

Obeyesekere develops this hermeneutic further, and in a direction that will become especially relevant for our own questions, in his chapter, "Virgin, Wife, and Mother," where he treats the theme of the virgin and the harlot in Hindu Indian and Buddhist Sinhalese culture. Freud had explored the phenomenon of his own European culture in which a man could only love a harlot-type figure, noting that psychic impotence is often experienced only with certain types of women, who unconsciously remind the man of his mother. Framed in these oedipal terms, sexual impotence is thus a psycho-physiological response to a symbolically incestuous dilemma. One resolution to such a psychosexual dilemma is the "splitting" of the woman into two radically different models, the pure mother and the sexually degraded whore or harlot. This then allows the man to create a disjunction between his affection (still tied to his mother or a mother-figure) and his sexuality (now freed for the harlot figure), which in turn allows him to surmount his impotence with a now sexually degraded woman who is obviously *not* his mother.

Ontogenetically, affection is prior to sexuality for Freud, as a child's first object-choices are always family members, and usually the mother. As the child matures, erotic components are added to these affective relationships until puberty, when biological changes and social taboos demand that sexuality attach itself to other objects. In the normal outcome, the male is able to attach himself to other women, and the affection he held and still holds for his family members is carried over into these sexual relationships. Affection and sexuality are united once again. However, this does not always happen, either because the male chooses (or has chosen for him) object choices that are not suitable to his desires, or, more important for our purposes, because the attachment to the original object-choice is simply too strong to relinquish. Because such an object-choice is incestuous, it cannot be expressed publicly and so remains unconscious: "In this way it may so happen that the whole current of sensual feeling in the young man may remain attached in the unconscious to incestuous objects, or, to put it in another way, may be fixated to incestuous fantasies."[41] Impotence is the result. If the fixation is less severe, however, the male may split his experience of women into two clearly demarcated patterns: a mother-image, with whom he cannot possibly have sex, and a harlot-figure, with whom he can.

Obeyesekere, pointing out that "erotic fixation on the mother" is a "widespread psychological problem" in Sri Lanka (as well as India), predicts the following sociological consequences: (1) incestuous feelings for the mother will result in castration fear as punishment for these wishes; (2) this fear will in turn result in a widespread fear of impotence among males; and (3) the erotic fixation on the mother will produce a splitting of woman into mother and harlot (Obeyesekere, pp. 453–55). All three observations, I should add, are directly relevant to Tantric culture and its handling of Kālī, the decapitating/castrating, sexually degraded woman par excellence. Indeed, it is remarkable how closely the psychoanalytic model fits the patterns of Tantric ritual, where the prostitute or low-caste woman is the ideal ritual consort (symbolically linked, through the Goddess, to the mother) and the drinking of menstrual blood or sexual fluids *(rajapāna)* becomes a kind of antinomian sacrament. Tantric ritual is thus a religious response to a set of psychosexual dilemmas produced by quite specific cultural child-rearing practices. On the psychological plane, at least, it is an attempt to resolve a modal oedipal crisis defined by an especially intense attraction to the (divine) mother.

Sarah Caldwell: Male Experiences, Female Frustrations (1999)

Sarah Caldwell's recent study of Kerala ritual theater, *Oh Terrifying Mother,*[42] both brings the twentieth-century psychoanalytic discourse on Kālī to something of a dramatic close and signals, in its unique academic and autobiographical styles, new theoretical directions and rhetorical possibilities. Breaking with a century of anthropological and analytic prose, in which the author seldom if ever interjects his or her own life-voice into the text, Caldwell adopts a postmodern reflexivity and intersperses her symbolic, psychoanalytic, feminist, and performative interpretations of Kerala ritual theater with disarmingly honest and dramatic journal entries from the field, revealing, in the process, her own mystical, sexual, and familial engagement with this remarkable Hindu art form of suffering, sexuality, and violence.

Muṭiyēṯṯu is a Kerala annual ritual art form in which a high-caste male dons a huge head-dress to become possessed by Bhagavati and act out the myth of her slaying of the male demon Dārika (also played by a male) in an all-night ritual drama. As the myth goes, Dārika is playing havoc in the three worlds to revenge Viṣṇu's slaying of his ancestors. Hearing of this, Śiva becomes enraged and creates Bhadrakāḷi out of his fiery third eye. Bhadrakāḷi then enlists the help of a female ghost named Vētāḷam, who helps slay the demon by extending her huge tongue to lap up his drops of seed-blood, each of which will spring up into another demon if allowed to touch the ground. With the help of Vētāḷam, Kāḷi decapitates the demon and returns to Śiva's abode, still enraged. In order to stop her advance, Śiva appears before her naked; she, after all, is his daughter, and since daughters are forbidden to see their fathers naked, she must finally turn back (Caldwell, pp. 19–21). What Caldwell sets out to explain in chapter 4 on "Male Experiences" is why the *Muṭiyēṯṯu* theatrical reliving of this myth is an almost exclusively male domain. The Goddess, after all, is *never* played by a woman but rather by a cross-dressed man.

Caldwell begins, like most psychoanalytic thinkers, with a discussion of Kerala child-rearing practices, particularly the mother's display of love through beating and feeding, the practice of prolonged breast-feeding (to between ages four and eight), and the intense pre-oedipal ties to the mother that lead to "a fixation on the feminine body as both irresistible and murderous" (Caldwell, p. 189). She then effectively applies such psychoanalytic insights to the ritual drama: "The 'heat' of real beatings is reenacted in the Kāḷi actor's rage towards Dārika. Kāḷi's gestures—left hand upraised to strike, accusatory right index finger pointing, popping eyes, and rolled back tongue—are easily recognized by Keralites as the gestures of an angry mother punishing her children" (p. 161). More important to Caldwell, however, are the frustrated sexual desires in the myths of the Goddess and their relationship to her rage. Perfectly aware that such readings go against the conscious explanations of the ritual actors (which psychoanalytic theory would, of course, predict), Caldwell turns to the theme of the *yakṣi* or dangerous demonic virgin. Virgin girls, she points out, are considered to be overheated due to their lack of sexual access and so are thought to pose a real danger to males. Such fears manifest in folk conceptions of the *yakṣi*s, "unhappy, seductive and bloodthirsty female tree spirits out to entice and destroy virtuous men" (p. 163), essentially a kind of female vampire. As one of Caldwell's male informants put it, "in the olden days people believed that when they slept . . . these [virgins] would come in dreams and have [sex] with us . . . [producing] nocturnal emissions. . . . These kinds of people enter our body, and cause us to ooze [fluid]. They drain us and drink it. That's the belief" (ibid.). Such conceptions of a frustrated virgin out to drain the powers of unsuspecting men are particularly relevant to contemporary Kerala, where, according to Caldwell, 30–40 percent of adult males leave the country to work in the Persian Gulf for long periods of time. Significantly, Bhadrakāḷi is also imagined as "an unmarried, virgin girl—beautiful, hot, and dangerous," and the drops of blood that her alter-ego Vētāḷam laps up are analogized to drops of semen by both the myth and Kerala's Malayalam language (p. 164). Essentially then, "Bhadrakāḷi is modelled on a virgin female who suffers from unfulfilled desire for sex and procreation, whose lack of fulfillment is one source of her anger, and who requires the blood sacrifice of a male to cool and satisfy her thirst" (p. 167).

It is to the women on the margins that Caldwell turns in chapter 5, "Female Frustrations, Women's Worlds." Employing an explicitly feminist lens, Caldwell is able to show that control of the female body is omnipresent in Kerala dress, social practices, and values, and that open discussions of sexuality are actively suppressed, rendering the sexually explicit myths and violent ritual actions of Bhagavati suspiciously "not female": "Who in the world was this Bhadrakāḷi," Caldwell asks, "shouting and running with long protruding teeth and tongue, her naked red breasts bouncing, chasing men wildly in the middle of the night? The sheer impossibility of Bhakrakāḷi's femaleness, combined with the reverent concentration of the audience as they watched her movements, seemed to cry out to me that something was very odd in this picture of female gender" (Caldwell, pp. 202–3). Clearly, Bhadrakāḷi is everything that a Malayali woman should *not* be (p. 204). Add to this the fact that because of their polluting menses, women can never play the role of the Goddess, and one is left with the troubling conclusion that "[t]hat which makes them female disqualifies them from embodying the divine feminine, or even from coming near the goddess at such times" (p. 205). Far from providing role models or empowering images for real women, Bhagavati's performances and myths "serve to reinforce cultural ideas about a woman's inherent danger *vis-à-vis* men, which she is responsible for containing and controlling" (p. 206). Little wonder that Keralite women find little resonance in the ritual theater, or perceive menstruation taboos, temple restrictions, and childbirth pollution laws to be "fairly arbitrary, incomprehensible, and imposed from without" (p. 208). These are almost entirely male constructions designed primarily to deal with male fears of and fantasies about female sexuality.

Certainly one of the most poignant examples of this radically asymmetrical system is the manner in which Kerala society defines female possession as "demonic inspiration" (*bādhā āvēśam*) and male possession as "divine inspiration" (*dēva āvēśam*). Historically speaking, the Bhagavati cult in ancient times was under the control of female shamans, whose roles were wrested from them by upper-caste males sometime after the fourth to seventh centuries C.E. Today, it is an entirely male preserve. Although males do sometimes experience *bādhā,* it is normally women who undergo this culturally defined "demonic" ordeal. Caldwell recounts what she saw at a local Bhagavati temple known for the healing of mental illness: "All rules of female propriety were controverted by the wild screaming and shameless jumping of the women, their matted hair flying about loose, dirt clinging to their faces, obscenities pouring from their angry tongues. . . . While I wondered what suffering could drive a woman to such extreme antisocial behavior, the obvious parallel to the dancing of Bhadrakali in mutiyettu . . . came painfully to mind" (Caldwell, p. 214). Often such possessed sufferers are instructed to pound large nails with their heads into a tree in the temple compound, which Caldwell poetically describes in her field journal as "the enormous tree full of pain and spirits, fairly groaning under the weight of its thousands of nails" (p. 215). Caldwell goes on to interpret such possession states, much like Obeyesekere and Castillo before her,[43] as symptomatic responses to the extreme repression of sexual and aggressive emotions that Kerala women must endure for most of their lives. Indeed, what Caldwell found in her interviewing was that women who suffered from "fits," "voices" and more serious disorders usually did so at times of sexual deprivation or emotional stress—that is, before or immediately after marriage, during pregnancy, or while suffering the extended absence of a husband—but seldom within a stable and complete nuclear household (p. 217).

Caldwell rejects the traditional Freudian reading of such states as stemming back to the incestuous wishes of the woman—effectively blaming the woman for her own trauma—and opts instead, with Castillo, to read them (and their common link to sexual dysfunction [Caldwell, p. 228]) as traumatic responses to actual sexual abuse. And indeed, as both Sered and Obeyesekere have suggested,[44] female possession states often look remarkably like sexual states, with a woman orgasmically shaking from being entered or penetrated by a male ancestral spirit. Kerala's traditional practice of adult-child marriage pairings, cultural restrictions on sexual access that lead to considerable frustration among both sexes, intimate familial sleeping arrangements, and a tropical climate demanding little clothing may all further undergird and support such possession states as culturally syntonic expressions of sexual trauma (p. 229) and religious healing (p. 224). The same may, moreover, be equally true with male spirit possession: "If the female's possession by aggressive male demons reenacts actual memories of childhood rape, then the male's possession by Kāḷi could likewise recall either a sexual seduction by an aggressive maternal figure or threatening homosexual contacts in childhood" (p. 231). Unfortunately, only the latter, male possession, is valued and legitimated by the culture as divine. Such rituals may, moreover, supply an outlet, even provide transforming spiritual experiences, but "they do not change the fundamental social causes of trauma, which remain hidden and flourish in secret" (p. 236).

Such a psychoanalytic model explains why only certain individuals are attracted to Kālī figures and why others—no doubt the vast majority of any culture, including Kerala—are left appalled, amused, baffled, or completely uninterested by her myths and rituals. As Obeyesekere has argued with his notion of the "personal symbol," there must be some resonance, some "fit" between personal idiosyncratic psychological experience and the cultural myth or ritual for the latter to "take." We thus cannot and must not confuse the public meaning of a *cultural symbol,* whose meanings are usually stylized, "safe," and publicly known (such as the *muṭiyēṯṯu* ritual or the Kālī Pūjā festival), with the intensely personal and somatic expressions of the *personal symbol* or somatized symptom, whose meanings have ideational value only to the individual experiencing it.[45] One might speculate, then, that individuals who have suffered sexual trauma might be particularly attracted to a Kālī-like goddess and become adept in her mythology, ritual, or possession states. It may also, I might add, tell us something about those scholars who give academic and intellectual devotion to her. Caldwell, for example, has spoken intimately and passionately to this provocative truth—in her case, and in her own words, a personal history of sexual abuse inflicted by males (her uncle and former husband) lie behind her research as the motivating and inspirational sources of her work. Inspired by her reflexive transparency, I too have written confessionally of a near-deadly anorexic adolescence and a painful crisis of religio-sexual orientation as the catalyzing process behind both my mystical life and my Kālī studies.[46] In the end, it was sexual suffering and physical violence that revealed to both of us the terrifying and liberating truths of the Goddess and her ritually possessed devotees.

WHY THE TĀNTRIKA IS A HERO

So why is the Tāntrika a hero? To begin to frame an answer to our question, let us first summarize what we have learned about the psychoanalytic perspective on the Goddess. Here we can do no better than quote Steve Derne's useful summary:

> Psychoanalytically oriented scholars . . . convincingly argue that the particular childhood experience of caste Hindus cause the child to perceive the mother as both loving and hating, nurturing and destroying, and that this is the psychological root of the salience of the symbol of the fierce goddess. The young wife's isolated, subservient role in the joint family is such that she may i) indulge her infant son, ii) form erotic attachments to the child, and iii) unknowingly display repressed rage toward the infant. Thus, the structural position of the young Hindu wife . . . creates a psychological disposition in her sons to perceive women as demanding, capricious, uncontrollable and terrifying—a perception that is projected on images of the fierce goddess.[47]

Certainly, the particular manners in which this model has been applied to specific case studies can and should be debated. We are dealing here, after all, with a hermeneutical art and a set of multivocal symbols and acts, not a hard science. Still, one thing seems unmistakably clear "after psychoanalysis," that the salience of Hindu goddesses is deeply rooted in, if never fully explained by, the psychosexual experiences of infancy and childhood within the Indian family. If the model seems extreme and excessive in places —and it no doubt does—we must remember that it is trying to explain some extreme and excessive mythological, ritual, and textual material; the method mirrors and reflects that which it is trying to understand. How, for example, can one possibly understand a mother goddess whose myths are filled with violence and sexuality without addressing explicitly the themes of mothers, violence, and sexuality? Is there any way to understand a goddess with fetus-earrings and a garland of decapitated heads having sex with a husband likened to a corpse in a cremation ground *without* being excessive? I do not see how.

But, strikingly, all of these phenomena make good sense once we understand them as psychological responses to the sexually powerful, emotionally blissful, and fearfully engulfing presence of the mother-figure, who has herself been constructed and formed by the broader culture and its construction of gender, mothers, fathers, power, and subjectivity. Indeed, in such a context (and South Asia is by no means alone here), we would *expect* them.

So, too, with the Tāntrika's heroism. Certainly, such a heroism is multivalent. His confrontation with death, his handling of potentially dangerous forces, and his transgression of powerful cultural taboos render any exclusivistic approach to the *vīra,* including a psychoanalytic one, simplistic at best. Take, for example, the problem of his antinomianism, that is, the Tāntrika's intentional and ritualized deconstruction of cultural taboos and purity codes, most famously summarized in the ritual of the Five M's. Certainly, the psychological and religious power of such acts cannot be explained without first contextualizing them within the sociological framework in which they were first conceived and practiced as taboo. To put it differently, transgression requires something to transgress. Tantric transgression is only "Tantric" and "transgressive" within a Brāhmaṇical value system that defines the substances and acts as highly polluting, impure, and dangerous. Tantrism, in other words, is dialectically related to, even dependent upon, Brāhmaṇical orthodoxy.[48]

Certainly, these sociological and cultural factors go a long way in explaining why the Tāntrika is a hero. But we can add more richness and depth to our explanation by listening to psychoanalysis and looking again at the hero. In this new light, the Tāntrika's courage appears as a brave refusal, against considerable psychological odds, to renounce his adult heterosexuality before the mother and her individuality-denying, if sexually blissful and loving, presence. He is a hero precisely to the extent that he refuses absorption, decapitation, castration (as a threat or a wish), or infantilization before the (mother) Goddess and insists instead on his own phallic adult identity. Quite unlike the cultural models of Gaṇeśa or Skanda,[49] both of whom renounce their adult sexuality before the mother, or the countermodel of the demon Mahiṣa, whose bold phallicism is punished with death at the hands of a similar goddess,[50] the Tāntrika boldly asserts his phallicism and literally has sex with the mother Goddess in the form of his ritual consort. He has become his father Śiva, the paradigmatic Tantric hero. Little wonder that such heterodox traditions lead a marginal, if nevertheless influential, life on the edges of Brāhmaṇical society. They both deconstruct the Brāhmaṇical values of society in their antinomian rituals and deny the oedipal norm in their central act of ritual intercourse with the mother (goddess).

And at what is Kālī's sword aimed? If we are to respect the images and myths, we must answer: directly at the male head. And how are we to interpret this threatened head? Psychoanalytically inclined Indologists have traditionally read decapitation as a symbolic form of castration, and with good reason (if through a remarkably poorly chosen term).[51] After all, in Tantric symbolism, the head is the storehouse of semen, the ascetic is literally "he whose semen is turned up" (*ūrdhvaretas*), and the rising of the *kuṇḍalinī* energy is imagined as an "upward displacement" from the genital region to the top of the skull, where it bursts out into a kind of mystical orgasm. Hugh Urban can thus rightly note that "[l]ong before Freud developed the idea of sublimation and upward displacement . . . Indians had been aware of the symbolic relationship between the genitals and the head, as well as between castration and beheading."[52] Along similar lines, Serena Nanda has pointed out in her study of Hijra emasculation that the mother goddess as "castrator" of her human lover or devotee is a common theme in Hindu mythology and ritual.[53] In one striking myth, for example, after the Goddess has slain the buffalo demon Mahiṣa by decapitating him, she finds a *liṅgam* on the severed neck in place of the now missing head: Mahiṣa's head and Śiva's phallus are thus symbolically equated in the myth itself.[54] Even more strikingly, we know that Hijras often become possessed by a goddess trance before they undergo the surgery that will literally take away their male genitals,[55] certainly one of the more dramatic confirmations of the general psychoanalytic perspective.[56] To read decapitation as symbolic castration/penectomy, then, need not be construed as a wild Freudian speculation imposed from without; quite the contrary, such a hermeneutic can be practiced in a way remarkably consistent with the culture's own symbolism. If anything, such a psychoanalytic hermeneutic *honors* that symbolism by taking it seriously. Such a hermeneutic can certainly help us understand—if never fully explain—why the male sense of Kālī is often filled with a certain anxiety and dread: the Goddess cuts off, takes away, and absorbs his masculine identity back into herself; indeed, she boldly wears a whole host of such male heads as her decorative garland.[57]

And we need not read such conclusions negatively. Girindrasekhar Bose, for example, long ago transformed the European "castration threat" into an Indian "castration wish," arguing that Indian men are more balanced in their gender identities and so often wish to become female.[58] It is also worth noting that the "French Freud," Jacques Lacan, felt that to be a truly great male mystic it is necessary to surrender one's maleness and experience "a jouissance that is beyond," that is, a polymorphous pleasure that is connected to being and that is beyond the phallic function.[59] In older and less precise psychoanalytic terms, that is, in the words of Jesus, one must castrate oneself "for the kingdom of heaven" (Matt. 19:11–12).

What is so remarkable about South Asian Tantra, particularly in its left-handed or "hard-core" models,[60] is that, against so many other mystico-erotic traditions in the world, it so often refuses this kind of mystical removal of the phallus/head and opts instead for an explicitly phallic affirmation. To the extent that he is a "hero," a *vīra,* a man (Latin *vir*), the Tāntrika engages the divine, not as a woman or through a feminine jouissance or a bullish death, but through an explicitly phallic, adult (hetero)sexual act. He has sex with the sword-wielding, head-wearing Goddess and comes back alive, with his head. From the perspective of comparative mysticism, this kind of assertive heterosexuality is both remarkable and rare: "heroic" seems an exactly right and perfectly accurate descriptor.

Psychoanalysis can also help us to understand Tantra's normative objectification of women. It is well known that Tantric texts and rituals often call for a low-caste or sexually illicit woman (that is, a "harlot" figure) for its central *maithuna* ritual. However troubling this may be to contemporary humanists or feminists (and it is troubling to me as well),[61] such a "splitting" makes psychological sense for the Tāntrika, as it allows him to have sex with a woman without making the incestuous connection between "woman" and "mother" that is so often made elsewhere in the culture and its salient myths. Indeed, the move accomplishes two important psycho-religious tasks at once: the woman is both socially dangerous (hence any contact, and especially sexual contact, with her is transgressive and so potentially liberating) and obviously *not* the Tāntrika's mother (who can thus remain idealized as pure and nonsexual). The Tāntrika phallicism thus preserves itself from the unconscious fear of incest and, at the same time, appropriates to itself through a transgressive act new dangerous energies and powers.

Another feature of Kālī's *cultus* that has puzzled interpreters for years is also illuminated by the psychoanalytic approach: the fact that, quite despite all appearances and a long textual history to the contrary, most contemporary devotees approach her as a sweet, consoling mother figure. She is "Kālī-Mā," "Kālī the Mama," a far cry indeed from the often outrageously sexy, violent, and macabre figure of Western appropriations (see, for example, McDermott's chapter in the present volume). How do we explain both this indigenous insistence on Kālī's motherly nature and this Western view of her as a supersexualized goddess? Psychoanalytically speaking, the two very different cultural appropriations again make good sense, as each speaks to and answers a particular oedipal and religio-cultural dilemma. In terms of South Asia, it is incorrect to speak of Kālī as simply the "fierce mother," for she possesses two radically different sides: a consoling, nurturing, protecting "right" side, and a violent, threatening "left" side. She grants boons *and* decapitates. She protects *and* threatens. What the devotional tradition has done is to reaffirm the positive, affective aspects of the mother over the sexual, potentially destructive ones, emphasizing the right over the left, if you will.[62] And this resonates with the Brāhmaṇical value system in which the vast majority of South Asian Hindu children no doubt experience the love and nurturance of their mothers in memorably positive ways.

But it makes little oedipal sense within a Western system of individuality, phallicism, open sexualities, and the search for a feminine divine. Western religious seekers are generally not looking for a way to sublimate their sexualities within the idealized innocence of devotion and the beauties of a childlike love. Quite the contrary, much like the left-handed Tāntrika and his consort, they are seeking to affirm their adult sexualities within a religious model that has a place for the divine feminine. This is why, I would suggest, the South Asian Kālī traditions so often appear devotional and gentle and the Western Kālī traditions so sexualized, extreme, and even offensive to Hindus. There is seldom, I would guess, any intended offense. Each culture is simply responding to a different set of psychological, religious, and cultural problems.[63]

Finally and most radically, the psychoanalytic model allows us to answer the question of why the Tantric traditions insist on linking sexuality with spirituality. Psychologically speaking, the instinctual powers of sexuality and affection were originally inseparably joined in the human being's first and most important relationship with an Other. Consequently, every quest for union, every longing for love, every mythology of mysticism is, in some very real sense, an attempt to recapture a state of being that, by virtue of time and human maturation, can never be fully realized again—that overwhelmingly blissful physically delightful merger with a Presence of truly mythological proportions, the infant's human mother. Tantric mysticism is thus a nostalgic song to the mother, a passionate longing for her body, an always frustrated effort to return to her loving embrace, however overwhelming and frightening that merger might be. It is an attempt to reunite affective and sexual powers back into a unitive experience of the (m)other.

WHY THE PSYCHOANALYTIC THINKER IS A HERO

With such thoughts, psychoanalytically inclined thinkers bestow dignity and meaning on those human beings whose sufferings they have encountered by accident or by plan. Perhaps it is worth listening here to one of Caldwell's informants, a male ritual specialist of *muṭiyēṯṯu* who spoke eloquently to the anthropologist about those who understand and those who do not: "No one thinks about what we suffer. They simply come and watch the performance and go home. Only we know what it is to live for this art."[64] What makes psychoanalysis so controversial (and so powerful) is that it listens carefully to such a confession of suffering, contextualizes it within the webs of myth and ritual in which it is found, and then interprets its dynamics, often against or beyond the self-understandings of the sufferer, in sociocultural and psychosexual terms.[65] It makes explicit what is only implicit in the religious phenomenon. In this, it is more radical, more "to the root," than any possession state or mystical experience.

And this is precisely where the tradition becomes a kind of mystical tradition in its own right, working through "the secret" (*to mustikon*), abreacting it in thought, writing it out on the page for the public. Little wonder that the tradition has always been infused with a genuine mystical sensibility: from Romain Rolland's "oceanic experiences," shared with a sympathetic but ambiguous Freud, to Jung's critical dialogue with *kuṇḍalinī yoga* and his conviction, in J. J. Clarke's words, that "psychoanalysis constitutes the first glimmerings of a modern Western form of [Tantric] yoga,"[66] through Sudhir

Kakar's self-described "liberal-rationalist" Hinduism "with a streak of agnostic mysticism" and Alan Roland's early formative experiences with the Western Hindu tradition of Vedānta embodied in the person of Ramakrishna and the writings of Swami Vivekananda[67] to Sarah Caldwell's mystico-sexual hermeneutical experiences of Bhagavati-Kāḷi, the psychoanalytic tradition has functioned as its own kind of Kālī-art, a culturally specific meditation on sexuality, violence and suffering with its own discursive rules, ritual techniques and esoteric communities—a psychoanalytic poetics of the goddess.

Within this same hermeneutical mystical vein, perhaps we could read the twentieth-century's psychoanalytic Kālī as a kind of embodied theorizing, as a century-long ritual gazing upon an iconography with which, as Lévi-Strauss might say, it is good to think. Surely such a vertiginous thought has not left us unchanged, for to think so long and deep about a subject is to become it in some sense. But "[w]hy would one wish to identify with, to actually become (in the logic of Tantra), a goddess such as Kālī . . . [who] dramatically embodies marginal, polluting, or socially subversive qualities?" David Kinsley asks us. The same could be asked of psychoanalysis itself: "Why would one wish to identify with, to actually become, a form of thought that dwells so obsessively, so obscenely, on sexual organs and acts, human aggression and ambivalence, and the deepest, darkest secrets of the human psyche?" The answer, I think, is the same for both questions: in order to be transformed, to lose one's egoic head and its hardened categories in an exhilarating experience of freedom and depth beyond the surface consciousness we mistakenly take as all we are.

For those of us still identified primarily with modern forms of individuality and consciousness, perhaps all we can finally do is acknowledge the psychological, erotic, and even ontological depths of the Goddess's forms as we nevertheless choose to live our lives well outside the fearful, if blissful, continuity of her embrace. But even this realization is itself a form of wisdom, a deep and honorable sense of respect for both the primordial truths of the Goddess and the integrity of the adult human worlds in which we must live now. There are many ways to be a hero, and it sometimes helps to keep one's head, especially after one has lost it.

NOTES

EPIGRAPH: David Kinsley, *Tantric Visions of the Divine Feminine: The Ten Mahāvidyās* (Berkeley and Los Angeles: University of California Press, 1997), pp. 7, 251, 252.

NOTE: In the notes that follow, *S.E.* = *The Standard Edition of the Complete Psychological Works of Sigmund Freud,* ed. James Strachey (24 vols.; London: Hogarth Press and Institute of Psycho-Analysis, 1953–74).

1. Sigmund Freud, *Introductory Lectures on Psycho-Analysis,* pt. 3, in vol. 16 of *S.E.* (London: Hogarth Press, 1961), pp. 284–85.

2. Sudhir Kakar, *Shamans, Mystics and Doctors: A Psychological Inquiry into India and Its Healing Traditions* (New Delhi: Oxford University Press, 1982), p. 153.

3. For another perspective on some of the same materials, with a helpful discussion of some of the Jungian materials (which space has prevented me from treating), see David Wulff, "Toward a Psychology of the Goddess," in *The Divine Consort: Rādhā and the Goddesses of India,* ed. John Stratton Hawley and Donna Marie Wulff (Boston: Beacon Press, 1982), pp. 283–97. I am deeply indebted to David Wulff's magisterial *Psychology of Religion: Classic and Contemporary* (New York: Wiley, 1997) for much that follows, both conceptually and bibliographically.

4. Sigmund Freud, letter to Romain Rolland, January 19, 1930, trans. in William B. Parsons, *The Enigma of the Oceanic Feeling: Revisioning the Psychoanalytic Theory of Mysticism* (New York: Oxford University Press, 1999), p. 176.

5. Sigmund Freud, *The Future of an Illusion* (1927), in vol. 21 of *S.E.* (London: Hogarth Press, 1961), pp. 1–56.

6. Rolland, letter to Freud, May 3, 1931, trans. in Parsons, *Enigma,* p. 178 (cf. p. 174): "But I do not aspire to anything more, for myself, other than repose and effacement, unlimited and total."

7. Romain Rolland, *The Life of Ramakrishna* (Calcutta: Advaita Ashrama, 1986), p. 6: "I myself do not believe in one personal God."

8. Rolland, letter to Freud, December 5, 1927, trans. in Parsons, *Enigma,* pp. 173–74.

9. Freud, letter to Rolland, January 19, 1930, trans. in Parsons, *Enigma,* pp. 176–77.

10. Parsons, *Enigma,* pp. 44–52.

11. Sigmund Freud, *New Introductory Lectures on Psycho-Analysis,* in vol. 22 of *S.E.* (London: Hogarth Press, 1961), pp. 79–80.

12. It was 1929 when the book was published. Rolland, disgusted with a demoralized postwar Europe, offers his book as an attempt to bring the sound of "the artery of Immortality" to the ears of fever-stricken Europe, "which has murdered sleep" (*Life of Ramakrishna,* p. 14).

13. Ibid., p. 29.

14. Ibid., p. 34.

15. Sigmund Freud, *Civilization and Its Discontents* (1930), in vol. 21 of *S.E.* (London: Hogarth Press, 1961), pp. 64–73.

16. Ibid., pp. 66–67.

17. Ibid., p. 68. I am indebted to William Parsons for pointing these passages out to me. See his *Enigma,* pp. 39–44, for a lucid exegesis of them.

18. Freud, *Civilization and Its Discontents,* p. 73.

19. For some background on Daly and the colonial background of his writing, see Christiane Hartnack, "Vishnu on Freud's Desk: Psychoanalysis in Colonial India," in *Vishnu on Freud's Desk: A Reader in Psychoanalysis and Hinduism,* ed. T. G. Vaidyanathan and Jeffrey J. Kripal (New Delhi: Oxford University Press, 1999), pp. 81–106. As of the submission of this chapter, Hartnack's monograph on the same topic, *Psychoanalysis and Colonialism in British India* (New Delhi: Oxford University Press, 2001), had not yet appeared. The latter work will surely add immeasurably to our understanding of the history of psychoanalytic approaches to Hinduism.

20. C. D. Daly, "Hindu-Mythologie und Kastrationskomplex," *Imago: Zeitschrift*

für Anwendung der Psychoanalse auf die Natur- und Gesteswissenschaften 2/3/4 (1927): 145–98; henceforth referenced in body of text. See also "A Hindu Treatise on Kali," *Samiksa* 1 (1947): 191–96. My thanks to Jake Erhardt for help with the German.

21. Hartnack has argued that the writings of Daly and Owen Berkeley-Hill, another British analyst practicing in India, helped stabilize colonial structures by portraying Hindu piety as childish and neurotic ("British Psychoanalysts in Colonial India," in *Psychology in Twentieth-Century Thought and Society,* ed. Mitchell G. Ash and William R. Woodward [New York: Cambridge University Press, 1987], pp. 233–51).

22. Gananath Obeyesekere tells this story in *Medusa's Hair: An Essay on Personal Symbols and Religious Experience* (Chicago: University of Chicago Press, 1981), pp. 6–7.

23. Alf Hiltebeitel, "Hair Like Snakes and Mustached Brides: Crossed Gender in an Indian Folk Cult," in *Hair: Its Power and Meaning in Asian Cultures,* ed. id. and Barbara S. Miller (Albany: State University of New York Press, 1998), pp. 145–76, explores remarkably similar connections.

24. Daly, "Hindu-Mythologie und Kastrationskomplex," p. 148. This same splitting pattern would be picked up by later thinkers, such as Lawrence Babb, Wendy Doniger O'Flaherty, Sudhir Kakar, and Stanley Kurtz, with significant effect.

25. Perhaps the best example of this is the menstruation motif. One could easily dismiss such a reading as a Freudian projection, but then what to do with a decidedly non-psychoanalytic thinker such as David Kinsley, who employs ethnography and the anthropological fact that Hindu women unbind their hair during menstruation to decode Kālī's disheveled hair as a likely symbol of her "impure" or "polluted" menstruation (Kinsley, *Tantric Visions,* pp. 83–84)?

26. Wulff, *Psychology of Religion,* p. 320.

27. Quoted in ibid., p. 327.

28. Ibid., p. 321.

29. Harald Schjelderup and Kristian Schjelderup, *Über drei Haupttypen der religiösen Erlebnisformen und ihre psychologische Grundlage* (Berlin: Walter de Gruyter, 1932).

30. Wulff, *Psychology of Religion,* p. 321.

31. Erik Erikson, *Young Man Luther: A Study in Psychoanalysis and History* (1958; New York: Norton, 1962), p. 264.

32. Schjelderup and Schjelderup, *Über drei Haupttypen,* p. 58; my translation.

33. See esp. Kakar, *Shamans, Mystics and Doctors,* ch. 6, "Tantra and Tantric Healing," pp. 151–90.

34. Kripal, "Re-membering a Presence of Mythological Proportions: Psychoanalysis and Hinduism," in *Mapping Religion and Psychological Studies: Contemporary Dialogues, Future Prospects,* ed. William B. Parsons and Diane Jonte-Pace (New York: Routledge, 2000), pp. 256–58.

35. See Gananath Obeyesekere, *The Cult of the Goddess Pattini* (Chicago: University of Chicago Press, 1984), pp. 427–50 and 451–82, respectively. Obeyesekere's writings on Kālī are especially rich. See also "Kali, the Punitive Mother," in Gananath Obeyesekere and Richard Gombrich, *Buddhism Transformed: Religious Change in Sri Lanka* (Princeton: Princeton University Press, 1988), pp. 133–62; and *Medusa's Hair.*

36. Obeyesekere, *Cult of the Goddess Pattini,* p. 428; henceforth cited in body of text.

37. Gananath Obeyesekere, *The Work of Culture: Symbolic Transformation in Psychoanalysis and Anthropology* (Chicago: University of Chicago Press, 1990). The earlier two books of the trilogy are cited in nn. 22 and 35 above.

38. Obeyesekere, *Pattini,* p. 430, referencing M. N. Srinivas.

39. Ibid., p. 440; cf. p. 449. Of course, numerous cases could be presented that refute or deny such a psychoanalytic reading, but this is hardly a refutation of the model, which asks questions of public myths and practices developed over large stretches of time by innumerable individual cases. The question is not "Does this model fit every case?" (the answer is "Of course not") but rather "How do we explain the broad cultural salience of these particular images?"

40. Diagrammatically, Obeyesekere's model looks like this: "the values of the society → the female role → mother-child relationship → perception of the deity by the child" (429).

41. Obeyesekere, *Cult of the Goddess Pattini,* p. 452, citing Freud.

42. Sarah Caldwell, *Oh Terrifying Mother: Sexuality, Violence, and Worship of the Goddess Kāḷi* (New York: Oxford University Press, 1999); henceforth cited in body of text.

43. Richard J. Castillo, "Spirit Possession in South Asia, Dissociation or Hysteria? Part 1: Theoretical Background," *Culture, Medicine and Psychiatry* 18, no. 1 (1994): 1–21, and "Spirit Possession in South Asia, Dissociation or Hysteria? Part 2: Case Histories," ibid., 18, no. 2 (1994): 141–62.

44. Obeyesekere, *Medusa's Hair,* and *Cult of the Goddess Pattini,* p. 33; and Susan Starr Sered, *Priestess, Mother, Sacred Sister: Religions Dominated by Women* (New York: Oxford University Press, 1994).

45. Obeyesekere, *Medusa's Hair,* p. 37.

46. Jeffrey J. Kripal, *Roads of Excess, Palaces of Wisdom: Eroticism and Reflexivity in the Study of Mysticism* (Chicago: University of Chicago Press, 2001).

47. Steve Derne, "Images of the Fierce Goddess: Psychoanalysis and Religious Symbols—a Response to Kondos," *Contributions to Indian Sociology* 22, no. 1 (1988): 89. Derne's essay is a critique of the psychoanalytic study of Hinduism and in particular of Vivienne Kondos, "Images of the Fierce Goddess and Portrayals of Hindu Women," *Contributions to Indian Sociology* 20, no. 2 (1986): 173–97.

48. I have been informed in my thinking here by the thought of Georges Bataille, particularly his *Erotism: Death and Sensuality* (San Francisco: City Lights, 1986), "Part One: Taboo and Transgression," pp. 27–146.

49. Sudhir Kakar, "The Maternal-Feminine in Indian Psychoanalysis," *International Review of Psycho-Analysis* 16 (1989): 335–62.

50. Carmel Berkson, *The Divine and the Demoniac: Mahiṣa's Heroic Struggle with Durga* (New Delhi: Oxford University Press, 1995).

51. As Gary Taylor has pointed out recently, what Freud and psychoanalysts are really talking about is penectomy (the surgical removal of the entire sexual organ), which they misidentified with castration (the removal of the testicles). Castration possesses a long and complicated history in Western culture—with some fascinating connections to Mesopotamian goddess traditions and Christian mystical thought (Jesus, for example, counseled his closest disciples to castrate themselves [Matt. 19:12])—revolving around issues of royal power and the protection of inheritance (hence the importance of eunuchs in royal administrations), animal and human re-

production, marginal or liminal sexualities (like homosexuality), the control of foreign peoples and slaves, and, later, the censorship of texts and birth control. See Gary Taylor, *Castration: An Abbreviated History of Western Manhood* (New York: Routledge, 2000).

52. Hugh B. Urban, "The Remnants of Desire: Sacrificial Violence and Sexual Transgression in the Cult of the Kāpālikas and in the Writings of Georges Bataille," *Religion* 25 (1995): 70.

53. Lawrence Cohen, "The Pleasures of Castration: The Postoperative Status of Hijras, Jankhas, and Academics," in *Sexual Nature, Sexual Culture,* ed. Paul R. Abramson and Steven D. Pinkerton (Chicago: University of Chicago Press, 1995), pp. 276–304; Serena Nanda, *Neither Man Nor Woman: The Hijras of India* (Belmont, Calif.: Wadsworth, 1990); and Wendy Doniger O'Flaherty, *Women, Androgynes, and Other Mythical Beasts* (Chicago: University of Chicago Press, 1980).

54. Ibid., p. 85; quoted and interpreted in Berkson, *Divine and the Demoniac,* pp. 126–27.

55. Cohen, "Pleasures of Castration," p. 276.

56. Ibid., p. 295. For three important essays exploring the connections between decapitation, eunuch penectomy, cock sacrifice, and hair-cutting in the Tamil folk cult of Aravāṉ, see Alf Hiltebeitel, "Dying Before the *Mahābhārata* War: Martial and Transsexual Body-building for Aravāṉ," *Journal of Asian Studies* 54, no. 2 (1995): 447–73; "Hair Like Snakes and Mustached Brides: Crossed Gender in an Indian Folk Cult"; and "Kūttāṇṭavar: The Divine Lives of a Severed Head," in *Ways of Dying: Death and Its Meanings in South Asia,* ed. Elisabeth Schömbucher and Claus Peter Zoller, Heidelberg University South Asian Institute Studies 33 (Delhi: Manohar, 1999), pp. 276–310.

57. Sudhir Kakar, *The Inner World: A Psycho-Analytic Study of Childhood and Society in India,* 2d ed. (Delhi: Oxford University Press, 1981), p. 102. There is one important caveat in all of this, however, and it goes back to Girindrasekhar Bose, who long ago argued that his Hindu male patients displayed no fear of a castration threat but, on the contrary, manifested clear signs of a castration *wish,* that is to say, they displayed a "desire to be female." This is an important point, and one supported by the remarkable series of Tantric ritual paintings that Indra Sinha has recently published, in which multiple decapitated heads (which appear along with ithyphallic sadhus and severed phalluses throughout the series) display a remarkable calmness and peace in their severed state, as if this is precisely what they wished to be (*The Great Book of Tantra: Translations and Images from the Classic Indian Texts with Commentary* [Rochester, Vt.: Destiny Books, 1993]).

58. "The Genesis and Adjustment of the Oedipus Wish" (1956), reprinted in T. G. Vaidyanathan and Jeffrey J. Kripal, *Vishnu on Freud's Desk: A Reader in Psychoanalysis and Hinduism* (Delhi: Oxford University Press, 1999), pp. 21–38.

59. See Jacques Lacan, "God and ~~Woman's~~ Jouissance," in *On Feminine Sexuality, The Limits of Love and Knowledge, 1972–1973,* ed. Jacques-Alain Miller, trans. Bruce Fink (New York: Norton, 1998), pp. 76–77. For an application of this hermeneutic to Indic materials, see Catherine Clement, *Syncope: The Philosophy of Rapture,* trans. Sally O'Discoll and Deirdre M. Mahoney (Minneapolis: University of Minnesota Press, 1994).

60. I am indebted to David Gordon White for his modern renditions of "right-handed" and "left-handed" as "soft-core" and "hard-core"; see his introduction to his edited *Tantra in Practice* (Princeton: Princeton University Press, 2000), p. 6.

61. These overwhelming androcentric and often misogynistic features of Tantrism are some of the most difficult for Westerners to understand and appreciate. Accordingly, Western appropriations of Tantra—both popular and scholarly—often try to reunite the affective and the sexual, effectively transforming the rites into a practice that is more isomorphic with Western oedipal resolutions, cultural values about romantic love, and contemporary concerns about agency, feminism, and reciprocal sexuality. Such a desire is all well and good and certainly understandable, but I have serious doubts about how well it reflects the traditional Indian patterns that it often claims to reproduce. David Kinsley, for example, in his recent study of the Tantric Mahāvidyās, could not find a single piece of textual or ethnographic evidence that suggested a female perspective (*Tantric Visions,* p. 250). Psychoanalysis here, as elsewhere, must insist, I think, on both the genuine otherness of the Tantric oedipal solutions and on their grounding in universal psychosexual dilemmas (i.e., the love of and for the mother).

62. For the definitive study of this process in Bengal, see Rachel Fell McDermott, *Mother of My Heart, Daughter of My Dreams: Kālī and Umā in the Devotional Poetry of Bengal* (New York: Oxford University Press, 2001).

63. Kinsley has noted and commented on this same phenomenon of the conservative-Hindu "insider" and the radical-Western-Tantric "outsider" readings of Kālī (*Tantric Visions,* p. 91).

64. Caldwell, *Oh Terrifying Mother,* p. 257.

65. For a brilliant analysis of this difference, see Peter Homans's discussion of Kakar's work, "Once Again, Psychoanalysis, East and West: A Psychoanalytic Essay on Religion, Mourning, and Healing," *History of Religions* 24, no. 2 (1984): 133–54.

66. J. J. Clarke, *Jung and Eastern Thought: A Dialogue with the Orient* (London: Routledge, 1994), p. 110. See also C. G. Jung, *The Psychology of Kundalini Yoga: Notes of the Seminar Given in 1932 by C. G. Jung,* edited by Sonu Shamdasani (Princeton: Princeton University Press, 1996).

67. Alan Roland, "Psychoanalysis and the Spiritual Quest: Framing a New Paradigm," in *The Unknown, Remembered Gate: Religious Experience and Hermeneutical Reflection in the Study of Religion,* ed. Elliot Wolfson and Jeffrey J. Kripal (New York: Seven Bridges Press, forthcoming).

CHAPTER 10

Doing the Mother's Caribbean Work

On Shakti *and Society in Contemporary Trinidad*

Keith E. McNeal

MOTHER KALI'S SECOND EXILE: DISCREDITED AT THE CENTER, RESURGENT ON THE MARGINS

To many diasporic Indians of the nineteenth-century Caribbean, it must have been painfully obvious that the world had progressed deeply into Kaliyug—that cosmic multimillion-year period when the world falls into decline and evil rules the day. At least this is how many of Kali's contemporary devotees in Trinidad see the matter. They are aware of the cruel hardships their ancestors endured in coming to the New World, and of the courage that survival through those times necessitated. And their own experiences vividly suggest that the worldly degeneration of Kaliyug is here to stay. Thus it is clear to them that one should seek the protection and blessings of Mother Kali, for it is her mysterious *shakti,* or power, that liberates us from suffering in this turbulent age.

This connection is actually not so obvious to many in contemporary postcolonial Trinidad. Indeed, something peculiar has happened to Mother Kali in the Caribbean regions of the vast Hindu diaspora. Put simply, she has fallen from grace; her worship is embarrassing to many respectable Hindus. Not only was she brought by her spiritual children to wander the wilds of the New World, far away from the homeland of Mother India; but she has also been exiled yet again, this time within the cauldron of the Caribbean itself. She has become highly marginalized over the past hundred years in Trinidad, and her worship is viewed with significant degrees of ambivalence, contempt, and fear by Hindus and non-Hindus alike.

This process of marginalization is particularly ironic when we realize that ritualized devotions in honor of Kali have not always been discriminated against on the island. During the period of East Indian indentureship (1845–1917), ritual supplications in honor of the Mother—as she is often called—were an important aspect of village *puja*s in many Trinidadian Indian communities. Thus from a societywide historical perspective, Kali *puja* has gone from being an openly practiced ritual performance observed on behalf of entire communities to a marginalized, somewhat clandestine therapeutic ritual carried out weekly on behalf of individuals and families in peripheral temples dedicated primarily to Kali and her most important spiritual associates.

The story does not end here, however, for there is a further dramatic twist in the Mother's local plot line. Following her midcentury fall from public grace, Kali worship and other closely related forms of *shakti puja* have undergone a noteworthy resurgence since the 1970s in Trinidad, but they are something of a subaltern practice enacted on the margins of late-twentieth-century mainstream Caribbean Hinduism. Thus despite her stigmatized spiritual status in the greater island society, Mother Kali's popularity and healing power have become revitalized in peripheral temples, and the number of her devotees has been growing significantly. Moreover, important *shakti* practitioners from Guyana on the nearby South American mainland have crucially influenced the resurgence of ecstatic Kali worship in Trinidad; indeed, the Guyanese influence on the Trinidadian scene should not be underestimated. Though the population of *shakti* practitioners is probably not growing at the rate it did during the 1970s and early 1980s, Kali devotions are certainly alive and well in contemporary Trinidad—only situated and therefore organized quite differently than they were a century before.

My aim here is to map out some of the historical and contemporary ethnographic contours of Kali worship in Trinidad. I describe the social organization and ritual structure of contemporary Kali *puja* as it is practiced on the island and attempt to convey some of the innovative ways these related forms of *shakti* worship have adapted to their changing New World context through dialectical processes of accommodation, appropriation, and hybridization. This is set within an analysis of the sociohistorical processes by which these forms of *shakti puja* became marginalized, only to become newly reincarnated in the postcolonial era (national independence was achieved in 1962) within the arena of contemporary temple-based Kali worship. In short, we need to understand how Kali has become simultaneously discredited at the center and yet resurgent on the margins of that center. But before doing this, we must first set the stage by turning to Trinidad and the deeper context of Caribbean colonialism.

COLONIALISM AND THE DILEMMAS OF CARIBBEAN HINDUISM

The twin-island Republic of Trinidad and Tobago is located at the southernmost point in the Caribbean archipelago, just off the northeast coast of Venezuela on the South American continent. The larger of the two, Trinidad, the republic's seat of government, banking, imports, and trade, is the fifth-largest island in the Caribbean region. Current statistics indicate that Trinidad and Tobago's population is approximately 1,400,000. About 40 percent of the population are of "African" descent, another estimated 40 percent are of "East Indian" descent, and the majority of the rest are "mixed," along with small but significant—also partially intermixed—minorities of Chinese, whites, "Portuguese" from the offshore islands of Madeira, Fayal, and the Azores, "Spanish" from Venezuela, and "Syrians" from Lebanon and Syria in the Near East.[1] Trinidad has also received significant population boosts from some of the smaller islands of the eastern Caribbean due to various regional migration dynamics.

The perceived need to locate Trinidad and Tobago geographically and demographically for readers of a volume of essays on Hindu centers and margins, and their relationship to that messy construct we call the "West," should give us pause. This is not simply because Trinidad is a relatively small player on the world's stage, or was never a crucial part of the Spanish, French, or British overseas colonial empires, all of which it was involved in along the way. These factors are certainly relevant, but more important is the fact that Hindu Trinidad is located at the margins of *two* global centers, not one: it is a small diasporic backwater vis-à-vis Mother India, and yet, however marginally, it is inextricably embedded in the West—especially western Europe, due to colonialism, and the United States, due to twentieth-century neocolonialism across the Americas. Indeed, this dual periphery-or-center situation should be seen as both reflective and generative of Caribbean Hinduism's ongoing diasporic dilemmas.

It is noteworthy that the Caribbean has stood in an awkward relation to anthropology in that it has had no surviving classically "indigenous" peoples to study and because it is and has always been "neither center nor periphery."[2] Caribbean societies are inescapably heterogeneous, and this heterogeneity is inescapably historical; thus investigation of Caribbean societies precludes the projection of "native" or "pure" cultures, because these societies are inherently colonial and are "nothing but contact" in their constitution.[3] The Caribbean is quintessentially modern, a region where "tradition" grew directly out of the colonial order.[4] Understanding how the Caribbean colonial dynamic influenced the course of New World Hinduism is not only crucial for grasping the twists and turns of Mother Kali's fate in Trinidad but also for gaining a deeper sense of the dilemmas and conflicts of being dually marginalized in relation to two quite different centers.

The development of plantations to produce commodities for European markets was a vital first step in the history of overseas capitalism. The Caribbean was the earliest focus of European colonial development in the New World: sugarcane, African slaves, and the plantation system were introduced into it within twenty years of its "discovery" in 1492. As Sidney Mintz writes: "The peoples of the Caribbean are the descendants of those ancestors dragged into European experiments, and of the Europeans who dragged them, at an early point in western history. Indeed, those peoples and this region mark the moment when 'the West' became a conceptual entity—for these were the West's first genuine overseas colonies."[5] In the Caribbean, slavery was practiced on agro-industrial plantations whose primary economic purpose was to fuel western European capitalistic expansion. Again, quoting Mintz: "The relatively highly developed industrial character of the plantation system meant a curious sort of 'modernization' or 'westernization' for the slaves—an aspect of their acculturation in the New World that has too often been missed because of the deceptively rural, agrarian, and pseudo-manorial quality of the slave-based plantation production."[6] The features of this plantation system—which include monocrop production for export, strong monopolistic tendencies, and a rigid, oppressive system of social stratification with a high correlation between racial and class hierarchies—have all contributed to the shared contours of Caribbean economies and societies.[7]

To mitigate and manipulate the labor problems prompted by emancipation of the slaves, many planters of the region resorted to the importation of nominally free laborers under contracts of indenture. Apart from the condition that they had a legally defined term of service and were guaranteed a set wage, these indentured servants were often treated not so differently from the African slaves they partially replaced in the fields and factories.[8] Between 1838 and 1917, over half a million South Asians came to work on the British West Indian sugar plantations—the majority going to the new sugar producers with fertile lands like Trinidad, which received about 144,000 indentured migrants. In the mid 1850s, more than 14,000 Chinese workers reached the shores of some of the very same islands. East Indians also went to work on plantations in francophone Martinique and Guadeloupe, as well as Dutch Surinam—with a significant number of Javanese joining them in the latter. Between 1841 and 1867, some 32,000 indentured or newly freed Africans also arrived in the British West Indies.

It is only with this dynamic sociohistorical context in mind that we can begin to appreciate some of the dilemmas of adaptation faced by Hindus in the Caribbean. The diasporic situation of being a criticized minority religion within a highly pluralistic, stratified colonial island society precipitated a sense of insecurity and self-consciousness about religious beliefs and practices among Hindus in Trinidad—dilemmas whose tensions and ambivalences have helped fuel the progressive marginalization of twentieth-century Kali worship on the island. Christianity, in a range of European and North American manifestations, all of which saw Indian religion as heathen idolatry, dominated the colonial environment for the Hindu in Trinidad.

Caribbean Hindus attempted to resolve the profound conflicts generated by the ongoing encounter with colonial Christianity through various kinds of compromise and reformulation. They, or at least a significantly influential group among them, were able to construct a standardized, Brahmanical form of Hinduism that came to be judged "orthodox."[9] Most important for our purposes here, this orthodoxy has sought to dissociate itself from particularly prominent religious modalities smacking of morally suspect, purportedly pagan practices such as animal sacrifice, spirit possession, and fire-walking—practices that have traditionally been deeply integral to various forms of *shakti* worship. Where the elimination of these has not been feasible, the predominant strategy has been to deem them peripheral, "low-caste" practices associated with the dark-skinned "Madrassi" immigrants from South India.

For the Caribbean Hindu, these ongoing experiences of inequality and suffering are unfortunately only to be expected in the present age of Kaliyug. What better way to understand such a 500-year period of high colonial drama than through a paradigm that sees the present world's discontents as signs of a degenerate cosmic cycle in which evil runs amok? Her spiritual children see Mother Kali as the ultimate arbiter of good and evil, and they turn to her in times of illness and suffering, hardship and need. We need to think about why this supreme patroness came to be discarded in the eyes of an emergent, constructed twentieth-century orthodoxy, for her second exile has been engineered through the efforts of her fellow victims from the first colonial exile. Paradoxically, then, we must also ask why Kali's *shakti* has been revitalized in the postcolonial era, and to do this I propose an ethnographic response. We have to understand what reincarnated shape her worship has taken in contemporary times, for only then will we understand patterns and variations in the ways she has become supreme Mother to her current devotees.

KALI WORSHIP IN ITS CONTEMPORARY TRINIDADIAN INCARNATION

As I have indicated, contemporary manifestations of Kali *puja* in Trinidad are highly marginalized religious activities that often stir up inchoate feelings of fear, ambivalence, and even contempt in the minds of nonpractitioners—whether Hindu or non-Hindu. From the outside, Kali is considered to be a capricious, malevolent goddess who lures people into her devotions and punishes them severely if they do not maintain the practice. The sacrificing of live goats and chickens has long been a central symbolic action in Kali *puja,* and these sacrificial practices continue in some of the more prominent modern Kali temples in Trinidad. Ecstatic manifestations of Mother Kali and several other related deities through the performances of possession-mediums are also central to contemporary Trinidadian Kali worship. Both the live sacrifice and spirit possession practices feed into "mainstream" public opinion, which sees Kali *puja* as demonic or dealing in *obeah* (black magic).

Kali *puja* services are often conducted on a weekly basis—typically on Sundays, but sometimes on Saturdays or even on a Friday night—in nonorthodox Hindu temples that range anywhere in size from a makeshift shack to compounds capable of holding hundreds of people at a time. I would estimate there to be approximately fifteen to twenty *shakti* temples in Trinidad; however, a handful do not hold active weekly services, and at least two of these less active temples are currently dormant. Most are symbolically oriented around a *murti* (statue) of Mother Kali, which is often housed within the most central sanctum of the temple compound.

Statues and chromolithographic images of other Hindu *deota*s (deities) of both orthodox and nonorthodox derivation often flank Kali in her temples. The most commonly found orthodox *deota*s include Ganesh, Surujnarayan, Hanuman, Shiva, Radha and Krishna, Rama and Sita, Saraswati, Durga, Lakshmi, and Ganga Mata; the nonorthodox divinities, not found in any of the other ostensibly mainstream Hindu temples on the island, include Kal Bhairo (Maduraviran), Dee Baba (Sanganni), Munesh Prem / Muni Spiren, Nagura Baba, and Mother Katerie.[10] Over time, there has therefore been a pattern of ritual consolidation of a very specific, unique pantheon of deities encountered solely in that configuration in Trinidadian *shakti* temples.

While some Kali temples maintain an adamant position against live animal sacrifice, ecstatic rituals of spirit possession undoubtedly occupy a centrally salient place in all temple-based centers of Kali worship in Trinidad. The spiritual manifestation of Mother Kali through an experienced possession-medium is a high point of Kali *puja* services, and many people visit the temple on *puja* days with the specific purpose of consulting with "de Mudda" (the Mother) about a wide range of existential problems such as illness, domestic or work conflicts, infertility, sexual dysfunction, and so on. Possession manifestation in these contexts is conceived of as the activation of *shakti,* a conceptualization of cosmic power or energy within Hinduism that is associated with the mother goddesses. The temporary activation of *shakti* in a human medium makes the practice of *jharaying*—spiritual purification and blessing—with neem leaves particularly powerful during spirit consultations in these temples.

Several of the other associated *deota*s found in Trinidadian Kali temples manifest via possession-mediums and likewise offer consultative *jharay* sessions: for instance, Kal Bhairo, Dee Baba, Mother Katerie, Mother Ganga,

Figure 10.1 *Shakti* play at an annual big Kali Puja, Trinidad. Photo by Keith McNeal, April 2000.

and Munesh Prem. Manifesting possession-mediums often take flaming cubes of camphor into their mouths as a sign that an authentic spirit manifestation is taking place. Lay members and visitors to the temples on *puja* days can also be possessed by *shakti* energy on a temporary, ritualized basis, but these manifestations are typically considered to be generalized episodes of *shakti* and are not necessarily identified with a specific possessing divinity (see fig. 10.1).

Devotees often arrive early on the morning of the weekly service armed with flowers, milk, fruit, and so on, which they offer to any or all of the various deities present in the temple before the official service begins. The general structure of the *puja* consists of the *pujari*s and an attending group of observers moving to each and every *deota* "stand" (place where the deity's *murti* or image is located) within the temple in order to make offerings of fruit, flowers, green and dry coconuts, incense, lit flame, and so forth, and

Figure 10.2 Performing the authenticity of one's *shakti* by undergoing the whip test. Photo by Keith McNeal, March 1999.

possibly to erect a spiritual flag (*jhandi*) representative of each *deota*'s power. Such deity *puja*s and offerings are accompanied by devotional songs sung in varying combinations of Hindi, Tamil, and English and musically driven by the rhythmic percussion of three to five *tappu* drums.[11] The round of *puja* offerings to the various deities typically culminates climactically in group devotional *puja* directed toward Mother Kali herself. If the temple conducts live animal sacrifice, it is at this point that the animals are beheaded as offerings to Kali and her associated divine attendants.

Although weekly services are the typical form of Kali *puja* practiced throughout the year in Trinidadian Kali temples, most devotees also perform a grand annual *puja* that takes place over an intense period of three days but involves many weeks of preparation. The structure of the annual "big *puja*" is similar to that of the weekly services, but the rituals, devotions, and offerings are more frequent and elaborate. This ritual period affords an opportunity for members to display the purity and authenticity of their devotions in either of two forms of "test," which they undergo under the gaze of the temple audience while experiencing the ecstatic influence of *shakti:* (a) receiving lashes from a whip without injury (fig. 10.2), or (b) walking or dancing through a fire pit without getting burned.

The issue of live animal sacrifice is actively contentious within the community of *shakti* practitioners in Trinidad, and has become something of a moral flashpoint. Blood sacrifice is perhaps the most immediate symbolic association that outsiders—Hindu and non-Hindu alike—make regarding Kali *puja* on the island, but most are not aware that a significant number of devotees and temples do not condone or observe the practice. Indeed, my experience leads me to believe that anti-sacrificial sentiments are gradually becoming the more prevalent ritual approach within local patterns of contemporary Kali worship. Those temples that perform live sacrifice stress that the goat or fowl must be ritually beheaded with a single stroke of the cutlass.

Kali worship as we encounter it today, in nonorthodox temples dedicated primarily to weekly ecstatic healing ceremonies of possession by Kali and other marginalized deities, emerged in its contemporary form in the mid 1970s and has experienced progressive growth since that time. This ritual system has attracted the majority of its devotees from among the island's Indo-Trinidadian rural and urban proletarians, but it is also important to note that it has recruited practitioners of African- and mixed-African descent, as well as from a handful of upwardly mobile spiritual seekers. The number of active Kali devotees reaches into the several thousands at least, but any kind of specific estimate would be difficult and probably misleading.

The emergence and rapid growth of modern Kali temples in postcolonial Trinidad must be seen in light of the country's topsy-turvy, late-twentieth-century socioeconomic experience—particularly the cycle of oil boom-and-bust in the 1970s and 1980s—and in relation to the increasing social anomie brought about by rapid industrialization and North American neocolonialism. In specifically religious terms, I believe the rise of modern Kali worship must be seen as analogous to the resurgence of Orisha religion and Shouter Baptism, as well as to the extraordinarily rapid spread of Pentecostalism and other forms of evangelical Protestantism within this multi-ethnic Caribbean island society.[12]

SHAKTI'S MANY FACES IN TRINIDAD: A BRIEF GENEALOGY

What is curious in the particular sociohistorical evolution of *shakti puja* on the island is that the goddess Kali was not considered a peripheral or wayward deity by Hindus of the indentured diaspora in colonial Trinidad. If anything, diverse textual and oral historical evidence suggests that she was one of the more commonly encountered divinities in the scattered array of Hindu ritual arenas and practices characteristic of that time.

Moreover, this evidence also suggests that what is generally referred to as "Kali *puja*" in contemporary Trinidad is a hybridized amalgam of various earlier, *shakti*-related folk practices, not all of which involved Kali. It is important to emphasize, not only that ecstatic forms of Hindu religious practice now take place solely in Kali temples in contemporary Trinidad, but also that the deities of the Hindu pantheon that do manifest through spirit possession—such as Kali, Kal Bhairo, Dee Baba, Mother Katerie, Munesh Prem, and the like—are also only found in these very same temples. At this point in time, in other words, ecstatic Hinduism is only conceivable in the local social imagination in temples devoted primarily to Mother Kali. Thus Kali has become metonymic for any form of charismatic or ecstatic Hindu practice on the island. I should therefore clarify that my usage of "Kali" and "*shakti*" tends to be interchangeable when speaking about the contemporary scene, whereas prior to the mid twentieth century, it is important to differentiate between "Kali" and "Mariamma" in terms of *shakti* as well as several other minor variant forms of folk devotional practice.

That previously autonomous traditions of *shakti puja*—at least the ones that have not been completely lost—have been incorporated into a more unified, compact, contemporary, temple-based system under Mother Kali's sacred canopy necessitates some understanding of what came before it. Perhaps the two most significant influences on contemporary Kali worship are the older community-based forms of Kali *puja* and the old-style Madrassi fire-pass ceremony; both have been transformed and readapted in hybridized relation to one another as mutual influences within Kali's current temple-based incarnation. What follows in this section are brief discussions of both, as well as a related critique of the local (scapegoating) ideology that attributes Kali worship to the dark-skinned, low-caste "Madrassi" immigrants from South India. With this important set of sociohistorical contextualizations, we can then map out some of the innovative contours of Kali's contemporary postcolonial landscape.

As observed above, what is curious in the particular development of Kali worship on the island is that Hindus in Trinidad did not consider Kali a wayward or peripheral deity during the period of their East Indian indentureship (1845–1917). In fact, a number of textual references suggest that she was one of the more commonly encountered divinities in the array of Hindu ritual arenas and practices characteristic of those times. For example, in *At Last, a Christmas in the West Indies,* originally published in 1871, the novelist Charles Kingsley offers a detailed description of an early Hindu shrine structure that singles out Shiva ("Mahadeva") and Kali as representative deities,[13] and Seepersad Naipaul offers a similar description in his series of fictionalized short stories, most likely written throughout the 1930s, collectively published as *The Adventures of Gurudeva.*[14] Mother Kali's relative centrality is implicit in Naipaul's description of a would-be *pundit*'s efforts at constructing a proper Hindu place of worship in rural Trinidad. These key texts indicate at least some degree of symbolic centrality for Mother Kali among Hindus of the early indentured diaspora in Trinidad.

One of the most prominent characteristics of the older-style Kali *puja* that emerges from mid-twentieth-century ethnographic reports and from the oral histories I have collected is that various village members conducted this *puja* openly on behalf of the entire community.[15] Not everyone in a village actually participated in the *puja* itself or the prior preparations, but they were certainly cognizant of its performance and usually contributed money, rice, and ritual paraphernalia in order to receive material and spiritual benefits. Collections were made during the weeks preceding the ceremony by groups of women, who would pass through a zone of five to seven neighboring villages, singing devotional songs accompanied by a *dholak* hand drum and carrying wooden trays on their heads for offerings, which they collected at each household. This practice was referred to as *Kalimai-ke-beekh,* "begging for Mother Kali."

Each group or community usually performed its *puja* at the home of the *panchayat* "captain," who often officiated as the head ritualist or priest.[16] It was carried out annually and at times of crisis in order to thank the Mother for her blessings, to seek her intervention for agricultural fertility, and to protect the community from sickness. The ritual's structure was characterized by the sacrificial immolation of a live goat (although chickens, or a pig, could also be offered), preceded by the ecstatic possession by Kali of the officiant before the sacrifice could take place. Upon completion of the *puja,* the meat of the sacrificed animal was cut up and divided among the *panchayat* and its associated families, who took it home to be cooked and eaten as *prasad* (food ritually offered to a deity and then ingested as a form of sacred blessing).

By the time of Morton and Sheila Klass's research in central Trinidad in the late 1950s, any form of Kali *puja* had already become associated with morally suspect, lower-status Indian religiosity. Klass encountered two forms of Kali *puja—panchayati-Kali-ki-puja* and *ghar-ki-puja*—that were basically similar in structure, except that the former was sponsored by a number of unrelated families and conducted on behalf of the entire community, whereas the latter was a semi-private, household (*ghar*) ceremony sponsored by individual families, but with friends, relatives, and neighbors in attendance upon invitation. Klass tells us that high-caste families contributed regularly to these *puja*s even though they expressed distaste for animal sacrifice.

Another important strand of influence in the development of Kali worship in Trinidad was the old-style Madrassi fire-pass ceremony. "Madrassi" is the generalized term for indentured labor migrants of varying regional and linguistic backgrounds in South India who sailed to the Caribbean from the southeastern port city of Madras. An average 80 percent of these "Madrassis" were equally divided between Tamil- and Telugu-speakers, and in the 1840s, there were far more Madrassi immigrants in Trinidad than those from the north of India who sailed from Calcutta to the Caribbean. Overall, for the period of East Indian indentureship (1845–1917), however, the number of South Indians who sailed from Madras to Trinidad only constituted approximately 6 percent of the total 144,000 indentured immigrants from India.[17]

The fire-pass—or fire-walking—ceremony is important because it was perhaps the most prominent religious ritual of the Madrassi indentured immigrants who came to the Caribbean from South India and came to be seen as an integral or paradigmatic aspect of early "Madrassi" identity in Trinidad. But the fire-pass performance is also important because it has had a significant influence on contemporary forms of Kali worship. Indeed, many Kali-*puja* practitioners and scholars alike often take it as confirmation of Kali worship's purported Madrassi origins.[18]

Certain aspects of the ceremony's ritual structure recur throughout many of the oral and written sources. These include periods of fasting and other purification disciplines; male participation only; prayers recited from atop a very tall pole erected near the fire-pass pit; preparatory river or sea baths taken just before crossing the hot coals; and the use of a specific type of thin, handheld drum. Several of these characteristics—fasting and purification, preparatory bathing in natural bodies of water, the specific type of drumming, and the fire-walking itself—are clearly related to similar practices in contemporary Kali temple-based *puja*. Moreover, it seems likely that ecstatic *shakti* manifestations were at least sometimes enacted within the space of the fire-pass performance. Regarding live animal sacrifice, however, a practice fundamental to the origins of contemporary Kali worship in 1970s Trinidad, evidence suggests that it was not integral to the Madrassi fire-pass; indeed, it is hardly mentioned at all in the early sources.

The simultaneous continuities and discontinuities between the old fire-pass ceremony and contemporary Kali worship remind us of her hybrid, heterogeneous origins. Although the fire-pass may have at times involved ecstatic possession-trance activities, we know that the older, community-based Kali *pujas* also involved ecstatic Kali manifestations. Indeed, they were much more integral in the old-style Kali *puja* than in the fire-pass. And there is no ambiguity whatsoever concerning the centrality of live sacrificial offerings to the Mother in the community Kali *pujas*. The important point here is that these sacrificial Kali *pujas* and Madrassi fire-pass ceremonies seem to have originally been part of different ritual performance traditions.

We thus begin to see the role of ideology when the Kali worship of today is simply and uncritically attributed to the legacy of the Madrassis. Elsewhere, I provide an extended critique that dismantles this ideology, which I call the Madrassi theory of contemporary Kali worship, exposing its latent scapegoating impulse in relation to the vested interests of an emerging twentieth-century "orthodoxy." To be clear, although there is no question of an important Madrassi influence on contemporary, temple-based Kali *puja* in Trinidad, the complexities and partialness of this influence have been erased within the Madrassi theory.[19]

SYNCRETISM AND INNOVATION IN THE MOTHER'S CARIBBEAN WORK

The ongoing dynamism of Trinidadian *shakti* worship should be increasingly apparent to my readers. This ritual performance system grows out of—and ultimately refracts—the many concerns, experiences, and ambivalences of its past and present practitioners. Kali has had to look after her children in a range of innovative ways given their ever-present, and yet ever-changing, New World context. Innovation here includes things like transformations or permutations in ritual paraphernalia, shifts in possession practice or explanatory discourse, co-identification or re-identification of deities or practices, the appropriation and reformulation of previously autonomous practices within the space of a consolidating meta-system, and so on.

This emphasis on innovation raises the specter of "syncretism," an important yet notoriously problematic concept in Caribbean and comparative religious studies. The complex and tricky details of this analytical category fall beyond the scope of this chapter. James Houk's description of syncretism is sufficient for our present purposes. One of the chief characteristics of syncretism, he observes, is that it represents "a compromise between the need to retain those things that give meaning to everyday life and the desire to embellish and broaden that meaning in the context of an ever changing sociohistorical and ecological matrix."[20] It is in this spirit of hybridized practice and the dialectics of syncretic compromise formation in contexts of power and inequality that I approach the innovative ways in which the Mother is doing her Caribbean work.

The Interface with Di Puja

As mentioned earlier, "Dee Baba," or simply "Di," is one of the nonorthodox *deotas* that commonly manifests through possession-mediums in most contemporary Trinidadian Kali temples. Some practitioners also identify him with the Tamil epithet "Sanganni," and one is often told that he is the owner or "Massa of de land." I have never encountered any image or *murti* of Di outside temple-based Kali worship, where his supplications are quite noteworthy. Indeed, Di regularly manifests during weekly Kali *puja* services, offering consultative *jharay* sessions to devotees and temple visitors hoping for healing. *Di* is a generalized name in Trinidad for protective village godlings (*gramadevata*) originally found in Bihar and eastern Uttar Pradesh in northern India. There was typically a separate Di for each village in India, but Steven Vertovec notes that "as new, isolated homesteads were founded in Trinidad following residence on estates, the propitiation of Dih came to be undertaken separately by individuals on their own plots of land."[21] Annual domestic Di *pujas* in Trinidad involving the sacrifice of fowl and the offering of cigarettes and alcohol have traditionally been undertaken to ensure good harvests and a healthy household. In a central Trinidadian village of the 1950s, Klass observed a distinction between private forms of Di *puja* performed without sacrifice for the benefit of agricultural fertility and a sacrificial form carried out for the sake of the household and property. He emphasized that sacrificial Di *puja* was the *rule* rather than the exception among high-caste families in his village of research, and noted that it was always performed before the main part of the community's Kali ceremonies began.[22]

My main point here regarding Di *puja* is to emphasize the transformations it has undergone from being a rural, folk-community practice in nineteenth-century northeastern India to a marginalized ecstatic practice performed under the eaves of Kali temples in contemporary Trinidad. Moreover, it was brought to Trinidad, at least in its *ur*-form, by indentured immigrants from north India and was also an important high-caste practice in mid-twentieth-century central Trinidad. Both of these points pose serious problems for the reigning ideology in Trinidad that attributes the origins of Kali worship to low-caste Madrassis from South India.

Appropriating Hog Puja for Parmeshwarie

Another dynamic that further subverts the Madrassi theory concerns the historically hidden, syncretistic accommodation of sacrificial hog *puja* for the goddess Parmeshwarie into contemporary Kali worship. Parmeshwarie is a North Indian low-caste *devi* often co-identified with Katerie Mata, or Mother Katerie, in local Kali temples. The latter is a particularly prominent goddess who—like Dee Baba and several others—is intimately associated with Mother Kali in Trinidad and who regularly manifests via possession-mediums to offer spiritual healing consultations during weekly temple services.

Ritual supplication of the goddess Parmeshwarie through sacrificing a hog or pig was traditionally connected to the domestic ritual life of low-caste Chamar families in Trinidad. "Chamar" is the term for a demographically large, low-caste group in India who were cobblers and leather workers and therefore considered ritually unclean. However, the term has been broadened throughout much of the Indian diaspora, including the Caribbean, to refer to low-caste Hindu persons more generally, and is likewise used at times as an insult. Thus it is noteworthy that people who want to conduct hog *puja* for Parmeshwarie to go to Kali temples in order to perform the ritual at the stand for Mother Katerie, who is of South Indian Tamil origin (Kātēriamma<u>n</u>, the Mother of [the town] Kātēri). Parmeshwarie and Katerie, although derived from different Indian geographic zones, meet at the Kali temple for those seeking the divine intervention of *shakti*.

Guyanese Connections and the Influence of Modern Psychiatry

Guyanese influences on Kali worship in Trinidad cannot be underestimated. *Shakti*-oriented sacrificial practices have been carried out relatively continuously in Guyana since the nineteenth century, where the tradition has also been seen as a "Madrassi" phenomenon. It has been gaining ground among increasingly wide segments of the Guyanese Hindu community and among Afro-Creoles as well.[23] Vertovec tells us that Kalimai *puja* became standardized in Guyana in the 1920s and 1930s, waned during the midcentury years, and has subsequently experienced resurgence under the leadership of Pujari Jamsie Naidoo since the 1960s.[24] There are now estimated to be anywhere between eighty and a hundred Kali "churches," or *koeloos,* throughout the country.

The rapid expansion of Kali worship in contemporary Trinidad can be traced quite specifically to the 1970s, when a group of Indo-Trinidadians (some, but not all, Madrassi) made contact with Jamsie Naidoo in Guyana. This group was particularly impressed with the work of Pujari Naidoo and his religious community, and thus began a series of exchange relationships that precipitated the emergence of modern temple-based Kali worship in Trinidad. The most significant Guyanese influences on contemporary Trinidadian *shakti* worship include use of the *tappu* drum and weekly *puja* services conducted in temples built especially for devotees and visitors in search of the Mother's healing power through ritualized possession performance.

The Guyanese connection is relevant here not only because it represents an added transnational—doubly diasporic, as it were—twist of influence in the complex evolution of Kali worship in Trinidad. It is also important because the Guyanese legacy brings its own unique and hidden dimension of hybridized transformation that has not been sufficiently appreciated and that completely sidesteps any presumed Madrassi connection. I am referring to the influence of modern psychiatry on the ritual healing techniques adopted by Naidoo's Guyanese community.

In 1963, Pujari Naidoo began a decade-long collaboration with an anthropologist and director of the country's only mental hospital at that time. During this period, patient referrals were made bidirectionally between the Kali temple and the mental hospital—located about fifteen miles apart—and there were important mutual influences between the practices carried out at each. Naidoo's years of observing psychiatric intake assessment and therapeutic interviews conducted dyadically between doctor and patient are of most importance here. This experience eventually led to significant creative intervention by Naidoo into his practice of Kali ritual performance and therefore into the patterns of *puja* currently done in Trinidad.

In 1973, Naidoo discarded the obscure sacred language of the possession-mediums, which required the services of a ceremonial interpreter. From this point onward, devotees could speak directly to Mother Kali and her spiritual associates in local English Creole during their spirit consultations.[25] This astonishing intervention—stemming from modern psychiatry and facilitated by anthropology—deserves far more reflection than is possible here. It should cause us to expand considerably upon how we think of syncretism, and it exposes a covert dimension of contemporary *shakti* practice that is not in any way connected to Madrassi origins.

The Charismatic Apotheosis of Hanuman

I would like to call attention to another recent innovation that also subverts the Madrassi theory; however, this innovation has emerged from within the sphere of Trinidadian practice itself and has not been imported from elsewhere. A relatively young Kali temple in the deep south of the island (Moruga area) regularly includes *shakti* manifestations of Lord Hanuman in most of its various types of *puja* services. In fact, the two largest *murti*s in the temple are those of Hanuman and Kali, whom the temple community refers to as "Father" and "Mother." And this temple is not alone, for it is possible to encounter ecstatic manifestations of Hanuman's *shakti* in a handful of contemporary Trinidadian Kali temples. Some of these manifesting mediums appropriately carry the *mukhtar* (club) wielded by Lord Hanuman in his mythic pursuits, representative of his power.

In these temples, we find the charismatic apotheosis of an unquestionably "orthodox" *deota* who is ubiquitous throughout all segments of Hindu Trinidad regardless of sect or status. Hanuman *puja*s are extremely common by any standard of measure, and at the beginning of the year 2000, the country's most powerful orthodox organization—the Sanatan Dharma Maha Sabha—held an extraordinarily large, new pilgrimage festival for Y2K in honor of Hanuman in southern Trinidad (Debe) called "Pooja 2000." This event attracted the attendance of both Prime Minister Basdeo Panday and President Arthur Robinson, among other important political and religious figures.

The point is that a young, active Kali temple—among others—has begun performing Hanuman *shakti* manifestations, something almost unthinkable to the Trinidadian Hindu imagination. Hanuman's symbolic centrality is reflected in the official name of the temple, "Shri Bandi Hanuman Shakti Mandir," and his orthodox status seems to lend legitimation within this dynamic religious sphere. Equally astonishing to mainstream Trinidadian society, this temple conducts regular ecstatic processions publicly along the main Moruga road, including anywhere from ten to twenty manifesting mediums—again, something almost inconceivable given local traditions of Hindu practice and the wider abhorrence of anything smacking of black magic. Indeed, on one occasion in 2000, Afro-Creole onlookers came out of their houses along the route of this procession, not only to observe what was happening, but also in some cases to mock the "simi-dimi" taking place practically on their doorsteps.[26]

Siparee Mai and Hindu-Catholic Syncretism

Another testament to the innovative capacity of *shakti* worship can be seen in the special pilgrimage tradition centered on Siparee Mai in southern Trinidad. What makes this islandwide pilgrimage devotion unique are the facts that her statue belongs to the Roman Catholic Church in Siparia, and that to Catholics she is the Blessed Virgin Mary, La Divina Pastora (Spanish for "The Holy Shepherdess"). She is the patron saint of the Catholic Capuchin monastic missionary order that Church historians believe brought the figure to the New World. Catholics perform their own entirely separate and equally elaborate set of ritual devotions in honor of the statue. But early on Holy Thursday afternoon, the statue is taken out of the church and into the parish hall, where it stands upon a temporary wooden altar until mid-afternoon on Good Friday. It is during this 24-hour period that thousands of Hindus make their way to spend a brief sacred moment in front of Siparee Mai.[27]

Siparee Mai's name means "Mother of Siparia" in Hindi, and she is well known for her healings and answered prayers. Mothers and barren wives come in particular, mothers praying for their children's health and barren women for fertility. Countless stories of miracles attributed to Siparee Mai circulate among her devotees, and pilgrims happily share their personal experiences of the Mother's compassionate power and grace. Pilgrims typically bring rice, olive oil, flowers, candles, and money to bestow upon Siparee Mai in supplication and thanksgiving. They also make *aarti* to her—a respectful offering of lit flame—and *charawe* her by touching her arms and feet and then transferring her power to themselves with a touch to their foreheads. The church keeps the candles, while the money is utilized to augment parish finances and charities. The olive-oil bottles are half-emptied by church assistants into large containers and then returned, half-full, to expectant devotees, who anoint themselves with the oil and use it at home throughout the year as a panacea.

Many stories claim to account for the origin of this miraculous statue—she comes from Spain, from Venezuela, from the native Amerindian Warao of Venezuela and Trinidad, or even autochthonously from Trinidad itself—but these reflect the disparate ethnic and religious backgrounds of her devotees more than historical fact. Given such a plethora of origin narratives, it is no wonder that the dark Mother of Siparia has been sought under many names. Among Hindus, for instance, she is not just Siparee Mai—she is also Mother Durga, Mother Lakshmi, Mother Mary, La Divin', and, every once in a while, Sita. But particularly important for our present purposes, we know that at least since the 1890s, she has been identified as Mother Kali, and her earlier twentieth-century devotions in Siparia are said to have included the ceremonial services of male transvestite "Kali dancers" who would dance with newborn babies on the front steps of the church to bless them during the auspicious Siparia pilgrimage time.[28]

Sai Satsang in Shakti*'s Playground*

Another hybridized refraction of Kali's *shakti* in contemporary Hindu Trinidad is occurring as a partial interface with the devotional sect of Sai Baba, an extraordinarily popular Indian religious leader who claims to be an incarnation of God. Widespread devotionalism to Sai Baba in Trinidad began in the 1970s and has continued into the present day. It is important to note that the bulk of devotees tend to be well-educated, urban or semi-urban, elite or middle-class Hindu Indians—the number of which swelled during the oil boom. His following has been less prominent in more rural areas, however.[29]

What I have been encountering within a subset of newer Kali temples is the recent appropriation of Sai Baba devotionalism—its discourses, practices, and imagery—especially within the central-or-south zone of Trinidad. This dynamic is so significant that one prominent southern temple in particular has incorporated an explicit reference to Sai in the temple's official name and apportions half of its annual ritual cycle to Sai *satsang*—devotional gathering centered on prayer and song. One is likely to encounter *murtis* of Jesus Christ or other Christian images, such as the Cross—and even the hymn "Jesus Loves Me"—in the *shakti* temples that have incorporated Sai *satsang* into their ceremonial arena. Thus the ecumenical spirit and one-love ethos of Sai devotionalism seems to be facilitating greater degrees of explicitly Christian symbolic absorption than that found in the other, non-Sai-oriented Kali temples on the island.

Equally important to the profile of these innovative Sai-*shakti* temples is their self-conscious opposition to the practice of live sacrifice, which they believe hinges on a misguided interpretation of Kali's sacred mythology. As strong supporters of *ahimsa* (nonviolence), they view animal sacrifice as a morally bankrupt practice. Thus the Sai Baba connection is especially important to keep in mind if my ethnographic impression is correct that antisacrificial trends are currently on the rise among contemporary Kali worshippers in Trinidad.

The spectrum of ongoing syncretism and innovation in contemporary Trinidadian *shakti puja* is thus wide and varied. Some Kali temples have introduced new patterns of possession performance, and these temples partially overlap with those whose commitment to Sai devotionalism bolsters a moral stance against animal sacrifice and not infrequently creates an open space for incipient Christian imagery. But not all contemporary *shakti* temples that delegitimize live sacrifice are connected to the Sai satsang, and I know of one prominent, older temple with an uninterrupted tradition of animal sacrifice that temporarily housed a Sai image and then dispensed with it after a time. And while Kali's *shakti* mediated by pilgrimage to Siparee Mai has been relatively independent from temple-based Kali worship in terms of explicit, institutionalized linkages, devotion to Siparee Mai has been an important source of transformative *shakti* for well over a hundred years. Thus the ongoing dynamism of Caribbean *shakti* worship is characteristic not simply of its past but also significantly of its present.

TRANSGRESSION, CONFORMITY, AND THE SACRED POLARITIES OF *SHAKTI*

The Brahmin-dominated ritual practices, dominant within the officially standardized, Sanatanist form of Hinduism in the larger Caribbean context, are associated with a subset of the Sanskrit-based pantheon of the great tradition in India (Vishnu/Krishna, Rama and Sita, Ganesh, Hanuman, Lakshmi, Shiva, Saraswati, etc.).[30] But since what can be considered "orthodox" in the New World has been profoundly influenced by Hindus' encounter with various forms of hegemonic Christianity over more than 150 years, Mother Kali has come to be seen as beyond the pale, even though, ironically, she is an important Sanskritic deity in India. This is partly because her devotions have traditionally included animal sacrifice, a practice considered abhorrent by colonial Christianity; partly because her ritual practices have been intertwined with the ecstatic possession-trance experiences so common in folk forms of Hindu *devi* worship; and partly because of connections with South Indian Madrassi fire-pass performances seen as "pagan" and "backward" under the colonial Christian gaze. Kali's dark iconographic color, moreover, most likely made her a prime target for moral scorn, given the demonic associations of the color black in Christianity and colonial and Indian racism.[31]

This helps to explain not only Mother Kali's marginalized fate but also the production of a scapegoating ideology that attributes her devotional rituals to dark-skinned "low-caste" Madrassis from South India. We can also see this same diasporic dialectic of transgression and conformity in a number of contemporary trends. I have already noted above my ethnographic impression of increasing anti-sacrificial commitments among the contemporary practices of Kali devotees. Consider also the fact that several temples have painted their Kali *murtis* pink rather than the traditional black or dark blue, their rationale being that Kali's standard iconographic color has scared too many visitors and potential devotees away from the temples. Thus the ambivalent legacy of colonialism continues to echo in Trinidad's dynamic postcolonial religious landscape.

That several earlier, relatively independent ritual traditions of *shakti puja* brought to the New World by a heterogeneous group of Indians from the subcontinent could withstand attack and transform themselves, only to become hybridized and amalgamated in a contemporary temple-based system under the aegis of Kali, should give us pause and make us reflect on the dynamic and innovative power of *shakti* worship as a cosmological system. This is perfectly resonant with how practitioners see the matter: Kali's sacred canopy is vibrant and expansive precisely because of her *shakti,* her power. So what exactly *is* this *shakti,* and how does its cosmology lend itself so powerfully to adaptive innovation? How does it mediate so effectively between the contradictions informing the life worlds of diasporic Hindus in the Caribbean?

Shakti is a Hindu conceptualization of cosmic power or energy that emanates from the *devi*s, or female goddesses, and that generates and continues to activate the universe. *Shakti* is thus conceived as feminine—whether in its benign or ferocious manifestations—and usually personified either as the dynamic, ultimate, independent Goddess (philosophically, the feminine ground of life itself; Shakti with a capital "S" and Devi with a capital "D") or as the divine consort of a male deity, whom she animates.[32] But as an independent feminine force, Shakti can be refracted—like a prism—into a plethora of differentiated goddesses, or *devi*s, each with their own individuated personalities and mythic *shakti* powers, and positioned by gradations along a single continuum. Thus Saraswati and Kali, Durga and Lakshmi, Mother Ganga, Mariamman, Draupadi, Parvati or Santoshi Ma, and so on, are all differentiated refractions of the one, ultimate Devi/Shakti/Goddess. *Shakti* cosmology is particularly salient in Trinidad's Kali temples because these are the sole contexts in which possession manifestation is conceived of as beneficial, as the incarnated activation of *shakti,* and this temporary amplification of *shakti* in a human body makes spirit consultations both possible and powerful in these temples. People seek to be *jharayed*—purified and blessed—by *shakti* mediums who wield handfuls of wet neem leaves that have been ritually presoaked for the *puja.*

We can now further appreciate the flexible and innovative power of *shakti* cosmology as a situated symbolic system. Take, as discussed above, the case of Siparee Mai. Here we encounter a statue owned by a Roman Catholic church in southern Trinidad that is worshipped as La Divina Pastora by her parishioners on an everyday basis and also on an islandwide basis during the annual Easter festival. But to many Trinidadian Hindus, she is the Mother Goddess of the local soil; as such, she has many dimensions and can also be known as Kali, Durga, or even Sita. This capacity for interidentification of *devi*s within an abstracted and encompassing concept of ultimate feminine power makes *shakti puja* traditions highly dynamic, contextually resourceful, and potentially adaptable. This dynamic can also be seen in the appropriation of hog *puja* for Parmeshwarie in Kali temples at the stand for Mother Katerie. Moreover, Katerie herself has been amalgamated under Mother Kali's canopy, for the former is referred to as "small sister" or "small mother" and Kali as "big sister" or "big mother."

But the flexible power of *shakti* cosmology can be apprehended on yet another, perhaps deeper level. Here what is important is the Goddess's astonishing ability to unite, however paradoxically, the opposite yet intimate poles of life and death, good and evil, order and chaos. In rising to the occasion of cosmic dominatrix, Shakti is encountered in her most resplendent, active, independent form—a form that exhibits simultaneous life-giving as well as life-consuming forces. This is why Kali's mythic iconography makes her such an integral part of *shakti* cosmology: she is a lone female warrior, her many arms loaded with weapons and ready for battle, unleashing her dance of divinely inspired destruction with her hair flailing in all directions and wearing nothing but a garland of skulls around her neck and a belt of severed human heads and limbs around her hips. Her outside detractors selectively focus upon her ostensibly "negative" characteristics—her ferociousness, her thirst for blood, her breaking of taboos, her subversive feminine power—and then castigate her through a studied effort at misinformation and willful ignorance of her more elusive profundities. But armed with a deeper understanding of Kali's complex personality, her devotees are able to appreciate *shakti*'s sacred polarities and therefore approach her in the context of divinely transgressive ecstasies.

What is difficult and yet so paradoxically powerful about *shakti* cosmology is that the great Goddess is the source both of worldly illusion and its bondage (*maya*) and of the knowledge that liberates and sets one free. Indeed, she is the *shakti* of bondage and the *shakti* of liberation—as Richard Brubaker so eloquently puts it: "the Divine playing hide-and-seek with Herself. And with us." Her energy continuously spins itself out in an infinite recursive cycle between positive and negative: life and death, health and disease, joy and sorrow, empire and exile. Again, as Brubaker observes: "India knows both the sacredness of order and the sacredness that abandons order; in fact she has given extraordinary emphasis to both and hence has a lively sense of their polarity." Thus we find in *shakti* a reciprocity between these two visions of sacred reality; the stronger either side of this polar tension becomes, the greater strength it calls forth on the other side. "Her left hand continually takes away what her right hand puts in place and her right hand continually replaces what her left hand removes. Thus she offers a choice—apparently between opposite visions of the sacred, but ultimately between experiencing them as schizophrenically split and rejoicing in their paradoxical oneness."[33]

Kali's worshippers in the Caribbean are certainly no strangers to these polarized tensions between order and disorder, wealth and poverty, well-being and despair, having "class" or being "common." One hears echoes of this polarity in the trials and tribulations of colonial and postcolonial Trinidad, and it can be related to the dialectically transgressive and conformative efforts of Caribbean Hindus and to the plight of *shakti* practitioners in a society and cosmos that unveil themselves as recalcitrantly stratified and quite unfair, even cruel. *Shakti*'s sacred polarities seem effective in not only expressing but also mediating the conflicts and dilemmas of her spiritual children in their search for a more secure place in the world. Like a good mother, Kali offers hope and release. Thus she does indeed devour, but then she always gives back—to those with the courage and commitment required in approaching her.

NOTES

This chapter constitutes part of a larger comparative doctoral research project concerning African- and Hindu-derived possession religions in Trinidad: "Ecstasy in Exile: Divinity, Power and Performance in two Trinidadian Possession Religions" (Emory University, Department of Anthropology). I gratefully acknowledge the financial support of the Social Science Research Council; the Fulbright-Hays Doctoral Dissertation Research Abroad Program; Wenner-Gren Foundation for Anthropological Research; and the Emory University Fund for Internationalization. My warmest thanks go to Jeffrey Kripal and Rachel Fell McDermott for their immediate, active interest in my work; their support and feedback have been crucial. I would also like to thank Katherine Frank, Yanique Hume, Gayatri Reddy, Cheryl Levine, Gregory Diethrich, Diana Finnegan, and Ronald Barrett for various amounts of critically constructive feedback upon last-minute coercion. The usual disclaimers apply.

Let me note here that I do not use any South Asian language-related diacritical marks in this chapter. Diacritics are almost completely irrelevant in Indo-Trinidadian language and culture; indeed, most words of South Asian origin are locally transliterated according to how they sound within Caribbean parlance. It is pertinent to note, as well, that these patterns of transliteration are themselves inconsistent, in flux, and not necessarily standardized. A very small handful of self-taught people may know a bit about Sanskrit diacritics (as with a unique, particularly learned *pundit*), but I have never encountered any significant use of diacritical marks in local forms of mass media, temple publications, public signs, etc.

1. The quotation marks here indicate how groups are referred to in local discourse. Trinidadians of South Asian descent have long been referred to in the Caribbean as "East Indians." Because Trinidad is in the West Indies and a local is therefore a "West Indian," the practice that tacitly codes Indo-Trinidadians as being from the "East" is part of a linguistic ideology that benefits certain Afro-"Creole" interests in the politics of nationalism and the state. Indeed, persons of African- or mixed-African descent have traditionally called themselves "Creoles"—a term that ties

them directly to Caribbean soil and makes them the more "natural" inheritors of the nation. With the rise and proliferation of ethnic politics in contemporary postcolonial Trinidad, the binarism of East Indian versus Creole has permutated into the related, but different binarism of Indian versus African. Thus I tend to use the term "Indian" when referring to Trinidadians of South Asian descent both because I contest the signification of Indo-Trinidadians as "East" as opposed to "West" and because this is the contemporary native terminology that is increasingly significant in Trinidad. On these very complex issues of ethnicity, race, nationalist politics and power in Trinidad and Tobago, see Aisha Khan, "Rurality and 'Racial' Landscapes in Trinidad," in *Knowing Your Place: Rural Identity and Cultural Hierarchy,* ed. Barbara Ching and Gerald Creed (New York: Routledge, 1997), pp. 39–69; Viranjini Munasinghe, "Culture Creators and Culture Bearers: The Interface between Race and Ethnicity in Trinidad," *Transforming Anthropology* 6 (1997): 72–86; Daniel A. Segal, "Living Ancestors: Nationalism and the Past in Postcolonial Trinidad and Tobago," in *Remapping Memory: The Politics of TimeSpace,* ed. Jonathan Boyarin (Minneapolis: University of Minnesota Press, 1994), pp. 221–39; and Kevin A. Yelvington, ed., *Trinidad Ethnicity* (Knoxville: University of Tennessee Press, 1993).

2. Michel-Rolph Trouillot, "The Caribbean Region: An Open Frontier in Anthropological Theory," *Annual Review of Anthropology* 21 (1992): 19–42; see also M. M. Horowitz, "Introductory Essay," in *Peoples and Cultures of the Caribbean,* ed. id. (Garden City, N.Y.: Natural History Press, 1971), pp. 1–13.

3. Sidney W. Mintz, *Caribbean Transformations* (New York: Columbia University Press, 1989), pp. ix–xxi.

4. Karen F. Olwig, "Between Tradition and Modernity: National Development in the Caribbean," *Social Analysis* 33 (1993): 89–104.

5. Mintz, *Caribbean Transformations,* p. xxi. See also Trouillot, "The Caribbean Region"; and *Caribbean Creolization: Reflections on the Cultural Dynamics of Language, Literature and Identity,* ed. K. M. Balutansky and M. A. Sourieau (Gainesville: University Press of Florida, 1998).

6. Mintz, *Caribbean Transformations,* p. 9. See also Sidney W. Mintz and Richard Price, *An Anthropological Approach to the Afro-American Past: A Caribbean Perspective* (Philadelphia: Institute for the Study of Human Issues, 1976).

7. O. Nigel Bolland, "The Politics of Freedom in the British Caribbean," in *The Meaning of Freedom,* ed. F. McGlynn and S. Drescher (Pittsburgh: University of Pittsburg Press, 1992), pp. 113–46; Franklin W. Knight and Colin A. Palmer, "The Caribbean: A Regional Overview," in *The Modern Caribbean,* ed. id. (Chapel Hill: University of North Carolina Press, 1989), pp. 1–20; Mintz, *Caribbean Transformations;* Raymond T. Smith, *The Matrifocal Family: Power, Pluralism and Politics* (New York: Routledge, 1996); and Trouillot, "Caribbean Region."

8. Bridget Brereton, "Society and Culture in the Caribbean: The British and French West Indies, 1870–1980," in *The Modern Caribbean,* ed. Franklin W. Knight and Colin A. Palmer (Chapel Hill: University of North Carolina Press, 1989), pp. 85–110; D. W. Galenson, "Indentured Servitude," in *A Historical Guide to World Slavery,* ed. S. Drescher and S. Engerman (New York: Oxford University Press, 1989), pp. 239–42; Knight and Palmer, "The Caribbean"; Walton Look Lai, *Indentured Labor, Caribbean Sugar: Chinese and Indian Migrants to the British West Indies, 1838–1918* (Baltimore: Johns Hopkins University Press, 1993); and F. A. Scarano,

"Labor and Society in the Nineteenth Century," in *Modern Caribbean,* ed. Knight and Palmer, pp. 51–84.

9. On the development of orthodox Hinduism in Trinidad, see John La Guerre, ed., *Calcutta to Caroni: The East Indians of Trinidad* (Trinidad and Tobago: University of the West Indies, 1985); Brinsley Samaroo, "Animal Images in Caribbean Hindu Mythology," in *Monsters, Tricksters, and Sacred Cows: Animal Tales and American Identities,* ed. A. J. Arnold (Charlottesville: University Press of Virginia, 1996), pp. 185–203; Peter van der Veer and Steven Vertovec, "Brahmanism Abroad: On Caribbean Hinduism as an Ethnic Religion," *Ethnology* 30 (1991): 149–66; and Steven Vertovec, *Hindu Trinidad: Religion, Ethnicity and Socio-Economic Change* (London: Macmillan, 1992) and "'Official' and 'Popular' Hinduism in the Caribbean," in *Across the Dark Waters: Ethnicity and Indian Identity in the Caribbean,* ed. David Dabydeen and Brinsley Samaroo (London: Macmillan, 1996), pp. 108–30.

10. Terms in parentheses here indicate the Tamil names of these deities, as attributed to them by some practitioners. Little has been written about Kali worship in Trinidad, but the following are particularly useful: William Guinee, "Suffering and Healing in Trinidadian Kali Worship" (Ph.D. diss., Indiana University, 1992); and Noor Kumar Mahabir and Ashram Maharaj, "Kali-Mai: The Cult of the Black Mother in Trinidad" (unpublished paper, University of the West Indies Archive, Trinidad and Tobago, 1985).

11. These are special, thin, goatskin drums held between the shoulder and forearm, played using two thin sticks, and found only in Kali temples in Trinidad.

12. Orisha is an African-derived (predominantly Yoruba) possession religion that has had to survive and adapt within the Trinidadian context under constant informal as well as official governmental forms of repression, and in varying degrees of syncretism with popular Catholicism. Spiritual, or Shouter, Baptism is another form of African-derived ecstatic religion, but one with a syncretized Protestant ideology.

13. Charles Kingsley, *At Last, A Christmas in the West Indies,* 3d ed. (1871; London: Macmillan, 1905), p. 300.

14. Seepersad Naipaul, *The Adventures of Gurudeva* (London: Heinemann, 1995), pp. 83–82. This author is the father of the acclaimed West Indian novelist V. S. Naipaul.

15. My two primary published ethnographic sources on old-style Kali *puja* were based on research conducted in the 1950s in central and southern Trinidad. See Morton Klass, *East Indians in Trinidad: A Study of Cultural Persistence* (1961; Prospect Heights, Ill.: Waveland Press, 1988), and Arthur and Juanita Niehoff, *East Indians in the West Indies,* Milwaukee Public Museum Publications in Anthropology, no. 6 (1960).

16. *Panchayat* is the old term referring to a neighborhood group committee consisting typically of five male village councilors, although in practice the number varied.

17. See Fr. Anthony de Verteuil, "Madrasi Emigration to Trinidad, 1846–1916," *Conference of Caribbean Historians* (University of the West Indies, Trinidad and Tobago) 22 (1990): 1–21.

18. For greater detail on the fire-pass ceremony, see my "'This is history that was handed down, we don't know exactly how true it is': On the Ambiguities of 'History'

in Trinidadian Kali Worship," *Oral and Pictorial Records Programme Newsletter* (University of the West Indies, Trinidad and Tobago) 39 (2000): 1–5.

19. For the fully elaborated details of this critical analysis, see Keith E. McNeal, "The Many Faces of Mother Kali: Caribbean Hinduism and the Moral Politics of Diaspora Ritual Performance in Trinidad," in *Asian Migrations to the Americas,* ed. Brinsley Samaroo (London: Hansib, forthcoming).

20. James T. Houk, *Spirits, Blood, and Drums: The Orisha Religion in Trinidad* (Philadelphia: Temple University Press, 1995), p. 170. Like "pluralism" and "creolization," "syncretism" is a gate-keeping concept in Caribbean ethnology that has attempted to confront the problematic relationship between heterogeneity and power in the constitution of Caribbean societies (see Trouillot, "The Caribbean Region"). While syncretism has generally referred to the hybridization or amalgamation of two or more sociocultural systems, it is important to emphasize that syncretic dynamism involves varying amounts of simultaneous cultural loss, retention and reinterpretation, imitation and borrowing, and creation—often within the framework of highly stratified power relations. The problem with the concept stems from the history of pejorative uses to which it has sometimes been put, in addition to implied and unnecessary reifications of parent traditions. Indeed, all cultural systems comprise a variety of diffused and borrowed elements; thus in this respect syncretism loses some of its descriptive precision.

21. Vertovec, *Hindu Trinidad,* p. 113.

22. Klass, *East Indians in Trinidad,* pp. 176–78.

23. See Dennis Bassier, "Kali Mai Worship in Guyana: A Quest for a New Identity," in *Indians in the Caribbean,* ed. I. Bahadur Singh (New Delhi: Sterling Publishers, 1987), pp. 130–55; Leslie Phillips, "Kali-Mai Puja," *Timehri* 11 (1960): 136–46; and Odaipaul Singh, "Hinduism in Guyana: A Study in Traditions of Worship" (Ph.D. diss., University of Wisconsin, Madison, 1993), pp. 82–94.

24. Vertovec, "'Official' and 'Popular' Hinduism in the Caribbean," p. 125.

25. Philip Singer, Enrique Araneta, and Jamsie Naidoo, "Learning of Psychodynamics, History, and Diagnosis Management Therapy by a Kali Cult Indigenous Healer in Guiana," in *The Realm of the Extra-Human,* ed. A. Bharati (The Hague: Mouton, 1976), pp. 347–48.

26. "Simi-dimi" is a local term for magical mumbo-jumbo that people are aware occurs in Trinidadian society but know very little about and view with a mixture of skepticism and fear.

27. The following are useful on the Siparee Mai phenomenon: Gerald Boodoo, "The 'La Divina Pastora/Suparee Ke Mai' Devotions of Trinidad," *International Review of Mission* 82 (1993): 383–90; Michele Goldwasser, "The Rainbow Madonna of Trinidad: A Study in the Dynamics of Belief in Trinidadian Religious Life" (Ph.D. diss., University of California, Los Angeles, 1996); Fr. John Thomas Harricharan, *The Feast of La Divina Pastora, Holy Shepherdess: Its Origin, Historical Development and Future Perspectives* (Trinidad and Tobago: General Printers of San Juan, 1981); Aisha Khan, "Sipari Mai," *Hemisphere* 2 (1990): 40–41; and Sr. Marie-Therese O.P., *Parish Beat* (Port of Spain, Trinidad: Inprint Caribbean, 1976).

28. While I have heard them referred to mainly as "Kali dancers," it seems clear that these male transvestite performers exhibited ceremonial behavior similar to the

hijras in India. Unfortunately, I have found it almost impossible to make contact with any of these older dancers or obtain any reliable, detailed information on their participation in the annual Siparee Mai pilgrimage of days gone by.

29. On Sai Baba religion in Trinidad as an ethnic-exclusive, elite revitalization movement, see Morton Klass, *Singing with Sai Baba: The Politics of Revitalization in Trinidad* (Prospect Heights, Ill.: Waveland Press, 1991).

30. A "Sanatanist" is a follower of *sanatan dharma,* which literally means "eternal duty, order or religion" and is used in reference to the form of generalized Hinduism that evolved in India and overseas, particularly since the nineteenth century; see Vertovec, *Hindu Trinidad.*

31. I should clarify that I do not intend to place blame for Kali's marginalization overwhelmingly upon the shoulders of colonialism, for I believe that the dynamic has also been influenced by what some Indianists call "Sanskritization" and the desire to emulate upper-caste practices. And yet, while I see the peripheralization of Kali worship as a complex, multiply determined process, I emphasize the legacy of the colonial encounter here as one particularly crucial factor motivating the marginalization of ecstatic *shakti puja* in Trinidad.

32. See John Stratton Hawley and Donna Marie Wulff, eds., *The Divine Consort: Rādhā and the Goddesses of India* (Boston: Beacon, 1982); David Kinsley, *Hindu Goddesses: Visions of the Divine Feminine in the Hindu Religious Tradition* (Berkeley and Los Angeles: University of California Press, 1986); and Ajit Mookerjee, *Kali: The Feminine Force* (London: Thames & Hudson, 1988).

33. Richard L. Brubaker, "The Goddess and the Polarity of the Sacred," in *The Divine Consort: Rādhā and the Goddesses of India,* ed. John Stratton Hawley and Donna Marie Wulff (Boston: Beacon Press, 1982), pp. 204, 206.

CHAPTER 11

Margins at the Center

Tracing Kālī through Time, Space, and Culture

Sarah Caldwell

In the South Indian state of Kerala, Kāḷi is everywhere.[1] Whether in the form of the goddess Bhagavati, or in her more fierce incarnation, Bhadrakāḷi, Kāḷi is at the center of every village, her shrine at the center of many homes, her presence the unseen force that grants both life and death. A dangerous, fearful, but fecund mother, she permeates the rich red soil, and seeps through the green rice and coconut plants as their lifeblood. Without her blessing, no undertaking can be successful, and under her curse, nothing can live. She brings both disease and harvest, drought and rain, pain and pleasure, death and life. She is both the ground of earthly existence and the means to salvation.

Kāḷi's embodiment of the fundamental, bipolar opposites that ground human existence is a familiar theme in the study of the fierce Goddess. This grounding in the deepest aspects of the human experience has led to a common scholarly characterization of Kālī as "marginal," a symbol of what is furthest from the ordinary, acceptable social world. Scholars have noted that Kālī's worship appears to be more prevalent at the edges of the Indian subcontinent (and in neighboring countries); she is also conceived of as originating in the extreme past, and in the religious practices of "marginal" social groups. Her iconography and worship have been portrayed as "extreme" in their violence and eroticism. However, such formulations of Kālī as "extreme" are positioned squarely within a dominant Sanskritic and

North Indian text-based critical tradition that is now being called into question. As we unravel some of Kālī's cloudy history, using Kerala as an example and focusing on the dimensions of gender and caste, we come to see her as the embodiment of core cultural values that were marginalized over time, but that have begun to reassert themselves. This process seems to have parallels throughout India. In the end, Kālī is neither marginal nor extreme in the places where she is worshipped. She is right at the center, the very source of life.

NOT A PRETTY PICTURE

One of David Kinsley's influential essays about Kālī, aptly entitled "Blood and Death out of Place,"[2] emphasizes her representation in the Hindu tradition as "terrible," "offensive," "destructive," "awful," and "dangerous," to choose only a few of her juicy appellatives. Kinsley notes that "Kālī has a long history of association with criminals and . . . murderous Thugs," even as early as the *Bhāgavata Purāṇa.*[3] Regardless of the truth value of this association with criminality, it is a sensational detail that also caught the imagination of colonial writers and early scholars of Hinduism. Numerous popular Western films have perpetuated this image of Kālī as the deity of bloodthirsty, maniacal sociopaths.

Kinsley rightly asserts that Kālī "is almost always associated with blood and death," and he goes on to state that "within the civilized order of Hinduism" blood, death, and Kālī herself are the supreme anomalies. Disruptive to all the carefully built up structures of Brāhmaṇical Hinduism, Kālī seems to represent chaos, lack of control, pollution, and disorder—that is, the ultimate danger threatening to undercut high-caste values. Kinsley explains the incorporation of Kālī into the orthodox pantheon as a philosophical compromise: "Kālī puts the order of *dharma* in perspective, or perhaps puts it in its place, by reminding the Hindu that certain aspects of reality are untameable, unpurifiable, unpredictable, and always threatening to society's feeble attempts to order what is essentially disorderly."[4]

This traditional characterization of Kālī as representative of disorder draws on numerous images of marginality: the social marginality (and antisociality) of criminals; the physical marginality of blood and death in a system that emphasizes bodily integrity and purity; the geographic marginality of the Goddess's haunts, which include cremation grounds, battlefields, borderlands, and inhospitable regions; and the philosophical marginality of a deity who exists mainly as a theoretical corrective to an overly ordered and patterned picture of reality. Kālī becomes a transcendent symbol of entropy as she enters the official Hindu pantheon. Her negative characterization and association with criminality suggest that those who worship her also run the risk of being relegated to the category of the marginal and repulsive from the point of view of an uncritical Indology.

In another important essay, Edward Dimock eloquently discusses the fierce Goddess's association with fever illnesses such as smallpox.[5] The Bengali Śītalā, like the Tamil Māriyamman̲, clearly embodies many aspects of Kālī's imputed marginality and extremism, which in Kerala are combined in the persona of Bhadrakāḷi. Despite its sensitivity to local nuances of meaning, the title of Dimock's essay, "The Theology of the Repulsive," once again emphasizes the predicament scholars of Western religious traditions have encountered in trying to explain the unfamiliar concept of a deity whose character appears to be almost entirely negative. Part of the difficulty some such scholars have faced is their reliance upon nineteenth-century Indology, which despite its pioneering brilliance was also heavily laced with Christian theology, colonial political motivations to establish the superiority of European culture, orientalist notions of the "exoticism" of Indian civilization, and outright racism.[6] Of all the myriad of Hindu deities who haunted the imagination of colonial scholars, Kālī, the naked, black eater of children, most pointedly added to the "white man's burden" of civilizing and moralizing uncouth heathens—as Cynthia Humes and Hugh Urban so vividly demonstrate elsewhere in this volume. Accounts of human sacrifice, reported in the Kālī cult as also among "tribals" (the ultimate heathens), were also exaggerated by nineteenth-century scholars. Taken entirely out of their cultural and religious context, such reports worked to justify the missionary and colonial aims of Europeans. It is no wonder that the only image of Kālī to filter down into American and British popular culture, from the Beatles' *Help* to *Indiana Jones and the Temple of Doom,* is that of orgies, thugs, and terrifying blood sacrifices.

But the picture of Kālī as morally, socially, and theologically extreme cannot be attributed exclusively to the dastardly machinations of colonial scholars, who were, after all, merely doing their job. As Cynthia Ann Humes vividly illustrates in chapter 7, early Indologists drew heavily on negative images of the Goddess drawn directly from indigenous South Asian texts. Whether Jain, Buddhist, or Hindu, the authors of these texts were located at the ideological centers of their religious worlds. In their efforts to enhance orthodoxy, these indigenous authors employed rhetorical strategies that deliberately marginalized the practices of nonelite groups, practices that often involved Kālī or goddesses like her. Thus even the earliest textual references to Kālī portray the Goddess as unusual, frightening, ambivalent, and hence powerful, particularly against demons. This characterization almost certainly reflects Kālī's origins outside the Sanskritic tradition, and attempts to tame and incorporate her (a process that continues to the present, as detailed below).

The treatment of Kālī even in recent textbooks perpetuates this traditional Indological stance. In a schematic summary of "the development of traditions of goddess worship" in his recent text on Hinduism, Gavin Flood lists "brahmanical Goddess worship," "Śrī Vidyā," "Kālī cults," and "village goddess worship" as four historical streams of Śāktism (Hindu worship of a supreme female deity).[7] This useful typology lists the various forms of goddess worship horizontally from left to right, in decreasing closeness to Brāhmaṇical tradition. Despite the apparent egalitarianism of a horizontal, rather than a vertical schematic, the left-or-right logic of the diagram still visualizes Kālī worship and village goddess worship as marginal, distant both in space and time from the elite center that defines the core of Hinduism. Summarizing the scholarly consensus on the subject, Flood tells us that "a general picture is suggested of low-caste, local goddesses becoming absorbed into, and resisted by, brahmanical tradition" through an "upwards" process of assimilation over time.[8]

We still know very little about this process of supposed assimilation. Other than a few Jain and Buddhist statues depicting voluptuous females, evidence for goddess worship in the period "between the composition of the Vedas and the Purāṇas" is scarce.[9] Histories of "Śākta religion" detail references to the Goddess in the Vedas, Purāṇas, Tantras, and epics, and speculate about their relation to historical realities, but with little concrete evidence.[10] What we do have in these Sanskrit texts are references to Kālī or Kālī-like goddesses, worshipped by naked or leaf-clad tribal groups (Śabaras), forest or mountain-dwelling tribes (Kuśikas), or "fierce Untouchables" (Caṇḍālas), who received offerings of wine, meat, and blood, including human sacrifice.[11] The accuracy of such portraits is, of course, impossible to verify, but their repeated appearance throughout the Vedic and Purāṇic periods certainly suggests that they contain some elements of fact. Texts from south India dating to the early centuries C.E. also contain plentiful references to bloodthirsty, fierce warrior goddesses such as Koṯṟavai, who dwelt in deserts, battlefields, and mountains.

The wide geographic and temporal distribution of such references leads us to believe that in fact a form of worship of a fierce goddess with many of the attributes of Kālī is extremely ancient and pervasive throughout South Asia. Despite their antiquity and ubiquity, however, such practices as blood sacrifice, possession, and offerings of meat and wine were described in unequivocally negative terms by most Sanskrit and Prakrit authors. As Humes details in chapter 7, the European colonial disgust shown for Kālī and her worshippers drew heavily on the negative characterizations of indigenous elite discourse. What we lack for the Vedic and Purāṇic periods is any record of the point of view of those "others" who worshipped Kālī.

During the growth of Śāktism in Northern India in the Gupta period, texts arose that incorporated these marginal practices and glorified the Goddess as the supreme Godhead.[12] The appearance in the fourth to seventh centuries of Śākta Tantrism (or its textual traces) seems to embrace these marginal practices as a legitimate form of spirituality. The specific incorporation of low-caste and tribal women into the rituals, and the worship of goddesses based on their images in esoteric Śākta Tantrism certainly betoken a phase of liberality and experimentation in high-caste Hinduism. The intriguing figure of the Mātaṅgī, one of the ten Tantric Mahāvidyās, is a particularly pointed example of such incorporation.[13] Depicted as a leaf-clad Caṇḍālī, Mātaṅgī's main function in the esoteric meditations of the Tantric practitioner is as an antinomian figure who inverts the Brāhmaṇical order of purity and pollution, an act that itself releases magical powers. Such images impute wild, uncontrolled, primal power to the marginal figures of tribal and low-caste females. The use of low-caste women in secret sexual Kālīkula practices to attain unusual magical strength and mystical consciousness was thus a deliberate attempt to incorporate power perceived to inhere in the bodies of marginal women, a process explored more fully below.

The South Indian textual record presents a somewhat different picture of Kālī and her antecedents. Mountain-dwelling groups who worshipped fierce deities with liquor and blood and became possessed in frenzied oracular dances were integral parts of the ancient cults of Murugaṉ and Koṟṟavai as represented in ancient Tamil literature. Vivid scenes of violence and bloodshed, drawing heavily on metaphors of forest beasts (elephants, tigers), abound in Caṅkam literature. While peripheral places are marked out as special zones of spiritual power, they are not regarded with the fear, fascination, and repulsion evident in many Sanskrit texts, but rather are essential parts of the early Tamil spiritual landscape. Peripheries feed centers through the person of the king, who ameliorates their dreaded powers for the renewal of life in the settled regions. Blood, liquor, and spirit possession are essential signs of this cyclic transaction.

The goddess Kāḷi (in the form of Bhagavati), has been the central deity of the south Indian state of Kerala at least since the Caṅkam age, some two millennia ago. The Caṅkam age is identified by scholars of Tamil literature as extending from the first until the fourth century C.E. After this time, Brahman influence began to be keenly felt due to extensive immigration of upper-caste Aryan groups into the south following the fall of the Gupta empire to the north.[14] A rich and sophisticated literary tradition in the ancient Tamil language gives us a window into a recognizably distinct linguistic and cultural complex from that of the Sanskritic, Aryan culture of North India.

Evidence from these Tamil and early Maṇipravāḷam (a medieval literary mix of Tamil and Sanskrit) sources strongly suggests that in ancient and even medieval times, women took actual roles of power in ritual and military activities of importance to society at large.[15] This is by no means to assert that a "matriarchy" ever existed; it is only to say that *śakti,* as well as the ancient Tamil concept of *aṇaṅku,* which preceded it, was channeled through real human female bodies in ritual roles at various times in the past. The exact extent of those roles is difficult to determine. We have textual evidence of women warriors, shamans, and oracles; some of the latter still exist today in remote areas of the Kerala foothills. But whatever the case in the past, such feminine figures of power are no longer an integral part of Kerala Hindu practice or social life. How and when it came to be that women were alienated from this tradition is still a mystery. Today, male ritual specialists dressed as the Goddess perform the rituals that once were the province of women. However, the centrality of low-caste females in so many of the origin myths of the Goddess and her shrines, as well as in contemporary South Indian rituals (described later in this chapter), seems to preserve a historical memory of the prior prominence of women, a role that is now almost entirely lost to women in Kerala as they attempt to raise their status by distancing themselves from everything connected to Bhadrakāḷi.

The major religious ideas that characterized Caṅkam culture have been succinctly summarized by various scholars to include, in Kalpana Ram's words: "(a) the absence of a clear awareness of transcendence, which allows for the visualization of the divine within the confines of earthly reality; (b) the sensual character of the worship; (c) the ecstasy of emotions in which the divine is felt to be present, which links (a) and (b); and (d) lastly the exclusively female cults of Caṅkam literature resurfacing in the later *bhakti* worship in which the psychology of religious awareness is female."[16] The concept of *aṇaṅku,* "in many ways a very early forerunner of the concept of *śakti,*" is summarized by Holly Baker Reynolds as "a malevolent, dangerous power" inhering in both the natural world and the bodies of humans and deities, particularly female.[17] George Hart identifies the predominant locus of *aṇaṅku* in Caṅkam literature as in the sexual parts of the female anatomy: breasts, loins, and genitals.[18] The goddess Bhagavati embodies all these aspects of *aṇaṅku:* malevolent female power that manifests as both violent and sexual energy.

Dramatic possession performances, still an important part of South Indian goddess worship, clearly developed from these ancient practices, which stressed the passionate and violent nature of supernatural energy. This power, because it inhered in the physical landscape as well as in the bodies of women, was essential for the nourishment of life and society and yet always threatened to get out of control, destroying life. Agricultural and human fertility were intimately related, so that rituals promoting the growth of crops developed using metaphors of the feminine reproductive cycle; the goddess Bhagavati herself embodies much of this symbolism. Much of ancient Caṅkam religion focused on the proper evocation and management of these ambivalent powers through war, bloodshed, sexuality, and possession performance. Contemporary rituals like *teyyam* (a ritual of masked spirit possession in northern Kerala) or the fire-walking cults seen in neighboring regions of southern India and Sri Lanka represent this strand of powerful devotionalism with direct links to this ancient past.[19]

Scholars concur in the opinion that Kāḷi derives in part from the ancient Tamil deity Koṟṟavai, a warrior goddess who delights in the blood of battle.[20] That Koṟṟavai is clearly an antecedent of Bhadrakāḷi in Kerala is demonstrated in her iconography in ancient Caṅkam literature: wearing a necklace of tiger teeth, riding a tiger, and shouting in victory (*kurava*), the Goddess comes to the battlefield to kill enemies, eat their flesh, and drink their blood. These iconographic motifs are still seen in modern lithographs of Kāḷi. Her blue skin (sometimes described as black) seems likely to describe the extremely dark skin hue of the residents of the mountainous regions between Kerala and Tamilnadu.

Devotees of the ancient war goddess Koṟṟavai included female dancers who accompanied male warriors to battle singing, dancing, and drumming.[21] Caṅkam period poems of war vividly describe the rituals performed on the battlefield, which was conceived of as the locus for "the most intense confrontation between man and the divine. . . . The Goddess Koṟṟavai dances on the battle-field accompanied by a host of demons, ghosts, and demon women" who feast on the bodies of the slain.[22] War poems describe battlefield rituals that included cooking of the bodies of defeated warriors "by a virgin, who stirs a huge pot containing blood and fat."[23] One ritual performer I interviewed in Kerala related this ancient battle sacrifice to the contemporary practice of *guruti,* or blood sacrifice, accompanying performances. The demonic female spirits that attended the war goddess Koṟṟavai were represented by human women dedicated to the service of the king. These sacred females had "the basic function of direct contact with the ambivalent power of the divine," which was channeled through their activities into the king's sacred power, the source of fertility in the realm at large.[24]

Female court bards called *viṟali*s and *pāṭiṉi*s sang, danced, and played music, glorifying the bravery of the king.[25] These chaste women were considered to channel supernatural forces such that they were said to have power over rain. The *viṟali*s accompanied the king and his male bards at celebrations of victory in battle, dancing the wild victory dance of *tuṇaṅkai* behind the king's chariot. "In certain instances we find the tuṇaṅkai performed during a feast . . . while the hero enters on his chariot accompanied by women who glorify his erotic exploits as well, drunk with toddy."[26] These female servants of the king were transformed in later eras into the *devadāsī*s (*nityasumaṅgalī*s) of South Indian temples. But their ritual roles included actions similar to the *veḷiccappāṭu*s of today: Tamil poems of the tenth century mention the Mātaṅkī, "a female who performs simultaneously three actions: *vāḷ vīci* ('swinging the sword'), singing the praise of . . . Murukaṉ . . . , and thirdly, beating [drums]."[27]

Friedhelm Hardy further describes the public religious activities of women in festivals during the Caṅkam period in South India: "On all the streets, (young women) get into a frenzy, dance, sing, and make a loud noise. . . . [T]he various forms of religion mentioned involve exclusively girls and women. Therefore it may not be accidental that in later *bhakti* religion, where these forms of worship appear again, the psychology of the religious awareness is 'female.'"[28] Women also participated in possession trances and divination. Female shamans are found in accounts of the social groups dwelling in the mountainous regions of the Western Ghats. Although research on these topics is scarce, enough evidence exists to indicate that the ancient precursor of Bhadrakāḷi was Koṯṯavai, the mountain-forest-dwelling war goddess; that she was accompanied by cannibalistic ghosts called *pey;* and that her ambivalent powers were recognized to inhere in young women, who performed important ritual roles embodying and expressing these powers. Frenzied orgiastic dancing, singing and drumming, eating of meat and drinking of liquor were integral parts of the ritual activities of these female practitioners.[29]

Oracles (ritual specialists through whom the Goddess speaks to her devotees) associated with temples today are exclusively male. Female oracles do exist, but only in the hilly tribal areas of Palghat region. These female oracles come to the Kodungallur Bhagavati Temple at Bharani and participate in the rituals of pollution, becoming possessed and cutting their heads along with the male oracles.[30] To my knowledge, no fieldwork has been done with these female oracles, who are reluctant to speak with outsiders. However, it is my impression that they are the last of the female shamanic priests who perform important ritual roles in these hilly regions. It is quite likely that the male oracles of high-caste temples in fact modeled their behavior on these female shamans, whose role was superseded in the Aryanized lowlands.

A historical shift then appears to have occurred over the past two thousand years in Kerala. Indigenous concepts of feminine power (the ancient Tamil *aṇaṅku* and the Sanskritic *śakti*), once firmly lodged in female bodies and celebrated by women, were marshaled in sacred military rituals to enhance the multivalent, mysterious power of the king and the realm. Over time, as Sanskritic and Brāhmaṇical values predominated, women were marginalized from the rituals of power, while their embodied feminine potency was co-opted and imitated by male ritual specialists. The essentially feminine character of the deity, with the concomitant values of sexual potential and violent rage still attached, became an attribute of men. The psychology of religious awareness identified by Hardy is indeed "female" in many important ways, but *women* are no longer central figures in the Bhagavati cult of Kerala.

As Kāḷi's worship came more under the control of Brahmanized elites, the earlier multivalent potency of the Goddess was reconfigured as danger, chaos, and pollution. The theme of danger thus appears in many contemporary South Asian ritual contexts where Kālī is worshipped. A Bengali friend explained to me that while Durgā is beloved as a visiting daughter during Navarātrī, Kālī herself is always regarded with awe, fear, and respect. Despite her "sweetening" over recent decades, Kāḷi's dangerous power is still recognized.[31] In my research on rituals of the Kāḷi cult in Kerala, high-caste men and women especially portrayed the Goddess as terrifying and antisocial. Many were not sure whether she was really a god or a demon (*deva* or *asura*). She is as unlike ordinary females as she could possibly be. As one woman from a royal family said jokingly about Kāḷi's fury, "It's not a pretty picture." A scholar visiting my house in Trichur, upon seeing my naive pastiche of Kāḷi images in the living room said to me in hushed tones, "You know, nobody has Kāḷi on their *pūjā* like that except black magicians [marginal religious figures who engage in harmful sorcery]."

Yet Kerala's Kāḷi (in the form of Bhagavati or Bhadrakāḷi) was ever-present, as a hidden potency. In the fields, Kāḷi's temple abutted the waving green paddy plants. In every town and village, one could find Bhagavati installed in a shrine; but her image was always enclosed in an inaccessible sanctum. Temple rituals I attended in the dead of night called her destructive force into the bodies of devotees, possessing them and receiving their offerings of blood, fire, and pain. In homes, the Goddess was hidden behind closed doors, dark and safe. Her mantras were inscribed on copper plates bound in secret closed capsules around babies' waists and necks. To place Kāḷi at the center of life was not unusual, but to display her openly was.

When they spoke of Kāḷi, people did not refer to her in an endearing, familiar manner, but guardedly, with a sense of awe. Their respectful worship was fueled by fear. Like dead relatives, worms underfoot, or snakes hidden in the grass, Kāḷi was always present as an unseen power that both enlivens and destroys. The times when attention was ritually focused on her were dangerous and anomalous, but inseparable from ordinary, mundane time as night from day. Like the dreamtime in aboriginal Australia, Kāḷi suffuses Kerala's life and landscape in a subtle manner. In this land where she is the predominant deity, we have a sense that the Goddess is not so much marginal or extreme as she is psychologically submerged. Like the unconscious mind or an underground stream, Kāḷi is always moving, always present, always informing what is on the surface. Pressing those surfaces reveals her directly, in extreme and unusual moments like those created by ritual possession. This complex, suffused landscape of power, which recalls the ancient Caṅkam worldview, still exists in on-the-ground religious practice throughout India.

Nuanced, critical, ethnographically informed studies of Kālī can therefore serve as a corrective to received understandings of the Goddess as "extreme" and "marginal." Such studies can also help us to reexamine the "repulsive" and "unacceptable" practices of blood sacrifice, possession, self-mutilation, and ritual sexuality, and understand them in more culturally sensitive terms. Many of these features of Kālī's worship have long been at the core of the religious practices and worldviews of aboriginal, Tantric, low-caste, and village traditions, particularly in the south and northeast of India. These nonelite traditions often center around conflictual models of divinity, immanent, embodied powers and a deep concern with death and sexuality. Intense, engaged physical and emotional experience, rather than detachment and ordered ritual purification, are their characteristic mode. From this point of view, Kālī is anything but marginal. She represents the essential and central values of the nonelite religious traditions.

The question that must be asked when we make statements about the Goddess is, "For whom is this true?" We must recognize that every vantage point is situated. To describe Kālī as a goddess of "outsiders" is to position ourselves as scholars alongside the elite Sanskrit texts that until very recently have been our main sources. By generalizing this elite viewpoint to represent "Hinduism" per se, we run the risk of perpetuating a skewed ideological stance. We also miss the more interesting truths about Kālī we can get by standing at the margins with aboriginal, Dalit (literally "oppressed," the term favored by people earlier called "Untouchables"), Tantric, or female persons. The richness of such multiple views is well worth the effort and may radically alter our understanding of Kālī.

This vast sea change in our approach to Hindu materials is already well under way. It is no longer possible to state what "the Hindu" thinks, as if there were in fact a Durkheimian "social mind" out there for us to probe. Reading only Sanskrit texts and talking only to Brahmans, as early scholars did, gave a very decided slant to the understanding of Kālī. This unitary view from above is no longer adequate. Our task now is to document the complex, multifaceted phenomena of religious belief and practice. The intentionality and position of the analyst as well as the informant must be taken into account. This is not to say that there is no truth about the Goddess, but only that it is not a simple one. The long history of cultural appropriation and marginalization of indigenous traditions by dominant Brāhmaṇical religion is part and parcel of what Kālī has become today, and it informs our characterization of her. It is time to reorient our vision and see Kālī, not as extreme or marginal, but as complex, subtle, and often misunderstood.

THE PUZZLE OF GEOGRAPHICAL EDGES

Keeping these caveats in mind, we must come to terms with some puzzling facts. There are several places where Kālī is most decidedly at the center of religious life, among Brahmans and Dalits alike. Oddly, those places are located at the geographical edges of the Indian subcontinent: Nepal, Assam,

Bengal, Bihar, Sri Lanka, Kerala, Himachal Pradesh. These geographically marginal regions of South Asia are notable for extensive public worship of Kālī (although often under other names), performed in Hindu temples by high-caste male religious specialists. But in what real sense are these places "margins"? They are margins of a contemporary nation-state arbitrarily established through political negotiations. Older sources refer to Kālī as dwelling in the Vindhyas, considered to be a liminal region at the boundaries of Āryāvarta, the then "civilized" world.[32] The many Purāṇas that refer to Kālī relegate her worship to distant or marginal areas such as forests, mountains, deserts, or the boundaries of villages, although these texts were composed in diverse geographical regions. This fact reminds us that "marginal" locations are relative to historical positionings of geography, invented boundaries, and social landscapes. Yet Kālī continually seems to have become associated with margins, even when those margins are constantly shifting.

Some of the areas where Kālī dominates the religious landscape, certainly, are at the edges of the physical subcontinent of India—at the seashore, in the Himalayan foothills, in remote and inaccessible areas. Śākta Tantra, considered an inversion of orthodox, Brāhmaṇical Hinduism, is strongly associated with Kālī's worship, especially in Bengal, Nepal, Assam, and Kerala. Within some of these regions (in the northwest, for example), Kālī's worship is prevalent among female religious specialists, in rural areas, and in low-caste and Dalit groups. However, if we look closely at more centrally located states of India, we find the same pattern. Low-caste, rural, and aboriginal males, as well as women of all castes, all worship fierce goddesses extensively. This is true from Kashmir to Uttar Pradesh, Gujarat to Tamilnadu. Unfortunately, insufficient ethnography has been performed within such populations to document the Goddess's prevalence and pervasiveness, but wherever students look, there they find her. The marginality of Kālī worship is, in fact, not so easily consigned to physical geography but may be a social and scholarly creation. It is perhaps worth considering who is left once we exclude such "marginal" populations as low-caste, rural, and aboriginal males, and women of all castes—in fact, only metropolitan, high-caste males! If all these groups are marginal, the center is very circumscribed indeed. The unfortunate fact is that this narrow center has dominated the textual traditions that formed the basis of Indological scholarship, providing a distorted viewpoint.[33]

The pioneering feminist work of scholars like A. K. Ramanujan and Gloria Raheja and Ann Gold inspired scholars to look for women's texts as a form of cultural contestation.[34] As large numbers of women and non-Europeans have entered the corps of professional students of Hinduism, ethnographic fieldwork is increasingly being conducted in places and among people who were once considered "marginal": low castes and women, in both rural and village settings. Work among these nonelite populations has turned up a wealth of examples of alternate interpretations of standard Brāhmaṇical religious texts.[35] Such "subaltern" texts appear to be everywhere, simply waiting to be heard.[36] The recent spate of scholarship on the Goddess easily proves this point. Kathleen Erndl's work in northwestern India uncovered female-centered traditions that were unknown to Western scholars a decade ago, simply because no one had yet had access to those populations.[37] N. Elaine Craddock, Karin Kapadia, Isabelle Nabokov, and Vijaya Rettakudi Nagarajan all have done recent fieldwork in Tamilnadu, elucidating forms of goddess worship, particularly among women.[38] In Uttar Pradesh, Orissa, Bihar, Maharashtra, Karnataka, Andhra Pradesh, Kerala, and Sri Lanka, Kālī and her incarnations are continually being encountered anew as divinities with enormous potency in people's everyday lives.[39] Where, in fact, is Kālī not at the center, the core, of religious sentiment?

These new sources of data are rapidly enriching our understanding of South Asian religion. Unfortunately, foreign fieldwork among South Asia's aboriginal populations (many of whom worship Kālī or female deities like her) is prohibited by the Indian government, precluding intensive study of traditions that might shed most light on our thesis about Kālī's origins. In recent decades, very few Indian ethnographers have shown any inclination to study the cultural traditions of tribal peoples either, focusing their efforts for the most part on physical anthropology. As Arjun Appadurai has aptly pointed out, edifices of theory generated by metropolitan "centers" often fail to take account of the intricate social and historical exigencies that lead to their own formation.[40] The relegation of the majority of South Asian religious practices to the margins of our theoretical discourse unfortunately reflects the haphazard course of colonial history and ethnography, which simply had no access to, little interest in, or outright hostility to such "marginal" populations. This enormous lacuna in the religious landscape of South Asia must be taken into account in our generalizations.

Of course, Thomas Coburn, David Kinsley, and Cheever Mackenzie Brown, the pioneers of Kālī studies, already recognized the importance of what were referred to in anthropology of the 1950s and 1960s as the "folk" or "little traditions."[41] Kinsley skillfully summarizes the ethos of these subaltern traditions in his essay on "village goddesses"; and Coburn and Brown acknowledge that such "village goddess" traditions predated Sanskritic attempts in the "Devī-Māhātmya" and *Devībhāgavata Purāṇa* to co-opt them under the guise of Devī, Durgā, and so on.[42] But scholarship over the past decade has revealed that what we usually identify with Kālī is also found in traditions that fall outside the rubric of "Hinduism." Worship of fierce goddesses who possess and sicken, who drink blood and provide fertility, who kill demons and consort with ghosts, is found throughout South Asia in Muslim and Buddhist traditions as well. In fact, the difficulties we face in positioning Kālī are inseparable from those arising from the rubric "Hinduism." An invented category that has taken on an amazing life of its own in the twentieth century, "Hinduism" attempts to unify a number of wildly diverse, often opposed traditions. By forcing such diversity into a single conceptual category, the originary becomes marginal and extreme.

The recent repositioning of our scholarly gaze to encompass more points of view explains why Kālī has never appeared to be central before. But it does not account for the fact that public, male, high-caste worship focuses so notably on Kālī in the geographical extremes of the subcontinent. One possible explanation is a historical "squeezed out from the middle" interpretation. According to this view, as successive waves of immigrants and dominating cultures from Aryans to Mughals entered South Asia, they imposed their languages, religions, and cultures on the central, dominant areas, the seats of political power. As Aryan and Mughal conceptions of deity were primarily male, an indigenous, older, female-centered religious tradition (typical of agriculturalists) might have been suppressed, forced into marginal areas and allowed to flourish in regions of less political influence and importance, such as those we see dedicated to Kālī now. As rulers moved into these regions, they co-opted existing goddess worship traditions, Sanskritizing them and appropriating them into high-caste temples. In such a model, Kālī worship was at the center of religious practice in the past, whereas its current marginal position is a product of history.

Is this just feminist fantasy or is there some evidence? The evidence from Kerala supports such a theory. The idea of an ancient shared goddess-worshipping culture is also suggested in older censuses, colonial ethnographies, and folklore studies that focus on "tribal" populations (noncaste organized groups). These studies reveal that in noncaste organized social groups everywhere throughout South Asia, Kālī-like deities are worshipped.[43] Ritual practices devoted to these goddesses include blood sacrifice (including head-hunting in the northeast), spirit possession, violence or self-mutilation, fertility rites, and the presence of female ritualists. A consistent core of specific beliefs is associated with the cults of "tribal" goddesses in regions as disparate as Assam, Bihar, Nepal, and Kerala, such as a belief in the magical properties of iron to neutralize demons, a connection of the Goddess with both death and menstrual blood, spirit possession, and the idea that the Goddess dwells in the sap of palm trees and mountain streams. Although detailed field studies of aboriginal religious traditions are still deficient, it would appear that they were part of an ancient goddess tradition in South Asia that has historically flourished on the edges of the subcontinent and other remote areas.[44]

The incorporation of indigenous non-Vedic practices into Brāhmaṇical Hinduism in the Gupta period and thereafter may have been inextricably linked to the growth of centralized political and social structures. Narendra Nath Bhattacharyya suggests that the incorporation of various local Kālī-like goddesses into the great Mahādevī was a strategy of the political center to incorporate noncaste tribal groups into the social mainstream.[45] Śāktism as a religious system developed and flourished between the second and twelfth centuries in South Asia perhaps largely in response to this increasing centralization and incorporation. During that millennium, Kālī, along with other manifestations of the Devī, may have been a far more central goddess than she was in either the Vedic or colonial periods.

When European colonizers entered South Asia, they did so by sea, constructing the major cities of Bombay, Calcutta, and Madras as their seats of power and commerce. Kālī worship was an integral part of the culture Europeans encountered in the erstwhile politically marginal seaport regions of South Asia. Calcutta, as the seat of power of the British colonial regime, became the site of intense cultural conflict in the sphere of religion.[46] Rachel Fell McDermott and Usha Menon and Richard Shweder have documented the impact of colonial values on the Kālī cult in Bengal, such that her ferocity was tempered by sweetness, domestication, and an emphasis on maternal aspects of the feminine persona.[47] The various reformist Hindu movements that arose in Panjab and Bengal in the nineteenth century, including the Arya Samaj, Brahmo Samaj, and Vedanta Society, all tried to expunge the more unacceptable, "extreme" and "marginal" aspects of their religious practice (blood sacrifice, Tantra, ecstatic emotionalism, sexual imagery), establishing masculinist, rational religion in its stead.[48] The "centralizing" forces of political and economic hegemony thus altered Kālī's persona in the very marginal regions where she had previously flourished, eliminating aspects of practice that were considered socially objectionable, including blood sacrifice and *vāmācara* ("left-handed") Tantric practices (practices that use such "prohibited" substances as meat, wine, blood, and sexual fluids).

Marginalization of Kālī worship thus seems to have taken place in two ways over the past two millennia: it was pushed to geographical margins and went "underground" locally. In both cases, the contemporary prevalence of Kālī worship among "marginal" populations signals great antiquity and a long history of conflict with dominant traditions. Geographic regions that continue to be heavily influenced by Kālī worship at all levels of the religious hierarchy may hearken back to religious centers that were pushed to the edges of the subcontinent over many centuries by religious elites. Where this form of worship survived and flourished, Brāhmaṇical elites used both textual and ritual strategies to incorporate and tame Kālī, bringing her into their realm of control. When colonial administrations arose in those very marginal geographic regions, the Goddess's ferocity was subject to a new set of "centralizing" and taming strategies. On the other hand, the persistence of the worship of Kālī and goddesses like her in women's domestic worship, and the presence of small, subordinate goddess shrines flanking those of male, Sanskritic deities in temples throughout India reflects a second, localized kind of marginalization: the suppression of older tradition. This theory contravenes the more popular assumption, derived from Sanskrit texts, that Kālī was always marginal and was incorporated over time into the theological center, taking her place within the triumvirate of deities that for the last millennium has included Mahādevī, the great Goddess.

Even if the latter is the case, the question arises as to why Brahman elites felt it necessary to incorporate a deity ostensibly worshipped only by marginal, low-status groups. Furthermore, why did such a change finally take place in the fourth to ninth centuries, when Kālī or deities like her had clearly coexisted with the Brāhmaṇic pantheon for at least a millennium before? Bhattacharyya has attempted to address this question in broad terms, but further close textual-historical and archaeological research is in order to clarify Kālī's historical relation to orthodox Brāhamaṇical religion. Rather than assuming a unilinear movement either away from or toward the center, the sketchy history we do have, as well as contemporary events, suggests a dialectic in which Kālī is incorporated and excluded, according to the needs of the time and place.

The puzzle of geographical edges can be resolved when we realize the constructed nature of landscapes, both social and physical. Poor people are historically pushed to the hilly regions, arid areas, and jungles where food is scarce and hard to obtain; low-status people are pushed to the edges of villages due to beliefs in their polluting potentiality; women are confined to homes; dangerous people are silenced and contained. Such marginal or hidden positions thus are visible accretions of continual historical processes of disenfranchisement. People socially and geographically at the edges have been pushed there by more powerful elites at the center. However, such a model takes a bird's-eye view appropriate to the mapping of the contemporary nation-state. The reality on the ground, in fact, is that there are centers everywhere, in every village, every roadway, every field, every house compound, centers where the Goddess dwells and is worshipped. Perhaps it is our scholarly perspective that needs to be reconsidered, such that we see that margins themselves have centers. Furthermore, those marginal centers have their own complex, contested forms of knowledge, in which goddesses like Kālī figure prominently.[49] Management of Kāḷi's fierce power is a highly valued cultural commodity in Kerala and other "edges" of the South Asian subcontinent, as we have seen, and more complex configurations of religious spaces everywhere are in order.

REIMAGINING THE CENTER

The interplay between peripheries and centers that is so central to the South Indian cult of the fierce Goddess is vividly demonstrated for a contemporary Andhra setting by Don Handelman.[50] In an elaborate annual ritual, the goddess Gaṅgamma appears in a variety of guises to the people of Tirupati, more famous for its wealthy Venkateśvara Temple. The Goddess is split into two forms, Tāllapāka and Tātayyaguṇṭa, whose temples are geographically located at the center and periphery of the town respectively. Tātayyaguṇṭa represents the dreadful, fearsome, violent protector of the village boundaries. Tāllapāka is explicitly referred to as a "'middle-of-the-street' Gaṅgamma," and her unassuming shrine is strategically placed "in the very middle of a busy thoroughfare next to a major intersection."[51] The two forms of the Goddess, although spatially separated, are essentially the same. Gaṅgamma is thus literally a center that is everywhere, as each street, each home, each family constructs her temporary image, while males of a variety of castes appear on the street dressed in her feminine guise during the festival. Handelman interprets the complex ritual transactions of Gaṅgamma's annual visit as a coaxing out of the Goddess from her inaccessible center into ever-widening circles of embodiment, within herself, within the village, within each home, and within the bodies of men.

Handelman's exegesis of Gaṅgamma's "middle" qualities presents us with a striking new paradigm for understanding the center-margins model of Kālī at issue here. The middle connotes both "the innerness of domestic space and family intimacy" and "the most transcendent of cosmic levels"; in South India, middles, whether external (street intersections, hearths) or internal (the innermost self, the womb) are spaces vulnerable to intrusions. According to David Shulman, the center is "a locus of movement, ambiguity and transformation, the place where doubts about reality arise."[52] This definition of centers is in vivid contrast to the Euro-American concept of centers as places of stability, control, dominance, and power; we tend to intuit margins, not centers, as places of "movement, ambiguity and transformation." Of course peripheries are also dangerous, liminal places in South Indian religion, but the relation between center and periphery is not one of dominance and exclusion. Center and periphery are both places of potentiality and power, closely related to each other, if not identical, as in the two forms of Gaṅgamma. The fluidity and ambiguity of South Indian rituals involving guising or possession allow center and periphery to fuse and then rearticulate as the festival defuses. The fusing that occurs in possession, and the violent emotions evoked by the rituals, infuse ordinary life with the power of the Goddess, always present but normally hidden.

The Goddess who appears simultaneously at the peripheries and in multiple centers also reveals a fundamental femaleness at the center of both human existence and the cosmos at large. The rituals of the Gaṅgamma festival suggest that at the heart of all humans is an essentially female center, which must periodically be affirmed and displayed in the open.[53] For this female center is normally kept hidden. Women, the metaphorical centers of their families, ideally remain in the interior, private rooms of the home's geography. The womb, at the center of both the female body and the Hindu temple, is the primal female space. The *garbha-gṛha,* or womb-chamber, is the enclosed, windowless room where the deity is kept in a Hindu temple. This ever-potent female center is dark, inaccessible, mysterious, fecund, frightening, dangerous, hot, life-giving when satisfied, the source of all. It must be honored, tended, nurtured, protected, and shielded, like a store of plutonium. The female core is not easily visible, but is rather a jewel that must be kept secret to be powerful. This conception of the qualities of the female that is at the center is neither "ambivalent" nor bipolar. It is a tightly woven net of associations, highly charged with emotion, that has been extrapolated to cosmic philosophical dimensions in Tantric and Śākta philosophy. Even at the simplest level, this provides us with an indigenous South Asian model that stands in clear contrast to the received image of the fierce Goddess as marginal, ambivalent, or extreme. She is, rather, at once central, hidden, and powerful.

The two forms of Gaṅgamma in Tirupati, the central and peripheral, are united at the heart of the festival through Gaṅgamma's possession of the body of the Mātaṅgī, a sweeper woman (significantly, in this case, a guise played by a male weaver). The living Mātaṅgī is a vivid character who has a long history (as evidenced by the tenth-century mentions of her in Tamil literature cited above) and may bear some relation to the Mātaṅgī of the Tantric Mahāvidyās (although evidence supporting this relation has yet to come to light). The Mātaṅgī, whose role is enacted by a middle-caste man in the festival described by Handelman, is a sweeper woman, a member of the lowest Untouchable caste in the South Indian caste structure. Handelman interprets her importance as arising from the fact that in sweeping the leavings of all other castes together, she recognizes no distinctions, and she thus becomes a symbol of profound unity. The fact that she is also the Goddess embodied in the form of the most despised and "marginal" person in the community, who during the ritual spits upon, abuses, and touches her buttocks to Brahmans and other venerable personages, seems to reveal other, more complex meanings of the Mātaṅgī that deserve further attention.

In earlier accounts, the Mātaṅgī was embodied in an actual female sweeper girl, who performed the simultaneously defiling and sanctifying ritual actions and became possessed by the Goddess.[54] In Richard Brubaker's account of South Indian village festivals to the Goddess performed in southern Karnataka in the 1970s, the Mātaṅgī still fulfilled an important role. A virgin of Untouchable caste was "initiated as a special representative or manifestation of the goddess."[55]

> Most . . . persons possessed by the goddess are male, for men perform most of the priestly roles in her festivals. But there is one very special role for a woman in many villages in Andhra Pradesh and adjoining areas of Karnataka,

> that of the Mātaṅgī. And possession is central to a Mātaṅgī's behavior and meaning. . . .
>
> There is only one Mātaṅgī in a village and she usually holds her office for life. Her successor is often designated by means of a ritual in which the prepubescent Madiga girls of the village are assembled, the goddess is invoked with much singing and drumming, and she enters into one of the girls, who later undergoes testing and initiation. Her subsequent life, in Elmore's delicate phrase, "knows no moral restrictions."[56]

The Mātaṅgī becomes possessed by the Goddess, drinking toddy and dancing in "wild frenzy" as she runs about spitting toddy on the assembled crowd, "uttering strange wild cries," and hurling obscene verbal abuse at all and sundry.[57] The suggestion by both Brubaker and W. T. Elmore that the Mātaṅgī performed sexual acts with high-caste men in village ritual contexts strongly recalls the employment of a low-caste female in certain forms of Śākta Tantrism, although again the precise nature of the relation is as yet obscure. What is notable in the comparison, however, is the degree of control and antinomian agency publicly asserted by the Mātaṅgī. The Mātaṅgī's visible, public humiliation of Brahman men stands in stark contrast to the Tantric rituals, in which females were made to serve male soteriologic aims through esoteric sexual practices in carefully controlled, highly secretive settings.

The fact that the Mātaṅgī is now enacted by a middle-caste man rather than a sweeper woman is not trivial. This fact points to the gradual transformation of religious practice over time, away from the inclusion of women and low castes, who were once central participants in ritual throughout South India. Men disguised as women are not the same as real women; just as women serving as partners to male Tantric practitioners are not the same as female gurus and teachers. Both transvestite masking and the ritual roles of "marginal" females in Śākta Tantrism and South Indian village worship reveal the efforts of men to absorb into their own bodies powers imputed to low-caste females.

This same transformation is alluded to in the many legends of temple origin in Kerala in which the Goddess is discovered accidentally through the agency of a low-caste female agricultural worker, who sharpens her sickle on a rock and causes it to bleed; alternatively, an ancient *mūrti* of rock or wood may surface while a "tribal" man is fishing or wading in the water.[58] In these legends, the essential originary power of the lowest-caste, most "polluting" persons (from a Brāhmaṇical point of view) is asserted; but a Brahman priest is then required to come to the spot, establish its divinity, and install the Goddess's idol properly in a temple. These temple legends insist simultaneously upon the Goddess's essential spiritual power inhering in the bodies of low-caste persons, and the need for purity, knowledge, and control by Brahmans. This Brāhmaṇical religious solution appears then to draw upon the religious practices and beliefs of the very lowest castes, who were then banned from approaching the temple premises. Along with that transformation, powers that once were celebrated in the bodies and minds of aboriginal women and men became the exclusive province of high-caste males. Excluded from entry into temples, low-caste and "Untouchable" persons are marginalized from Kāḷi worship, while their religious practices are emulated and incorporated into regular high-caste temple worship.

It is fairly easy to see the ways in which upper-caste religious ideology transforms indigenous practices to fit its own worldview and values. A growing literature on South Asia has begun to demonstrate the myriad forms of resistance and subversion of "subaltern" groups, whose religious practices and texts often work directly to counter negative stereotypes from above. In the field of Hinduism, particularly, a number of scholars have been at pains to show resistance by women to male domination in the religious and expressive spheres.[59] However, as I have noted, far more ethnography has been conducted with high castes than with those on the bottom. This is especially true for Kerala, where the fascination Nāyar women hold for ethnographers seems endless. Deborah Neff is a valuable exception, providing an in-depth ethnography of Puḷḷuvans, low-caste ritual specialists hired by superior castes (Īḻavans and Nāyars) to propitiate serpent deities in Kerala.[60] Kapadia's study also provides invaluable comparative data for a wide spectrum of caste groups in Tamilnadu.[61] Her detailed ethnography convincingly supports her thesis that the underlying values, as well as the ritual particulars, of the Brahman and non-Brahman castes are deeply divergent and separate, despite the many apparent similarities between them.

The sea change in religious studies I have alluded to, moving away from exclusive reliance on elite texts and incorporating the perspectives of diverse groups, is already drastically reconfiguring the landscape of Hinduism. Recent work in South Asian religion, mostly by women scholars, is beginning to turn up evidence of the preeminence of Kālī among low castes and female religious specialists, who incorporate possession, blood sacrifice, and violence into their worship. While these populations may be considered marginal by those with greater socioeconomic power and education, Kālī is quite central among them. High-caste, high-status religion either moves away from these practices, transforming Kālī into a philosophical necessity or a tamed wife of a male Hindu god, or Kālī's power is incorporated into high-caste rituals from which women and low castes are excluded. Some reclaim Kālī's original violent power as a source of strength in times of social change. For example, Patricia Lawrence has found her to be a truly subaltern figure of political resistance in Sri Lanka.[62]

Kālī's continual repositioning to suit the needs of her devotees can also be seen in recent Hindu reform movements such as the Bharatiya Janata party (BJP), where female orators exhort cowardly, impotent males to violence in the name of Hinduism.[63] The Goddess's power and autonomy has also proven extremely appealing to Western feminists.[64] Some Indian feminists are also beginning to envision Kālī as a role model, contrary to traditional attitudes of high-caste women.[65] In these new accounts, Kālī is certainly not marginal, although she can be subversive. As Kālī is recognized as a valuable image of liberation and empowerment, she again emerges at the center. As India throws off the mantle of the colonial gaze, perhaps it can reclaim its ancient inheritance of *śakti,* female power. And as scholars, we can assist in that move by ceasing to refer to Kālī as a goddess only of the extreme, repulsive, and unacceptable. It is time to reorient our vision and see in Kālī instead the power for human transformation that her complex truths contain.

NOTES

1. The name Kālī is generally spelled using Sanskrit diacritics in this chapter, except where I am referring specifically to her role in Kerala myth and ritual. The appearance of the spelling Kāḷi, rather than Kālī, thus indicates transliteration from Malayalam, the language of Kerala.

2. David R. Kinsley, "Kālī: Blood and Death out of Place," in *Devī: Goddesses of India,* ed. John S. Hawley and Donna M. Wulff (Berkeley and Los Angeles: University of California Press, 1996), pp. 77–86.

3. Ibid., p. 78.

4. Ibid., p. 84.

5. Edward C. Dimock Jr., "A Theology of the Repulsive: The Myth of the Goddess Śītalā," in *The Divine Consort: Rādhā and the Goddesses of India,* ed. John Stratton Hawley and Donna Marie Wulff (Boston: Beacon Press, 1982), pp. 184–203, 349–52.

6. Ronald Inden, *Imagining India* (Cambridge: Blackwell, 1990).

7. Gavin Flood, *An Introduction to Hinduism* (Cambridge: Cambridge University Press, 1996), p. 180, fig. 7.

8. Ibid., pp. 180–81.

9. Ibid., p. 179.

10. See Narendra Nath Bhattacharyya, *History of the Śākta Religion,* 2d rev. ed. (1973; New Delhi: Munshiram Manoharlal, 1996) and Pushpendra Kumar, *Śakti Cult in Ancient India* (Varanasi: Bhartiya Publishing House, 1974).

11. Bhattacharyya, *History of the Śākta Religion,* pp. 76–77.

12. Tracy Pintchman, *The Rise of the Goddess in the Hindu Tradition* (Albany: State University of New York Press, 1994).

13. See David R. Kinsley, *Tantric Visions of the Divine Feminine: The Ten Mahāvidyās* (Berkeley and Los Angeles: University of California Press, 1997).

14. Friedhelm Hardy, *Viraha-bhakti: The Early History of Kṛṣṇa Devotion in South India* (Oxford: Oxford University Press, 1983), p. 123.

15. See Sarah Caldwell, *Oh Terrifying Mother: Sexuality, Violence, and Worship of the Goddess Kāḷi* (Oxford: Oxford University Press, 1999), ch. 1.

16. Kalpana Ram, *Mukkuvar Women: Gender, Hegemony and Capitalist Transforma-*

tion in a South Indian Fishing Community (1991; New Delhi: Kali for Women, 1992), p. 69.

17. Holly Baker Reynolds, "To Keep the Tāli Strong: Women's Rituals in Tamil Nadu" (Ph.D. diss., University of Wisconsin, Madison, 1978).

18. G. Hart, "Woman and the Sacred in Ancient Tamilnad," *Journal of Asian Studies* 32, no. 2 (1973): 233–50.

19. See also Elizabeth Fuller Collins, *Pierced by Murugan̠'s Lance: Ritual, Power, and Moral Redemption among Malaysian Hindus* (De Kalb: Northern Illinois University Press, 1997); Alf Hiltebeitel, *The Cult of Draupadī,* vol. 2: *On Hindu Ritual and the Goddess* (Chicago: University of Chicago Press, 1991); and Bruce Kapferer, *A Celebration of Demons: Exorcism and the Aesthetics of Healing in Sri Lanka* (1983; Washington, D.C.: Smithsonian Institution Press, 1991).

20. Hardy, *Viraha-bhakti,* p. 223.

21. Saskia C. Kersenboom, "Vir̠ali," *Journal of Tamil Studies* 19 (1981): 19–41; and Saskia C. Kersenboom-Story, *Nityasumaṅgalī: Devadāsī Tradition in South India* (Delhi: Motilal Banarsidass, 1987).

22. Kersenboom-Story, *Nityasumaṅgalī,* p. 14.

23. Ibid., p. 10.

24. Ibid., p. 16.

25. Kersenboom, "Vir̠ali."

26. Kersenboom-Story, *Nityasumaṅgalī,* p. 15.

27. Ibid., p. 22.

28. Hardy, *Viraha-bhakti,* p. 140.

29. Ibid., p. 620.

30. Caldwell, *Oh Terrifying Mother,* p. 26 photo.

31. Rachel Fell McDermott, "Evidence for the Transformation of the Goddess Kālī: Kamalākānta Bhaṭṭācārya and the Bengali Śākta Padāvalī Tradition" (Ph.D. diss., Harvard University, 1993).

32. See Cynthia A. Humes, "Vindhyavāsinī: Local Goddess yet Great Goddess," in *Devī: Goddesses of India,* ed. John Stratton Hawley and Donna Marie Wulff (Berkeley and Los Angeles: University of California Press, 1996), pp. 49–76.

33. See Vasudha Narayanan, "Diglossic Hinduism: Liberation and Lentils," *Journal of the American Academy of Religion* 68, no. 4 (2000): 761–79, and Gail Omvedt, *Dalit Visions* (New Delhi: Orient Longman, 1995).

34. A. K. Ramanujan, "Toward a Counter-System: Women's Tales," in *Gender, Genre, and Power in South Asian Expressive Traditions,* ed. Arjun Appadurai, Frank J. Korom and Margaret A. Mills (Philadelphia: University of Pennsylvania Press, 1991), pp. 33–77, and Gloria G. Raheja and Ann G. Gold, *Listen to the Heron's Words: Reimagining Gender and Kinship in North India* (Berkeley and Los Angeles: University of California Press, 1994).

35. Paula Richman, ed., *Many Rāmāyaṇas: The Diversity of a Narrative Tradition in South Asia* (Berkeley and Los Angeles: University of California Press, 1991); Appadurai, Korom, and Mills, *Gender, Genre, and Power in South Asian Expressive Traditions;* and Donald S. Lopez Jr., ed., *Religions of India in Practice* (Princeton: Princeton University Press, 1995).

36. Stanley N. Kurtz, "Who is Kālī? Gender Hierarchy as Sacrificial Dominance" (unpublished paper presented at the conference on the Goddess Kālī at Barnard

College, New York, September 19–22, 1996), and Usha Menon and Richard A. Shweder, "The Return of the 'White Man's Burden': The Moral Discourse of Anthropology and the Domestic Life of Hindu Women," in *Welcome to Middle Age! (And Other Cultural Fictions),* ed. Richard A. Shweder (Chicago: University of Chicago Press, 1998), pp. 139–88, suggest that the focus on individual agency and political contestation may simply reflect the ethnocentric tendencies of feminist scholarship. While such a critique may have some validity, the discovery of multiple viewpoints arising from attention to populations subject to social inequalities cannot simply be dismissed.

37. Kathleen M. Erndl, *Victory to the Mother: The Hindu Goddess of Northwest India in Myth, Ritual, and Symbol* (New York: Oxford University Press, 1993), and "The Goddess and Women's Power: A Hindu Case Study," in *Women and Goddess Traditions in Antiquity and Today,* ed. Karen L. King (Minneapolis: Fortress Press, 1997), pp. 17–38.

38. N. Elaine Craddock, "Anthills, Split Mothers, and Sacrifice: Conceptions of Female Power in the Māriyamman̲ Tradition" (Ph.D. diss., University of California, Berkeley, 1994); Karin Kapadia, *Siva and Her Sisters: Gender, Caste, and Class in Rural South India* (Delhi: Oxford University Press, 1996); Isabelle Nabokov, *Religion against the Self: An Ethnography of Tamil Rituals* (New York: Oxford University Press, 2000); and Vijaya Rettakudi Nagarajan, "Hosting the Divine: The Koḷam as Ritual, Art and Ecology in Tamil Nadu, India" (Ph.D. diss., University of California, Berkeley, 1998). See also Hiltebeitel, *Cult of Draupadī,* vol. 2: *On Hindu Ritual and the Goddess.*

39. For Uttar Pradesh, see Humes, "Vindhyavāsinī: Local Goddess yet Great Goddess" and "Glorifying the Great Goddess or Great Woman? Hindu Women's Experience in Ritual Recitation of the *Devī-Māhātmya,*" in *Women in Goddess Traditions in Antiquity and Today,* ed. Karen L. King (Minneapolis: Fortress Press, 1997), pp. 39–63; and William S. Sax, *Mountain Goddess: Gender and Politics in a Himalayan Pilgrimage* (New York: Oxford University Press, 1991). For Orissa, see Cornelia Mallebrein, "Tribal and Local Deities: Assimilations and Transformations," in *Devi: The Great Goddess: Female Divinity in South Asian Art,* ed. Vidya Dehejia and Thomas B. Coburn (Washington, D.C.: Smithsonian Institution Press, 1999), pp. 137–55; and Usha Menon and Richard A. Shweder, "Kālī's Tongue: Cultural Psychology and the Power of Shame in Orissa, India," in *Emotion and Culture: Empirical Studies of Mutual Influence,* ed. Shinobu Kitayama and Hazel Rose Markus (Eugene: University of Oregon Press, 1994), pp. 241–84. For Maharashtra, see Anne Feldhaus, *Water and Womanhood: Religious Meanings of Rivers in Maharashtra* (New York: Oxford University Press, 1995). For Karnataka, see Peter J. Claus, "Ritual Transforms a Myth," *South Indian Folklorist* 1, no. 1 (1997): 37–57. For Andhra Pradesh, see Don Handelman, "The Guises of the Goddess and the Transformation of the Male: Gangamma's visit to Tirupati, and the Continuum of Gender," in *Syllables of Sky,* ed. David Shulman (Delhi: Oxford University Press, 1995), pp. 283–337. For Kerala, see Caldwell, *Oh Terrifying Mother;* and John Richardson Freeman, "Purity and Violence: Sacred Power in the Teyyam Worship of Malabar" (Ph.D. diss., University of Pennsylvania, 1991). Finally, for Sri Lanka, see Patricia Lawrence, "Kāḷi in a Context of Terror: Tasks of a Goddess in Sri Lanka's Civil War," chapter 5 in this volume; and Dennis B. McGilvray, "Sexual Power and Fertility in Sri Lanka: Batticaloa Tamils and Moors,"

in *Ethnography of Fertility and Birth,* ed. Carol P. MacCormack (London: Academic Press, 1982), pp. 25–74, and "The 1987 Stirling Award Essay: Sex, Repression, and Sanskritization in Sri Lanka?" *Ethos* 16, no. 2 (1988): 99–127.

40. Arjun Appadurai, "Theory in Anthropology: Center and Periphery," *Comparative Studies in Society and History* 28, no. 2 (1986): 356–74.

41. See McKim Marriott, "Little Communities in an Indigenous Civilization," in *Village India* (Chicago: University of Chicago Press, 1955), pp. 171–222.

42. David R. Kinsley, *Hindu Goddesses: Visions of the Divine Feminine in the Hindu Religious Tradition* (Berkeley and Los Angeles: University of California Press, 1986); Thomas B. Coburn, *Encountering the Goddess: A Translation of the Devī-Māhātmya and a Study of its Interpretation* (Albany: State University of New York Press, 1991); and Cheever Mackenzie Brown, *The Triumph of the Goddess: The Canonical Models and Theological Visions of the Devī-Bhāgavata Purāṇa* (Albany: State University of New York Press, 1990).

43. Wilber Theodore Elmore, *Dravidian Gods in Modern Hinduism: A Study of the Local and Village Deities of Southern India* (1915; Madras: Christian Literature Society, 1925), A. A. D. Luiz, *Tribes of Kerala* (New Delhi: Bharatiya Adimjati Sevak Sangh, 1962), and Edgar Thurston, *Castes and Tribes of Southern India* (1909; Delhi: Cosmo Publications, 1975).

44. See Mallebrein, "Tribal and Local Deities: Assimilations and Transformations."

45. Bhattacharyya, *History of the Śākta Religion,* pp. 38–84 passim.

46. See Urban and Humes, chapters 7 and 8 in this volume.

47. McDermott, "Evidence for the Transformation of the Goddess Kālī," and Menon and Shweder, "Kālī's Tongue"; see also J. N. Tiwari, "An Interesting Variant in the *Devī-Māhātmya,*" *Purana* 25, no. 2 (1983): 235–45.

48. See Jeffrey J. Kripal, *Kālī's Child: The Mystical and the Erotic in the Life and Teachings of Ramakrishna,* 2d ed. (1995; Chicago: University of Chicago Press, 1998).

49. Anna L. Tsing, in "From the Margins," *Cultural Anthropology* 9, no. 3 (1994): 279–97, makes this case eloquently in a different cultural context.

50. Handelman, "Guises of the Goddess and the Transformation of the Male."

51. Ibid., p. 286.

52. Personal communication, quoted in Handelman, "Guises of the Goddess and the Transformation of the Male," p. 286.

53. The Goddess is portrayed in both male and female guises by men during the festival. Handelman's analysis of the "continuum of gender" interprets this intensive male meditation on femaleness as a finding of a female core within the male body; simultaneously, the female deity finds "maleness" within her self as both achieve spiritual wholeness. For a different interpretation of male embodiment of the Goddess in South India, see Sarah Caldwell, "Bhagavati: Ball of Fire," in *Devī: Goddesses of India,* ed. John Stratton Hawley and Donna Marie Wulff (Berkeley and Los Angeles: University of California Press, 1996), pp. 195–226.

54. Richard L. Brubaker, "The Ambivalent Mistress: A Study of South Indian Village Goddesses and Their Religious Meaning" (Ph.D. diss., University of Chicago, 1978), and Elmore, *Dravidian Gods in Modern Hinduism.*

55. Brubaker, "Ambivalent Mistress," p. 267.

56. Ibid., pp. 267–68.

57. Ibid., p. 269. See Craddock, "Anthills, Split Mothers, and Sacrifice," for a description of similar events at Māriyammaṉ shrines in Tamilnadu.

58. K. R. Vaidyanathan, *Temples and Legends of Kerala* (Bombay: Bharatiya Vidya Bhavan, 1988), and C. A. Menon, *Kāḷi Worship in Kerala,* 2d ed. (1943; Madras: University of Madras, 1959). Despite its English title, Menon's text is in Malayalam.

59. Ram, *Mukkuvar Women;* Raheja and Gold, *Listen to the Heron's Words;* Debra Skinner, Dorothy Holland, and G. B. Adhikari, "The Songs of Tijj: A Genre of Critical Commentary for Women in Nepal," *Asian Folklore Studies* 53 (1994): 259–305; Velcheru Narayana Rao, "A Rāmāyaṇa of Their Own: Women's Oral Tradition in Telugu," in *Many Rāmāyaṇas: The Diversity of a Narrative Tradition in South Asia,* ed. Paula Richman (Berkeley and Los Angeles: University of California Press, 1991), pp. 114–36; A. K. Ramanujan, "Two Realms of Kannada Folklore," in *Another Harmony: New Essays on the Folklore of India,* ed. Stuart H. Blackburn and A. K. Ramanujan (Berkeley and Los Angeles: University of California Press, 1986), pp. 41–75; and Lindsay Harlan and Paul B. Courtright, eds., *From the Margins of Hindu Marriage: Essays on Gender, Religion, and Culture* (New York: Oxford University Press, 1995).

60. Deborah Neff, "Fertility and Power in a Kerala Serpent Ritual" (Ph.D. diss., University of Wisconsin, Madison, 1995).

61. Kapadia, *Siva and Her Sisters.*

62. Lawrence, "Kāḷi in a Context of Terror."

63. Paola Bacchetta, "All Our Goddesses Are Armed: Religion, Resistance, and Revenge in the Life of a Militant Hindu Nationalist Woman," in *Against All Odds: Essays on Women, Religion, and Development from India and Pakistan,* ed. Kamla Bhasin, Nighat Said Khan, and Ritu Menon (New York: Kali for Women, 1994), pp. 133–56; and Lise McKean, "Bhārat Mātā: Mother India and Her Militant Matriots," in *Devī: Goddesses of India,* ed. John Stratton Hawley and Donna Marie Wulff (Berkeley and Los Angeles: University of California Press, 1996), pp. 250–80.

64. Rachel Fell McDermott, "The Western Kālī," in *Devī: Goddesses of India,* ed. John Stratton Hawley and Donna Marie Wulff (Berkeley and Los Angeles: University of California Press, 1996), pp. 281–313.

65. Lina Gupta, "Kali the Savior," in *After Patriarchy: Feminist Transformations of the World Religions,* ed. Paula M. Cooey, William R. Eakin, and Jay B. McDaniel (Maryknoll, N.Y.: Orbis Books, 1998), pp. 15–38; and Humes, "Glorifying the Great Goddess or Great Woman?"

CHAPTER 12

Kālī's New Frontiers

A Hindu Goddess on the Internet

Rachel Fell McDermott

CHASING A DISGUISED GODDESS ON THE ELECTRONIC HIGHWAYS

I want to start with a visual introduction to the theme of this chapter: two depictions of Kālī, both by Western women, exemplifying the extremes of possible interpretation. Figure 12.1 is similar to the Indian "calendar art" style of portraying the four-armed Goddess, whereas figure 12.2 is reflective of Western views of the Goddess as powerfully sexual. The first illustration is typical of the types of Kālī images one would find in Bengal, in eastern India. Although she holds an instrument of death, is adorned with decapitated remains, and stands in a cremation ground, Kālī is nevertheless serene: with two of her hands she signals calmness and generosity, and her face is beautiful, attractive, alluring. I first saw the second picture in a periodical called *Tantra: The Magazine,* which for several years was devoted to the proliferation of Tantric understanding, lore, and practice in contemporary America.[1] The figure is dynamic, seductively engaging, and obviously able to arouse; unlike the face of figure 12.1, which is sweet and almost childlike, this face is that of a woman, with emotions and independent power.

Both images have a context. As a bookstore watcher, I have since the early 1980s seen an explosion of literature in sections of bookstores labeled "Women's Studies" and "The New Age."[2] The New Age sections of some bookstores are larger than their entire holdings on non-Western history.

Figure 12.1 Pen and ink, line drawing of Kali by Margo Gal, 2001. Reproduced by permission.

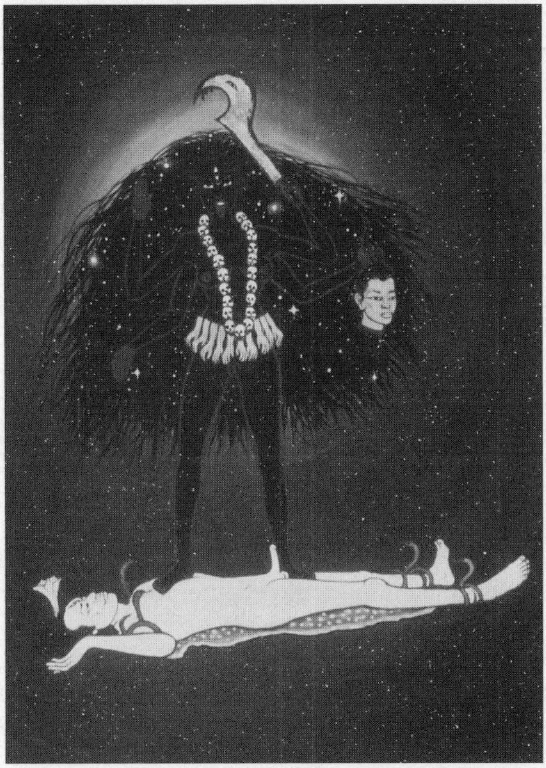

Figure 12.2 *Young Kali, Cosmos in Her Tangled Hair,* by Penny Slinger, 1994, acrylic and gold leaf on wood panel, 27." × 20.5". Reproduced by permission.

Such books deal with astrology, Tarot cards, channeling, gurus and meditation, the power of crystals, alternative diets, resources for women among the ancient goddess traditions, and testimonials of those who have found health and healing through self-help techniques. They also introduce the Western reader to a number of living Asian religions, such as Hinduism.

In 1991, I decided that it would be an interesting project to investigate such feminist and New Age literature in order to see what it was saying about Kālī. The result was an essay called "The Western Kālī," published in a volume edited by John S. Hawley and Donna M. Wulff, *Devī: Goddesses of India* (1996).[3] Very generally, I found that this Hindu goddess was being viewed as a model: since she is a union of opposites, combining within herself the poles of creation and destruction, love and fear, modern women should also learn to recover and reclaim this wholeness in themselves. Moreover, because Kālī embodies those characteristics which patriarchy has repressed and demonized—the potent, sexual, dark sides of women—claiming Kālī is also a way of owning female energy and empowerment. I concluded "The Western Kālī" by applauding the way in which this Kālī of female wholeness and rage was helping women to heal divisions in their lives, but also wondered whether, in the hands of her new interpreters and enthusiasts, she would soon become unrecognizable to the culture from which she sprang.

More recently, I have embarked on a similar project: to update my findings, given two important new media of knowledge transmission, the electronic resources of Internet newsgroups,[4] and the World Wide Web.[5] While continuing to search more traditional genres, such as books and magazines, I have used my computer to explore these two other avenues of communication. How is the presentation of Kālī being affected by the democratization of knowledge sources through the Internet and the Web? Are people's ideas of Kālī continuing to veer away from what might be considered her "genuine" cultural moorings? Or is the Kālī of India resurfacing to challenge her new Western devotees? Figures 12.1 and 12.2 hint at the answer.

Within the framework of this comparison between Kālī of the late 1980s and Kālī of the third millennium, this chapter also addresses four theoretical concerns: the reasons for persisting Western fascination with Kālī; the increasing impact of Indianization in the United States and Europe; the evolution in self-identity among convert groups;[6] and the potential influences of computer resources upon religious understanding. But before we get to theory, let us see more of Kālī.

NEW DIRECTIONS SINCE 1991: THE WESTERN KĀLĪ MEETS THE INDIAN KĀLĪ

In relation to my discoveries of a decade ago, my present research has yielded two main trends, the first of which is a continuation, in perhaps an even more bizarre form, of directions seen in the earlier literature. As (1) a symbol of female empowerment, (2) a guarantor of sexual pleasure, (3) a recipient of ritual worship, and (4) an object of artistic ingenuity, today's Kālī has inherited the mantle of the Kālī of 1991.

Old Themes, New Genres

Kālī and Female Empowerment. A World Wide Web site known as "I am the Bitch from Hell" begins with the following poem:

I am the Bitch from Hell
I think you know me well
I am the dark goddess
Kali, Hecate, Lilith, Morrigan, Ereshigal.

The text then explains that "the dark goddess lives in us all. Often suppressed and denied she will eventually leak out in hostility and sarcasm, with sly cutting digs, nagging, gossip, and put downs. She reveals herself at her most ugly in our closest relationships. . . . The energy of the dark goddess brews and bubbles in the belly." One can then click onto a subsidiary page called "The Bitch Board," where one is invited to write down all the aggravating things in one's life. "The Bitch Board is a place to let off steam, to express your bitch with no holds barred. Once you let her have her say then maybe she will leave you in peace!"[7]

To me, this unique home page illustrates what I see as a reinforcement, in an electronic medium, of trends identified in my earlier research. Kālī is taken as a symbol of the darkness and anger within, and acknowledging her is the route to healing. Such fascination with a deity who combines everything within herself is attested by two personal witnesses on a webpage called "The Dark Goddess and me."[8] The first writer describes how he watched his cat play with a terrified wounded mouse and realized that "my cat, paradoxically, loved the mouse." Thereafter, seeing the parallel implications with respect to the Dark Goddess, he becomes willing to love Kālī, "to face that there is a force, a being if you like, who has the power to inflict terrible sufferings on us as She calls us back to Her, and who may very well do just that." The second writer explains how he has been able to come to terms with his AIDS diagnosis through an acceptance of the Dark Goddess. Note, likewise, a poem by Mel Lyman, also appearing on a "Kali" webpage. The Goddess is speaking:

> I am going to burn down the world
> I am going to tear down everything that cannot stand alone
> I am going to turn ideals to shit
> I am going to shove hope up your ass
> I am going to reduce everything that stands to rubble
> And then I am going to burn the rubble
> And then I am going to scatter the ashes
> And then maybe SOMEONE will be able to see SOMETHING as it really is
> WATCH OUT[9]

Continuing this association of ferocity, passion, and danger with the Goddess, one finds Kālī the hag,[10] Kālī the vampire,[11] Kālī the inspiration behind a group of airline stewardesses who strangle their passengers, like the Thugs,[12] and Kālī the patron of lesbian terrorists who guillotine their victims' pensises off.[13] Indeed, as stated in the webpage, "Warrior Goddesses and Women," it is only "womyn's" violence, as illustrated in these Kālī-esque savage, merciless figures, that can stop male violence and supremacy.[14] A computer-generated picture of Kālī, from another page, sums up the allure of this coincidence of beauty and death: a young wise woman called "Kali" holds a skull at her throat.[15]

In addition to balancing the emotions, Kālī can also bring into equilibrium the hormonal swings in a woman's body,[16] consecrate birth and sex,[17] and even make the act of housekeeping enjoyable: "I sing praises to Kali, the only goddess capable of sanctifying housework. ' . . . *Om Namo Kali Om* . . . Oh Kali cleanup home . . . *Om Namo Kali Om* . . . I praise you when I mop the floors . . . *Om Namo Kali Om* . . . I praise you when I scrub the toilet . . . *Om Namo Kali Om.*' "[18]

Thus Kālī endures as a reminder of the possibilities and depths of one's being, which she can help to bring to light and heal.

The Tantric Kālī: Sex as the "Path to the Queendom of Goddess." One of the biggest developments, within the general rubric of continuity, in the conceptualization of Kālī over the past several years concerns Tantra and sex.[19] Interest in Tantra, while strong in the past decade, has recently skyrocketed, with magazines championing it, websites whose sole purpose is to explicate and illustrate it,[20] and newsgroups whose conversations center around its proper use.

As a Tantric goddess par excellence, Kālī is tied to Tantric rituals of self-empowerment, many of which, in this literature, seem to revolve around sex.[21] Newsgroup conversationalists refer to Kālī as their lover,[22] even revealing on the Internet their personal sexual experiences with her: "She decided to throw me to the ground and have sex with me in a dream. She also cut off my head and tossed it somewhere. Scared the hell out of me until I figured out what it meant."[23]

In the following poetic excerpt, another man makes explicit the link between Kālī and sex with a real woman:[24]

> a little while ago i was reading
> about a pilgrim who was with a crazy saint in india
> and they went to the temple of the goddess kali
> and the saint put his hand on top of the pilgrim's head
> and his other hand under the dress of a statue of mother kali
> and the pilgrim felt a bolt of electricity
> running thru his body
> and i thought to myself
> if there's so much energy to receive from even a statue
> how much more so from an other human being who
> is also a god/goddess.

Kālī and other Hindu goddesses' association with sex is everywhere, in all genres surveyed: Kālī is depicted as a playboy centerfold on the Web,[25] *Tantra: The Magazine* used to have a regular column of questions and answers on sex, called "Dear Tantric Goddess," translations of Sanskrit Tantras that bear on ritual intercourse are advertised on Home Pages,[26] and various workshops and audiocassettes—such as "Freeing the Female Orgasm: Awakening the Goddess,"[27] "Tantra: Indian Rites of Ecstasy,"[28] and "Tantra: The Art of Conscious Loving,"[29]—are routinely offered.[30] It is in this context that figure 12.2 makes sense.

Before leaving the topic of Tantra, it is intriguing to note that from the perspective of sexual liberation, Kālī and the other goddesses are viewed almost entirely as beneficent and merciful in their encouragement of their votaries' self-fulfillment. One can see this in the final paragraph of the advertisement for an American Tantra workshop by Paul Ramana Das and Marilena Silbey: "we intend to co-create neo-tribal, post-dysfunctional, multidinzensional [*sic*], sex and spirit positive, loving and juicy generations of gods and goddesses in the flesh. On the Starship Intercourse, we greet and part with 'ORGASM LONG AND PROSPER!'"[31] This positive, sweetness-and-light depiction of Kālī as a patron of sexual fulfillment represents a New Age shift away from the primarily feminist-oriented Kālī of dark, angry, female power.

Rituals: Come Into My Cauldron. If, in preparing my former essay, I had to search hard to find any examples of Kālī-centered New Age rituals, my task is easier this time around. The Kali Issue of *Tantra: The Magazine* explains how to worship the Goddess on Tuesdays, after midnight;[32] a Kālī-centered new moon ritual is available on the Internet;[33] the Witches Web of Days, to be found in either paper or electronic form, has identified February 17 as Kālī's birthday;[34] Rowena Kryder offers a mix of poetry, ritual, and illustrations to encourage the worship of Kālī, the Gorgon of Death and the Dark Mother;[35] and D. J. Conway claims that Kālī is the best known Crone Goddess, or goddess representing the decay, and wisdom, of old age. In Conway's Crone Meditation, the initiate is led to Kālī, who asks her to leap into her inky cauldron, where she experiences rebirth.[36] A group of women who call themselves The Daughters of Kali spend their time worshipping Kālī, performing life-cycle rites, learning Sanskrit, receiving magical and martial arts training, conducting animal sacrifices, and running a shelter for abused women in London.[37] More cerebral types of ritual involve the adoration of the Goddess through webtemples. In the "Temple of Kali" website, for instance, one is invited into a temple, shown graphically as a garden with a beautiful woman lying suggestively on the ground. A naked man leans over her. The caption reads, "Welcome to the Temple of Kali, the Goddess of Vice and Destruction."[38]

Kālī in Dance, Theater, Art, and Advertising. Songs, poetry, and rituals are not the only expressions of the conviction that Kālī liberates, empowers, and challenges. The same message is also increasingly portrayed though art forms, such as dance, theater, painting, and advertising. Some productions are obviously influenced by Indian art and Indian dance teachers, but most

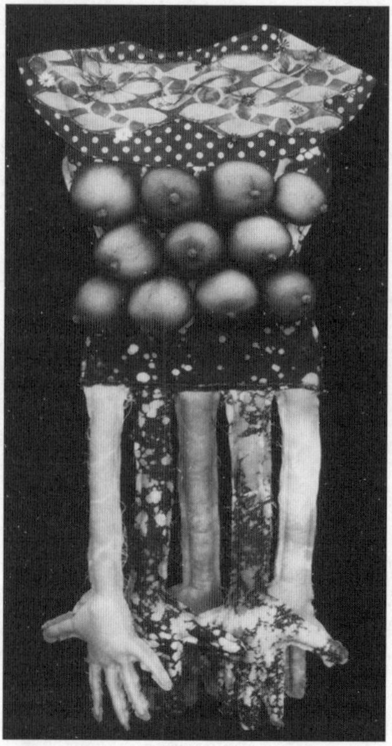

Figure 12.3 Apron made from symbols of abundance from the ancient goddess Diana of Ephesus and symbols of freedom and power from the Hindu goddess Kali Ma, by Susan Black-Keim, 1998, fiber. Reproduced by permission.

have been developed by people inspired to create their own styles. Le'ema Kathleen Graham, a teacher of movement and meditation classes called "Goddess Empowerment Dancing," has developed a repertory called "Healing Goddess Dances." Early in life, she says, it was Isis, Aphrodite, Green Tara, and Pandora who appealed to her; in midlife, however, the Black Madonna and Kali made their appearance, and now they dominate her dance forms completely: "I realize now that Kali has had hold of me most of my life. Kali has sunk her fang-like teeth into me and will not let go until she devours me whole. I feel her chasing me with sabre in hand keeping me on the conscious path. Since my path is the dancing one, I created a devotional dance to this goddess."[39]

Figure 12.4 *Economist Review of Books and Multimedia,* June 21, 1997, cover by Chris Brown. Reproduced by permission.

Even more noticeable than Kālī-centered dance and theater productions, however, are drawings and paintings of Kālī in books, covers of magazines, CDs, posters, ads, and websites. Kālī sells. Her face and body have become far more noticeable in the public arena than they were ten years ago. This is true not only for what one might call the New Age market, through which one can buy a Goddess Kali box or Goddess Kali incense burner,[40] Kali pendant and matching earrings,[41] or a Kali tattoo,[42] but also —and this is more revealing as an indicator of her growth in Western societies—in contexts *not* governed by New Age and feminist concerns. To cite a few examples: Kālī inspires contemporary artisans such as Susan Black-Keim, who has created a Kali Ma Apron (fig. 12.3),[43] and adorns the cover of a rock band's new CD release;[44] an ad for a nightclub in San Francisco;[45] a "New York Press" article on New Orleans cooking;[46] an ad for a copier machine, called "Improve Office Karma";[47] the cover of the *Economist*'s prestigious *Review of Books and Multimedia* (fig. 12.4);[48] and even the cover of *Immunology Today,* to depict the many-facetedness—many-armedness—of deadly proteases.[49] In general, these reflect the desire on the part of the artists to create a sensual, powerful goddess; some of the images are so sexually explicit as to shock a normal Indian devotee (see fig. 12.2).[50]

In sum, what I found ten years ago is still in evidence: the Western Kālī—Goddess of female power, sex, ritual, and art—is becoming even more at home.

The New Kālī of the Internet and the World Wide Web

What I find even more fascinating than all these oddball things people are writing about Kālī is a second trend, new since 1991: contrasting and argumentative voices. Partly this is due to the entrance into the conversation of people who have traveled to India or who have read academic books about the Goddess. Such people not only challenge the type of literature surveyed above by offering alternative information sources; they also—mainly on the Internet—articulate issues and questions regarding cross-cultural borrowing. In what follows, I give a brief overview of both such strategies.

Showcasing Another Kālī: Perspectives from India. It is obvious, especially from the World Wide Web, that even among nonacademics, there is a new awareness of Indian traditions of worship and devotion to Kālī. The home pages that bear titles such as "The Goddess Kalika," "Kali," and "The Tantra Goddess," all include photos of genuine Indian Kālīs, with correct identification and annotation, and the information given in these websites is more or less accurate. For instance, selections from various Tantras are translated into English;[51] regional variations, for instance between the goddesses of Bengal, Nepal, and Tamilnadu, are noted and explained; and the differences between the iconographic conventions of various goddesses are described, often with accompanying pictures.[52]

One of the reasons for this new direction in the depiction of Kālī is the experiences of Westerners with Hindus, not only in India but also in the United States and Europe. Some are Hindu priests and devotees associated with the numerous Hindu temples appearing all over the Western world, many of which have developed their own websites. Others are gurus like Mata Amritanandamayi from Kerala, who claims to be a living manifestation of Kālī and who has her own website, and the Brooklyn-born guru Ma Jaya Sati Bhagavati, who offers retreats in which one can receive her "Kali Shakti Gaze."[53] Says Ma Jaya, "I have brought her out for the world to see her, for the world to know that Kali has come to the West."[54] One can also click onto a site posted by the Indian State Government of West Bengal, which explains about Durgā and Kālī festivals, gives photos of the goddesses, and even includes Bengali script.[55]

Some non-Indian but India-inspired groups have also begun to popularize Kālī in the West. The best example is Kali Mandir, the most ambitious of the electronic groups.[56] Kali Mandir was formed by Elizabeth Harding, author of *Kali: The Black Goddess of Dakshineswar,*[57] as a group of people united by the love of God in the form of Kālī. Although they are hoping to build a physical temple for the performance of Kālī-centered worship, in Laguna Beach, California, at present they have two substitutes: a Kālī temple on the Web, where they urge viewers to "come and make an offering to the Divine Mother of the Universe"; and regular meetings in rented spaces in Laguna Beach, for songs, fellowship, and an annual Kālī Pūjā. This Pūjā is performed authentically by priests brought especially from the Dakṣiṇeśvar Temple in Calcutta. Perhaps most impressive is the stamp of legitimation accorded Kali Mandir's activities by Bengalis living in this country; one often finds exhortations to visit the Mandir, as well as directions on how to reach Laguna Beach, on their newsgroups.[58]

How do these organizations, gurus, and temples—most of South Asian origin, and all deeply informed by South Asian traditions—respond to the depictions of Kālī prevalent in feminist and New Age circles? Few of these groups actively try to combat erroneous Western conceptions. However, by presenting a competing goddess—an "authentic" Kālī, as channeled through Indian books, computer resources, centers of worship, and religious adepts—they certainly bypass the angry and sexually permissive deity. But not all spokespeople for the South Asian perspective are so muted in their responses. A second way of downplaying or counteracting the overly Westernized interpretations of Kālī is to argue against them explicitly. This is the subject to which I now turn.

Polemics: Can One Be "Too NewAgeish"? South Asian voices are becoming more and more vocal in protecting what they see as an endangered and misunderstood "true" vision of Hindu deities like Kālī. One recent example of the success of this monitoring or anti-defamation watchdog activity concerns an episode of the TV serial *Xena, Warrior Princess,* in which Kṛṣṇa and Hanumān aid Xena in escaping from a demon king by transforming her into a black-skinned Kālī figure, who is then able to decapitate her enemy. The storm of outrage over this portrayal by Hindus and Hindu sympathizers was so strong that Studios USA and Renaissance Pictures agreed to pull the segment out of worldwide circulation.[59] Another similar instance involves the toilet seat company, Sittin' Pretty Designs, which, until American Hindus against Defamation vigorously protested, was selling toilet seats imprinted with the images of Gaṇeśa and Kālī. The furor whipped up against the company's owner-artist, Lamar Van Dyke, is a perfect example of the disparity between liberal feminist and traditional South Asian American attitudes toward the importation of Hindu deities into Western contexts. Said Van Dyke: "We feel that it is important to put strong female images out there in the universe in an attempt to counteract the negativity that is, and has been, directed towards women throughout the millennia. Goddess Kali is one of the strongest female images to have survived the deliberate distortion that patriarchy has placed upon all of our history."[60]

This time, anyway, South Asian arguments have won out; Sittin' Pretty has discontinued its Sacred Seat Collection. Note that much of the protest on both of these issues—Xena and toilet seats—was communicated and aired on the Internet, which has become a powerful lobbying tool.

Indeed, it is correspondents on the Internet who provide the most intriguing counterpoints to the prevailing views on Kālī, as typically articulated by the New Age and women's spirituality literatures. In the little over six years since I began tracking such conversations, I have observed two points in particular worth noting: (1) an Indian perspective is being brought to bear on the discussion, and (2) what is being criticized is *both* the feminists' Rage Kālī *and* the sweetened and homogenized Sexual Cheerleader Kālī of the New Age.[61]

In mid April of 1995, for instance, two Internet users debated whether Kālī is or is not solely a "woman's deity," is or is not a representation of aggression and rage.[62] Wrote one: "I too rail when exposed to literature either trying to white-wash or stereotype Ma Kali as some kind of child-eating demon. In Her homeland She has a rich and varied iconography. She defies reduction by Western writers seeking to absorb her in some mushy composite."[63]

If this debunks the feminists' Kālī of anger and power, the New Age Goddess also comes under fire, for other writers reproach the literature for focusing too heavily on women and on sex: "There is one thing I want to make clear, real Tantra is 1% sexual rites (symbolic and/or literal) and 99% training and practicing. So if you are looking for a [*sic*] sex, you are looking at the wrong place," one said.[64] "Portraying Mother Kali as one who impales herself in a wild erotic frenzy on Lord Shiva's erect lingam or as the Great Virgin and the Great Whore is sad. This is a clear example of us mortals creating God/Goddess in our own image," another commented.[65]

A third example of the rather far-sighted discussions occurring on the Internet concerns the issue of cross-cultural borrowing itself. In response to someone who writes that "modern neo-Pagan interpretations of Kali don't even remotely match the [genuine? and if so, why?] Hindu interpretations of her," another correspondent answers that there are *many* Indian perspectives on Kālī, and that maybe the neo-Pagans aren't as far off as it might appear. Besides, why can't a god "venture beyond those artificial boundaries into other cultures? . . . I think to some extent we do a disservice to our world and to the gods when we establish some sort of standard of 'genuineness' which shall be taken as 'correct.' Kali expresses Herself to many people in many ways."[66]

So what was implicit as a methodological principle in the 1990s is now being voiced, and sometimes criticized, as an explicit postulate: cross-cultural borrowing *is* appropriate and a natural by-product of religious globalization—although such borrowing ought to be done responsibly and self-consciously. If some Kālī enthusiasts, therefore, careen ahead, reveling in a goddess of power and sex, many others, particularly since the early 1990s, have decided to reconsider their theological trajectories. These, whether of South Asian descent or not, are endeavoring to rein in what they perceive as excesses of feminist and New Age interpretations of the Goddess by choosing to be informed by, moved by, an Indian view of her character.

CONCLUSION: ASSESSING THE TRENDS

The comparative and descriptive materials presented above beg for some sort of methodological discussion. How are we to interpret (1) the increasingly Western and idiosyncratic interest in Kālī by feminists and New Age groups, and, by contrast, (2) her new Indianization? Although there are doubtless many perspectives from which to understand these phenomena, here I present four. They are not explanations so much as contexts—religious, demographic, historical, and commercial—that may shed light on the phenomena through the establishment of comprehensible frameworks.

Still Turning East for Individual Healing

The first way of understanding the continuing New Age infatuation with Kālī is to see this desire as yet another example of Western interest in Indian spirituality. This fascination with things Eastern can be traced back to the nineteenth century, with the Transcendentalists, the Theosophists, and the Spiritualists, and into the early twentieth century, through the writings of William James and the appreciation in the West of the messages of Hindu monks such as Swami Vivekananda and Paramahamsa Yogananda. However, the more immediate predecessors of the contemporary interest in Indian spirituality and mysticism are the Beats, Hippies, and various other counterculture groups since World War II who, highly influenced by Aldous Huxley, Jack Kerouac, Allen Ginsberg, Alan Watts, and even Maharishi Mahesh Yogi, in the 1950s, 1960s, and early 1970s, hungered for high states of consciousness, an organic community life, a respect for the earth, and a "new age" or an "Aquarian Age," in which each person could flower in his or her own unique way. Like their counterparts in the late 1990s, these earlier counterculture enthusiasts had a craving for the occult, for magic, and for exotic ritual, without an ascetic element. Instead, their mysticism was this-worldly, affirming the body and the earth, in a vision akin to that of the Indian *Kāmasūtra* and Indian Tantra. "Nothing," said Theodore Roszak in 1969, in describing this phenomenon, "is so striking about the new orientalism as its highly sexed flavor."[67]

Other aspects to the movements of the 1950s and 1960s that are reminiscent of their modern heirs are: their lack of institutionalization, dogmatization, or criteria for membership; their typical origins in affluence; and their eclecticism. Intrigued by symbols and the esoteric, young men and women created what Roszak called an "occult Jungian stew,"[68] or a random, piecemeal conglomeration of religious elements centered on personal growth, without necessarily knowing much about their cultures of origin. One is reminded of Robert Bellah's now classic description of what he called "Modern Religion," in which the ability to make meaning and to find a workable synthesis resides in the individual.[69]

In this vein, Gananath Obeyesekere's study of personal symbols and religious experience is also illuminating.[70] He explains how individuals whom he studied in Sri Lanka creatively manipulated cultural symbols—whether belonging principally to the majority or the minority community (Sinhalese Buddhist or Tamil Hindu, in this case)—to express and eventually resolve their personal psychic conflicts. Obeyesekere defines "subjectification" as the process by which cultural patterns and symbol systems are "put back into the melting pot of consciousness and refashioned to create a culturally tolerated set of subjective images. These images are often protoculture, or culture in the making, though not all of them end up as culture, since this depends on the acceptance of the imagery by the group and its legitimization."[71] Indeed, not all symbols, even if healing for an individual or a small group of individuals, are successful in providing a bridge back to the community at large; Obeyesekere gives the example of a Muslim named Abdin, who becomes a hook-swinger and tongue-piercer for Kālī.[72] Although respected and even consulted for his spiritual powers, Abdin is accepted neither by the Hindus at Kataragama, for he is a Muslim who eats meat and drinks alcohol, nor by the Muslims, who decry his unorthodox brand of syncretistic Islam. In this case, other people's symbols help him overcome certain psychological traumas in a very innovative way but do not win him a steady income or a stable community home.

Applying these insights to the case of Western feminists and New Age practitioners who look to Kālī for strength and inspiration, one can see that they have drawn upon a symbol largely but not entirely foreign to their home culture and imbued it with an innovative meaning. Not only does the raging, sensuous Kālī look different from the Kālī of her homeland, but the use of this Goddess to express Western women's feelings is unprecedented. Because they are non-Hindus, because Kālī is still not recognized as a common symbol in a Western cultural context, and because their use of the symbol is bizarre to those for whom it is familiar, the feminist and New Age goddess worshippers—like Abdin—meet criticism from Hindus and non-Hindus alike. Nevertheless, insofar as they have been able, through the subjective appropriation of this symbol, to create a subcommunity of women and men who find peace and resolution of inner conflict, the symbol has been successfully and creatively manipulated. One speculates, from Obeyesekere's model, that true acceptance of the Woman's Kālī would require both a more normative use of the symbol and a wider cultural understanding and acceptance of that symbol. These two conditions may yet prevail —particularly if the Kālī-worshipping community or communities become more mainstream.[73]

There are three scenarios that might possibly push certain subsections among such people toward stricter group identity: the desire to use the courts to safeguard Hindu ritual practices deemed unsafe or undesirable according to the current legal system; persecution by the society at large;[74] or such success in generating enthusiasm among Westerners, whether of South Asian descent or not, that survival depends upon systematization. Given that at present, at least, there appears to be no aspiring leader to put his or her umbrella of authority over the entire set of groups, this last option seems somewhat improbable. Unlike Guru Mayi's Siddha Yoga, Swami Bhaktivedanta's ISKCON, or Maharishi's Transcendental Meditation, all of which became organized after tremendous popular triumphs centered around a charismatic guru, the people and groups examined in this chapter are still at a formative, diffuse stage of development, in many ways like the hippies and seekers of recent generations past.

Indianization and the New Postcolonial Critique

The second lens through which one can view the phenomenon under study —particularly the new fascination with the Goddess's Indian origins and indigenous meanings—is the ever-increasing influence of South Asians in the United States and Europe. Hindu temples, the availability of Indian videos and newspapers, the opportunities for instruction in Indian dance, music, and art, and introductions to Indian food through ubiquitous groceries and restaurants, have all created a new awareness in the West of Indian religious vocabulary, customs, and beliefs, not only among the public at large, but even among those who, perhaps for generations, have been looking East for inspiration already. One can see this, for instance, in the Indianization of the Hare Krishna temples, of the Ramakrishna Vedanta Societies, and even of the Siddha Yoga retreats; Indian devotees are both attracted by these organizations and eager to make them more "authentic" in ritual style and theological message.

Knowledge about and influence from South Asia do not simply result in the active Indianization of Western religiosity. They also lead to new judgments of that religiosity. Some critics, whether South Asian themselves or deeply identified with South Asian history, view the rather novel interpretations of Kālī by feminists and New Age groups as a form of neocolonialism. In this view, the refashioning of the Goddess according to upper-class, typically white women's agendas does violence, not only to Kālī herself, but also to the Hindu tradition as a whole and to the representatives of that tradition who have made their homes in the West. This new form of the orientalist gaze is indicative of the still pervasive tendency of Westerners to take what they want from the Other, transforming it in tandem with their own idiosyncratic, selfish needs and robbing Kālī of her voice in the process. Every time I teach about the New Age Kālī in my "Hindu Goddesses" seminar at Barnard College, for instance, my students are outraged and offended; they often link the "inappropriate" cultural borrowing of Kālī with inaccurate and condescending British attitudes toward goddess worship during the Raj. In other words, what partly fuels the heated Internet discussions about the "correct" interpretation of Kālī worship is a desire to rescue her from further colonial butchering.

The Indianization of Kālī worship, therefore, is natural and is only to be expected, given the maturation of the immigrant population since the 1960s. South Asians have settled in this country, the first crop of second-generation kids are now in college or beyond, and, as the most economically successful of all American minorities, South Asians' voices are articulate, powerful, and influential. I expect this Indianization of religious groups, especially those claiming some link to Hinduism, only to increase.

The Search for Fundamentals

The third perspective I bring to bear is comparative, and places the concern for authenticity, among certain of the feminist and New Age groups considered here, within the context of other convert groups who, after a time of self-assertion, begin to sense the need to explore the cultural roots of their new religious traditions. In other words, participants desire to get to the "core" of their spiritual path.

A few examples: the Hare Krishnas, who, after an initial period from 1965 to 1977 as a charismatic and sometimes unwieldy movement, became a more settled, Indianized, institution; Ambedkar's Dalit Buddhists in India, who have tried to reach out to the world Buddhist community and have successfully attracted Buddhists from countries outside India to their cause; the Nation of Islam, whose members have become more and more interested in conventional (or Sunni) Islam since the time of Malcolm X;[75] the rise in numbers of converts to ultra-orthodox Judaism, either from reform and conservative Jewish families or from non-Jewish backgrounds;[76] and Christian fundamentalists, many of them new converts to Christianity or refugees from more liberal, mainstream denominations.

Hence the interest in Kālī's Indian iconography, Indian priests and rituals, and Indian "authenticity," new to the Western literature on Kālī since 1991, can also be understood as a step taken by most groups who have embraced a religious tradition different from that of their births: after a time, and for varied reasons, as an indicator of their commitment to their new paths, they evince enthusiasm for knowledge about the lands and traditions now claimed as their spiritual birthrights.[77]

Virtual Kālīs, Virtual Communities

Given the character of the Internet—decentralized, universal, and pluralistic—it is not surprising that its presence has encouraged the proliferation of new and competing voices on the subject of Kālī. As a democratizing and socially *dis*-embedding mass medium, which is freed from the social constraints of caste and is largely unmediated by specialists, it has allowed for goddess worship to become unlinked from its original Hindu contexts and to be moored in new communities. Since newsgroups and websites provide ample opportunities for consumer input and interaction, as well as dissent and freedom of expression, one would expect religious symbols to become mobile, stamped with the personalities of their several interpreters. This process accounts for the bitch goddess of feminist reclamation, for the "sweetness and light" Goddess of neo-Tantra, and for the more traditional, Bengali-ized Kālī of Indian-influenced voices: Kālī fills several new Western demands, in a new "public space." What we are seeing, therefore, are the journeys of a goddess into unknown territory on the electronic highways; due to the nature of the medium traveled, her itinerary is public, fought over, and even manipulated for commercial benefit.[78]

To conclude, let me return to the two pictures with which I began this chapter. Publication trends since 1991, whether in paper or electronic media, indicate that two simultaneous trajectories are being followed by those who include Kālī in their own, a-traditional, spiritual journeys. The first, represented by figure 12.2, "Young Kali" by Penny Slinger, indicates that the fascination with sex, women's power, and individualized conceptions of the Western goddess, continue unabated since the 1980s, and in even more extreme forms. However, what is new to the general picture, and to me signals new vibrancy and health in the several movements termed New Age, Feminist, and Women-centered, is the entrance into the dialogue of Indian voices, Indian perspectives, and even Indian iconography, as represented by the other picture, figure 12.1, Kālī in the style of Bengali calendar art. As such, I laud the democratization of publication opportunities afforded by the Internet and World Wide Web, for they have provided the Indian goddess Kālī with a certain ease and speed of travel, so that she can come to the West to visit her counterpart. If I ended my research in 1991 with the question as to how long it would take before Kālī lost all moorings to her land of origin, now I find myself musing on the degree to which the Bengali Kālī will transform her sister, here in the bookstores, wicca covens, and minds of those who turn to their computers for stimulation and inspiration.

NOTES

I am grateful to the participants of the Columbia University Seminar on Religion (April 1996), to the members of the Kālī Conference at Barnard College (September 1996), and to seminar respondents at Sarah Lawrence College (February 1998), who gave me excellent feedback on earlier drafts of this chapter.

1. *Tantra: The Magazine,* Kali issue, no. 9 (1994): 41.

2. While there is an overlap between the themes and concerns of women's spirituality, literature of the New Age, and goddess spirituality, the three are by no means the same. Western women and men who are sensitive to issues of gender within religious contexts follow a wide variety of approaches: some remain within their existing, usually Jewish or Christian, religious traditions, and work to reform oppressive attitudes and revive forgotten valences that are healing for women; some leave their birth traditions and turn instead to goddess figures, whether Graeco-Roman, Asian, or Native, finding new freedom outside the male-dominated imagery of Judaism or Christianity; and still others, while they affirm the need for women's spirituality, do not find the worship of any external deity, male or female, to be empowering.

3. McDermott, "The Western Kālī," in *Devī: Goddesses of India,* ed. John S. Hawley and Donna M. Wulff (Berkeley and Los Angeles: University of California Press, 1996), pp. 281–313.

4. The nine used for this chapter were alt.fan.kali.astarte.inanna; alt.magick .tantra; alt.magick.tyagi; alt.pagan; alt.religion.goddess; alt.religion.triplegoddess; alt.religion.wicca; soc.culture.bengali; and talk.religion.newage.

5. Sample titles include "Calcutta," "Church of Tantra," "The Dark Goddess," "The Goddess Kalika," "The Heart of Kali," "Hindu Image Library," "Hindu Tantrik Home Page," "I am the Bitch from Hell," "Kali," "Kali Gallery," "Kali Mandir," "Kali Pictures," "Kali Sanctuary," "Tantra Goddess," "Tantrik Texts and Links to Related Sites," "Warrior Goddesses and Women," and "Who is Kali?" Note that many of the websites accessed in 1996 were already defunct by 1998, and new ones discovered in 1999 had often disappeared by 2001. In what follows, I give the correct addresses as they appeared at the date of access.

6. I use the word "conversion" very loosely, and do not mean to suggest by it what is classically understood as the Christian conversion experience: a once-and-for-all change of heart and doctrine, which separates like a chasm from what came before. As modern Western Kālī devotees are quick to point out, they are often eclectic in their religiosity, and, while they may have included Kālī in their sphere of spiritual

empathy, they would not necessarily identify themselves as "converts" in the sense of eschewing all other forms of religiosity.

7. Http://yoni.com/bitch.html, accessed April 7, 2002, p. 1 of 2.

8. Http://www.feed.com/~rschenk/dmarshal/darkma.html, accessed February 19, 1998, pp. 1–3.

9. Http://home.earthlink.net/~persepha/Kali.html, accessed March 8, 2001, p. 1.

10. Http://www.dreamwv.com/muse/muses/hag.html, accessed April 7, 2002.

11. "Welcome to Darkyde: Vampire Myths and Legends," at http://www.geocities.com/Area51/Hollow/1610/index.html, accessed April 7, 2002, p. 2.

12. "The Destroyer: The Arms of Kali," at http://www.xnet.com/~acpinc/sinanju/59remo.htm, accessed April 7, 2002.

13. Diane DiMassa, *The Revenge of Hothead Paison: Homicidal Lesbian Terrorist* (Pittsburgh: Diane DiMassa and Giant Ass Publishing, 1995).

14. Http://www.csulb.edu/~persepha/violence.html, accessed February 19, 1998, p. 1.

15. Http://www.cei.net/~jwocky/Kali.html, accessed June 24, 1996, p. 1.

16. "I utilize her 'bloody and destructive' aspects as a metaphor for my own 'female rage'—for instance, in a self-mocking but ultimately transcendent way, I consider her the embodiment of my own pre-menstrual syndrome outbursts. By allowing myself these monthly Kali-like dances of destruction, I remain aware of my hormonal ebb and flow, and do not become caught up in the maya of it." From Cyronwode@aol.com on April 28, 1995, in answer to "A Survey of Kali Worship," posted on the Internet by Hussein Rashid, Columbia College senior.

17. In "Kali's Dance," *Tantra: The Magazine,* Kali Issue, no. 9 (1994): 56, Le'ema Kathleen Graham says, "Kali is a force that says 'Yes!' to primal instinctual energy. To me Kali is very much a goddess of the body. She is not some lofty out-of-reach, intellectual, out-of-body deity. She is not removed from the human condition. I see Kali in the flesh, blood, bones, and bowels of humans. Each time my baby sucks my breasts for milk, or I water my garden with my sacred menstrual blood, or I feel my lover's lingam inside my yoni uniting us in Tantric bliss, I know that I am enacting Kali's holy rites. And I rejoice! Thank Goddess!" As a champion of motherhood, Kālī also states, via her medium Lawrence Edwards, that while "both virgins and mothers can mature into wise women, . . . child birth is an initiation which gives access to realms of experience and wisdom which virgins don't have." From "World Light Articles: The Great Goddess on Women's Rites and Menopause," at http://www.worldlightcenter.com/prsn_art/ritesle.htm, accessed April 7, 2002.

18. Graham, "Kali's Dance," p. 56.

19. The section subheading quotes Kenneth Ray Stubbs, in "Sacred Orgasms," http://www.tantra.org/sacrorgs.htm, accessed April 7, 2002.

20. The following four are among the most frequented: "The Church of Tantra" (http://www.tantra.org); "Tantra.com" (http://www.tantra.com); "Tantraworks" (http://www.tantraworks.com/tantrawk.html); and "Hindu Tantrik Home Page" (http://www.hubcom.com/magee/tantric).

21. Ritualized sex is not the only context through which one can meet Kālī; as "The Kali Home Page" states, "Her worship, therefore, consists of fertility festivals as well as sacrifices (animal and human); and her initiations expand one's conscious-

ness by many means, including fear, ritual sexuality, and intoxication with a variety of drugs." It is sex, however, which most often appears in the published and electronic media.

22. "I actually like interacting with Her as Mother at times, though my preference is as Lover" (Nagasiva, April 17, 1995, posted on alt.fan.kali.astarte.inanna, alt.religion.wicca, alt.pagan, and talk.religion.misc).

23. From Mashani@ibm.net, May 5, 1995, in answer to "A Survey of Kali Worship."

24. "Love Poem to the Goddess and Comments," by Tom Rex, at http://www.azstarnet.com/~trex/togoddss.htm, accessed April 7, 2002.

25. See the opening caption to the Home Page called "Video Releases" (http://www.ids.net/picpal/trailr13.html, accessed April 7, 1996, p. 1).

26. See n. 51 below.

27. "Freeing the Female Orgasm: Awakening the Goddess," *Tantra: The Magazine,* Mother of the World Issue, no. 11 (1995): 57.

28. "Tantra: Indian Rites of Ecstasy" is a re-release by Mystic Fire Video of a film originally produced in 1969. It is quite disappointing, especially given that it is advertised as showing an authentic Tantric five-m ritual performed in Tarapith, West Bengal. When the couple, who are quite elderly, get to the fifth m, the camera switches to shots of a whirling duo, who are professional dancers.

29. "Tantra: The Art of Conscious Loving " is the title both of a workshop offered by Charles and Caroline Muir, Directors of Hawaiian Goddess Inc., and of a video produced for home instruction.

30. As a subscriber to *Tantra: The Magazine,* I receive periodic flyers for interesting weekends: one such memorable offering was for "Sacred Sex in Miami with Jwala" (a three-day workshop on the Tantric Arts). For more of same, see "The Church of Tantra" website (http://www.tantra.org), where one can find an array of advertised courses, workshops, and self-help instructions on sacred orgasms, yoni and lingam massage, aphrodisiacs, and sexual magic. In 1999, books from their gift shop that were marked with an erect phallus were highly recommended. One can run personal ads through this service as well.

31. Http://www.AAArt.com/tantra/amertan.htm, accessed February 21, 1998, p. 5.

32. One is instructed to purify oneself before worshipping the Goddess by taking a bath or shower, rubbing oils onto the body, and doing "aarati" to one's head, heart, navel, sexual region, and limbs. Kālī's mantra, "hring shring kring" (incorrect for "krīm krīm krīm hūm hūm hūm hrīm hrīm hrīm Dakṣiṇe Kālīke krīm krīm krīm hūm hūm hrīm hrīm svāhā"), is repeated seven times, after which one intones her many names. Following meditation, one closes with a suggested prayer. (Inside front cover.)

33. Kālī-centered new moon ritual: http://www.uark.edu/studorg/stpa/kali.htm, accessed April 7, 2002.

34. Http://www2.witchesweb.com/february.html, accessed on March 25, 1999.

35. Rowena Kryder, *Faces of the Moon Mother* (Mount Shasta, Calif.: Golden Point Productions, 1991), pp. 61–67. The two pictures are from pp. 61 and 65.

36. D. J. Conway, *Maiden, Mother, Crone: The Myth and Reality of the Triple Goddess* (St. Paul, Minn.: Llewellyn Publications, 1994), pp. 142–45. Conway's directions for the Crone Ritual, p. 153, go even further. "You will need a black candle, incense, a

chalice of juice, a small dish of salt, pencil and paper, and a metal bowl. Decorate with black cats, owls, wolves, ravens, cauldrons, and black stones. Invoke her, write your wishes on the piece of paper, then do the Crone Meditation. You may at this time cast the runes or lay out the Tarot cards, for divination. Then burn the paper in the metal bowl. Thank her and dismiss her."

37. For Daughters of Kali, see http://www.necronomicon.org/clandestyne/world/kali.html, accessed April 7, 2002.

38. "Temple of Kali" website: http://www.eden.com/~poke.Kali/temple.html, accessed February 19, 1998.

39. Graham, "Kali's Dance," p. 56.

40. Both are offered by Abaxion, a company in Chico, California, at http://www.abaxion.com, accessed on March 18, 1999.

41. Http://www.bellalumina.com/html/goddess/allfour/kali10.html, accessed April 7, 2002.

42. Http://www.daremore.com/godtat.html, accessed on May 4, 1999. As of 2001, the tattoo line had been discontinued, and by 2002, the webpage no longer existed.

43. I am grateful to Dr. Black-Keim for allowing me to reproduce her apron here. It may also be seen at http://www.elsawachs.com/apron/black.htm.

44. Genetic Drugs, *Karma Club.* I am grateful to Mark Seibring for bringing this to my attention.

45. Http://www.home.pacbell.net/jeffie, accessed on February 21, 1998.

46. Darius H. James, "A Gumbo: Way Down Under New Orleans," September 25–October 1, 1998, p. 1.

47. "Improve Office Karma," produced by Anderson Lembke ad agency for the Agfa Scanner/Copier. See "Hinduism Today," April 1998, p. 8.

48. *Economist Review of Books and Multimedia,* June 21, 1997.

49. *Immunology Today* 19, no. 1 (January 1998).

50. The best illustrations of the sexually explicit Kālī are by Penny Slinger; see *Tantra: The Magazine,* Kali Issue, pp. 41–44. Two others not reproduced here are her "Radiant Kali" and "Kali Union."

51. See Mike Magee's translations of the *Bṛhadnīla, Kālī, Mahānirvāṇa, Śakti-saṁgama, Yoginī,* and *Yoni Tantra*s on links to his website, http://www.hubcom.com/tantric. It is unclear to me at present how "accurate" these translations are.

52. One can find a wide variety of reproductions: Indian paintings, sculptures, and temple images, as well as calendar art depictions.

53. Says Ma Jaya about her first meeting with Kālī: "The Mother Kali came to me in 1974, and I was terrified of her. She appeared on Easter Sunday on 1974. She actually had me hiding; she was so intense. Yet even in that intensity, I recognized beauty. I was terrified, and I called up my teacher at that time who was Hilda Charlton. She said, 'Oh my darling, just ask the Mother to 'unzip' herself.' I went to the Mother and I cried, 'Oh, Mother, please show me. Please unzip yourself.' She almost looked like she was unzipping her chest straight down to her belly. She climbed out of herself and there was the most beautiful of women, the Golden Mother. I have never seen such beauty before or after. That was Kali." See *Tantra: The Magazine,* Kali Issue, pp. 58–61 and 76. For her site, see http://www.kashi.org.

54. "Kali Mandir Newsletter" 5 (May 1997): 3.

55. See, for instance, http://www.westbengal.com/puja, accessed May 26, 1999, and http://www.westbengal.com/puja/puja2k, accessed on March 8, 2001.

56. Http://www.kalimandir.org, accessed April 7, 2002.

57. Elizabeth U. Harding, *Kali: The Black Goddess of Dakshineswar* (York Beach, Me.: Nicholas-Hays, 1993).

58. E.g., soc.culture.bengali.

59. The episode in question of *Xena, Warrior Princess* aired on Saturday, February 27, 1999.

60. See Arthur J. Pais, "Off With the Lid," *India Today* 25, no. 49 (4 December 2000): 24g. For a photograph of National Congress Party activists burning American flags and porcelain toilets in Mumbai after hearing of Sittin' Pretty Designs, see *Times of India,* November 20, 2000, p. 7.

61. "Are you sick of New Age-ers who portray the Goddess as a Cosmic Barbie doll, all sweetness and light? I am. . . . There are some very good reasons to be afraid of the dark." "The Dark Goddesses," at http://home.earthlink.net/~persepha/DarkGoddess.html, accessed March 8, 2001, p. 1.

62. April 12–20, 1995, on alt.fan.kali.astarte.inanna.

63. Jody Radzik, April 20, 1995, on alt.fan.kali.astarte.inanna.

64. Kspitz@bigfoot.com, on alt.religion.wicca (February 26, 1998).

65. Ethan Walker, in ibid.

66. Nagasiva, February 7, 1995, on alt.fan.kali.astarte.inanna, alt.magick.tyagi, alt.pagan, and talk.religion.newage.

67. Theodore Roszak, *The Making of a Counter Culture: Reflections on the Technocratic Society and Its Youthful Opposition,* with a new introduction (1969; Berkeley and Los Angeles: University of California Press, 1995), p. 135. This book, especially the "Introduction to the 1995 Edition" and "Journey to the East . . . and Points Beyond: Allen Ginsberg and Alan Watts," pp. xi–xlii and 124–54, are useful overviews of these various protest groups and their motivating ideals.

68. Ibid., p. 144.

69. Robert Bellah, "Religious Evolution," *American Sociological Review* 29 (1964): 358–74.

70. Gananath Obeyesekere, *Medusa's Hair: An Essay on Personal Symbols and Religious Experience* (Chicago: University of Chicago Press, 1981).

71. Ibid., pp. 169–70.

72. Ibid., pp. 142–59.

73. At present, however, none of the currently active groups that include Kālī as part of their worldviews or rites are as "organized" as, say, the various Ramakrishna Vedanta Centers, the International Society for Krishna Consciousness, or even the *satsaṅgas* formed around Mata Amritanandamayi. There may be individual covens, therapy centers, magazine teams, or informal support groups who consider her to be an important part of their spiritual universes, but one is hard-pressed to find a Kālī sect or cult with definable distinguishing characteristics.

74. New Age Kālī devotees have experienced little persecution, apart from denunciations of their "pagan proclivities" by Christians and Jews, and have not had to defend their legitimacy through legal battles, as have the Mormons over polygamy, the Jehovah's Witnesses over American patriotism, the Nation of Islam over abstention from pork in prisons and conscientious objection to army duty, the Amish over

the right to prevent their children from secular schooling after the age of fourteen, and Scientologists over brain-washing. However, because of their ties to the Indian-American communities of this country, Kālī worshippers may one day find themselves in support of, or even at the center of, court cases on issues such as the permission to perform *homas* (fire ceremonies) or blood sacrifice. That Indian-Americans are already using the courts to fight for religious rights is evidenced by a landmark judgment in the Federal courts, lifting the ban on all-night Navarātrī festivities in Edison, New Jersey. See "Cleared to Celebrate," in *India Today,* August 15, 1996, p. 60k.

75. See C. Eric Lincoln, *The Black Muslims in America,* 3d ed (1961; Grand Rapids, Mich.: Eerdmans, 1994), and Clifton Marsh, *From Black Muslims to Muslims: The Transition from Separatism to Islam, 1930–1980* (Metuchen, N.J.: Scarecrow Press, 1984).

76. The Israeli movie star Uri Zohar is a famous example of this trend among young people of turning away from their secular Jewish lives to that of the Haredi (ultra-orthodox) world. For an overview of ultra-orthodoxy, including the recent growth in its appeal, see Samuel C. Heilman and Menachem Friedman, "Religious Fundamentalism and Religious Jews: The Case of the Haredim," in *Fundamentalism Observed,* vol. 1 of *The Fundamentalism Project,* ed. Martin E. Marty and R. Scott Appleby (Chicago: University of Chicago Press, 1991), pp. 197–264.

77. The search for roots, says Tu Wei-Ming, is "a perennial human concern." It does not have to be "a yearning for the past nor an attachment to a threatened life style. Rather, it is a deliberate attempt to mobilize traditional symbolic resources to bring them to bear on the critical issues generated by the modernizing process" ["The Search for Roots in Industrial East Asia: The Case of the Confucian Revival," in *Fundamentalism Observed,* vol. 1 of *The Fundamentalism Project,* ed. Martin E. Marty and R. Scott Appleby (Chicago: University of Chicago Press, 1991), pp. 742, 772]. Likewise, T. N. Madan, writing about Islam in South Asia, states that attention to orthodoxy and orthopraxy is a normal part of acculturation, both in a new environment and on behalf of new converts ["From Orthodoxy to Fundamentalism: A Thousand Years of Islam in South Asia," in *Fundamentalisms Comprehended,* vol. 5 of *The Fundamentalism Project,* ed. Martin E. Marty and R. Scott Appleby (Chicago: University of Chicago Press, 1995), pp. 288–320].

78. Excellent studies on this topic include Lawrence A. Babb and Susan S. Wadley, eds., *Media and the Transformation of Religion in South Asia* (Philadelphia: University of Pennsylvania Press, 1995); Peter Manuel, *Cassette Culture: Popular Music and Technology in North India* (Chicago: University of Chicago Press, 1993); and Jeffrey Zaleski, *The Soul of Cyberspace: How New Technology Is Changing Our Spiritual Lives* (New York: Harper*Edge,* 1997).

APPENDIX

Documentary Film and Video Resources for Teaching on Kālī and Fierce Goddesses

Sarah Caldwell

Ball of Fire: The Angry Goddess (Sarah Caldwell, 1999, 58 minutes). University of California Extension Center for Media and Independent Learning. Ethnographic study that explores rituals and gender dynamics of *muṭiyēṯṯu,* a dramatic ritual performed as an offering to Kāḷi in Kerala, in which men impersonate and are possessed by the spirit of the fierce goddess.

Bearing the Heat: Mother Goddess Worship in South India (Kristin Oldham, 1995, 50 minutes). Center for South Asia, University of Wisconsin, Madison. Documents Hindu celebrations that center around mother goddess worship in South India.

Divine Madness: Trance, Dance and Healing in Guyana (Philip Singer, 1978, 60 minutes). Distributor: Singer-Sharrette Productions. Ritual healing at a Kali temple in Guyana. Presents therapeutic aspects of rituals.

Eyes of Stone (Nilita Vachani, 1989, 90 minutes, 16 mm film). Doordarshan. Intimate portrait of a North Indian woman who is troubled by the spiritual attentions of a *dakan* (witch). She undergoes exorcism at local goddess temples and is temporarily cured. Film shows relation of possession to family tensions and psychological difficulties in women's lives.

Fire of Kali (Patricia Lawrence, 1997, 52 minutes). Ray Fitzwalter Associates Ltd., Lloyds House, 22 Lloyd Street, Manchester, M2 5WA, U.K. Produced as a BBC-TV documentary film, aired on "Everyman." Overcoming rigid censorship, this film offers a profile of a young Tamil mother's struggle with "disappearances" in Sri Lanka's cordoned-off war zone and details increasing acts of intense devotion for Kāḷi, including oracular possession and fire-walking.

The Goddess Bhagavati: Art and Ritual in South India (Clifford Jones). Columbia University South Asia Center.

Hail Mother Kali: A Tribute to the Traditions and Healing Arts Brought to Guyana by Indentured Madrasi Labourers (Stephanos Stephanides, 1988, 60 minutes). Distributor: Singer-Sharrette Productions. Documents a healing ceremony in Guyana from the perspective of religion, cultural history, and performance.

Lady of Gingee: South Indian Draupadi Festivals (Alf Hiltebeitel, 1988, 113 minutes). Center for South Asia, University of Wisconsin, Madison. Describes celebrations of a Draupadī festival in two villages in northern Tamilnadu in May–June 1986.

The Living Goddess (Frank Homans, 1979, 50 minutes). University of California Extension Center for Media and Independent Learning. Film about the Kumārī cult in Nepal, made with the assistance of Michael Allen of the Department of Anthropology, Sydney University.

Śītalā in Spring: Festival of the Bengali Goddess of Health and Illness (Joseph Elder, 1960, 40 minutes, black and white). Center for South Asia, University of Wisconsin, Madison. A historical film of an annual festival held in West Bengal to honor Śītalā, the Hindu Goddess of health and illness.

A Song of Ceylon (Laleen S. B. Jayamanne, 1985, 51 minutes). Women Make Movies, New York. Exorcism of a young Sri Lankan woman is recounted in a study on performance and hysteria.

Worship of God in the Form of Mother Kali. Adventures in Awareness, P.O. Box 5316, Fullerton, CA 92635. Kālī worship at the Southern California Ramakrishna Mission temple.

SELECT BIBLIOGRAPHY

Appadurai, Arjun, Frank J. Korom, and Margaret A. Mills, eds. *Gender, Genre, and Power in South Asian Expressive Traditions.* Philadelphia: University of Pennsylvania Press, 1991.

Ashcroft, Bill, Gareth Griffiths, and Helen Tiffin. *The Empire Writes Back: Theory and Practice in Post-colonial Literatures.* London: Routledge, 1989.

Bacchetta, Paola. "All Our Goddesses Are Armed: Religion, Resistance, and Revenge in the Life of a Militant Hindu Nationalist Woman." In *Against All Odds: Essays on Women, Religion, and Development from India and Pakistan,* edited by Kamla Bhasin, Nighat Said Khan, and Ritu Menon, pp. 133–56. New York: Kali for Women, 1994.

Ballhatchet, Kenneth. *Race, Sex, and Class under the Raj: Imperial Attitudes and Policies and Their Critics, 1793–1905.* New York: St. Martin's Press, 1980.

Banerjea, J. N. *Pauranic and Tantric Religion, Early Phase.* Calcutta: Calcutta University, 1966.

Bassier, Dennis. "Kali Mai Worship in Guyana: A Quest for a New Identity." In *Indians in the Caribbean,* edited by I. Bahadur Singh, pp. 13–155. New Delhi: Sterling Publishers, 1987.

Basu Roy, Indrani. *Kālighāt: Its Impact on Socio-Cultural Life of Hindus.* New Delhi: Gyan Publishing House, 1993.

Bataille, Georges. *Erotism: Death and Sensuality.* Translated by Mary Dalwood. 1962. San Francisco: City Lights Books, 1986. Originally published as *L'Érotisme* (Paris: Éditions de Minuit, 1957).

Berkson, Carmel. *The Divine and the Demoniac: Mahiṣa's Heroic Struggle with Durga.* New Delhi: Oxford University Press, 1995.

Bharati, Agehananda. *The Tantric Tradition.* London: Rider, 1965.

Bhattacharya, Brajamadhaba. *The World of Tantra.* New Delhi: Munshiram Manoharlal, 1988.

Bhattacharyya, Narendra Nath. *History of the Śākta Religion.* 2d rev. ed. 1973. Reprint. New Delhi: Munshiram Manoharlal, 1996.

Boodoo, Gerald. "The 'La Divina Pastora/Suparee Ke Mai' Devotions of Trinidad." *International Review of Mission* 82 (1993): 383–90.

Bose, Girindrasekhar. "The Genesis and Adjustment of the Oedipus Wish." 1956. Reprinted in *Vishnu on Freud's Desk: A Reader in Psychoanalysis and Hinduism,* edited by T. G. Vaidyanathan and Jeffrey J. Kripal, pp. 21–38. New Delhi: Oxford University Press, 1999.

Brown, Cheever Mackenzie. *God as Mother: A Feminine Theology in India.* Hartford, Vt.: Claude Stark, 1974.

———. "Kālī, the Mad Mother." In *The Book of the Goddess, Past and Present: An Introduction to Her Religion,* edited by Carl Olson, pp. 110–23. New York: Crossroad, 1983.

———. *The Triumph of the Goddess: The Canonical Models and Theological Visions of the Devī-Bhāgavata Purāṇa.* Albany: State University of New York Press, 1990.

Brubaker, Richard L. "The Ambivalent Mistress: A Study of South Indian Village Goddesses and Their Religious Meaning." Ph.D. diss., University of Chicago, 1978.

———. "The Goddess and the Polarity of the Sacred." In *The Divine Consort: Rādhā and the Goddesses of India,* edited by John Stratton Hawley and Donna Marie Wulff, pp. 204–9. Boston: Beacon Press, 1982.

Bruce, George. *The Stranglers: The Cult of Thuggee and Its Overthrow in British India.* London: Longmans, 1968.

"The Buddha-karita of Asvaghosha." Translated by E. B. Cowell. In *Buddhist Mahayana Texts.* Vol. 49, pt. 1 of *The Sacred Books of the East.* Oxford: Clarendon Press, 1894.

Butulia, Urvashi, and Tanika Sarkar, eds. *Women and Right-Wing Movements: Indian Experiences.* London: Zed Books, 1995.

Caldwell, Sarah. "Bhagavati: Ball of Fire." In *Devi: Goddesses of India,* edited by John Stratton Hawley and Donna Marie Wulff, pp. 195–226. Berkeley and Los Angeles: University of California Press, 1996.

———. *Oh Terrifying Mother: Sexuality, Violence and Worship of the Goddess Kāḷi.* New Delhi: Oxford University Press, 1999.

Carstairs, G. M. *The Twice-Born: A Study of a Community of High-Caste Hindus.* Bloomington: Indiana University Press, 1958.

Chakravarti, Chintaharan. *Tantras: Studies on Their Religion and Literature.* Calcutta: Punthi Pustak, 1963.

Chatterjee, Bankim Chandra. *The Abbey of Bliss.* Translated by Nares Chandra Sen-Gupta. Calcutta: Cherry Press, n.d.

Chirol, Sir Valentine. *Indian Unrest.* London: Macmillan, 1910.

Choudhuri, Keshub. *The Mother and Passionate Politics.* Calcutta: Vidyodaya, 1979.

Christ, Carol. *Rebirth of the Goddess: Finding Meaning in Feminist Spirituality.* New York: Routledge, 1998.

Coburn, Thomas B. *Devī-Māhātmya: The Crystallization of the Goddess Tradition.* Delhi: Motilal Banarsidass, 1984.

———. *Encountering the Goddess: A Translation of the Devī-Māhātmya and a Study of Its Interpretation.* Albany: State University of New York Press, 1991.

Cohen, Lawrence. "The Pleasures of Castration: The Postoperative Status of Hijras, Jankhas, and Academics." In *Sexual Nature, Sexual Culture,* edited by Paul R. Abramson and Steven D. Pinkerton, pp. 276–304. Chicago: University of Chicago Press, 1995.

Colebrooke, Henry T. *Essays on History, Literature, and Religion of Ancient India: Miscellaneous Essays.* 2 vols. 1837. Reprint. New Delhi: Cosmo Publications, 1977.

Craddock, N. Elaine. "Anthills, Split Mothers, and Sacrifice: Conceptions of Female Power in the Mariyamman Tradition." Ph.D. diss., University of California, Berkeley, 1994.

Daly, C. D. "Hindu-Mythologie und Kastrationskomplex." *Imago: Zeitschrift fur Anwendung der Psychoanalse auf die Natur- und Geisteswissenschaften* 2/3/4 (1927): 145–98.

———. "A Hindu Treatise on Kali," *Samiksa* 1 (1947): 191–96.

Daniel, E. Valentine. "The Individual in Terror." In *Embodiment and Experience: The Existential Ground of Culture and Self,* edited by Thomas J. Csordas, pp. 229–47. Cambridge Studies in Medical Anthropology. Cambridge: Cambridge University Press, 1994.

Dare, M. Paul. *Indian Underworld: A First-Hand Account of Hindu Saints, Sorcerers, and Superstitions.* New York: Dutton, 1940.

Das, Veena. "Moral Orientations to Suffering: Legitimation, Power, and Healing." In *Health and Social Change in International Perspective,* edited by Lincoln C. Chen, Arthur Kleinman, and Norma Ware, pp. 139–67. Boston: Dept. of Population and International Health, Harvard School of Public Health, 1994.

———. "Sexual Violence, Discursive Formations and the State." Paper presented at the conference "Violence against Women: Victims and Ideologies." Sri Lanka Foundation, Colombo, Sri Lanka, March 1996.

Dāsa, Sāralā. *Caṇḍī Purāṇa.* Cuttack: Dharma Grantha, n.d.

Dāśgupta, Śaśibhūṣaṇ. "Kālī-Debī o Kālī Pūjār Itihās." In id., *Bhārater Śakti-Sādhanā o Śākta Sāhitya,* pp. 63–89. Calcutta: Sāhitya Saṃsad, 1960.

Derne, Steve. "Images of the Fierce Goddess: Psychoanalysis and Religious Symbols—A Response to Kondos." *Contributions to Indian Sociology* 22, no. 1 (1988): 89–93.

Devī-Māhātmyam: The Glorification of the Great Goddess. Edited and translated by Vasudeva S. Agrawala. Ramnagar: All India Kashiraj Trust, 1963.

Dimock, Edward C., Jr. "A Theology of the Repulsive: The Myth of the Goddess Śītalā." In *The Divine Consort: Rādhā and the Goddesses of India,* edited by John Stratton Hawley and Donna Marie Wulff, pp. 184–203. Boston: Beacon Press, 1982.

Dubois, J. A., Abbé. *A Description of the Character, Manners, and Customs of the People of India; and of Their Institutions, Religious and Civil.* 2d ed. Madras: Thacker Spink, 1862.

Duff, Alexander. *A Description of the Durga and Kali Festivals Celebrated in Calcutta, at an Expense of Three Millions of Dollars.* Troy, N.Y.: C. Wright, 1846.

———. *India and India Missions: Including Sketches of the Gigantic System of Hinduism, both in Theory and Practice.* 1839. Reprint. Delhi: Swati Publications, 1988.

Eliade, Mircea. *Yoga: Immortality and Freedom.* Translated by Willard R. Trask. 1958. 2d rev. ed. Bollingen series, 56. Princeton: Princeton University Press, 1969. Originally published as *Le Yoga: Immortalité et liberté* (Paris: Payot, 1954).

Eller, Cynthia. *Living in the Lap of the Goddess: The Feminist Spirituality Movement in America.* New York: Crossroad, 1993.

———. *The Myth of Matriarchal Prehistory: Why an Invented Past Won't Give Women a Future.* Boston: Beacon Press, 2000.

Elmore, Wilber Theodore. *Dravidian Gods in Modern Hinduism: A Study of the Local and Village Deities of Southern India.* 1915. Reprint. Madras: Christian Literature Society, 1925.

Erndl, Kathleen M. "The Goddess and Women's Power: A Hindu Case Study." In *Women and Goddess Traditions in Antiquity and Today,* edited by Karen L. King, pp. 17–38. Minneapolis: Fortress Press, 1997.

———. *Victory to the Mother: The Hindu Goddess of Northwest India in Myth, Ritual, and Symbol.* New York: Oxford University Press, 1993.

Foucault, Michel. *The History of Sexuality.* Vol. 1: *An Introduction.* Translated from the French by Robert Hurley. New York: Vintage Books, 1980.

Freud, Sigmund. *The Standard Edition of the Complete Psychological Works of Sigmund Freud,* edited by James Strachey. 24 vols. London: Hogarth Press and Institute of Psycho-Analysis, 1953–74. Cited as *S.E.*

———. *Civilization and Its Discontents.* 1930. *S.E.,* 21: 77–145.

———. *The Future of an Illusion.* 1927. *S.E.,* 21: 1–56.

———. *Introductory Lectures on Psycho-Analysis. S.E.,* vols. 15 and 16.

———. *New Introductory Lectures on Psycho-Analysis. S.E.,* 22: 1–182.

Gadon, Elinor. *The Once and Future Goddess: A Symbol for Our Time.* New York: Harper & Row, 1989.

Goldwasser, Michele. "The Rainbow Madonna of Trinidad: A Study in the Dynamics of Belief in Trinidadian Religious Life." Ph.D. diss., University of California, Los Angeles, 1996.

Gombrich, Richard, and Gananath Obeyesekere. *Buddhism Transformed: Religious Change in Sri Lanka.* Princeton: Princeton University Press, 1988.

Gordon, Leonard A. *Bengal: The Nationalist Movement, 1876–1940.* New York: Columbia University Press, 1975.

Goudriaan, Teun, and Sanjukta Gupta. *Hindu Tantric and Śākta Literature.* Vol. 2, fasc. 2 of *A History of Indian Literature,* edited by Jan Gonda. Wiesbaden: Otto Harrassowitz, 1981.

Griffin, Wendy, ed. *Daughters of the Goddess: Studies of Healing, Identity, and Empowerment.* Walnut Creek, Calif.: AltaMira Press, 2000.

Guinee, William. "Suffering and Healing in Trinidadian Kali Worship." Ph.D. diss., Indiana University, 1992.

Gupta, Lina. "Kali, the Savior." In *After Patriarchy: Feminist Transformations of the World Religions,* edited by Paula M. Cooey, William R. Eakin, and Jay B. McDaniel, pp. 15–38. Maryknoll, N.Y.: Orbis Books, 1991.

Gupta, Roxanne Kamayani. "The Politics of Heterodoxy and the Kina Rami Ascetics of Banaras." Ph.D. diss., Syracuse University, 1993.

———. *A Yoga of Indian Classical Dance: The Yogini's Mirror.* Rochester, Vt.: Inner Traditions, 2000.

Gupta, Sanjukta. "Tantric Śākta Literature in Modern Indian Languages." In Teun Goudriaan and Sanjukta Gupta, *Hindu Tantric and Śākta Literature,* vol. 2, fasc. 2 of *A History of Indian Literature,* edited by Jan Gonda, pp. 178–80. Wiesbaden: Otto Harrassowitz, 1981.

———, trans. *Lakṣmī Tantra: A Pāñcrātra Text.* Leiden: E. J. Brill, 1972.

Gupta, Sanjukta, Dirk Jan Hoens, and Teun Goudriaan. *Hindu Tantrism.* Leiden: E. J. Brill, 1979.

Hallstrom, Lisa Lassell. *Mother of Bliss: Ānandamayī Mā (1896–1982).* New York: Oxford University Press, 1999.

Hartnack, Christiane. "British Psychoanalysts in Colonial India." In *Psychology in Twentieth-Century Thought and Society,* edited by Mitchell G. Ash and William R. Woodward, pp. 233–51. New York: Cambridge University Press, 1987.

———. *Psychoanalysis and Colonialism in British India.* New Delhi: Oxford University Press, forthcoming.

———. "Vishnu on Freud's Desk: Psychoanalysis in Colonial India." In *Vishnu on Freud's Desk: A Reader in Psychoanalysis and Hinduism,* edited by T. G. Vaidyanathan and Jeffrey J. Kripal, pp. 81–106. New Delhi: Oxford University Press, 1999.

Hawley, John Stratton, and Donna Marie Wulff, eds. *The Divine Consort: Rādhā and the Goddesses of India.* Boston: Beacon Press, 1982.

Hazra, R. C. *Studies in the Upapurāṇas.* Vol. 2: *Śākta and Non-Sectarian Upapurāṇas.* 1963. Calcutta: Sanskrit College, 1979.

Hiltebeitel, Alf. *The Cult of Draupadī.* Vol. 2: *On Hindu Ritual and the Goddess.* Chicago: University of Chicago Press, 1991.

———. "Hair Like Snakes and Mustached Brides: Crossed Gender in an Indian Folk Cult." In *Hair: Its Power and Meaning in Asian Cultures,* edited by Alf Hiltebeitel and Barbara S. Miller, pp. 145–76. Albany, N.Y.: State University of New York Press, 1998.

———. "Kūttāṇṭavar: The Divine Lives of a Severed Head." In *Ways of Dying: Death and Its Meanings in South Asia,* edited by Elisabeth Schömbucher and Claus Peter Zoller, pp. 276–310. Heidelberg University South Asian Institute Studies 33. Delhi: Manohar, 1999.

Hiltebeitel, Alf, and Kathleen Erndl, eds. *Is the Goddess a Feminist? The Politics of South Asian Goddesses.* Sheffield: Sheffield Academic Press; New York: New York University Press, 2000.

Homans, Peter. "Once Again, Psychoanalysis, East and West: A Psychoanalytic Essay on Religion, Mourning, and Healing." *History of Religions* 24, no. 2 (1984): 133–54.

Humes, Cynthia Ann. "Glorifying the Great Goddess or Great Woman? Hindu Women's Experience in Ritual Recitation of the *Devī-Māhātmya.*" In *Women in Goddess Traditions in Antiquity and Today,* edited by Karen L. King, pp. 39–63. Minneapolis: Fortress Press, 1997.

———. "Rājās, Thugs, and Mafiosos: Religion and Politics in the Worship of Vindhyavāsinī." In *Render unto Caesar: Religion and Politics in Cross-Cultural Perspective,* edited by Sabrina Petra Ramet and Donald W. Treadgold, pp. 219–47. Washington, D.C.: American University Press, 1995.

———. "Vindhyavāsinī: Local Goddess yet Great Goddess." In *Devī: Goddesses of India,* edited by John Stratton Hawley and Donna Marie Wulff, pp. 49–76. Berkeley and Los Angeles: University of California Press, 1996.

Hurtado, Larry, ed. *Goddesses in Religion and Modern Debate.* Atlanta: Scholars Press, 1990.

Inden, Ronald. *Imagining India.* Oxford: Blackwell, 1990.

Iyengar, K. R. Srinivasa. *Sri Aurobindo: A Biography and a History.* 2 vols. 3d rev. ed. 1950. Reprint. Pondicherry: Sri Aurobindo International Centre of Education, 1972.

Jones, Sir William. *The Letters of Sir William Jones.* Edited by Garland Cannon. Oxford: Clarendon Press, 1970.

Jones, Sir William, and Lady Anna Maria Jones. *The Works of Sir William Jones.* 6 vols. London: G. G. and J. Robinson and R. H. Evans, 1799. Reprint. Delhi: Agam Prakashan, 1977.

Kakar, Sudhir. *The Analyst and the Mystic: Psychoanalytic Reflections on Religion and Mysticism.* Chicago: University of Chicago Press, 1991.

———. *The Inner World: A Psycho-Analytic Study of Childhood and Society in India.* 2d ed. Delhi: Oxford University Press, 1981.

———. "The Maternal-Feminine in Indian Psychoanalysis." *International Review of Psycho-Analysis* 16 (1989): 335–62.

———. *Shamans, Mystics and Doctors: A Psychological Inquiry into India and Its Healing Traditions.* New Delhi: Oxford University Press, 1982.

Kapadia, Karin. *Siva and Her Sisters: Gender, Caste, and Class in Rural South India.* Delhi: Oxford University Press, 1996.

Kapferer, Bruce. *A Celebration of Demons: Exorcism and the Aesthetics of Healing in Sri Lanka.* 1983. Washington, D.C.: Smithsonian Institution Press, 1991.

Kersenboom-Story, Saskia C. *Nityasumangali: Devadasi Tradition in South India.* Delhi: Motilal Banarsidass, 1987.

Khan, Aisha. "Sipari Mai." *Hemisphere* 2 (1990): 40–41.

Kinsley, David R. *The Goddesses' Mirror: Visions of the Divine Feminine from East and West.* Albany: State University of New York Press, 1989.

———. *Hindu Goddesses: Visions of the Divine Feminine in the Hindu Religious Tradition.* Berkeley and Los Angeles: University of California Press, 1986.

———. "Kālī: Blood and Death Out of Place." In *Devī: Goddesses of India,* edited by John Stratton Hawley and Donna Marie Wulff, pp. 77–86. Berkeley and Los Angeles: University of California Press, 1996.

———. *The Sword and the Flute: Kālī and Kṛṣṇa: Visions of the Terrible and the Sublime in Hindu Mythology.* Berkeley and Los Angeles: University of California Press, 1975, 2000.

———. *Tantric Visions of the Divine Feminine: The Ten Mahāvidyās.* Berkeley and Los Angeles: University of California Press, 1997.

Klass, Morton. *East Indians in Trinidad: A Study of Cultural Persistence.* 1961. Prospect Heights, Ill.: Waveland Press, 1988.

———. *Singing with Sai Baba: The Politics of Revitalization in Trinidad.* Prospect Heights, Ill.: Waveland Press, 1991.

Kondos, Vivienne. "Images of the Fierce Goddess and Portrayals of Hindu Women." *Contributions to Indian Sociology* 20, no. 2 (1986): 173–97.

Kopf, David. *British Orientalism and the Bengal Renaissance: The Dynamics of Modernization, 1773–1835.* Berkeley and Los Angeles: University of California Press, 1969.

———. "An Historiographical Essay on the Idea of Kali." In *Shaping Bengali Worlds,*

Public and Private, edited by Tony Stewart, pp. 112–27. East Lansing: Michigan State University Press, 1989.

Kripal, Jeffrey J. "A Garland of Talking Heads for the Goddess: Some Autobiographical and Psychoanalytic Reflections on the Western Kālī." In *Is the Goddess a Feminist? The Politics of South Asian Goddesses,* edited by Alf Hiltebeitel and Kathleen Erndl, pp. 239–68. Sheffield: Sheffield Academic Press; New York: New York University Press, 2000.

———. *Kālī's Child: The Mystical and the Erotic in the Life and Teachings of Ramakrishna.* 2d ed. 1995. Chicago: University of Chicago Press, 1998.

———. "Pale Plausibilities." Preface to the 2d edition of *Kālī's Child: The Mystical and the Erotic in the Life and Teachings of Ramakrishna.* Chicago: University of Chicago Press, 1998.

———. "Re-membering a Presence of Mythological Proportions: Psychoanalysis and Hinduism." In *Mapping Religion and Psychological Studies: Contemporary Dialogues, Future Prospects,* edited by William B. Parsons and Diane Jonte-Pace, pp. 254–79. New York: Routledge, 2000.

———. *Roads of Excess, Palaces of Wisdom: Eroticism and Reflexivity in the Study of Mysticism.* Chicago: University of Chicago Press, 2001.

Kurtz, Stanley N. *All the Mothers Are One: Hindu India and the Cultural Reshaping of Psychoanalysis.* New York: Columbia University Press, 1992.

———. "Who is Kālī? Gender Hierarchy as Sacrificial Dominance." Unpublished paper presented at the conference on the Goddess Kālī at Barnard College, New York, September 1996.

La Guerre, John, ed. *Calcutta to Caroni: The East Indians of Trinidad.* Trinidad and Tobago: University of the West Indies, 1985.

Lacan, Jacques. "God and ~~Woman's~~ Jouissance." In id., *On Feminine Sexuality: The Limits of Love and Knowledge,* translated by Bruce Fink, pp. 61–77. The Seminar of Jacques Lacan, edited by Jacques-Alain Miller, 20. New York: Norton, 1998.

Lawrence, Patricia. "Violence, Suffering, Amman." In *Violence and Subjectivity,* edited by Veena Das, pp. 171–204. Berkeley and Los Angeles: University of California Press, 2000.

Li, Hwui. *The Life of Hiuen-Tsiang.* Translated by Samuel Beal. London: Kegan Paul, Trench, Trubner, 1914.

Lopez, Donald S., Jr., ed. *Religions of India in Practice.* Princeton: Princeton University Press, 1995.

Loseries-Leick, Andrea. "Kālī in Tibetan Buddhism." In *Wild Goddesses in India and Nepal,* edited by Axel Michaels, Cornelia Vogelsanger, and Annette Wilke, pp. 417–35. Bern: Peter Lang, 1996.

MacMunn, Sir George Fletcher. *The Underworld of India.* London: Jarrolds, 1933.

The Mahābhāgavata Purāṇa (An Ancient Treatise on Śakti Cult). Edited by Pushpendra Kumar. Delhi: Eastern Book Linkers, 1983.

Mahabir, Noor Kumar, and Ashram Maharaj. "Kali-Mai: The Cult of the Black Mother in Trinidad." Unpublished paper, University of the West Indies Archive, Trinidad and Tobago, 1985.

Mahapatra, Manamohan. *Traditional Structures and Change in an Orissan Temple.* Calcutta: Punthi Pustak, 1981.

Mallebrein, Cornelia. "Tribal and Local Deities: Assimilations and Transformations." In *Devi: The Great Goddess: Female Divinity in South Asian Art,* edited by Vidya Dehejia and Thomas B. Coburn, pp. 137–55. Washington, D.C.: Smithsonian Institution Press, 1999.

Manogaran, Chelvadurai, and Bryan Pfaffenberger. *The Sri Lankan Tamils: Ethnicity and Identity.* Boulder, Colo.: Westview Press, 1994.

Marglin, Frédérique Apffel. "Types of Sexual Union and Their Implicit Meanings." In *The Divine Consort: Rādhā and the Goddesses of India,* edited by John Stratton Hawley and Donna Marie Wulff, pp. 307–13. Boston: Beacon Press, 1982.

———. *Wives of the God-King: The Rituals of the Devadasis of Puri.* Delhi: Oxford University Press, 1985.

Marshall, Peter J. *The British Discovery of Hinduism in the Eighteenth Century.* Cambridge: Cambridge University Press, 1970.

Masters, John. *The Deceivers.* New York: Viking, 1952.

Mayo, Katherine. *Mother India.* 1927. London: Jonathan Cape, 1930.

McClintock, Anne. *Imperial Leather: Race, Gender and Sexuality in the Colonial Conquest.* New York: Routledge, 1995.

McDaniel, June. *The Madness of the Saints: Ecstatic Religion in Bengal.* Chicago: University of Chicago Press, 1989.

McDermott, Rachel Fell. "Evidence for the Transformation of the Goddess Kālī: Kamalākānta Bhaṭṭācārya and the Śākta Padāvalī Tradition." Ph.D. diss., Harvard University, 1993.

———. "Kālī at the Crossroads: New Directions in the Eighteenth- to Nineteenth-Century Śākta Padāvalī of Bengal." *Bulletin: Center for the Study of World Religions* (Harvard University) 16, no. 1 (1989–90) : 22–42.

———. *Mother of My Heart, Daughter of My Dreams: Kālī and Umā in the Devotional Poetry of Bengal.* New York: Oxford University Press, 2001.

———. *Singing to the Goddess: Poems to Kālī and Umā from Bengal.* New York: Oxford University Press, 2001.

———. "The Western Kālī." In *Devī: Goddesses of India,* edited by John Stratton Hawley and Donna Marie Wulff, pp. 281–313. Berkeley and Los Angeles: University of California Press, 1996.

McGilvray, Dennis B. "The 1987 Stirling Award Essay: Sex, Repression, and Sanskritization in Sri Lanka?" *Ethos* 16, no. 2 (1988): 99–127.

———. *Tamils and Moors: Ethnic Minorities in Sri Lanka's War Zone.* Forthcoming.

McKean, Lise. "Bhārat Mātā: Mother India and Her Militant Matriots." In *Devī: Goddesses of India,* edited by John Stratton Hawley and Donna Marie Wulff, pp. 250–80. Berkeley and Los Angeles: University of California Press, 1996.

McLean, Malcolm. *Devoted to the Goddess: The Life and Work of Ramprasad.* Albany: State University of New York Press, 1998.

McNeil, Keith E. "The Many Faces of Mother Kali: Caribbean Hinduism and the Moral Politics of Diaspora Ritual Performance in Trinidad." In *Asian Migrations to the Americas,* edited by Brinsley Samaroo. London: Hansib, forthcoming.

———. "'This is history that was handed down, we don't know exactly how true it is': On the Ambiguities of 'History' in Trinidadian Kali Worship." *Oral and Pictorial Records Programme Newsletter* (University of the West Indies, Trinidad and Tobago) 39 (2000): 1–5.

Menon, C. A. *Kāḷi Worship in Kerala.* 2d ed. 1943. Madras: University of Madras, 1959.

Menon, Usha, and Richard A. Shweder. "Kali's Tongue: Cultural Psychology and the Power of 'Shame' in Orissa, India." In *Emotion and Culture, Empirical Studies of Mutual Influence,* edited by Shinobu Kitayama and Hazel Markus, pp. 241–84. Eugene: University of Oregon Press, 1994.

———. "The Return of the 'White Man's Burden': The Moral Discourse of Anthropology and the Domestic Life of Hindu Women." In *Welcome to Middle Age! (And Other Cultural Fictions),* edited by Richard A. Shweder, pp. 139–88. Chicago: University of Chicago Press, 1998.

Meyer, Eveline. *Aṅkāḷaparamecuvari: A Goddess of Tamil Nadu, Her Myths and Cult.* Wiesbaden: Franz Steiner Verlag, 1986.

Mintz, Sidney W. *Caribbean Transformations.* New York: Columbia University Press, 1989.

Mookerjee, Ajit. *Kali: The Feminine Force.* London: Thames & Hudson, 1988.

Mookerjee, Ajit, and Madhu Khanna. *The Tantric Way: Art, Science, Ritual.* Boston: New York Graphic Society, 1977.

Morinis, E. Alan. *Pilgrimage in the Hindu Tradition: A Case Study of West Bengal.* Delhi: Oxford University Press, 1984.

Müller, Friedrich Max. *Anthropological Religion.* 1891. Reprint. New Delhi: Asian Educational Services, 1977.

Nabokov, Isabelle. *Religion against the Self: An Ethnography of Tamil Rituals.* New York: Oxford University Press, 2000.

Nandy, Ashis. *The Intimate Enemy: Loss and Recovery of Self under Colonialism.* Delhi: Oxford University Press, 1983.

Neevel, Walter. "The Transformation of Śrī Rāmakrishna." In *Hinduism: New Essays in the History of Religions,* edited by Bardwell L. Smith, pp. 53–97. Leiden: E. J. Brill, 1976.

Neumann, Erich. *The Great Mother: An Analysis of an Archetype.* Translated from the German by Ralph Manheim. Princeton: Princeton University Press, 1955.

Obeyesekere, Gananath. *The Cult of the Goddess Pattini.* Chicago: University of Chicago Press, 1984.

———. *Medusa's Hair: An Essay on Personal Symbols and Religious Experience.* Chicago: University of Chicago Press, 1981.

———. *The Work of Culture: Symbolic Transformation in Psychoanalysis and Anthropology.* Chicago: University of Chicago Press, 1990.

Obeyesekere, Gananath, and Richard Gombrich. "Kālī, the Punitive Mother." In id., *Buddhism Transformed: Religious Change in Sri Lanka,* pp. 133–62. Princeton: Princeton University Press, 1988.

O'Flaherty, Wendy Doniger. *Śiva, the Erotic Ascetic.* Oxford: Oxford University Press, 1973.

———. *Women, Androgynes, and Other Mythical Beasts.* Chicago: University of Chicago Press, 1980.

Olson, Carl. *The Mysterious Play of Kali: An Interpretive Study of Ramakrishna.* Atlanta: Scholars Press, 1990.

Oman, John Campbell. "Kalighat and Hinduism in Bengal." In id., *Brahmins, Theists, and Muslims of India,* pp. 3–23. London: T. Fisher Unwin, 1907.

Orme, Robert. *Historical Fragments of the Moghul Empire, of the Morattoes, and of the English Concerns in Indostan, from the Year MDCLIX.* 1782. Reprint. New Delhi: Associated Publishing House, 1974.

Parks, Fanny. *Wanderings of a Pilgrim in Search of the Picturesque.* 1850. Reprint. Karachi: Oxford University Press, 1975.

Parry, Benita. *Delusions and Discoveries: Studies on India in the British Imagination, 1880–1930.* London: Allen Lane, 1972.

Parson, William B. *The Enigma of the Oceanic Feeling: Re-visioning the Psychoanalytic Theory of Mysticism.* New York: Oxford University Press, 1999.

Payne, Ernest A. *The Śāktas: An Introductory and Comparative Study.* Calcutta: Y.M.C.A. Publishing House, 1933.

Pintchman, Tracy. *The Rise of the Goddess in the Hindu Tradition.* Albany: State University of New York Press, 1994.

Purani, A. B. *The Life of Sri Aurobindo.* 4th rev. ed. Pondicherry: Sri Aurobindo Ashram, 1978.

Purohit-Darpaṇ. Compiled and edited by Surendramohan Bhaṭṭācārya. 38th ed. Calcutta: Satyanārāyaṇ Library, 1393 [1986].

Puttick, Elizabeth. *Women in New Religions: In Search of Community, Sexuality, and Spiritual Power.* New York: St. Martin's Press, 1997.

Rahejia, Gloria G., and Ann G. Gold. *Listen to the Heron's Words: Reimagining Gender and Kinship in North India.* Berkeley and Los Angeles: University of California Press, 1994.

Rashid, Hussein. "A Survey of Kali Worship." Unpublished paper. Columbia College, 1995.

Rawson, Philip S. *The Art of Tantra.* Rev. ed. 1973. Reprint. London: Thames & Hudson, 1978.

———. *Oriental Erotic Art.* New York: A and W Publishers, 1981.

Rolland, Romain. *The Life of Ramakrishna.* Calcutta: Advaita Ashrama, 1986.

Roy, Manisha. *Bengali Women.* Chicago: University of Chicago Press, 1975.

Said, Edward. *Orientalism.* New York: Pantheon Books, 1978.

Samanta, Suchitra. "The Self-Animal and Divine Digestion: Goat Sacrifice to the Goddess Kālī in Bengal." *Journal of Asian Studies* 53, no. 3 (1994): 779–803.

Sarkar, Sumit. *The Swadeshi Movement in Bengal, 1903–1908.* New Delhi: People's Publishing House, 1973.

Sarva-deva-devī-pūja-paddhati (*Method of Worshipping All Gods and Goddesses*). Edited by Vāmadeva Bhaṭṭācārya and corrected by Prabhākar Kāvyasmṛtimīmāṃsatīrtha. 4th ed. Calcutta: Calcutta Town Library, 1355 [1948].

Sax, William S. *Mountain Goddess: Gender and Politics in a Himalayan Pilgrimage.* New York: Oxford University Press, 1991.

Scarry, Elaine. *The Body in Pain: The Making and Unmaking of the World.* New York: Oxford University Press, 1985.

Schjelderup, Harald, and Kristian Schjelderup. *Über drei Haupttypen der religiösen Erlebnisformen und ihre psychologische Grundlage.* Berlin: Walter de Gruyter, 1932.

Shaw, Miranda. *Passionate Enlightenment: Women in Tantric Buddhism.* Princeton: Princeton University Press, 1994.

Shweder, Richard A. *Thinking through Cultures: Expeditions in Cultural Psychology.* Cambridge, Mass.: Harvard University Press, 1991.

Singer, Philip, Enrique Araneta, and Jamsie Naidoo. "Learning of Psychodynamics, History, and Diagnosis Management Therapy by a Kali Cult Indigenous Healer in Guiana." In *The Realm of the Extra-Human,* edited by A. Bharati, pp. 345–70. The Hague: Mouton, 1976.

Singh, Odaipaul. "Hinduism in Guyana: A Study in Traditions of Worship." Ph.D. diss., University of Wisconsin, Madison, 1993.

Sinha, Indra. *The Great Book of Tantra: Translations and Images from the Classic Indian Texts with Commentary.* Rochester, Vt.: Destiny Books, 1993.

Sinha, Surajit. "Kali Temple at Kalighat and the City of Calcutta." In id., *Cultural Profile of Calcutta,* pp. 61–72. Calcutta: Indian Anthropological Society, 1972.

Sircar, D. C. *The Śākta Pīṭhas.* 2d ed. Delhi: Motilal Banarsidass, 1973.

Sleeman, William Henry. *Ramaseeana.* Calcutta: G. H. Huttmann, 1836.

———. *The Thugs or Phansigars: Comprising a History of the Rise and Progress of that Extraordinary Fraternity of Assassins; and a description of the system which it pursues, and of the measures which have been adopted by the Supreme Government of India for its suppression.* Philadelphia: Carey & Hart, 1839.

Steel, Flora Annie. *The Law of the Threshold.* New York: Macmillan, 1924.

———. *On the Face of the Waters.* London: W. Heinemann, 1896.

———. "On the Second Story." In *Indian Scene: Collected Short Stories of Flora Annie Steel,* pp. 292–26. London: Edward Arnold, 1933.

Suleri, Sara. *The Rhetoric of English India.* Chicago: University of Chicago Press, 1992.

Tambiah, Stanley Jeyaraja. *Buddhism Betrayed? Religion, Politics, and Violence in Sri Lanka.* Chicago: University of Chicago Press, 1992.

———. *Sri Lanka: Ethnic Fratricide and the Dismantling of Democracy.* Chicago: University of Chicago Press, 1986.

Tantra: The Magazine, Kali issue, no. 9 (1994).

Taussig, Michael T. *Mimesis and Alterity: A Particular History of the Senses.* New York: Routledge, 1993.

Taylor, Kathleen. "Arthur Avalon: The Creation of a Legendary Orientalist." In *Myth and Mythmaking: Continuous Evolution in Indian Tradition,* edited by Julia Leslie, pp. 144–64. Richmond, U.K.: Curzon Press, 1996.

———. *Sir John Woodroffe, Tantra and Bengal: "An Indian Soul in a European Body"?* Richmond, U.K.: Curzon Press, 2001.

Thomas, Paul. *Christians and Christianity in India and Pakistan: A General Survey of the Progress of Christianity in India from Apostolic Times to the Present Day.* London: George Allen & Unwin, 1954.

Thompson, Edward, and Arthur Spencer, trans. *Bengali Religious Lyrics, Śākta.* Calcutta: Oxford University Press, 1923.

Thornton, Edward. *Illustrations of the History and Practices of the Thugs and Notices of Some of the Proceedings of the Government of India, for the Suppression of the Crime of Thuggee.* London: William H. Allen, 1837.

Two Prakrit Versions of the Maṇipati-carita. Edited by Robert Williams. London: Royal Asiatic Society, 1959.

Urban, Hugh B. "The Remnants of Desire: Sacrificial Violence and Sexual Transgression in the Cult of the Kāpālikas and in the Writings of Georges Bataille." *Religion* 25 (1995): 67–90.

Vaidyanathan, T. G., and Jeffrey J. Kripal, eds. *Vishnu on Freud's Desk: A Reader in Psychoanalysis and Hinduism.* New Delhi: Oxford University Press, 1999.

Vertovec, Steven. *Hindu Trinidad: Religion, Ethnicity and Socio-Economic Change.* London: Macmillan, 1992.

Ward, William. *The History, Literature, and Mythology of the Hindoos.* 4 vols. 3d ed. 1817–20; Delhi: Low Price Publications, 1990.

White, David Gordon, ed. *Tantra in Practice.* Princeton: Princeton University Press, 2000.

Wilson, H. H. *Essays and Lectures on the Religions of the Hindus: Selected Works.* Collected and edited by Dr. Reinhold Rost. 2 vols. (1861–62). Vol. 1: *Religious Sects of the Hindus.* Reprint. New Delhi: Asian Publication Services, 1976.

Woodroffe, Sir John. *Hymns to the Goddess and Hymn to Kali.* London: Luzac, 1913.

———. *Principles of Tantra.* 2 vols. London: Luzac, 1914.

———. *The Serpent Power, Being the Ṣaṭ-Cakra-Nirūpaṇa and Pādukā-Pañcaka.* London: Luzac, 1918.

———. *Shakti and Shākta.* London: Luzac, 1918.

Wulff, David. *Psychology of Religion: Classic and Contemporary.* New York: Wiley, 1997.

———. "Toward a Psychology of the Goddess." In *The Divine Consort: Rādhā and the Goddesses of India,* edited by John Stratton Hawley and Donna Marie Wulff, pp. 283–97. Boston: Beacon Press, 1982.

Wurgaft, Lewis. *The Imperial Imagination: Magic and Myth in Kipling's India.* Middletown, Conn.: Wesleyan University Press, 1983.

Zaleski, Jeffrey. *The Soul of Cyberspace: How New Technology Is Changing Our Spiritual Lives.* New York: Harper*Edge,* 1997.

Zimmer, Heinrich. *Myths and Symbols in Indian Art and Civilization.* Princeton: Princeton University Press, 1974.

CONTRIBUTORS

Sarah Caldwell is visiting assistant professor of the history of religions at Harvard Divinity School. Her training is in cultural anthropology, and her work focuses on South Indian goddess traditions and spirit possession rituals, Śākta Tantrism, and contemporary guru movements in the United States. Her publications include *Oh Terrifying Mother: Sexuality, Violence, and Worship of the Goddess Kāḷi* (1999) and the ethnographic film *Ball of Fire: The Angry Goddess* (2000).

Patricia Dold is a lecturer in the religious studies program at the University of Alberta, Edmonton, and a Ph.D. candidate at McMaster University in Hamilton, Ontario. Her research focuses on Sanskrit texts of goddess worship from northeastern India. Her dissertation is a translation and analysis of narratives from the *Mahābhāgavata Purāṇa.*

Roxanne Kamayani Gupta is assistant professor of religious studies at Albright College in Reading, Pennsylvania, where she teaches courses in Asian and comparative religions, Goddess traditions, yoga philosophy and practice, and ecological spirituality. Her research interests include Indian ascetic traditions and Śākta Tantrism. She is an Indian classical dancer and the author of *A Yoga of Indian Classical Dance: The Yoginī's Mirror* (2000).

Sanjukta Gupta has been senior lecturer at the Institute of Oriental Languages and Culture at the University of Utrecht in the Netherlands. At present, she is a member of the Oriental Faculty of the University of Oxford and fellow of the Oxford Centre for Vaishnava and Hindu Studies. Her areas of research are nondualistic Vedanta, ancient Vaiṣṇavism and Tantrism, Sanskrit literature, and gender studies as related to the Hindu tradition. Her publications include *Studies in the Philosophy of Madhusūdana Sarasvati* (1966); *Lakṣmī Tantra: A Pāñcarātra Text* (1972); *Hindu Tantrism* (1979), with Dirk Jan Hoens and Teun Goudriaan; and *Hindu Tantric and Śākta Literature* (1981), with Teun Goudriaan.

Cynthia Ann Humes is associate professor in the Department of Philosophy and Religious Studies at Claremont McKenna College in Claremont, California. Her publications concern the contemporary use of Sanskrit literature, modern ritual in North Indian goddess worship, the political and economic dimensions of Hinduism, and issues of gender in world religions. Recently, she has co-written a book on the history of the Transcendental Meditation movement in the United States and translated and annotated the popular discourses of Shankaracarya Brahmananda Saraswati.

At the time of his death in April 2000, *David R. Kinsley* was professor in the Department of Religious Studies at McMaster University in Hamilton, Ontario. During his long and distinguished career, he published voluminously on subjects ranging from a general introduction to Hinduism and a monograph on Krishna to comparative books on healing and religion, ecology and religion, and goddesses in cross-cultural perspective. His books on Kālī include: *The Sword and the Flute: Kālī and Kṛṣṇa: Visions of the Terrible and the Sublime in Hindu Mythology* (1975 and 2000), *Hindu Goddesses: Visions of the Divine Feminine in the Hindu Religious Tradition* (1986), and *Tantric Visions of the Divine Feminine: The Ten Mahāvidyās* (1997).

Jeffrey J. Kripal is Lynette S. Autrey Associate Professor of Religious Studies at Rice University, Houston, Texas. His publications include *Kālī's Child: the Mystical and the Erotic in the Life and Teachings of Ramakrishna* (1995), which won the American Academy of Religion's History of Religions Prize, and *Roads of Excess, Palaces of Wisdom: Eroticism and Reflexivity in the Study of Mysticism* (2001). He has also co-edited four volumes, which include *Vishnu on Freud's Desk: A Reader in Psychoanalysis and Religion* (1998), with T. G. Vaidyanathan, and *Crossing Boundaries: Essays on the Ethical Status of Mysticism* (2002), with G. William Barnard. He is at present working on a social history of the Esalen Institute in Big Sur, California.

Patricia Lawrence is a Rockefeller Fellow at the Kroc Institute for International Peace Studies, Notre Dame University, where she is completing a manuscript on goddess worship in Sri Lanka's war zone. Her ethnographic research speaks about altered lives of activists, oracles, survivors, and healers in Sri Lanka. She was the anthropological consultant for the BBC documentary film *Fire of Kali.*

Rachel Fell McDermott is associate professor in the Department of Asian and Middle Eastern Cultures at Barnard College, New York. She works on goddess worship in eastern India, in particular, the devotional literature and public ritual focused on Kālī, Durgā, and Umā, as well as on its hybrid forms in the West. Her publications include *Mother of My Heart, Daughter of My Dreams: Kālī and Umā in the Devotional Poetry of Bengal* (2001) and *Singing to the Goddess: Poems to Kālī and Umā from Bengal* (2001).

Keith E. McNeal is assistant professor of anthropology at the University of California, San Diego. He is completing a comparative study of African- and Hindu-derived possession religions in Trinidad, West Indies. He works at the intersection of anthropology, psychoanalysis, and comparative religion and has written on drag performance, Pentecostalism in the southern United States, and the anthropology of emotion.

Usha Menon is assistant professor of anthropology in the Department of Culture and Communication at Drexel University, Philadelphia. She writes on Hindu morality, popular, contemporary understandings of the goddess Kālī, family dynamics and gender relations in Oriya Hindu society, and Hindu-Muslim relations. She is currently working on a book that examines the rise to national prominence of political parties like the Bharatiya Janata Party and its allies.

Richard A. Shweder is a cultural anthropologist and professor of human development in the Committee on Human Development at the University of Chicago. He works on topics in cultural psychology, comparative ethics, and culture theory. He is the author of *Thinking Through Cultures: Expeditions in Cultural Psychology* (1991), *Why Do Men Barbecue? Recipes for Cultural Psychology* (in press), and *Engaging Cultural Differences: The Multicultural Challenge in Liberal Democracies* (2002), edited with Martha Minow and Hazel Markus.

Hugh B. Urban is assistant professor in the Department of Comparative Studies at Ohio State University, Columbus. He is primarily interested in the study of secrecy in religion, particularly in relation to questions of knowledge and power. Focusing on the traditions of South Asia, he is the author of *The Economics of Ecstasy: Secrecy and Symbolic Power in Colonial Bengal,* with an accompanying volume of translations, *Songs of Ecstasy: Tantric and Devotional Songs for Colonial Bengal* (2001). His book *Tantra: Sex, Secrecy, Politics and Power in the Study of Religion* is forthcoming from the University of California Press.

INDEX

The index follows the transliteration and italicization principles set out in "Notes on Transliteration" (xvii–xviii). Rather than impose an artificial uniformity on the volume, we have done our best to follow the different conventions and practices of the individual essayists.

Compositor:	G&S Typesetters, Inc.
Text:	10/12 Baskerville
Display:	Baskerville
Printer and binder:	Thomson-Shore, Inc.